D0855412

PLOWSHARES INTO SWORDS
MANAGING THE AMERICAN DEFENSE ESTABLISHMENT

5
5N
17
65

PLOWSHARES INTO SWORDS

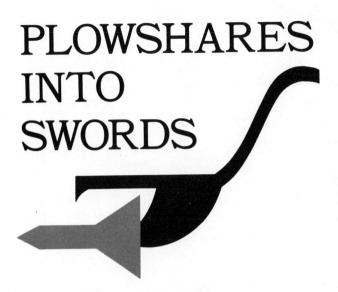

MANAGING THE AMERICAN DEFENSE ESTABLISHMENT

J.A.Stockfisch

Mason & Lipscomb PUBLISHERS   NEW YORK

Copyright © 1973 by J. A. Stockfisch

All rights reserved

No part of this book may be reproduced in any form
without permission in writing from the publisher

ISBN: 0–88405–008–4

Library of Congress Catalog Card Number: 73–84883

Printed in the United States of America

FIRST PRINTING

Robert Manning Strozier Library

JUN 25 1975

Tallahassee, Florida

to Charles J. Hitch

CONTENTS

PREFACE

During recent years the public has been made increasingly aware of difficulties the Defense Department has had with weapon system development and procurement. Most attention is drawn to the facts of cost overruns and failures to meet technical performance objectives. The rising cost of sophisticated weapons is also beginning to cause a less publicized but serious concern over the future security of the country itself. The purpose of this book is to provide the interested citizen with a better understanding of the dimension and complexity of the weapon development process, how it evolved to its present state, and how it may be better managed and controlled.

The subject of weapons selection is a key element of peacetime military management in its broadest sense. The quality and effectiveness of weapons is a reflection of military management. Such management is a result of an interaction between elected and politically-appointed officials, the uniformed military, the scientific-technical community, and the citizenry as both taxpayers and the beneficiaries of government spending. Hence the fields of politics, public administration, military organization and tactics, and scientific endeavor and analysis are interwined. This book tries to illuminate these diverse strands and, especially, their interactions. In one way, the effort may be regarded as a "case study" of the problems encountered in the effort to control and manage an instrument of the State in the setting of modern, advanced technology. Initially, this book presents a "theory" of political-bureaucratic behavior as it impacts upon government budgeting and spending. It then examines the historical evolution of the major strands of military affairs, force planning, and weapons technology that brought us to the present condition, with special emphasis given to American experience to include adaption of European precedents.

The peculiar problems of weapon system procurement are due to the combination of high levels of peacetime defense spending, modern technology, and the emergence of extreme specialization as between diverse military combat specialities, in the context of a democratic political system. This combination is uniquely an American experience of the past twenty-five years. Hence the rich and abundant experience of Western European countries provides only limited insight on how to manage military affairs in the present United States setting.

The flaws of the present system are primarily due to a failure to work out a coherent division of labor between political decision-makers (including Congress and those in the executive branch), and specialists, including the uniformed military. Given this shortcoming, the military bureaucracies operate under perverse incentives, wherein the process "makes sense" if weapons are viewed as means to justify budgets rather than items with which to equip troops so that they can most effectively conduct military operations should the need arise. It is further contended that only if these incentives are changed will defense management improve much.

The incentives impacting upon government bureaucrats, including the uniformed officer corps, are overwhelmingly a product of how the political masters, including Congress, conduct business in the budgeting process and in the identification of policy objectives. Thus the behavior of subordinates, like that of a child who responds to the incentives created by his parents, is largely determined. For this reason it is unfair and potentially dangerous to attribute major blame for the faults in the system to the uniformed military. Only the political leaders in the Congress and the executive branch can change this subtle but powerful set of forces. Moreover, the need to improve the system is greater than even the well-publicized shortcomings of weapon-system cost overruns and failures to meet technical performance objectives might suggest, because of a more serious fault. That fault is that, even if there were no cost overruns and even if the systems met their technical design objectives, many of them would still not be worth their cost because they possess dubious combat utility. Hence it is vital and urgent for the country's national security that the weapon acquisition process be changed. A way to achieve this is suggested in this book.

This book was written to enhance understanding of a complex and difficult subject, in the belief that better understanding in a democratic society contributes toward improvement in public administration and policy-making. By "improvement" I mean increasing the efficiency of our military management which, in turn, means getting the most fighting capability for the resources spent, or getting a given level of fighting capability for the least amount of scarce resources. To some, this efficiency objective is distasteful because armed forces exist to be used for war, and war entails killing and social waste. But acknowledgment of this point leads nowhere unless it be advocacy of a zero military budget. For the present, at least, the civilian economy will be most effectively served by decreasing defense spending and by increasing the efficiency of our weapons procurement system. Unfortunately, the world remains a dangerous place. Only those who accept this somber and sad truth are apt to find this book useful or relevant.

PLOWSHARES INTO SWORDS
MANAGING THE AMERICAN
DEFENSE ESTABLISHMENT

1

THE BUREAUCRATIC ANIMAL AND OTHER ACTORS

> The pukka Civil Servant kowtows to his Minister until he nearly makes you sick. But he doesn't worry. He knows that one day the Minister will be flung out on his neck. But the civil servant won't. He's there for keeps.
>
> Nigel Balchin, *The Small Back Room*, p. 137

The terms "bureau" and "bureaucracy" as used in this book refer to an organization or group of specialists that obtains its resources by means of the coercive financial instruments of the state. Taxation, and the inflationary money-creation powers of a national state, are these financial instruments. A government bureau contrasts with an industry in the private sector that obtains its financing by selling its output or product to consumers who are free to buy as little or as much as they individually want. In the case of a bureau, the consumer (as a taxpayer) exercises control over the amount and composition of the output through an indirect political process, in which his preferences must compete with those of powerful producer groups, elected officials, and bureaucrats. For a private-producing activity, consumer control is direct and exercised in an impersonal marketplace. For a bureau, competence of specialists producing the output is often determined by members of a peer group or through examination. For a private industry, dollar-profit performance, the absence of which has the incidental but important by-product of eliminating "losers," is the relevant measure of competence. In varying degrees, bureaucrats enjoy privileges and bear responsibilities that a farmer or businessman does not. As compared to private activities bureaus are "closed systems." Activities into which entry is free possess a quality of "openness." The "closed" quality of a government bureau poses severe problems affecting the information available to policy makers and citizens

1

regarding the conduct of bureau operations. In the private sector, one need not concern himself with the operations of the firm itself; only information about the quality of products, which he can gain by trial and error or by word-of-mouth from other consumers, is relevant.

The "military bureaucracy" is the professional, uniformed officer corps. Society must look to it for critical skills if it is to produce and possess military forces. However, it is only one of several groups of "actors" who play critical and necessary roles in the production of military force. Other key actors are the constituted policy makers—"politicians" in both the Executive and Legislative branches of the government—technologists and scientists who are the source of new developments that impact upon weapon design, and analysts who serve both policy makers and bureaucrats.

Views on bureaucratic organizations are varied.[1] On one hand are images of organizations that are well organized and highly effective, made up of members who are professional and dedicated. The U.S. Strategic Air Command, the Federal Bureau of Investigation, and the German army of the past, have been well-publicized examples of effective organizations. On the other hand a conception of "bureaucracy" is prevalent that almost renders the term an epithet. Visions of a modern counterpart of a Byzantine court, characterized by gross inefficiency at worst or mere bumbling at best, are often evoked in treatment of the subject. One might think of organizations and institutions that in certain contexts warrant esteem as not being bureaucratic, when obviously they are. Conversely, the term "bureaucracy" might be applied only to organizations that serve no social functions or that serve such functions in only a limited way, at best. But the Strategic Air Command, the Federal Bureau of Investigation,[2] or even one's favorite church or university are indeed bureaucracies, and they display all the behavior that evokes critical thought on the subject when it is treated in the abstract. Where lies the contradiction that leads to these apparently conflicting views on the subject? Or is it possible there is no contradiction at all? To develop some of the many facets of bureaus is our task in this chapter.

The ideal conception of bureaucracy—as described by Max Weber, the German sociologist—is an organization characterized by (1) a well-ordered system of stable and exhaustive rules governing the behavior of officials discharging their duties, (2) a hierarchical system of internal organization, and (3) management based on written documents ("the files").[3]

Particularly important in this concept of bureaucratic organization are its implications for officials, that is, for the bureaucrats, including the following:
(1) the officeholder is a full-time careerist, who moves up through the hierarchy; [4] (2) he enjoys status and social esteem, which is identified with the office he holds; (3) he acquires office on the basis of his educational or technical qualifications; and (4) he receives "regular pecuniary compensation of a normally fixed salary and the old-age security provided by a pension."[5]

These attributes, describing officials, also imply "professionalism." The essential qualities of the "concept of profession" are (1) expertise, for which there are objective standards for separating the competence of professionals and laymen; (2) responsibility toward performing a role that is essential to the client, where the "client" is society; and (3) corporateness, by which the profession's members develop and share a sense of themselves as being a group apart from laymen.[6]

Corporateness further implies a system of rules or "norms," or a professional ethic, that governs the behavior of the members of the group toward each other and toward "laymen." "Responsibility" implies an ethic of rendering service for its own sake and of purposefully eschewing exploitation of the monopoly possession of expertise for personal profit. Hence, "financial remuneration cannot be the primary motivation of the professional man *qua* professional man."[7]

The opportunity to move through (or "upward" in) the hierarchy means that senior positions are open to the aspirant who sharpens his expertise and develops an ability to lead. The status and social esteem of an office or position are partial compensation for receiving a salary (including the pension) that may be less than one might earn in business. Expertise, based on educational or technical qualification, also suggests an appeal to individuals who are motivated to acquire and apply expertise for its own sake and who desire to render service to society. Well-ordered rules, a hierarchical system, a management based on written documents—all taken together constitute an institutional harnessing and organization of professionalism on the basis of expertise so as to perform social services. Because it can perform many tasks, bureaucracy has become a major institution through which industrialized society functions.

A skeptic may indeed question Weber's ideal conception of bureaucracy (but as we shall see, by his emphasis upon a "secrecy syndrome" that bureaucrats display, his thought also contains the sufficient seed for a less flattering view of bureaucracy). However, Weber's model of bureaucracy treated the modern, Western European form that began to emerge most sharply in the seventeenth and eighteenth centuries. His broad view of social and political processes suggests that "authoritarian" political forms, of which feudalism was the principal variant, had dominated. The "rules of the game" or "laws" were usually embedded in custom, and administered and interpreted by either local barons or the satraps of a distant ruler. Political power sprang from the point of a lance or the edge of a sword that was wielded locally, and the "rights" of the individual and the safety of his property were susceptible to variable interpretation, particularly over large geographic areas. The emergence of modern bureaucracy, therefore, was part and parcel of the rise of government based on explicit and written laws, due process, and the associated predictability that these institutions provided for political and economic subjects. The modern form of bureaucracy was the key instrument that enabled kings to gain the upper hand over autonomous barons. These governmental devices were also part of the same "package" that included money rather than "in-kind" taxation. With money came "accountability," extending from business to government affairs. In its early forms, modern bureaucracy was an adjunct to "opening up" society, of which early modern capitalism was also an element. In the process the power of the instruments of the state was constrained by the "bureaucratization" of the officials. And subsequently, the power of the king was also curbed by the rise of parliamentary systems. Modern democracy, including its republican forms, could have never gotten underway had not the main elements of Weber's conception of bureaucracy been adopted both in form and substance. Although skepticism toward the "ideal" conception is warranted, the overall perspective of Weber's view also has a very high empirical content.

Yet the popular image of bureaucracy is hardly a favorable one. C. Northcote Parkinson, in a pseudoscientific derivation of "laws," develops a pattern of organizations that achieve and sustain their height of activity (and size) long after the purpose for which they have been created has either considerably diminished or disappeared. In short, the bureau absorbs more and more resources to do less and less.[8] Among the examples cited are the British Colonial Office, which continues to grow while the Empire declines, and the U.S. Department of Agriculture, whose level of employment continues to rise even as the number of farmers in the United States decreases. (In the same humorous vein, it has been observed that if a major monument were erected in Washington for every federal bureau or agency that has been disestablished since the founding of the Republic, the skyline would not change very much.) The same forces that cause entire organizations to grow and survive in accordance with Parkinson's laws also operate with respect to the subelements of an agency, particularly in the staff functions of the head office.

A somewhat different, but related, line of criticism of bureaucracy focuses upon individual and group behavior within the organizations,[9] in this instance described as a Machiavellian "model" of bureaucracy and easily extended to business organizations.[10] In such a system there is the chief, or "sovereign." There are also peers, courtiers, and barons. And finally, there are the followers, subordinates, and inferiors. The principal objective governing individual behavior is to please the sovereign. The major activity is the generation of information that simultaneously evokes the sovereign's pleasure and serves one's own ends, the whole frequently being accomplished by contriving to cause the sovereign to view one's peers or immediate superiors with displeasure. In this setting, behavior is, at best, amoral. At worst, the prevailing individual ethic resembles that displayed in a pig pen.

The major force of the Machiavellian model of bureaucracy is an activity that is so "political" that the energies of its job incumbents are mainly absorbed by political infighting, at the expense of "efficiency" in performing the tasks for which the organization exists. Moreover, the organization's promotion process operates in such a way as to select people who are adroit at wielding political knives or pleasing the boss, or who are simply good "organization men." For example, drawing upon his State Department experience, one student notes that members of our Foreign Service learn that it is critical to "get along" with their peers and superiors in the Foreign Service, knowledge and expertise on foreign cultures and operations being of secondary importance.[11]

Central to this conception of bureaucracy is the idea that a large organization consists of a chief who, like a sovereign, is surrounded by barons. Each baron asserts a territorial imperative with regard to his division or staff section, which resembles a feudal fiefdom. In his description of the old, prewar State Department, Dean Acheson notes that "the heads of all these divisions, like barons in a feudal system weakened at the top by mutual suspicion and jealousy between king and prince, were constantly at odds, if not at war."[12] The principal weapon of a baron is information, or more accurately, a lack thereof—information that is withheld from the boss regarding the resources within the baron's fiefdom. Such a condition permits the baron freedom of action within his own domain, which is in fact another way of defining power. But the chief executive, in his own turn, can deal with his barons in different ways: he can buy them off or ruthlessly crush them, or he can use a variety of tactics between these extremes.[13] That this Machiavellian image of bureaucracy has much popular appeal perhaps testifies to some kind of foundation in fact. It also suggests that the elements of ancient and medievel feudalism were not entirely eliminated by the rise of the modern organizational contrivances.

The Machiavellian conception of bureaucracy focuses on interpersonal relationships, which can be characterized as "gaming," or playing games. The situation is one in which there is a struggle or rivalry between the involved parties. An individual, as an actor, behaves in such a way toward his rival or superior as to try to evoke a favorable response on the part of his opponent. Ambush tactics, bluffing, and other stratagems are part of the scenario, although outright lying is not normally considered good form. But clever players do not have to lie, at least most of the time, since concealment and omission of information, along with other tactics, serve their purposes quite adequately.

This conception of bureaucratic behavior serves useful purposes because it has much explanatory worth; but it has only limited relevance, because of its very richness. The interpersonal phenomena encountered in a government bureau or large corporation are the same as those experienced in all interpersonal relationships. For it is not true that the relationships, for example, between husband and wife, parent and child, lover and loved, farmer and hired hand, pedestrian and motorist, and teacher and student all have a gaming quality? Everyone has his secrets and tries to preserve some of them, while seeking to provide suggestions to others about the remainder. Everyone has his unrevealed motives, as well as his stated intentions; and everyone communicates by signals and actions, as well as by the explicit word. In one sense, every social relationship is bureaucratic, to the extent that a Machiavellian conception of bureaucracy is one in which all the principals play games.

What remains then of the purely bureaucratic problem, particularly for its least popular form—the public bureaucracy—apart from aspects inherent in the human condition? Public bureaucracies are, of course, the instruments of the government and manage resources obtained by coercive financial devices that are the monopoly of the state. Those financial devices are the powers of creating money and of taxation.

The difference in financing separates business organizations, exhibiting many of the trappings and forms of bureaucracies, from their public counterparts. Business organizations are compelled to compete with each other in the marketplace. Apart from the effects of patent laws, expert knowledge of production techniques and organizational innovations are revealed to competitors (existing or potential) by attempts to profit from special knowledge. Competition diffuses both knowledge and the benefits it provides in the form of lower-priced goods and improved products and services. Similarly, the selection of personnel is based, in part at least, on performance and competence in conducting "operations"—production, sales, and so forth—which can be measured in terms of monetary profit and loss. Although there may be a marked Machiavellian behavior pattern in a business corporation, the share of the market gained by the competitor is likely to affect adversely the status of executives judged to be responsible for the adverse change. Whatever else may be said about business bureaucracy, operating expertise continues as an ongoing characteristic, if only because business firms lacking it are driven out of business. Economic competition—including the social and institutional apparatus that permits, fosters, and sustains competition—renders the business bureaucracy a "special case." It is not an especially interesting one, as far as the subject of "bureaucracy" is concerned. If effective competition occurs in the marketplace, then the nature of the internal workings and interpersonal relationships of an organization is of no concern to the public.

The bureaucracy problem in its purest form is a "monopoly problem," unique to instrumentalities of the state. The expertise embodied in its structure and mastered by its officials endows the organization with a monopoly of knowledge, which is a source of power. "The power position of a fully developed bureaucracy is always overtowering," and "the 'political master' finds himself in the position of a 'dilettante' who stands opposite the 'expert.' " Moreover "every bureaucracy seeks to increase the superiority of the professionally informed by keeping their knowledge and intentions secret."[14] The power derived from secrecy becomes operational when coupled with the monopoly that is inherent in the taxing and related coercive power of the state.

That the monopoly power of a "civil servant" (a more kindly term than bureaucrat) inherent in his specialized and professional knowledge can be converted into an economic force is a well-established idea and historical phenomenon. However, its generally acknowledged form is associated with graft, corruption, and venality. That is, the official actively employs his position to obtain a personal monetary payoff. But the rise of professional bureaucracies—most of which occurred in the United States during the present century as a result of the civil service and related reforms inspired by Woodrow Wilson and his followers—has eliminated large-scale venality. Nevertheless, the monopoly power of the bureaucrat can be used to exert a profound economic effect in a more subtle way. A bureaucrat monopolist is much like a private, discriminating monopolist. Up to a point, both kinds of monopolist behave the same way; but then a difference occurs that gives the bureaucratic animal's behavior a peculiar feature. It should be emphasized that the behavior pattern can occur without the slightest whiff of corruption that so characterized public administration in a past era.

Consider a thirsty desert traveler encountering a water vendor who possesses the only available water within miles. Let us assume that the cost of water, to include a going wage to the vendor for his effort and a fair return on his investment, is one dollar a quart. Our traveler may be so thirsty that he would be willing to pay $5 for only one quart; thus the $5 is also an index of the utility or satisfaction that one quart would provide him. Similarly, at $4 a quart, he would buy two quarts; at $3, he would take three; at $2, four; and at $1 per quart, he would take five quarts.

Implicit in this consumer-valuation scale is the economist's concept of consumer surplus. If the consumer could buy the water at a dollar a quart, the five he acquires for a total cost of $5 provides him fifteen units of "utility" (recall, he would have been willing to pay $5 for one and only one; $8 for two, and only two, and so on.) But at one dollar, at which price he would buy five, he gives up five dollars. Nevertheless, the 5 quarts gives him fifteen units of satisfaction. Hence, the net benefit, or consumer surplus, is 10—(5−1) + (4−1) + (3−1) + (2−1).

If our monopolistic vendor is perceptive, he could make an "all-or-none, take-it-or-leave-it" deal with our traveler: five quarts for $10. Since the cost of five quarts is $5, the vendor enjoys a monopolistic profit of $5, and thereby personally enriches himself. Such an event would not happen, of course, if there were a "large number" of sellers at the watering place. In that case, competition between them would cause the price to converge toward its production cost of $1, and at this unit price the consumer acquires his desired quantity.

The bureaucrat/monopolist behaves much like the private discriminating monopolist.[15] He, in effect, is able to offer an "all-or-none" package. However, he cannot legally enrich himself like the private monopolist. But he is nevertheless a "maximizer," even though money profit is not his maximand. Rather, as Parkinson suggests, the bureaucrat seeks to maximize the size of his organization, in this fashion deriving personal fulfillment and the feeling of power. The larger the amount of a society's resources available, the greater is his power and the capability to perform his mission in life. Stemming from this, the greater is his prestige and that of his colleagues.

Thus, continuing our parable of the watering place, the bureaucrat could extract $10 from the traveler. Given the cost of $1 per quart, he will use that $10 to produce 10 quarts (perhaps giving the traveler a light shower as part of the package deal). A larger activity, of course, means a larger organization, more power, and more means to do "good," like keep the world clean, or healthy, educate the young, build highways, defend the country, and so on. Thus, at a theoretical limit, a government bureau can be twice the size of a comparable private operation.

It was stated earlier in this chapter that a government bureaucrat or head of a bureau attains his power through the secrecy that he can derive from his expertise. No bureaucrat can offer his sovereign or the legislature that controls appropriations an all-or-none package, as might a private, discriminating monopolist dealing with a consumer. Such behavior would be at least impudent, if not arrogant. Instead, the bureau head tries to maximize his budget by taking advantage of his superior's lack of knowledge of demand and cost (or supply) conditions that might constrain the bureau's operations. This lack of knowledge stems partly from inherent complexities bearing upon the bureau's activity, and it is sustained by purposeful obfuscation and the employment of various public relations and information-generating skills. These techniques are focused on the cost and production aspects of the bureau's affairs as well as on the demand for the bureau's output.

It is to a bureau's advantage to make the cost of production appear less than it is, an impression that can be encouraged by three techniques. The crudest of these is to understate the dollar outlays by failing to identify all the relevant inputs and to be overoptimistic in cost estimation. With regard to complex, yet-to-be-developed technical systems, it is easy to be optimistic about the talents of one's engineers or designers, especially when the optimism is self-serving; and failure to take account of all cost inputs is endemic to a bureaucratic organization. Military advocates of new weapons having higher rates of fire or larger ordnance payloads than the current ones tend to overlook the increased costs of munitions that follow from the higher rates of ammunition expenditure permitted by the new systems. Again, sophisticated systems of increasingly complicated design often necessitate costlier training for the personnel who will man them, and these costs, too, tend to be underestimated.

Underpricing certain service inputs lowers the apparent cost of a bureau's program, a misconception that is especially easily fostered when capital costs are being considered. Normally, governments can borrow money at interest rates of between 5 and 6 per cent (or even lower for state and municipal governments, which can issue bonds paying interest that is not subject to federal income tax). The social cost of capital, however, is in the neighborhood of 10 per cent, since capital investment in the private sector of the economy yields on the average a 10 per cent rate of return before property and corporate income taxes are subtracted. The use of a rate of return in the neighborhood of 5 or 6 per cent when evaluating and costing government investments leads to a gross understatement of the capital-cost component of a program. Such costs weigh very heavily in "capital intensive" projects, such as for highways, reclamation and flood control projects, and airports. Because inappropriately low discount rates are used in measuring the cost of capital, many projects and investments that would not be undertaken in the private sector of our economy are in fact undertaken by the government.

Another technique for making the projected cost of some government programs appear lower is to avoid explicitly taking account of the "technical external diseconomies" associated with a government program. Many production processes generate byproducts that impose damage or unpleasantness on the community, and these often are not taken into account by the producer. Smoke from factory chimneys or sewage dumped into streams and lakes are examples often encountered in private enterprise. Airport noise is a further example. Dealing with such external diseconomies can pose a number of subtle difficulties in the private sector.

Where government operations generate nuisances, it is sufficient to recognize their existence, make some quantitative estimate of their magnitude, and view the resulting amount explicitly as a "cost" of the program. But although these full costs, including the shadow costs, should be compared with other uses to which the resources could be put, this is seldom done by government bureaus. On the contrary, there is usually a great effort to avoid such a comparison. This is particularly true with regard to transportation facilities, wherein the highway programs responsible for the ingression of large numbers of vehicles to urban areas, creating enormous congestion problems, provide a prime example of such offense. Highway and port authorities seldom, if ever, take account of the costs in terms of this congestion. Neither is the additional noise generated by increased air traffic often reckoned as part of the cost of programs designed to serve aircraft operators. Many students suggest that the widespread nature of technical external diseconomies in the private sector is so great that a business economy breaks down in performing a role in serving social wants and objectives. The implication of the suggestion is that the state should play a more directive and, indeed, active role in the allocation of resources. However, the extent to which the state's own instruments fail to account for the external diseconomies they spawn does not give rise to optimism that government, which must necessarily operate through bureaucratic instruments, can efficiently cope with these problems.

Obfuscation and propaganda techniques are both used to exaggerate the demand for the output of a bureau. Military organizations, for example, tend to exaggerate the strength and capability of a potential enemy, although it must be admitted that these exaggerations are advanced in good faith by the military professionals. After all, in the judgment of historians and politicians it is the generals who lose battles and wars, not the politicians whose job it is to determine the budgets.

Although both bureaucratic and private advocates of particular government programs are normally silent on the subject of external diseconomies, one cannot accuse them of being ignorant about the general concept of "externalities." This is manifest in the great emphasis placed on the external benefits attributed to many programs. One hears much, for example, about the "fallout" that will accrue to the civilian economy from the advanced technology generated by the space program. And with equal facility, the academic-scientific community touts increased federal funding of basic research on the basis of the great benefits that will result therefrom. (Considering the source of these statements, the evidence thus far, scientific or otherwise, to support the assertions seems scanty.) It is seen, then, that the claims for external benefits to be derived from a wide variety of programs—including public housing, transportation services, public health, and others—are extensive. These claims perhaps are exceeded only by those often made to the effect that the benefits cannot be measured. So far, there has been but little pursuit of the hypothesis that such an extreme difficulty of measurement frequently suggests a lack of anything to measure.

Secrecy, unclear information, and misinformation are tools that enable the head of a bureau to tap the taxing power of the state so as to get the resources. But there are also other reasons for maintaining his secrets.

One of these exists in organizations that are complex because they comprise subgroups specializing in narrower operating or technical skills. Divisive struggle may arise among the subgroups, thus harming the operating effectiveness of the larger organization. In armies, for example, perennial struggles among infantrymen, cavalrymen, and artillerymen are prevalent; in navies there are struggles among destroyermen, aviators, and submariners; and in a tax-collecting agency differences emerge among lawyers, accountants, and the law-enforcement components. Universities are scenes of extreme divergencies of views (as between, say, the chemistry and physics departments) regarding broader educational objectives whenever changes in those objectives entail changes in the relative budgets of the departments.

In organizations like these, the leadership instinctively tends to head off or suppress such controversy, for if it "gets out of control" the resulting bitterness and ill feeling can injure the morale and, hence, the effectiveness of any important subgroup that suffers a decline in status. This in turn dilutes the organization's effectiveness in performing its broader mission. Differences might be suppressed also to avoid their resolution by superior authority from outside the group. Such a resolution would, of course, involve an extensive investigation of the conflicting claims, in the course of which the outsiders would learn more about the internal workings, technology, and production processes of the organization. And the power issuing from operational secrecy and possessed by the bureaucratic leadership (or the corporate body) would be diminished accordingly.

The operational worth and payoff of the power inherent in the bureaucrat's monopolistic possession of knowledge comes to the forefront in the government-budgeting arena. Here, however, he is cast with other important actors. Although the federal-government budgeting process apparently had a lively quality in the early days, as evidenced by the appearance of such descriptives as "pork barrel" during the nineteenth century, the business did not get really serious until the period beginning with the end of World War II. For most of the nineteenth century, the scope of federal-government resource-using activities was small compared to revenues that were raised from protective tariffs dictated by internal-development policy and from the sale of public lands. The revenue yields were more than ample for financing federal public works and occasional cash dividends to the several states, both of which were necessary to avoid the adverse deflationary consequences of unspent federal surpluses. This state of affairs continued into the twentieth century, when World War I cast up an awareness of the need to rationalize the federal spending process. It was only as late as 1921 that the Bureau of the Budget was created as a part of the Treasury Department.

The New Deal and the 1930's, which saw the growth and proliferation of federal agencies, provided a setting of substantially unemployed resources in which any increment of federal spending, provided it was not financed by increased taxes, was better than none.[16] World War II (and to a lesser extent, World War I) was "financed" by a combination of money creation, price controls, and a constraint on consumption by recourse to the required use of red and blue coupons. During the wars, the relevant resource constraints for government planning and budgeting were physical inputs such as critical raw materials, shipping space, and infantry replacements.

Only the experience since Wold War II provides useful insights into the management of high-level federal-government spending, in which setting strong sentiments about the associated levels of taxation necessary to finance that spending are also operative. Observation of the federal-government budgeting process suggests that the prime emphasis may not be on efficiency, as implied by the model of the maximizing household. Rather, budgeting and budgets reflect political aspirations; they constitute political information and communication systems and set political precedents.[17] "If politics is regarded as conflict over whose preferences are to prevail . . . then the budget records the outcome of the struggle."[18] Politics explicitly brings up the question as to "who gets what," or as to the distribution of power, property rights (and obligations), and benefits that can be derived from government spending programs. It also entails the specification of objectives, whose attainment or nonattainment can affect the status quo among different groups in the society.

Struggle over these questions comes to a focal point in Washington, where it takes the form of a complex set of interactions by which Congress, the executive branch, the bureaus, and the constituents mutually adapt to and accommodate each other. We try to depict these interactions in Figure 1.1:

Figure 1.1   Schematic View of the Political Budgetary Process

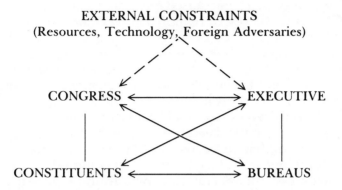

The top of the figure indicates that all parties must adapt to basic external constraints: scarce resources, a technology that does not solve all the problems caused by scarcity, and foreign adversaries who do not accommodate us. The figure also makes explicit that the "sovereign," or policy-making and budgeting, power is divided between the executive branch (the President) and Congress.

The "bureaus," shown at the lower right hand corner of the figure, constitute "the bureaucracy." Here is concentrated the expertise of the bureaucrats. Straightaway, an important consideration in the conduct of government business centers around the role of presidentially appointed Cabinet officers and where they stand on the figure. Nominally, they are part of the President's "team" or of the Administration, and they might accordingly be so located. But Cabinet officers may in fact closely identify with and become almost indistinguishable from the bureaus composing their respective departments. More accurately, a Cabinet officer may be better described as being an advocate for his agency, except when he is under pressure from the Executive. Secretaries of the Army and Navy in a past era traditionally functioned as "civilian spokesmen" before Congress on behalf of their military bureaucracies. And Secretaries of such departments as Health, Education, and Welfare, Housing and Urban Development, and Transportation appear to be advocates of programs promulgated by their respective line agencies. The Secretaries of HUD appear to have felt that their primary role is to sponsor and support the building of new houses; the Secretaries of the Department of Transportation

have shown evidence of regarding themselves in the role of
providing services for the major transportation sectors of the
economy. Such behavior caused one practicing student of politics, Charles G. Dawes, to remark that "members of the cabinet
are a President's natural enemies."[19]

The "constituents" elements of the figure represents the diverse interest and pressure groups in the society, who interact
strongly with the Executive, particular elements of Congress,
and bureaus. The concept of a constituency as it bears upon
these relationships is often noted explicitly when it is observed,
for example, that the Secretary of the Interior should be a
"Westerner" or that the Secretary of Agriculture should be from
the Midwest and should have a strong agricultural background.
That many Treasury Secretaries come from the banking community is reason enough for some to suggest that the Treasury,
too, represents a particular segment of the society.

An important force driving many Bureau/Constituency interactions is that bureaus primarily provide instrumental services to certain sectors of the economy at very low, or even zero,
cost. An instrumental service is, after all, an intermediate product or service, which in turn is an input for the production of
some end product that contributes to consumer satisfaction and
welfare. Irrigation projects, for example, provide the water that
contributes to the growing of lettuce, tomatoes, and cotton;
air-traffic control, airports, and supersonic transport programs
are instrumental inputs for airline transportation, which in turn
is an input for other activities, to the extent that it is used for
business travel. The Bureau of Reclamation and the Corps of
Engineers have a long-standing record of providing low-cost
water, electric power, flood control, and navigation facilities to
particular regions and groups.[20] The airline industry requires
the air-traffic control service provided by the Federal Aviation
Agency, and it finds very worthwhile a variety of programs that
operate to provide more and larger airport facilities. The airline
industry regarded with dismay the reorganization that brought
the Federal Aviation Agency under the cognizance of the newly
created Department of Transportation. Such an "integration"
of federal transportation functions, in the view of the airlines,
might reduce the benefits realized by the industry relative to
those realized by other transportation media.[21]

The relationship between Congress and its constituency is of
a double nature. On the one hand, Congressmen are sensitive

to the public's aversion to paying taxes and the anguish in private households when inflation occurs. As the "guardian of the treasury" and controller of the "pursestrings," Congress also has a strong interest in controlling the power and size of the executive branch and is thus responsive to a traditional American philosophy that seeks to limit the size and scope of state activities. The American legislative branch also inherited a philosophy from England that emerged from a long struggle whereby Parliament was ultimately able to obtain the upper hand in the control of the tax revenues. Through most of the Republic's history, Congress was the dominant "branch" in the federal policy-making process, and individual Congressmen were the principal "personifications" of the federal government to the average citizen. But with the growth of the federal bureaucracy and of the power of its officials since the 1930's, Congress has been on the "defensive." To maintain its power and status, it has imposed constraints on the executive branch and it employs a committee system to control the government's bureaus and agencies.[22]

On the other hand, individual Congressmen, mainly those occupying key positions on powerful committees, become advocates of the activities of bureaus that serve their respective constituencies. Individual Congressmen can acquire expert knowledge of a particular functional area and develop a sincere belief that a particular program contributes vitally to the country's welfare, and consequently may vigorously support larger budgets for such programs. Moreover, substantive expertise itself— which a Congressman acquires during years of service on a committee—tends to generate an attitude of advocacy.

Career bureau officials are sensitive to the attitudes prevailing on "the hill," to constituents served by their bureaus, and to the relationships of those constituents to key Congressmen. A primary function of the lobbyists in Washington is to provide an "intelligence" or "communications system" that ensures that all three parties—Congressmen or their staffs, officials, and constituents—receive "relevant" information.[23] Bureau officials are adroit at conducting bureau affairs so as to minimize any adverse budgetary effects inflicted by congressional appropriations subcommittees or by constraints imposed in the authorizing legislation. Indeed, the hallmark of an "effective agency official" in the Washington setting is his ability to achieve these objectives. A historian of the Army's experience in aircraft procurement "in two world wars and the years in between . . ." notes with regard to military procurement affairs that "hill tactics [Capitol Hill] are profoundly important. Officers inexperienced in this specialized function, no matter how . . . meritorious in every other respect, operate . . . to the detriment of the service they represent."[24]

The posture of high career officials with respect to the Executive branch, and particularly in their attitudes toward the President, has been described as one of "respect for power, a degree of resignation, and a tinge of contempt."[25] Judgment concerning a new Cabinet officer is withheld until he demonstrates whether he will advocate the bureau's programs, be passive, or ask tough questions and implement ideas of his own. The best that could happen is to acquire an advocate, the second best to acquire someone who can be converted to an advocate. Nevertheless a passive Cabinet officer is also acceptable, for then the bureau officials can manage on their own.

The setting suggests specific roles for the "actors," who must accommodate each other in such a way that substantive business gets done. The accommodation, however, must permit each actor to maintain the image suggested by the formal roles: Congressmen must economize; bureaucrats must advocate. The Office of Management and Budget (OMB) can play an economizing role on behalf of the President, but such action can harm congressional constituents and, hence, Congressmen. And since the President must have sufficient political currency with Congress to obtain support for his legislative program, the OMB cannot act vigorously unless it has very clear signals from the President. Finally, Congressmen must serve their constituents.

From all of this an equilibrium emerges. The roles are played, and long-range commitments are honored. Agencies ask for more than they expect, but not "too much" more. The OMB trims some agency requests, but it does not advocate changes that would disrupt the activities that Congressmen favor, for to do so would evoke positive congressional action that would discredit that office. Then agency bureau officials would look to Congress even more for guidance and support, and this would diminish what influence the OMB does have over them. The net result would be that the President's total budget would have little meaning.[26] It is not surprising then that the Office of Management and Budget often takes its cues from previous congressional behavior.

The congressional budgetary process is itself highly fragmented, initially residing in House appropriations subcommittees, each of which makes marginal adjustments to existing programs, with only limited consideration being given to basic policy choices.[27] Appeals may be made to the Senate Appropriations Committee, both formally and informally. Altogether, the budgetary process, whatever else it might be, is one in which each of the actors engages in strategies that take into account the response of other actors to those strategies. What this means is that one's own action is designed to evoke a preferred behavior on the part of other actors. Political persuasion, advertising and salesmanship, threats, power plays, and political blackmail pervade the entire budgetary process, including the manner in which programs are designed and evaluated.

The total budget and its division among the bureaus nevertheless remains highly stable.[28] Only a few activities, each subject to a narrow range of increases or decreases, are intensively scrutinized in any given year. Policies may indeed be chosen for their intrinsic merit, but they are also chosen for the political support they generate for agencies and, in turn, for the politicians. Political support thus becomes operational when it is translated into funding for the agencies. How the agencies use the funds, in turn, importantly affects the political support.

The political budgeting process described above is driven by a strong economic force, which is complicated by ethical and political factors that are peculiar to American society. An underlying ethic in the American setting is that people should receive income in proportion to their contribution to the total output, that contribution being due perhaps to their labor or to the yield from the capital they own and manage. This criterion has been termed "productivity ethics." One gets dollars for working and for being thrifty and a good manager of capital, and one votes in the marketplace when he spends his dollars, with a single dollar being worth a single vote. Appropriately enough, then, the system has also been termed "dollar democracy."

The economic force is the phenomenon of "rising supply price," combined with the motives of individual workers and property owners in maximizing their earnings. Rising supply price occurs with increased spending on a particular product or service, because the increased spending forces the product's price up. Higher profits and earnings accrue to its producers, and this leads to an expansion of output, which may then mitigate the tendency for the price to rise. But as long as the industry requires specialized resources, the later price will be somewhat higher than the one that existed before the increased spending took place, and the higher unit price of the product will afford the owners of specialized resources permanently higher earnings.[29] But the phenomenon is symmetrical: a lower level of spending for an item causes a lower unit price and lower earnings for the owners of specialized resources used in its production.

The implication of the rising supply price phenomenon is critical to the government spending-taxing processes. Suppose, for example, that the government decides to budget an additional $5 billion a year for higher education. Simultaneously, then, it imposes taxes that constrain the money demand that consumers can exert for all other products. The higher-education industry intensively utilizes skilled academic workers such as Ph.D. scientists and scholars. Other industries, on whose products the consumers must economize, also use these resources to some extent and they can thus release some inputs to the expanding higher-education industry. But the earnings of scientists and scholars will nevertheless rise relative to the earnings of, say, dairy farmers, agricultural workers, and automobile mechanics. Some of the latter may also find employment in the expanding industry as handymen or janitors or even in their old trades. As the universities expand, or as new ones are established, businessmen and landowners in the particular locations benefit from the increased spending of students and staff. All of the human resources peculiar to the expanding industry thus benefit from the changed pattern of spending. Owners of other resources experience a reduction in *before tax* earnings in a way that is determined by the workings of the revenue-raising system, which directly reduces the people's money income and cash holdings and causes a decrease in spending on products and services that the individuals would have purchased in the absence of the higher taxes.

The phenomenon of rising supply price—which has a technological-economic foundation—has a happy consequence for those who embrace the concept of productivity ethics, but who can nevertheless bring political techniques to bear in improving their economic status and power in the community. The system can still be viewed as a form of dollar democracy; but by taxing and spending the government becomes a major voter in its own right. In a past age, a powerful prince or potentate could dispense favors and riches among favorite subjects. Modern methods are not so direct or crude, although their effects are similar. They are greatly complicated, however, by the uncertain operative features of the political democracy.

The system of dollar democracy that characterizes market organization and exchange processes in the private sector of our economy accords each dollar one vote (apart from some of the effects of racial discrimination). However, for a variety of reasons—such as different degrees of effort, natural endowment, the chance of parentage, which affects cultural and material inheritance—the possession of dollar votes varies widely among individuals and families. The term "property" best describes the combination of the possession of earning power, talent, and claims against assets that determines the number of dollar votes one may have.

Modern political democracy, on the other hand, provides each man one nominal political vote, and so nominal political votes are distributed equally. Dollar votes or property can be, and are, distributed very unequally. Such discrepancy in the distribution of the different kinds of votes contains the seed of instability. Because the state, most notably through its taxing and spending power, can affect both the before- and after-tax dollar votes among different groups, it is possible to exchange dollar votes for political votes and vice versa.[30] The object of the exchange process is to change the economic status quo: on one hand, those who possess little property try to vote themselves some property. This is one way of describing egalitarianism. On the other hand, those who possess much property use their dollars to buy votes in an effort to avert egalitarianism tendencies and thereby maintain the status quo. Nor are those who are amply endowed with property above using their purchase of votes to influence the taxing-spending in such a way as to sweeten their holdings. Politics can thus be viewed as an exchange process. Politcians are the brokers; bureaucrats are instruments; with the aid of this conception, it is possible to sharpen the roles of the main actors in the scenario: powerful producer-oriented groups play supporting roles (literally as well as figuratively); and the citizens, as a whole, pay the bill and, perhaps, write the scenario itself. Unlike many dramas, however, there is no clear-cut "villain." Although it may be tempting to so label the bureaucrat, he might be more appropriately regarded as a "victim" of the process. But whatever, his role is a very difficult one.

2

THE DUAL ROLE
OF BUREAUCRATS

> I have come to the conclusion that there must be two
> separate mailing lists for distributing instructions to
> Government personnel. On one list, you get instruc-
> tions to be economical; don't waste Government
> funds; the President urges you to cut down costs, and
> so forth. On the other list, you get instructions to pay
> higher profits; spend more money than you need to;
> look out for industry because industry is not capable
> of looking out for itself. My problem is, I am on both
> mailing lists.
>
> Testimony of Adm. H. G. Rickover before the Subcommittee on
> Economy in Government of the Joint Economic Committee, U.S.
> Congress, November 14, 1968, p. 70.

Although legislative and elective political processes are the focal
points of attempts to influence the distribution of economic
power by political means, much of the effort becomes operative
through the action of government bureaus. The role of bureaus
is particularly critical in spending programs. Indeed, bureaus
are created to spend; and established bureaus continually design, advocate, and acquire new spending programs.

Central to much of the discussion of bureaucracy and bureaucrats is the concept of expertise, which can be described as the
composite of knowledge and skills that an individual or group
of individuals possesses, so as to permit the performance of a
specialized function or activity. Bureaucrats possess much expertise, which enables them to be secretive about their operations.

The term *expertise* itself is unclear, however. Some observers
appear to equate expertise with efficiency,[1] so if one is skeptical
about the efficiency of bureaus, then one might accordingly
doubt the aptness of the term in application to bureaucrats.

Many people have the idea that bureaucrats are inherently maladroit; but on the other hand, the Machiavellian conception of bureaucracy suggests an opposite view. Finally, one hears much, usually in a different context, about "dedicated" public officials, among whom are generally included the military officer corps and the faculties of universities.

In varying degrees, each of these diverse views of bureaucrats and career public officials is correct. The seeming contradictions among them can be resolved by recognizing that there are important differences among different bureaus, and that an important distinction can be made between military organizations on the one hand and many civil government agencies on the other. Perhaps a clarification of the issue can be facilitated by sharpening our conception of expertise.

Distinctions must be made among the three kinds of expertise encountered in varying degrees in various bureaucratic organizations: operating expertise, bureaucratic expertise, and political expertise.

Operating Expertise. Operating expertise describes the ability to perform a task, mission, or function for which an organization exists, as is illustrated by the ability of military organizations to organize for war and carry it out. The military has many facets and it draws upon a variety of specific operational skills. There are the "pure" combat skills possessed by a general officer and his staff, which enable them to handle large forces in intricate and wide-ranging operations. Encompassed by these skills are the abilities to appoint subordinate commanders, to know and to motivate them, and to organize them in ways wherein the personal qualities of each are complementary to those of the others. To operate effectively also requires a knowledge of equipment systems operated by friend and foe alike and an ability to improvise in the field as the strengths and weaknesses of the equipment and tactics on both sides are revealed.

Highly specialized operational expertise is required for naval and air operations, for which a knowledge of the narrower engineering and physical performance characteristics of aircraft and ships is also required. But it is a blending of this narrower technical knowledge with warriorlike qualities that constitutes the unique attributes of the operating/technical expertise of naval and air officers.

Another form of operating expertise comprises the ability to create and train organizations. The creation of an army division, for example, requires pulling together components with narrower specialties from among the many "combat arms" and services that make up an army. These subcomponents already possess specialized operating and technical expertise, plus often a "narrow" indoctrination. But training them to function as a team so that their diverse specialties complement each other verges on being a high art.

The creation of an air force, as illustrated by Gen. Curtis LeMay's development of the Strategic Air Command to its present level of professionalism and competence, is a form of operating expertise. Operational expertise also includes high-level staff work, as was epitomized by the decisive capability of the Railway Division of the German General Staff for mobilization and major strategic deployment and redeployment of the German armies in two nineteenth-century wars, as well as by a nearly similar capability in World War I. Operating expertise is also encountered in other bureaucracies—law enforcement, public-health service, tax collection, and wild-life preservation, to mention but a few. The capacity of a university for teaching and research falls into the same category.

The capabilities that individuals and groups have for performing such specialized functions are valuable social resources. In varying degrees, these capabilities require that individuals participating in an organization be dedicated to the organization's function. And conversely, the organization must institute special selection processes for acquiring people who can be "indoctrinated" in the performance of the activity.

A by-product of this selection and indoctrination process is the frequent emergence of a "subculture," the members of which are oriented inward. The professional military officer corps, for example, is judged to have this introversive quality within the American society.[2] The tendency may be particularly acute if the values and modal personality characteristics of the group are at variance with those prevailing in society in general. From these differences can arise attitudes which range from the feeling that one's profession is "misunderstood"[3] to feelings that verge on a sense of alienation. The resulting tensions can be severe, and they can be extremely troublesome for the society as a whole.[4]

Bureaucratic Expertise. This type of expertise is a composite of organizing skills and thorough knowledge of one's organization. Modern bureaucracy is based on written documents and formal procedures, with skill in "office management" also being relevant. As related to a specific organization, bureaucratic expertise bears upon information channels, reporting procedures, functions of various subparts of the organization, the rules governing efficiency reporting, and the prerogatives and responsibilities associated with various positions in the hierarchy. A possession of a certain amount of bureaucratic expertise is necessary for anyone who is to function in a given organization, and the possession of a high degree of this type of expertise is the mark of an accomplished bureaucrat per se.

Bureaucratic expertise importantly bears upon making organizational changes or modifications when necessary, in response both to changing external conditions and to personnel capabilities and capacities within the organization. It involves paying attention and devoting energy to matters that may seem trivial to an inexperienced outsider but that are vital to the performance of an organization's mission. Involved in all of this is the creation of an organizational environment wherein there can be an effective division of labor among specialized subcomponents. The formulation of clear statements of individual and group responsibilities and obligations (both upward and downward in the hierarchy), the expeditious processing of paper work, the specification of forms and formats so that information can be distributed efficiently and succinctly to points where it is needed, "keeping the record" so that actions and decisions can be tracked and eventually subjected to future accounting, if necessary—all are manifestations of bureaucratic expertise.

Effectiveness in performing the organization's operating functions depends importantly upon bureaucratic expertise. There are marked differences among various organizations in the degree of bureaucratic expertise their members exhibit, with professional military officers no doubt being the most highly sophisticated and tax collectors perhaps running a close second. The reason may be that in military administration there is much experience to draw upon, with numerous examples of poor combat effectiveness and low morale in operations when careful attention was not paid to such matters as command relationships, efficiency reporting, and countless other details that are in many respects the essence of armed forces. In tax collection a fiduciary trust accountability, plus adherence to predictable rules, must exist if there is to be an effective tax-collection system at all. Conversely, in many organizations where "administrative" or "bureaucratic" matters are given short shrift or are handled in a sloppy way, there is apt to be a great deal of ineffective operation, poor morale, and unhappy customers. Many civilian bureaucracies, including those in the government, manifest these characteristics partly because senior management has a disdain for bureaucratic detail or is simply bureaucratically naive.

Political Expertise. An important characteristic of bureaucratic leadership is a tendency to maintain secrecy so as to exploit a monopoly position in an attempt to maximize the budget. Maintenance of secrecy requires purposeful activity, which can be denoted by the verb "obfuscate." To obtain resources, an agency also seeks political support from groups in the society that can influence political decision makers and the budgetary process. This activity requires public relations to build up the organization's image. Another objective of public relations is to assure the political decision makers that the organization is performing in the most efficient possible manner. Much staff work and intellectual and analytical endeavor are employed in performing this function.

Bureaucratic political expertise is also directed inward, so as to maintain internal political stability. Complex organizations, consisting of diverse technical or operating subgroups whose leaders lead strong, well-knit constituencies, may operate essentially under a "group sovereign" arrangement, with the nominal head occupying a position of *prima inter pares.* His heads of groups or deputies have status that is comparable to that of feudal barons, and they struggle among themselves to gain a larger relative share of the organization's budget for their own fiefdoms. Also, since there is often a strong likelihood that one of the barons may one day inherit the sovereign's throne, there are ample opportunities for members of the sovereign's immediate staff to contemplate some sporting options.

There are important interrelationships among the types of expertise described above, and there are differences among organizations at a given time or within an organization over a period of time, all of which can be explained in terms of mixes of the three kinds of expertise.

The interrelationships among operating, bureaucratic, and political expertise are subtle, and they determine qualities of the bureau itself. Bureaucratic expertise occupies a critical middle ground. Insofar as it encompasses organizing skills, it complements and enhances operating expertise. On the other hand, however, bureaucratic technique can be an effective tool for playing the politico-budgetary game, with special reference to maintaining secrecy and obfuscating. When directed outside of the bureaucracy, political expertise is practiced primarily by the head of the bureau and, in some cases, by the barons. Also, it is practiced mainly in the headquarters—for example, at the Pentagon. On the other hand, the United States Post Office, because of congressional prerogatives, was caught up in external politics in both its headquarters and field operations as a result of the patronage system of postmaster appointments.[5] Inner-directed political behavior, too, is a major activity in the headquarters, but this can also filter down to the headquarters of subordinate agencies.

An awareness of the different kinds of expertise permits a distinction between two types of bureaucracies: mature and immature. A mature bureaucracy has a clear and well-defined mission or role to perform. This is typified by the military services, a tax-collecting agency like the Internal Revenue Service, the management of a state-owned railroad, or some postal systems. An important characteristic of such mature bureaucracies is that they generally know how to perform their missions well. Thus, an army in the field displays a high degree of professionalism and operating expertise. Conversely, the headquarters of the larger organization may at the same time exhibit all the manifestations of a Byzantine court. In all of this, an important question arises as to how the behavior pattern prevailing in headquarters may affect behavior in the field.

Operating expertise should not be confused with efficiency in the broader economic and social sense. For although without operating expertise an organization cannot be efficient in an economic sense, the presence of operating expertise does not guarantee efficiency. An organization may be able to perform a given mission with a high degree of effectiveness, dispatch, and professionalism, but the mission it performs may not be socially relevant or its capability for performing a given mission may be too great relative to social needs or priorities. Or, it may operate on too large a scale because its budget is too large.

Similarly, organizations like the Rural Electrification Administration and the Savings Bonds Division of the Treasury Department have developed their operating expertise to a high degree. Yet their existence continues, in a fashion suggested by Parkinson, despite a negligible social need for their output. "Social efficiency" of a bureaucracy, then, is not exclusively identified with operating expertise; rather, it is a budgeting or resource allocation problem. The possessors of operating expertise are invariably advocates of their endeavor, so society cannot expect to receive useful, or even rational, advice from them with respect to the budgeting question. At most, they only provide some inputs for budgetary deliberations.

Immature bureaucracies are those in which the leadership has not yet crystallized its efforts in performing a specified role. These are usually organizations that have been newly created to cope with emergencies or new problems, for whose solution there is little experience or knowledge. In the United States, starting with the New Deal and continuing through the Fair Deal and the Great Society, there has been a proliferation of such agencies. In these new organizations there is very little operating expertise, in the sense of being able to cope with, say, the problems of urban blight and poor housing. And it may be that bureaucratic expertise of a high level is also lacking. Such organizations do display a fairly high degree of political expertise, however, since they must struggle to retain budgets that initially may have been liberal in the flush of the emergency. Also, their budgets may be expended in efforts to maximize the agency's political good will vis-à-vis Congress, and to gain constituents at the grass-roots level.

An important characteristic of such agencies is a tendency toward program proliferation. The Department of Housing and Urban Development, for example, sustains a variety of housing programs for both low-income groups and especially for middle-income groups, college students, and urban renewal, all of which tend to benefit local business interests; open-space programs, which benefit landowners and please nature lovers; and programs for city planning and urban-transportation development.

Such a proliferation of programs has the interesting side effect of ensuring that no single "need" is adequately met, and the resulting "unfilled requirements," in turn, serve to justify larger future budgets and the longevity of the bureau. But since there is no really clear and well-researched understanding of the intricacies of the nation's "urban problem," there is little basis for evaluating the programs. Hence, the behavior of an immature bureau bureacracy is overwhelmingly political, inasmuch as its major functions consist of political log-rolling and the distribution of favors that can flow from the Federal fisc.

Like most people, bureaucrats have many motives, one of which is to perform a function that has social relevance. But this objective can only be achieved if the organization itself can operate effectively. Effective operational performance—whether it be in the conduct of research or in the command of an infantry battalion—is a derivative of expertise and of pride in that expertise, a quality that can be viewed as a form of the more generally noted pride of workmanship.

But to be able to give expression to such operating expertise, one must be sustained in some way by the rest of society, and government bureaus obtain this sustenance through a political, rather than impersonal, market process. It is necessarily an income-redistribution process. Money allocations, or income and services in kind, are exchanged for votes in the legislative budgetary process, and these votes in turn attract both popular votes at the ballot box and the other forms of support from which politicians and political parties gain sustenance. Included in this other support are campaign contributions (in money and in kind), editorial backing from communications media, and intelligence from various private-interest groups. The exchange can take place with little of the "corrupt politics" that may have characterized past eras, although we should recognize that standards of behavior are changing, as is the degree of sophistication of the techniques employed. In any event, primarily because they have a constrained view of society and social processes, all, or at least most, parties to the process play their roles with perfectly good faith in the notion that whatever they do directly serves some socially worthwhile purpose.

Senior bureaucrats must perforce be politicians to the extent that their activities—whether they be spending or providing services to private groups—have consequences for income distribution. They must be politicians insofar as they and their bureaus are instruments in the game played by elected politicians. To elected politicians, who may be egalitarian or generally conservative or favorably disposed toward special-interest groups, the income-redistribution process is a more or less purposeful affair. But it is a rare Congressman or Senator who will openly acknowledge any intention to redistribute income or property purposefully. (However, such intents *are* inferentially acknowledged at election time through reference to federal actions that benefit a Congressman's district or state.) Because of the predominance of productivity ethics in the United States, any action that can be construed as undue interference with the "normal" distributive processes is associated with alien attitudes. Thus, the income redistribution process that takes place by political means is carefully submerged from view, surfacing explicitly only in the formulation of tax policy.[6] As a result, government spending programs must be rationalized on the ground that they contribute to the "general welfare."

Senior bureaucrats, and career officials in the Office of Management and Budget, understand this income- and property-redistribution process, and they are highly adroit at playing the game with elected politicians. But this is not their primary endeavor: other objectives are paramount. The bureaucrat's primary objective is to further the operating expertise of his bureau and apply it to practical matters. A secondary objective is political, in that an effort is directed inward toward the effective harnessing of rivalries that may exist among leaders of important subgroups in his bureau. This secondary objective may not pose a serious problem in some bureaucracies; but in others, particularly in the military services, where senior officers are selected and conditioned to be independent and aggressive, the inward-directed politics can be most demanding. Such control is easier if the bureau obtains ample funds and especially so if increasing resources are made available through the budgetary process. The outward-directed political behavior of the bureau head, with its consequences for income and property distribution, is a means that serves the end of obtaining resources from elected officials.

Bureau heads are thus often indifferent to the social implications in terms of achieving egalitarian or conservative income-distribution goals of the income-redistribution process to which they are parties. In this regard a "nonpolitical" attitude is in perfect harmony with the image of the well-behaved bureaucrat, who defers to the politician or policy maker on matters of broader political significance. It is also a prudent attitude to the extent that he wishes to assure the future of his organization.

The role of a senior bureaucrat is therefore very difficult. In few endeavors is a comparable duality required. The business executive can focus on profit and loss, the politician seeks the political power provided by an independent constituency, the academician strives to build up an impressive (or at least, long) list of publications. But the senior bureaucrat must be adroit at the politician's game while at the same time not appearing to be a politician. He must possess a high order of professional expertise, and moreover, he and his subordinates must have a high degree of organizational and bureaucratic expertise. The latter requirement is especially demanding, because the bureau itself must possess dual qualities if its head is to play his dual role.

A recognition of this duality of bureaucracy can shed light on several of the observed features of bureaucratic organizations, which bear upon the concepts of efficiency, knowledge, and communication systems.

When it is said—and it frequently is—that bureaucracy is "inefficient," such an assertion can have several meanings. One of these meanings, that "too much" is being spent on the activity, may be quite appropriate. But if we recognize that the bureau is a creature of the duality described above, then the term "inefficient" may miss the mark. The bureau's objective is to participate in an unobstrusive way in the political income-distribution process. It generally performs this role with a high degree of adroitness and efficiency. Lobbying and public relations are skillfully employed; and these skills, combined with the political guidance of the bureau chief, intermesh with the similar skills of the decision makers and their staffs at the Capitol and in the Executive offices.

The political decision-making process also operates in ways that are highly predictable. All one needs is a knowledge of who the "players" are, including the Congressmen on key committees and their constituents, plus a knowledge of the activities the bureau has or might like to have that might be of benefit to private groups who are of interest to the Congressmen. With respect to military "hardware" programs, a knowledge of civil-servant scientists located at arsenals or laboratories or in key Pentagon offices plus a knowledge concerning the current hierarchical standing of military officers who in earlier years advocated certain programs enables one to make good predictions about forthcoming scenarios, including occasionally how the engineering and test reports will come out. Such organizational behavior assuredly does not result from the efforts of bumbling or maladroit people. And yet, simultaneously, the same organizations can produce a capability in the field that exhibits a high order of operational expertise.

To maintain such a dual operation requires special communications systems, and most organizations have two of these. One is the formally prescribed system, suggested by the hierarchical structure and made explicit by the manuals on procedure. The second is the informal communications system, which operates through oral expression or the use of certain signals.[7] A principal advantage of the informal communication system is that it entails no "record," and it is therefore ideally suited to the bureau chief's need for communicating directives to those members of his staff who implement his outward-directed political actions.

In the military services, oral briefings have become a critical part of the informal communications system. They permit an "upward flow" of information, with the kind of information actually flowing upward depending partly upon the quality of superiors and the signals they emanate regarding their preference for information about the true state of affairs or simply what they like to hear. The upward flow of information at briefings also depends on how many "sports" there are who will argue with a superior. But perhaps a more important function of the formal, oral briefing is that it provides an opportunity for the superior—by means of the questions he asks, his criticism of specific points, and his scowls and smiles—to make known throughout the system his preferences without actually recording them. That is why attendance at such briefings is a privilege that is coveted by subordinates.

Simultaneously with the operation of the informal information system, formal directives and memoranda constitute a record that demonstrates the bureau head's intention of implementing his superior's desire for economy or of conducting an objective analysis of the issue at hand. Thus, a great many formal directives have been issued in Washington during recent years, instructing subordinates to make use of modern, rational management techniques, including the Planning, Programming, Budgeting System (PPBS) and its associated cost-benefit or cost-

effectiveness analytical techniques. But the senior people sign-
ing those same directives, collectively at least, have made
enough bad jokes about the new tools and their champions in
higher offices to have conveyed to the troops the idea that things
be changed not too much and not too quickly.

A high premium is placed on the ability of subordinates to
perceive the desires of the bureau head with regard to the latter's outward-directed political requirements. In a setting peo-
pled by many individuals with strong egos, weak principles, and
the drive of personal ambition, the demand is readily supplied.
It is gauche, if not actually bad form, to ask the bureau head to
state explicitly his outward-directed political objectives. It is
risky to render a cost-effectiveness study suggesting that a program having a high external political payoff will not meet the
magic criterion of 1.0 or better. But the risk of such a thing
happening can be minimized by careful selection of the persons
or contractors that do the studies.

The informal communications system becomes tied into a
total system that generates information, misinformation, and an
absence of information, all serving and feeding the bureau's
outward-directed political endeavors. High on the positive information list is intelligence on the bureau's activities that can
impact various Congressional districts either favorably or unfa-
vorably. Great care is exercised to facilitate the announcement
by the interested Congressmen of favorable actions impacting
in a given area, when this is deemed appropriate or useful. Care
is also given to maintaining ties with trade associations and
other groups in the private sector of the economy that may
support the agency. The positive information that is gathered
and retained for use in the agency's political and public relations
endeavors compares in quality with that generated by a first-rate
combat intelligence network in time of war. And well it should,
since such information is critical to the bureau's survival.

Despite the impact of government spending upon the distribution of income, the amount of information generated with
regard to that impact is astonishly small, although perhaps this
meagerness of information should not be surprising at all. One
reason it is not readily available is that it often requires analysis
or extensive grubbing and compilation of data. Putting such
information in a usable form is often avoided, although an occasional effort is made to do so with respect to the income-distribution effects of selected programs, usually by students outside

the bureaucracy.[8] The Johnson administration's "War on Poverty" focused much attention on the measurement of the "poverty gap" and a determination of how selected welfare-oriented income maintenance programs fail to cope with the poverty problem. And occasionally, an enterprising journalist may research the subject of land transactions that occur prior to the announcement of an urban renewal program or the route selection of a federally supported beltway around a large urban area. But such endeavors are striking for their rarity.

Indeed, the explicit generation of information revealing how special groups or individuals benefit from political decisions may be purposefully avoided, because of the embarrassment it can create for all of the parties concerned. Furthermore, it may be that such information is not purposefully sought and made explicit because the informal system adequately serves the political decision-making process. As a former Director of the Bureau of the Budget has observed, "There are thousands of individuals whose full-time occupation is the careful examination of proposed legislation or executive actions, seeking to discover implications for the interests of groups they represent."[9]

Bureaucrats have to play a dual role. On one hand, they are impelled by the natural motive of practicing their profession. On the other hand, they are parties to and instruments in a political process that operates to influence the distribution of income and property. But this latter, higher-level, political game is a tacit affair; and the knowledge affecting it is quasi-private, although it is generally held by all with a modicum of political sophistication. Since as critical instruments in the process, the heads of bureaus must perform their dual roles, then their bureaus, in turn, must have dual communications systems and even organizational structures for playing the dual role. As has often been observed with regard to military organizations, bureaucracies reflect the values and characteristics of the societies from which they spring, and to heap criticism on bureaucrats for their lack of efficiency is therefore likely to miss the mark. Indeed, an interesting question centers on why the country is served with the degree of professional competence it does get from most of its bureaucrats.

The primary force behind this duality in bureaucracies appears to be the requirement for influencing income distribution by political means so as to buy and sell votes. In some unknown way income is redistributed, but by no means is it always done in an egalitarian fashion. The real cost of such a process is a certain amount of waste, by which we mean an allocation of resources that is inefficient in both an economic and technical (engineering) sense.

So far as national security is concerned, bureaucratic behavior and its related resource allocation problems assume a special character. In the resource-using activities of the civil agencies of government, pork-barrel tactics can be handled emotionally and even rationalized intellectually, provided one either is willing to accept them as part of the price of a democratic society or is sufficiently sophisticated or both.[10] In military affairs, however, there are some differences. The activities for which military force (which is the major component of national-security out-lays) is employed perhaps most vividly display the rigor of com-petititon that business firms encounter in the market place. War provides a partial test as to whether or not good resource-alloca-tion decisions have been made. But the price of experience gained through warfare can be costly for the nation at any time, and poor decisions made even in peacetime in the selection of weapons and equipment of forces can be overcome only be taking casualties. This being so, to view military-resource alloca-tion as an aspect of the pork-barrel tradition greatly taxes our ability to be "sufficiently sophisticated," a proviso mentioned earlier in this paragraph.

Political and institutional problems may be more difficult to treat intelligently in the military than in civilian government, because of cultural/bureaucratic differences between the professional military officer corps on the one hand and civilian policy makers and the citizenry on the other. Through most of United States history, those members of the professional officer corps who must go into the field in time of war have been able to insulate themselves from the elements of domestic politics impacted by small military budgets. This insulation is no longer possible, both because of larger military budgets in the absolute and relative senses and because of the impact of modern tech-nology on military systems. The increased technological content of military affairs has also beclouded the ability of laymen and civilian policymakers to relate resources to military capability. Accordingly, the opportunity for military bureaucrats, including technologists, to obfuscate is greater than it has ever been.

To the degree that the military professionals could insulate themselves from the domestic politics associated with spending, it was also possible for them to concentrate on nurturing and preserving the traditional military values of duty, loyalty, and honor. Intertwined with honor is truthfulness, including honesty with one's self. Moreover, the effective conduct of military field operations also requires objectivity and an information system that is geared to providing relevant facts. By no means is it clear that organizations can long maintain an apparatus that is well suited to playing the politico-budgetary game while simultaneously preserving the military values and the information apparatus required for the effective conduct of military operations.

In military affairs we witness extreme cycles of emotionalism that are seldom experienced with regard to, say, the medical profession, central bankers, or intellectuals in general. Our involvement in Vietnam and its associated high-resource cost, for example, suggests that our principal policy makers, as well as the citizenry as a whole, had higher expectations regarding the effectiveness and efficiency of our military force than might have been warranted. The resulting disappointment has been bitter. Present frustrations and general discontent suggest that the problems of military management, force planning, and weapon-system selection cry more than ever for hard thinking and deep thought. What follows directs our concern from bureaucratic behavior in general to the problems of military management.

3

ELEMENTS OF MILITARY MANAGEMENT: POLITICIANS, PROFESSIONALS, AND TECHNOLOGISTS

> It was the policy of the ablest generals, and even of the emperors themselves, to encourage these military studies by their presence and example; and we are informed that Hadrian, as well as Trajan, frequently condescended to instruct the unexperienced soldiers, to reward the diligent, and sometimes to dispute with them the prize of superior strength or dexterity.
>
> Edward Gibbon, *The Decline and Fall of the Roman Empire* (Modern Library, vol. 1, p. 11.

Central to the subject of military management is the concept of civilian control, which clearly implies two ideas. First, military professionals should be so "housebroken" or otherwise controlled that there is no danger of a military takeover of the civilian government. The Founding Fathers were keen students of Roman and English history, and their attention must have been arrested by the adventures of Caesar and Cromwell, for they were greatly concerned about the problem of civilian control of the military. One way of solving the problem was to rely mainly on a volunteer militia and generally take a dour view of military professionalism or activities that would nurture professionalism.

Another way to minimize the possibility of a military coup was practiced by Hitler, who encouraged the development of an independent Air Force to counter the monopoly control of force that the German Army otherwise would have had. To play this role more effectively, the Luftwaffe had antiaircraft guns that could be handy against army tanks in street fighting, and it also owned parachute infantry. As additional insurance, Hitler permitted organization of the Schutzstaffel (SS) troops, first in regiments and later in Panzer divisions.[1] Both the Luftwaffe and the SS were commanded by Nazi henchmen who were more or less loyal to Hitler, and both organizations recruited and attracted personnel with strong pro-Nazi political sentiments. The resulting proliferation of military organizations greatly complicated the mechanics of achieving a military coup.[2]

A second unambiguous aspect of civilian control of the military apparatus is the idea that military operations and wars should be started only by civilian authorities. Civilian control of military operations also extends to major or potentially sensitive phases of operations once a war is under way, often creating differences of viewpoint between civilians and the military. To handle the resulting stress between the two groups intelligently requires knowledge of military capability by the higher civilian officials. Civilian political leaders must also possess knowledge about military capability to make intelligent decisions about initiating military operations. This requirement poses some subtle problems of its own, inasmuch as acquisition and possession of such knowledge could lead to civilian intervention in decisions the military bureaucracy may feel should be its exclusive preserve.

Another sensitive and difficult aspect of military management centers around the politics that are internal to the military establishment. These can be termed interservice and intraservice politics, as contrasted with the politics of military-civilian relationships, so that the former can be described as "internal" politics and the latter as "external." The internal politics has two major facets, which interact in complicated ways. A major military service, like an army, navy, or air force, actually consists of a number of subcommunities, if not actual subcultures, which represent specialties in different combat functions or specialized combat missions. Armies have their infantry, cavalry (armor in the modern setting), artillery, and combat engineer specialties (the U.S. Army again has its own air arm), and there are usually latent rivalries among the practitioners of these specialties. Often the rivalries are healthy, if not jovial, but they do have their serious and troublesome aspects. During the American Civil War, cavalrymen on both sides were the butt of much ribald humor on the part of infantrymen, as in this rhetorical question posed by Union General Hooker: "Whoever saw a dead cavalryman?" On the Confederate side, it is reported that the manifestations of this humor were serious enough that General Lee felt constrained to admonish one of his corps commanders to control the wit of his infantrymen. And as naval forces became more specialized with respect to surface, submarine, and air components, similar rivalries emerged. These rivalries erupt frequently in headquarters struggles over dollars, weapon design, and procurement decision making. Much of this dispute often comes to a head in controversy over "roles and missions" of the different services, or of the combat branches of a given service. In turn, weapon development and acquisition is a key to roles and missions issues. Conversely, the uniformed military more generally adhere to a "gentleman's agreement" to avoid raising roles and missions issues. This arrangement has the beneficial result of minimizing divisiveness and rancor that could destroy the spirit of cooperativeness essential for the operating effectiveness of the larger organization. But the failure to raise the technical and operating questions implicit in roles and missions issues can trammel innovation, and the reallocation of resources that innovation invariably calls for. Hence many critics have belabored the "conservatism" of military bureaucracies. The charge is valid. But the critics often fail to appreciate that some degree of conservatism is perhaps a partial price that must be paid for institutional stability, some of which is essential if there is to be a viable operating instrument at all. Moreover, it should be recognized that for each innovation delayed by "mossbacks," an equal number of instances can be uncovered of attempted ones that turned sour, and entailed a "waste" of resources, including troops that were lost in war. In addition, for each innovation attempted, countless others have been proposed, and often forcibly advocated and supported by influential parties, that were just plain nonsense. Although crank inventors dominate this group, uniformed military zealots and politicians have played the same role. In brief, since new "ideas" seem to be in almost unlimited supply, there is often much to be conservative about.

In addition to being the incubator of many new ideas, the rise of modern technology and the specialization it required contributed to creating two major elements of a military service: the military "user," or consumer, and the military "producer." In armies, distinctions emerged between combat arms or branches, such as infantry, artillery, and so forth, on one hand, and "technical services," such as quartermaster, ordnance, and transportation specialists, on the other. And in navies, there is the distinction between "the fleet" and "the shore establishment." Initially, the technical services handled procurement and hence became the focal point of an ongoing interface between the military services and the civilian sector, as it bears upon spending of the dollars allocated to military purposes. But as the business of war became more technical, the technical services and elements of the shore establishment became more important and powerful, to the point where their influence is now critical to the weapons-development process. At the same time, the problems of communication between the users and the military technical communities have become severe, and indeed, interservice and intraservice struggle and politics have increasingly characterized and dominated their interrelationships.

What with interservice, intrabranch, and consumer-producer rivalries within a service, military decision making has a very high *internal* political and social content, quite apart from the politics of government spending as it bears upon Congressional–Executive Branch–Constituent relationships. Now the two brands of politics—internal and external—can interact in very complicated ways; and the resulting complications critically affect the relationships among political decision makers, military professionals, and technologists. The purpose of this and the following two chapters is to develop an insight into some of these interactions.

The problems that dominate military management, under conditions other than in a major war, center around spending the dollars and equipping the troops. Involved are a complex of activities including formulation of national security policy, budgeting of dollars and manpower, programming force elements, developing and selecting weapons, innovating and formulating new tactics, training military personnel and units, and, finally, operating forces in the field. Technologists—consisting of scientists, engineers, and designers—play a key role in this complex of activities, along with political officials, including Congress, and the uniformed military professionals. The difficulties of military management may be viewed to be those of achieving a workable division of labor between these groups with respect to the different activities. This is hard to do because the activities are so closely interrelated.

The idea of a division of labor derives its justification and foundation from the fact that each of several specialist groups can exert primacy in the decision making of at least one critical activity. However, a primary decision maker must often rely on other specialists for knowledge. He may also have to rely upon other specialists to implement a decision. Occasionally, a party may make decisions outside of his normal area of competence, either because he enjoys a position of higher authority or because a superior may not perform his normal function and thereby permits a subordinate to fill the void. For example, a field commander may deploy his forces in a provocative way, but nevertheless believe he is discharging his military mission in the spirit desired by his civilian superiors and in that fashion defeat the intent of his superiors. High authorities, including Presidents and Congressional committees, have directly concerned themselves with very fine-grained procurement and force-structure decisions.

Thus the President and Congress share primacy of decision-making in formulating national-security policy. Congress dominates the budgeting process by its Constitutional power to appropriate funds. The professional military exert primacy in the procurement of weapons, in innovating and tactics formulation, and in training, programming and operating the forces. Professional military provide political leaders critical knowledge about both our own and rival military capability. Technologists provide both political leaders and the military knowledge about weapons and potential weapons. Technologists also implement, by participation in the development process, decisions to procure weapons. Related to provision of knowledge is the function of advocacy, which is critical to the budgetary process. The military operator is traditionally an advocate for larger budgets; and the technologist, if only because of his expertise and his faith in that expertise, is generally an advocate of new weapons. Frequently, the President and, more frequently, the Secretary of Defense are advocates before Congress with regard to military budgets.

A vast number of management problems come to a head in programming, which is closely associated with procurement. Programming is the complex of actions and specific processes by which resources are translated into actual military capability. Programming includes a wide variety of activities, each being highly complex and requiring a high order of expertise. As we use the term, it includes, for example, the decision to procure a force of air transports designed to support land operations, which in turn requires the procurement of many items of equipment, the procurement and training of support manpower and crews, the provision of maintenance and other supporting resources, and the building or allocation of bases. It also requires the development of tactical procedures and doctrine in the use of the system.

One might object to the assertion that military operators exert primacy with regard to programming, and the objection gains some force from the fact that, under Robert McNamara's administration of the Defense Department, a Programming Office was introduced as an adjunct to the comptroller's function in the Office of the Secretary of Defense.[3] The OSD programming system is an accounting and auditing system augmenting the dollar and manpower budgeting system, which in turn is used as a tool for controlling decisions made by the military programmers. The program format is useful for planning or for the dialectic and study processes that are the essence of the activities implied by the term "planning." A program format, however, should be distinguished from the activity of "programming," which encompasses a large variety of activities in which both the spirit and the letter of the higher decision-makers' intentions must be followed and which only the operators can carry out. Through programming activities, the operators—either purposefully or unintentionally, cleverly or crudely—can, because of the ample opportunity provided by the complexity of large systems, frustrate the objectives of their superiors. To allocate funds to the Air Force for air transports for supporting Army operations, for example, requires that the crews be trained in ways to carry out those special operations. But if the Air Force is indifferent about such a mission and if it finds that the aircraft can profitably be used in support of its own operations—as by providing logistic support for its Strategic or Tactical Air Commands—the capability for support of the Army that was intended by the policy makers will not be attained. Programming, as a complex of many highly detailed actions, must perforce be carried out by operators; and their decisions regarding the complex of actions, including failures of omission, endow them with a position of primacy in the programming function.

For certain purposes, the word "administration" might be interchanged with "programming," and the above discussion would be supported by much of the literature that emphasizes the critical role of administration. We prefer the term "programming," however, because in the Department of Defense the word "program" encompasses activities and associated dates at which an activity begins and ends. The diverse activities contributing to a larger objective—e.g., the training of people, the procurement of equipment, and so on, which are necessary to provide a new air wing—must mesh, or some waste occurs. The activities must also be funded, and therefore consistent with a financial "plan," or budget. Decisions, or "plans," cannot, of course, be implemented unless they can be programmed; thus "programming" and "planning" are interdependent. The emphasis on timing is traditional and well founded in military management because of its vital importance in war. In our view, the word "programming" captures this quality better than "administration." Nevertheless, administrative skill is a necessary ingredient for good programming.

Programming is critically related to and dependent upon the selection, development, and procurement of weapons, the latter entailing the creation of force-structure elements, such as battalions and air wings, and an associated set of programming actions. The weapons-acquisition process should be kept conceptually separated from programming, because it is through weapons that technology and technologists impact the decision-making process. Entailed in the selection and procurement of weapons is the evaluation of their effectiveness, and weapons effectiveness, in turn, holds critical and important implications for the elements of the force structure that might be programmed.

It is also important to identify an activity termed "innovation." Although the innovative process is imperfectly understood, an innovation should be held in sharp contrast to a technical invention. Military innovations are usually combinations of new equipment, changes in tactics, and often, changes in organizational structures, and they may also be functions of how personnel are trained and motivated. Often, the significance of improvements in weapons performance is that they permit tactical innovations; and through this nexus, technological developments create the possibility of producing military force more effectively for a given amount of resources. Innovation, as applied to military affairs, requires explicit decision making by the military operators, and this is a critical area wherein operating military expertise is applicable.

The management of military affairs in the United States before World War II was affected, if not dominated, by two forces that interacted in subtle ways and gave the concept of civilian control a flavor differing from that of the European experience. One was a general disdain for military professionalism, fueled by the increased technical content of war that became apparent around the turn of the nineteenth century. This force, along with the underdeveloped state of the nation's industrial capability during much of the nineteenth century, contributed to the development of the "bureau" and associated "arsenal" system in both the War and Navy departments, a system that acquired a singular quality in the United States, inasmuch as it provided an apparatus on which to build a division of labor between civilians and military decision makers. The "bureau system" became the second force to influence decision making. The system contained flaws, however, that persist into the contemporary setting. This section examines the rise of military professionalism in the United States, while the next section treats various aspects of the military bureau or technical service system.

During most of the history of our nation, our continental insularity permitted the maintenance of a small military establishment and provided only limited cause to the civilian policy makers for concern about our military effectiveness. Central to American military management during the Republic's formative period was the Jeffersonian notion that a citizenry, organized as a militia, could spring to arms and cope with a professional soldiery.[4]

This hypothesis was tested in the American Revolution and the War of 1812. It appears that the operational lessons of the Revolution—including the order of battle at Yorktown, where most of the artillery and sappers (critical ingredients for conducting a siege) were French professionals—were promply forgotten. And the War of 1812, as an experiment, yielded mixed results. James Madison's Secretary of War, John Armstrong— taking literally the Constitutional proviso that the President was Commander-in-Chief of the armed forces and drawing from this the inference that he was the President's deputy—personally took to the field on two occasions and aspired to be a thunderbolt of war, in the fashion of Cincinnatus. On his first endeavor he attached himself to an expedition that was to seize the St. Lawrence valley. But he apparently had enough military acumen to perceive that the venture would go badly and accordingly detached himself from the operation in sufficient time for the onus of failure to fall upon the heads of the regular officers initially designated as commanders. The second command venture of this civilian paladin took place in the defense of Washington, where the results were less ambiguous.[5]

The War of 1812 actions at Lundy's Lane and Chippewa revealed that regular American infantry could slug it out with British regulars.[6] The findings of these battles were rendered ambiguous, however, by the results of the Battle of New Orleans, where a mixture of frontier militiamen, pirates, and a few regulars inflicted heavy casualties on and defeated a contingent of Wellington's peninsular veterans. The British force was commanded by the Duke's brother-in-law, Sir Edward Packenham, who was also one of the fatalities. Although Packenham was with Wellington throughout the Peninsular Campaign, he apparently failed to observe the lessons his brother-in-law consistently taught Napoleon's marshals, one of which was to avoid head-on confrontations unless one carefully selected his ground. Nor can it be maintained that Sir Edward was ignorant about rifles. The British had for many years equipped their own light infantry with rifles and used them effectively to counter French light infantry skirmish tactics. However, Packenham may not have possessed a high learning ability—a possibility suggested by Wellington, who had a penchant for extreme understatement, when he said that "Ned" was not brilliant (a shortcoming which in Wellington's view was more than compensated for by loyalty). Yet it must be noted in Packenham's defense that his line of attack at New Orleans was dictated by the admiral who selected the troop debarkation point, despite Packenham's objection. It has been suggested that this selection was motivated by the desire to permit the Royal Navy to be in a better position to participate in the sacking that would immediately ensue after the capture of New Orleans.[7] Thus British decision makers—by selection of officers to command American operations in two wars —contributed to fostering and preserving the military management corollaries of Jeffersonian (and later Jacksonian) political philosophy.

An underpinning of the Jeffersonian approach was the idea that a military officer "was expert in one of several technical specialties, competence that separated him from other officers trained in different specialties and at the same time fostered close bonds with civilians practicing his specialty outside the military forces."[8] This philosophy was long reflected in the curriculum of the U.S. Military Academy. During a large part of the

nineteenth century, when military schools in Europe were concentrating on applied tactics and staff training, and hence turning out young officers who could handle companies and battalions, West Point was producing future civil engineers and
railroad presidents.[9] The philosophy was comforting and compatible with the idea that every citizen was a soldier and every
soldier a citizen. With a blending of civilian and military callings,
the dichotomy between civilian and military need not appear,
nor could there be a problem of civil-military relationships if, in
fact, no distinction existed between the military and civilians.

The Jeffersonian concept of military men as technical specialists had a superficial foundation in events that acquired sharp
focus in Europe, especially in France with the advent of the
French Revolution. The French Army had a strong tradition in
military engineering, which went back to Louis XIV's Marshal
Vauban, who mastered the art of designing fortifications and
laying siege to them.[10] Vauban was not only innovative in such
technical areas as fortress design and the construction of paral-
lels by which fortresses could be taken, but he also developed
techniques for mining and for enfilade fire.[11] In addition, Vauban hand-picked and trained the first infantrymen to employ a
new weapon—the grenade—in assulting fortresses.[12] (The appellation "grenadier" came to refer to elite infantry in all European armies). But although Vauban was what today would be
termed a technician, he was also a fighter and tactician.

The advent of the military engineer was accompanied by that
of the artilleryman, who in that day possessed technical knowledge in such areas as metallurgy and applied chemistry. These
callings also provided avenues by which commoners could become part of the officer corps, of which those having such a
proletarian background and technical competence also moved
in eighteenth-century intellectual circles that were the seedbed
of the ideals of the French Revolution. The faith in rationalism
was institutionalized with the founding of the École de Polytechnique during the flush of postrevolutionary zeal. This school
took on a paramilitary quality, including in its founding faculty
Lazare Carnot, himself a military engineer who moved alter-
nately between academia and high government position. And by
about 1810, it had become the European center of rationalism
and scientific achievement.[13]

The contribution of military men to the founding of the École
de Polytechnique and the contribution of some of its faculty to

the French war effort could not have gone unnoticed by Jefferson, who sympathized with French institutions and culture. And Sylvanus Thayer, who dominated West Point during its formative years, viewed France as "the repository of military science,"[14] a notion no doubt sustained by the achievement of French arms under Napoleon. There was an important difference, however, between the French model of military management and its attempted American copy. As was illustrated by Vauban and, later, by the French artillerists with their technical expertise, the French achieved a blending of combat and technical skills in their officer corps. But they also had strong traditions in the less technical military vocations of infantry and cavalry, with their firm cores of professional officers and enlisted men. True, the École de Polytechnique continued to produce military engineers and artillerists; but the French also created St. Cyr, with a curriculum that concentrated on infantry tactics. Americans chose to focus only on those aspects of French experience compatible with the grass-roots American concept of politics and war. The effect of adopting only a part of the French model contributed to a split in the American officer corps when it finally did acquire a professional element during the post-Civil War period. This split contributed to and was promoted by the bureau system that became characteristic of American military management.

The naval forces caused no fears among those whose sensitivities to possible military takeover were stimulated by imaginative readings of the adventures of Caesar and Cromwell (and, one must note, such fears were not purely fanciful). A characteristic of a wood-and-sail navy was that, although it required a professional officer corps, it did not require specialist seamen for its men-of-war. Merchant seamen with only limited additional training could man naval ships,[15] and hence it was possible to maintain only a small naval force in peacetime (with gratifying budgetary consequences), which would have only a limited capability, if indeed it had any capability at all, for seizing and holding the civilian apparatus.

Naval forces in the age of wood and sail possessed other qualities that facilitated clear-cut military-civil relations. The technology of naval weapons had a base in common with the civilian maritime industry; and the technical and operating differences between merchant ships and men-of-war were minor, with naval officers and civilian authorities sharing much knowledge about handling ships at sea in an age when merchantmen were armed as a protection against piracy. However, the command of naval ships and, especially, the handling of fleets became the special domain of the professional naval officer. Procurement, including ship construction, could be dominated by civilians ashore, and in the main, it could be a natural and easygoing relationship.

Nor were naval operations at sea greatly complicated by technicalities. The weapons were simple, and they were carried by comparatively simple ships. As late as 1830, the basic qualifications required in the naval profession "were still almost entirely such abstractions as valour, leadership, discipline, devotion and experience: not technical knowledge of highly specialized and complicated installations."[16] The tactics were also simple. In reply to a friend who was sending Nelson "a man who had an idea about aiming guns," Nelson wrote back, "as to the plan . . . I shall of course look at it, or be happy, if necessary, to use it: but I hope we shall be able, as usual, to get so close to our enemies that our shot cannot miss the object."[17] Hence, in navies there was neither a basis for military-combat subcommunities like those in infantry, cavalry, and artillery nor a major bifurcation between technical and combat branches. The distinction between technology and operation was rapidly to engulf the naval forces, however, with the advent of steam and iron and, later, of steel, as well as of advances in ordnance.

The United States did not acquire a truly professional element in its officer corps until the post-Civil War period. In the Civil War, itself, which was the seedbed of this element, officers of both the Navy and the Army were confronted by the requirement to handle large-scale military operations, and they rose to the necessity. Knowledge in the command of divisions, corps, and armies, in the integration of separate combat arms, and in joint naval-land force actions (Vicksburg and Sherman's campaign from Savannah into South Carolina) was acquired the hard way. Similarly, the generals who could do these jobs well were few and hard to discover. Happily for the Union, however, President Lincoln was an empiricist, and he employed the expedient of firing losers until he found winners, the principal and most successful of whom was General Grant. But the star pupil was Sherman, who in some ways excelled the teacher, as was illustrated by his march from Tennessee through Georgia to the sea. It was Sherman and other officers like him who created the American professional officer corps.

The American officer corps acquired its professional quality in a setting that superficially was inimical to the armed services, for after the Civil War the nation turned to making money. Pressures exerted by civilians to acquire commissions through political means withered away, and to minimize taxes the armed services were cut drastically. Civilians and military technical officers, through the Navy's bureaus and the Army's technical services, handled administration. And so the elements of the officer corps who aspired to line or operating-command functions turned inward, isolating themselves from the mainstream of American life and commencing the serious study of war. A number of "postgraduate" schools were created. For the Army, Sherman took on the role of a Loyola: he protected and revived the Artillery School at Fort Monroe, he fathered an infantry and cavalry school at Fort Leavenworth, and he fostered an increased military emphasis in the curriculum at West Point.[18] Sherman's counterpart in the Navy was Admiral Luce, who had worked with Sherman in joint operations during the Civil War, and who later became a commandant of midshipmen at Annapolis, a founder of the Naval Institute, and a promoter of the Naval War College. These, then, were the predecessors of a generation of officers who viewed war as being the real business of the military, who developed a detachment from politics, and who created the environment that was to produce the officers capable of handling the armies and fleets of the two world wars.

The bureau-technical service and associated arsenal system that emerged in America had a precedence in European practice. It rested on the valid foundation that military organizations must have administrative apparatuses and suborganizations consisting of specialists who procure inputs from the civilian society. With increasing specialization, the functions of quartermasters were institutionalized, and further divisions of labor were called for with advances in weaponry, which spawned Departments of Ordnance for both the Army and Navy. For the Navy, shore facilities had to be operated (Bureau of Yards and Docks) and ships had to be designed and procured (Bureau of Ships).[19] The procurement and "housekeeping" functions of bureaus were formally recognized by the Congress insofar as budgetary accounting categories were specified as appropriations to the particular bureaus. This budgetary classification was used until about 1950, at which time the present budgetary categories of "personnel," "operations and maintenance," "procurement," and so forth were introduced.

During the nation's early history, force was placed on the creation of a system of arsenals, or in-house manufacturing facilities, by our low state of industrial development. In this respect, the United States resembled France in the latter's formative period of nationalism and even in its later periods of development. French industry, even by the late eighteenth century, was not attuned to mass-production techniques, as was British industry of the same period. But the British, too, had their arsenals, as well as the Royal Dockyards that constructed and repaired ships.

As western countries became increasingly industrialized, private firms entered the armaments production business and existed side by side with government-owned arsenals. The division of labor varied. In England, for example, government arsenals manufactured heavy land armaments, especially artillery and small arms, while Vickers was the principal producer of naval guns and mountings. On the Continent, France retained its old arsenal system, but the government also provided business for firms like Schneider and Creusot. Elsewhere on the Continent, firms like Fabrique National, Skoda, Krupp, Bofors, Oerlikon, and Hispano-Suiza came to be words in the military lexicon.

Bureau systems and arsenal systems are not necessarily related. Nevertheless, there is a historical correlation between them. The record of the overall performance of arsenals is mixed, although a good comparative study of those of different countries is yet to be made. Yet historical evidence portrays the arsenal system both at its best and at its worst. There may be extremes that have not yet been developed, but some elements of the French and American systems can illustrate extremes in performance. The weapons development and acquisitions of artillery in France on one hand and of small arms in America on the other provide such a study in contrasts.

It was an arsenal in Strasbourg that developed the foundry and machining techniques in 1739 that permitted more efficient and lighter cannon for field artillery;[20] and this development in turn revolutionized artillery tactics and Army organization by the time of the eve of the French Revolution. Later, prodded by defeat at the hands of the Prussians, who placed the Krupp breech-loading cannon in opposition to the French muzzle loaders, the French arsenal system turned to developing and producing an optimum field-artillery piece. The end product incorporated a number of generally known principles, the most critical of which was a hydropneumatic recoil system that permitted a "long recoil" of the gun, which minimized displacement of the piece by absorbing the shock of firing. Since it was no longer necessary to reaim, or "lay," the piece after each firing, quick firing, registration by firing, firing over one's own infantry, and rolling and box barrages now became standard artillery practice, leading to the prodigious ammunition consumption rates of World War I, as only one result. The weapon was the "French 75."[21]

Although French military ways provided the model for Americans during the nation's formative years, neither the U.S. arsenal system nor its technical officers matched French performance in developing and producing weapons. As a contrast to the French experience, the worst example of our own in-house system was the Army's Department of Ordnance (later, its Ordnance Corps) and its Springfield Arsenal. On occasion, there were some competent designers at Springfield, but the unhappy workings of the Ordnance Department and its arsenal with respect to small arms was striking. Indeed, it was astonishing, when one considers that practically all major technical improvements in small arms and automatic weapons of the nineteenth century and the early twentieth century were made by American inventors, many of whom were either reared a short distance from Springfield or employed by New England firms.

Although American inventors were far in the lead in producing repeating rifles, major bureaucratic wars had to be waged during the Civil War to get repeating weapons such as the Spencer rifles and carbines into the Union Army. It was only the personal intervention of President Lincoln that permitted the procurement of enough repeaters to equip Sheridan's cavalry, whose resulting large volume of fire permitted the turning of the Confederate flank at Petersburg and thus contributed to the fall of Richmond.[22] Other than this, only a scattered number of militia units procured improved small arms, purely through their personal financial sources or through the efforts of state governors. It was not until thirty years later that the Army finally got a magazine loading rifle—the Danish Krag-Jorgensen rifle, which was available in limited numbers for the Spanish-American War. The Springfield Arsenal promptly undertook its own development, which led to the 1903 Springfield, a fine clip-fed rifle that many ex-soldiers and marines regard with fondness.[23] However, the 1903 Springfield was so much like the German Mauser that the Germans obtained damages for patent infringement.

Overall, the American small-arms development and procurement performance on behalf of its armed services has been sad. Although America was the source of most of the technical improvements of small arms during the nineteenth century, American designers like Hotchkiss and John Browning found Europe more receptive to their creations. It was only after he established his reputation in Europe and after World War I revealed that the U.S. Army had neither a satisfactory machinegun nor an automatic rifle of its own design that Browning was able to apply his skills (under the auspices of private American firms) to the development of the Browning Automatic Rifle and the .30- and .50-caliber machine guns, which proved to be mainstays for the World War II American forces.

Nor did the country's nineteenth-century ordnance establishment, wherein both the Army and Navy operated its respective bureaus, sparkle in the cannon department. Indigenous design was dominated by such "cannon kings" as Parrott, Rodman, and Dahlgren, all of whom were or had been bureau officials, who developed rifled artillery. (However, for its mainstay field piece the Army had adopted in 1857 the twelve-pounder "Napoleon," sponsored by Louis Napoleon III, who sought to inherit his uncle's luster.)[24] During most of this period, recrimination and ill feeling between artillerymen and military-ordnance specialists, on one hand, and between civilian inventors and bureau officials on the other, dominated relationships. Artillerymen, chafing under Ordnance Bureau regulations in peacetime and a seeming lack of support in war, labeled the bureau as "invincible in peace, invisible in war."[25] Quality control bearing on procurement left much to be desired, as indicated by bursting guns and such arresting statistics as that provided in one Union-fleet bombardment, in which five shipboard accidents of bursting Parrott guns produced 45 friendly casualties against 11 owing to enemy fire.[26] At this point in time, Parrott was operating a private firm; however, arsenal-produced Rodman and Dahlgren cannon also inspired fear on the part of crews selected to man them.[27] Yet ordnance officials could point to much sharp practice on the part of civilian producers to make a seemingly plausible case for arsenal production. Conversely, ordnance officials established a consistant record of ignoring any inventions or ideas that emanated from civilian sources. Meanwhile in Europe, the title of "cannon king" was held by civilians—Armstrong, Krupp, and Whitworth.[28]

In other land armaments the United States also lagged behind Europeans. Although the United States was the world leader in automative development, American tank design and concepts through World War II were not the equal of those of either the Germans or the Russians. An American designer such as Walter Christie, finding the Ordnance Department automotive experts unreceptive toward his ideas,[29] found the Russians to be much less so. Our World War II basic artillery weapons either were derived from French or British design (the 155-mm. and the 8-inch howitzers) or were modifications of the World War I German 105-mm. gun/howitzer. We had nothing that compared favorably with the German 88-mm. dual-purpose gun. One bright spot in weapons was the semiautomatic Garand rifle, which permitted more rapid rates of fire than did the enemy's bolt-action rifles. But even this advantage was partially offset by the Germans' light, belt-fed machinegun (the design of which provided the model for our present standard M60 machinegun), which was employed to a greater extent by the German infantry than the less portable, tripod-mounted Browning machinegun was by our own troops. The only major area in which American land-forces equipment excelled during World War II was jeeps, trucks, and earth-moving equipment, contributions that only in a limited way reflected the inspiration of our military technologists.

Gen. George C. Marshall, in his final World War II report, was moved to defend the Army's record, and that of the Ordnance Department in particular, with regard to materiel development and procurement. He shouldered the blame for materiel deficiencies by stating that the Ordnance Department produced "what it was told to produce, and these instructions came from the General Staff of which I am the responsible head."[30] The problem ran much deeper, however, and it had its roots in a history of poor management, combined with too much politics.

The Navy's Bureau System was the basis for one-half of the dichotomy that arose between its "shore establishment" and the "fleet." The fleet was to be concerned with operations and "effectiveness," while the shore establishment was to support the fleet. One of the functions of the shore establishment was to provide active-duty command slots for senior officers; and another was to provide political pork for the districts in which the navy yards were located. In the post-Civil War era, for instance, navy yards were sustained by repair work on old wooden ships: "Don't give up the ship!" became a navy-yard slogan as the workers did their best to stretch out each repair job.[31] Thus, the United States in the first half of the 1870's was spending half as much on its navy as was Britain; and yet in 1875 a British observer wrote that "there never was such a hopeless, broken-down, tattered, forlorn apology for a navy as that possessed by the United States."[32] This behavior, however, in large part stemmed from an assertion of authority by line officers over technical specialists and their staff departments, in the immediate post-Civil War period. Although the Navy conducted numerous joint operations during the war, and extensively used such new-fangled gadgets as steam-propulsion systems and iron-clad ships, it strongly reinstituted its pre-Civil War doctrine, which was essentially oriented to commerce-raiding. Sail was regarded the preferred propulsion for such a function, given the cantankerous quality of steam engines at that time, although steam engines were also tolerated on ships for the purpose of providing emergency power. Thus for an extended period, ship commanders were enjoined not to burn coal; and training focused on individual ship handling, rather than on coordinated use of ships in squadrons or fleets. This doctrine combined with a political ethic like that of the Grant administration served to assure that the Navy's main role was to function as an input to the pork barrel.[33]

The U.S. Navy's entry into the age of steam and steel contained many trails. It began to occur in earnest during the 1880's, during which period the foreign-policy-making "establishment" was advancing the idea that the nation should take an activist or imperial role in world affairs. The concept of a navy consisting mainly of cruisers for commerce raiding and monitors for coastal defense gave way to that of a blue-water fleet structured around "capital" ships. Yet the technical and administrative skills impacting upon ship design and construction did not match the aspirations and the resources Congress provided. The failure of the different Navy Bureaus to coordinate their efforts was judged to be responsible for grave design deficiencies, whereby new battleships of the *Kentucky* class came to possess uncovered ammunition hoists, inadequate steaming range because space for fuel was consumed for purposes specified by the competing bureaus, and other deficiencies.[34] Gunnery technique, highly dependent on technical design of mountings, badly lagged behind that of the British. Only after these deficiencies were called to the attention of President Theodore Roosevelt by the maverick Captain Sims were vigorous steps taken to remedy them. Fortunately for that officer's future, the President also took steps to protect Sims from a limited career that the dominant encrusted element of the Navy would have prescribed.[35]

Central to the Navy's organizing and personnel policy as it accommodated itself to the technological impact of steel and steam was the emergence of the distinction between "line" and "staff" officers. In the Navy lexicon, a "staff officer" was a specialist in a technical function like construction, engineering, medicine, or supply. As such, he could not command a ship or a fleet, as could a line officer.[36] Simultaneously with this bifurcation of its officer corps, the Navy's Bureaus emerged, with two key ones remaining under the domination of line officers. One of these was the Bureau of Personnel (originally established as the Bureau of Navigation in 1861), which controlled personnel assignments. The other was the Bureau of Ordnance, one of the five original bureaus established in 1842, whose domination by line officers was an approach opposite to that of the Army, wherein the Ordnance Department was a province of uniformed technicians.

In principle, the Navy's logic was sound, being based on the simple notion that those who were to use weapons should know them: "Our ships are designed by men who do not go to sea; and our planes by men who do not fly; but by gadfrey, our guns are made by the men who'll fire them."[37] The "Gun Club," as it came to be known, was a power in internal Navy politics, and heads of the Bureau often went on to greater things, particularly fleet commands. (Accordingly, the term "Gun Club" was extended to include the battleship-oriented admirals who dominated the command hierarchy). Promising young midshipmen were often admonished "to get behind the big guns and stay there."[38]

The Gun Club developed and produced fine big guns, including their mountings and fire-control systems, and it also turned out a good twin-mount, five-inch, .38-caliber, dual-purpose gun that was used extensively in the war on destroyers and as secondary armament on larger ships.[39] But in other areas of naval armament, the Club's performance was not good. For close air defense, the Navy had to scramble to take advantage of British experience and to acquire through licensed manufacture both the Oerlikon 20-mm. and Bofors 40-mm.[40] antiaircraft guns, struggling at the same time to transform the metric design specifications into the English system.[41]

The Bureau's experience with submarine-launched torpedoes was unhappy. Central to the story was the government torpedo station at Newport, which both developed and manufactured the weapon. The use of this torpedo in World War II revealed unpredictable and unreliable performance. Instead of getting kills with hits or near misses (kills were theoretically attainable from near misses by means of a magnetic exploder for a torpedo running under a ship's bottom), the submarine crews too often revealed their position to the enemy on firing because of unreliable depth control, premature explosions or duds, and "low order explosions that failed to cause lethal damage to enemy ships."[42]

The principal reason for the torpedo debacle was a failure to conduct tests on the weapon during peacetime. Such tests were expensive, since they required the destruction of costly torpedoes; and as the Navy's official historian notes, "One basic reason for not making the tests . . . was perhaps the pressure from the civilian employees of the Torpedo Station and from the commercial and political interests in the vicinity of Newport to spend available funds on keeping as large a force as possible employed."[43] It is to the Navy's credit, however, that Admiral Blandy, wartime head of the Bureau of Ordnance, noted that it was the Bureau's responsibility, inasmuch as "no one either in the Bureau or at Newport apparently questioned the inadequacy of the design without such tests."[44] Admiral Blandy's apparent last word on the subject of torpedoes also possessed a singular quality (which is greatly lacking in the contemporary weapon system acquisition process): "The Chief of the Bureau therefore directs that as a matter of permanent policy, no service torpedo device ever be adopted as standard until it has been tested under conditions simulating as nearly as possible those which will be encountered in battle."[45]

The criticism and defense of technical military subcommunities and their "in-house" production and development facilities is a perennial sport, in which all practioners and students of military management engage.[46] This technical community in turn is factionalized, as is its military counterpart in the line or combat branches. In varying degrees and in different settings and times, a blending of technical and operating or combat skills has occurred, but never in a way that has been, or can be, complete or universal. This divergence of subcommunities leads to high-level management problems, and indeed these problems have been a major focus of civilian authority in all major countries. Differences of view within the military community have also been a source of information for civilian leaders; and the ways in which civilian authorities have used these sources of information and have coped with ruptures within the seemingly monolithic military bureaucracy is central to military-civilian relationships. Such turbulence provides ample opportunity for civilian leadership either to exert a statesmanlike and healing role or to intensify ill feeling and mistrust. Thus, "civilian control of the military" can exist in both instances.

From the 1850's onward, the American bureau system became the focal point of involvement of the civilian secretariat and Congress in the affairs of military departments, although the bureaus themselves were headed by career military officers in a tenure pattern that frequently resembled that of U.S. Supreme Court Justices. Civilian Secretaries of War and of the Navy involved themselves primarily with procurement. The chiefs of bureaus became "staff advisers" to the civilian secretaries, and some, often simply by virtue of long tenure in Washington, established channels with the various congressional committees. In some instances, the chiefs developed close ties with powerful individual Congressmen, and conversely, some Congressmen came to regard the military or some phases of its management as their personal fiefdoms.

The system worked in such a way as to permit civilian secretaries to play any of several roles. Some, like Grant's second Secretary of War, W. W. Belknap, could override Sherman's attempt to run the Army (including the War Department bureaus), causing him to leave Washington in disgust and transfer his office to St. Louis, and then go on an extended trip to Europe. One of the issues between Belknap and Sherman involved the appointments of sutlers, an aspect of military management in which the Secretary's interest was keen, as was attested by his hasty resignation when evidence was made public that he was selling sutlerships for private gain.[47] Other Secretaries of War, like Donald Cameron, could use the position "in training for his father Simon Cameron's Senate seat and the political boss-ship of Pennsylvania."[48] (Meanwhile, Sherman had returned to Washington and was left alone by this statesman.) Woodrow Wilson's Secretary of the Navy, Josephus Daniels, viewed his likely major contribution as being that of converting the Navy into an extension of the Boy Scouts, by way of uplifting the character and education of the enlisted men. At least it must be conceded that he improved the sobriety of the officer corps, if his success in ending the age-old naval practice of serving liquor in the shipboard officers' mess is any criterion.[49]

Other service secretaries, like Elihu Root, could combine political acumen and organizational insight to try by the necessary legislative means to provide the Army a staff apparatus designed to cope with that service's "bureau problem." Root's endeavor was stimulated by the example of the German general staff, which excelled in formulating mobilization and strategic deployment plans (for which railway planning and scheduling were critical elements). By contrast, the American mobilization for the Spanish-American War was plagued by poorly if noncoordinated endeavors by the separate War Department bureaus, which had responsibility for different components of procurement and logistic support of the field forces, and this experience provided a negative element that motivated Root's effort.[50] But even so, the problem remained and came to be called the "Technical Service problem" up to and after World War II.

Thus, even after the outbreak of World War II, the Headquarters Staff of the Army was pervaded with bureaucratic red tape, facilitated by the fact that at least 61 officers—including the Chiefs of Technical Services and Combat Arms—had access to the Chief of Staff. Although the Army's Technical Services chiefs posed serious difficulties in any effort to integrate materiel and logistics activity, the chiefs of Infantry, Cavalry, Field Artillery, and Coast Artillery had long exercised power and "insisted on being consulted about any order that might conceivably pertain to their special preserve."[51]

A partial glimpse of Gen. George Marshall's stature and ability is revealed by the fact that he reorganized the Army's General Staff on the eve of World War II so as to cope with the problems posed by an Army consisting of fiefdoms.[52] The Headquarters-Staff reorganization was followed in early 1942 (implemented by an Executive Order of the President, and legally sustained by the President's war powers), which effected a massive reorganization of the Army itself.[53] Both a well-planned strategy on Marshall's part and the support of Secretary of War Stimson facilitated the change. In the process, the heads of the Combat Arms (organizationally speaking) were lopped off, and the Technical-Service chiefs were subordinated to the head of the newly created Army Service Forces.[54] After the war, however, the Technical-Service chiefs were reinstated to their prewar status, which testifies to the strong hold of tradition. The Navy partially met its own bureau problem through congressional insight and support in the face of coolness on the part of the leadership of the civilian executive branch by creating the Office of the Chief of Naval Operations in 1915. Nevertheless, enough of the old problems remained to absorb fully the administrative talents of a James Forrestal on the eve of World War II, as well as during that conflict.

The role of Congress in American military management prior to the end of World War II exhibited many facets, although certain major strands emerged. That the nation came into being as a result of war against a seemingly high-handed king who sought to levy taxes to support military forces imposed on the Colonies profoundly affected the writers of the Constitution. This document clearly reflects an intent to foster an adversary relationship between the Executive and Legislative branches. To strengthen the position of Congress, it expressly vested in it both the power to raise armies and to declare war. Since the major resource-using activity of a limited central government would be national defense, the power of appropriating money further strengthened the position of Congress. Finally, the Constitution provided Congress the power to specify rules and regulations governing both the armed forces and their organization. Yet the need for an Executive function was recognized, and the President was designated Commander-in-Chief. On such matters as whether the President has to spend monies Congress appropriates, and the role of Congress in the conduct of military operations and administration, the Constitution is silent. Ample scope was therefore wisely provided to work out or modify the division of labor impacting on carrying out day-to-day business. Yet even the power of Congress was limited: the two-year term of the House of Representatives, from where the appropriations emanate, and the explicit Constitutional proviso that "no appropriation of money to that use [the raising and supporting of armies] shall be for longer term than two years" provide checks against congressional abuse of authority.[55]

In the War of 1812, and especially, the Civil War, Congress took a keen interest in military operations. The Committee on the Conduct of the [Civil] War was established and dominated by the radical wing of the Republican Congress, and was energized by the suspicion that too many Union generals (many of whom, like McClellan, were Democrats) harbored Southern sympathies. It also seemed to feel that the President himself might be laggered in pursuing the war. By use of its investigative power, generals were called upon to testify; moreover, subordinates of high-ranking officers were invited to offer information about their commanders. Although the Committee took a lively interest in all matters of military management, its tactics bearing upon operations served to prod some officers into ill-advised actions, to inhibit others, and to enhance the apparent opportunities for ambitious "political" officers in all military headquarters. Counsel on strategy and high-level organization was offered to the President, generals were praised and criticized, and a considerable amount of sharp procurement and selling practices was exposed.[56] The overall effect of the Committee, however, must have been worth several divisions to the Confederacy, because in subsequent wars Congress did not repeat the performance. Investigative committees were set up in time of war, of which the World War II Committee headed by Senator Truman was an outstanding example. It served the country and the executive branch well because it adhered strictly to matters bearing upon procurement and spending dollars. Although such a "watchdog" activity has a heavy content of "second guessing" in a context in which it is difficult to judge the extent to which errors are due to either imperfect information or incompetence, it nevertheless generates no small amount of information useful to the Executive branch as well as to signal to administrators that incompetence has a higher probability of being exposed.

Apart from performing such an auditing function, Congress in time of major war has been "passive" insofar as it generally appropriates more funds than can be possibly spent.[57] This behavior is no doubt motivated by a mixture of patriotism, a desire to absolve itself of any future responsibility that could follow from a charge it constrained a war effort, and a tacit, if not explicit, recognition of the fact that "raising armies"—once the enemy is clearly identified—has a very high administrative and programming content.

Because dollars are no longer constraining, both major policy and minor administrative decisions fall into the province of the executive branch. Physical constraints dominant decision making—steel, aluminum, manpower, and numerous smaller ones. Identifying physical constraints, the points in time at which different ones will become operative and subsequently mitigated (to be supplanted by new ones), is necessarily dependent on programming, and related feasibility of programs implied by alternative plans and strategies. Both the available information and the expertise to do these things is concentrated in the Executive branch. Thus, Congress is perforce relegated to performing a post-audit function in time of major military operations.

During peacetime, of course, dollars acquire their normal role of being the principal constraint on resource allocation. Congress, partly motivated to spare constituents the anguish of paying taxes and perhaps instinctively seeking to maintain its status relative to aggrandizing executives, finds itself on nearly equal terms with the executive branch. In this circumstance, the congressional role has been very mixed.

Prior to World War II, Congress appeared to exert an "economizing" role on the armed services, but not in all categories of spending. In most years, it would "trim" the total requests in the President's budget.[58] How much of this was the exercise of a true economizing function, however, is difficult to gauge. Remember, Executive budgets are submitted to Congress with the knowledge that Congress must give the appearance of "economizing." This may have been more pronounced in the past, when Congress reflected highly conservative sentiments about government spending. Parsimony regarding the aggregate budget, however, was accompanied by keen interest on what the money was spent for and, especially, where it was spent. Construction, in particular, received close and critical scrutiny. Perhaps this was partly motivated by a suspicion that, unless carefully watched, the military would build plush officers' quarters and club facilities. It may have been more profoundly influenced by the view that new construction at only one or a few installations would be the beginning of a strategy to change the geographical allocation of the forces, with resulting dire consequences for the payrolls and land values in communities adversely affected. Other input items, like the acquisition of staff cars and small arms ammunition drew extensive examination, perhaps because these were items that Congressmen, like many civilians, have occasion to purchase as consumers. The resulting knowledge facilitates a display of expertise without having to do too much homework.

Although total budget requests would often be cut back, Congress on many occasions would authorize and appropriate more than what was requested for modern weapons and equipment.[59] This behavior was prevalent during the 1930's on Army appropriations, whereby Congress was signaling that perhaps the Army should mechanize its forces at a faster rate. The Army, for its part, appeared less reluctant to give up its horses. Perhaps this was because of inherent conservatism, although it is equally plausible to assume that spending for horse feed and animals served to generate support from a politically powerful agricultural sector, to say nothing of influential citizens who comprise the fox-hunting and equestrian sets.[60] Thus, it was not until 1948 that the Army ceased spending funds for "improving the breed," at which time the function was transferred to the Department of Agriculture. Another consideration that may have given the Army an incentive to adhere to the horse is that mechanized units are more costly, and under a constrained dollar budget this would mean a smaller Army and fewer command slots.

Navy appropriations did not contain the large variety of diverse items, the precise procurement of which could shape the force structure, as do Army appropriations. New ship construction, and especially its composition, is the key to Navy appropriations. And ship design, embedded in naval architecture, determined manpower requirements and spending. In this field, Congress displayed a willingness to enter the imperial age, the hankering for which in America also coincided with the emergence of lusty steel and metallurgical industries during the 1880's and 1890's. (A similar set of developments, during roughly the same period, was occurring in Imperial Germany, where it was maintained that expenditures for ships were more "productive" than the Army's outlays for meat and horse feed.) Nevertheless, Congress was parsimonious in providing operating funds to faciliate concentrated gatherings of ships for the purposes of fleet exercises. Given the fact that experience in handling different kinds of ships in large groups is indispensable for effective operations, this form of economy meant that for a long period the country had a fleet but no fleet. This budgetary action was nevertheless consistent with a sensitivity on the part of Naval bureaucrats to the idea that the larger number of "home ports", the larger the number of grateful constituents. Thus it was only after World War I, at which time it was no longer credible to hold to the idea that Britain could be a future naval enemy and that Japan might someday pose a real threat, that the battle fleet was concentrated in California waters.

Thus the interaction of congressional interests and those of military bureaucrats could produce peculiar results. A clear example was provided with the newly created Army Air Corps during the 1920's. Congress in the 1926 Air Corps Act authorized the Army eighteen hundred "serviceable" aircraft. But ambiguity could prevail over whether that number specified included only those in combat units or total aircraft, which would include training and other requirements. And did that number include "obsolete" aircraft, and, if not, what were the criteria by which obsolescence is defined? Legislation also specified manpower positions for the combat arms. But bomber units require more men than do fighter units. And funding—determined by the appropriations committees—was seldom adequate to implement the authorization legislation. Hence, Air Corps planners were willing to stretch the definition of an obsolete aircraft to approximate more closely the number of aircraft authorized. Moreover, although the airmen had a predilection for bombers because they sought to develop aircraft as a quasi-independent military capability, they had strong financial and budgetary incentives to program less costly fighters to achieve the authorized numbers. Thus doctrine, as well as operational and logistic planning factors, came to be modified to accommodate the budgeting and legislative constraints in ways that were complex and seldom explicit.[61]

All in all, the civilian control of the military services before World War II as it impacted on resource management was not very impressive, and the Roots, Stimsons, and Forrestals were rare. By controlling funds, Congress exerted the dominating influence on most decisions, including those that had major force-structure implications; and generally, congressional influence and attempts by bureau heads to influence Congress operated mostly in such a way as to provide even less military effectiveness than the parsimonious congressional appropriations might have provided. And yet, there were occasions when congressional interest exerted a wholesome influence. One such instance was its prodding to establish the Office of the Chief of Naval Operations during the Wilson administration. Navy Secretary Daniels viewed the autonomous Navy Bureaus as a mechanism that enabled him (and the executive branch) to maintain tighter control over the Navy vis-à-vis Congress, and he feared that a Chief could more effectively bypass the Secretary in dealing with the Congress. Conversely, in the previous decade, the Congressional Military Committee regarded War Secretary Root's establishment of an Army Chief of Staff and its associated General Staff with some dismay because the similar Army Bureaus were the mainstay of the Army, being a congressional fiefdom.

The combined picture of military management prior to World War II is therefore very mixed. Whatever else it was, it was highly "political"—a product of an occasional activist President, a large number of civilian secretaries who were less than inspiring, entrenched and often encrusted bureau chiefs, an occasional Elihu Root, whose success in achieving a major reform was in large part forced by the fact that the system cried for reform, and Congressmen to whom all the rest had to cater. Anything but a mixed performance would be astonishing. Management of the system lacked coherency.

That management lacked coherency may in large part have been because coherent management of military forces requires a "force plan," or a set of military objectives that are related to foreign policy. From these, it is possible to derive a force structure which in turn impacts upon organization, tactics, and even military innovations. Prior to World War II, Americans had to look primarily to Europeans for guidance in these latter departments. These subjects will be discussed in the next chapter.

4

PROGRAMMING THE FORCES, INNOVATIONS, AND TACTICS

> If I had rice and bullocks I had men, and if I had men
> I knew I could beat the enemy.
>
> Wellington, Quoted in Philip Guedalla, *Wellington*, p. 106.

The preceding chapter examined the military decision-making process in terms of the roles and relationships among the principal actors. Special attention was directed to the organizational, administrative, and political problems bearing upon the interaction between technicians and military operators, with special reference to American experience.

The same subject can be profitably examined in another way, characterized by a deeper dimension that might be viewed as a major province of the military professional. This dimension is the area of military innovations and tactics, two concepts that are also critically important for their organizational implications. The complexities of innovations, tactics, and military organization is what military doctrine—a much used, and in some cases abused, phrase—is about.

The meaning of the term "doctrine" is often misunderstood, particularly by civilians. To military men it means a composite of things, which in civilian life encompasses everything from the general philosophy of a business organization to the detailed procedures as to how the workers should tighten the bolts on items flowing along an assembly line. The rules of thumb that a bank branch manager employs in determining the kinds of loans he can make to different customers are similar to military doctrine. Determining such rules and procedures, promulgating them, and enforcing them (through punishments and rewards) is a large part of what the management of complex organizations is about. In the military context, the term "doctrine" incorporates all of these things.

Military doctrine can range between dogma and well-struc-

66

tured and well-conceived management principles based on evidence and experience. Usually, the body of doctrine for any given military service contains some mixture of both of these, which can vary in time and among different military organizations. Doctrine is also critical to the way in which weapons and elements of the force structure are to be used in war, and it is central to the formulation of *concepts* that influence the design of new weapons, for doctrine lays down rules as to how weapons are used in the field. This element of doctrine, along with the rules of management that govern areas such as logistics and organization, is critical to military management, whether it be involved with programming and designing the force or in other activities. This chapter strives to illustrate some of the complexities of military management in these terms, with special reference to land and naval forces. Air forces are treated in our next chapter.

The programming of military forces requires that two major questions be addressed. First, how large should the force level be? And second, what should its composition be in terms of major subcomponents, including active and reserve elements? Throughout much of the modern experience, it was found that these questions could be addressed by applying a few basic principles that were easily understood by civilian policy makers and were simple for use with both land and naval forces.

For the design of land forces, Karl von Clausewitz, writing in 1830–32, could provide the following guidance and planning (including cost) factors.[1] Infantry was at once the most important and most independent of the three combat arms, artillery was entirely dependent upon infantry to protect it, and cavalry could most easily be dispensed with; but a combination of the three arms gave the most strength.[2] At the time he wrote, a Prussian 800-man infantry battalion, a 150-horse cavalry squadron, and an eight-gun battery of six pounders "cost nearly the same, with respect to both the initial expense of equipment and its maintenance."[3] In his view, if one intended to fight in the plains, where the battle can be decisive, then the army should have ample cavalry to screen its maneuvering and turn any tactical enemy withdrawal into a rout. An emphasis on defense and passive warfare dictated a greater amount of artillery, which, being costly, might be employed more intensively by wealthy countries. But if the state were strong in the sense that the population identified with it, a militia and an ample national levy could permit a force to be intensive in infantry, so that the standard ratio of one eight-gun field artillery battery to one battalion of infantry might fall to one battery per two or three battalions .[4] Thus, Clausewitz—in terms of concepts of modern production concepts—treated the production processes for "capital intensive" and "labor intensive" land forces.

Clausewitz also pointed out that the proportion between cavalry and infantry from the Middle Ages onward had remained rather constant, although cavalry in the early period "was the stronger arm, composed of the flower of the people."[5] In the modern period, the ratio remained from a fourth to a sixth as much cavalry as of infantry, with Austria and Russia ("because they have in their dominions the fragments of a Tartar organization") being on the heavy side in terms of cavalry.[6]

Clausewitz's "model" for designing land forces can be applied to consideration of the contemporary land-force structure, wherein tanks are the modern counterpart of calvary and tactical air and artillery can be close substitutes for each other. One can also substitute "poor man's artillery," like mortars and man-portable rockets, for both artillery and tactical air—an apparent practice of the Viet Cong and North Vietnamese. In summarizing his offerings on force structure design, Clausewitz noted that a lack of "the two subordinate arms" (cavalry and artillery) can "be compensated for, provided we are so much stronger in infantry, and the better the infantry, the more easily this may be done."[7] The fundamental question in programming land forces thus became "How much artillery can we have without inconvenience, and what is the least proportion of cavalry with which we can manage."[8]

In other words, land warfare is primarily infantry warfare. There are limited possibilities for substituting artillery (including airborne fire support) and cavalry (or armor) for infantry. And conversely, infantry, depending on its quality, can be substituted for the other branches. But when the three elements are used in cooperation, they mutually complement each other; and obtaining the kind of cooperation and coordinated use of the three arms that is needed is the special province of military expertise. It is also the focal point of tactical innovation and technical improvement as these bear upon land warfare.

The size of the force "is determined by the government."[9]

The military man had to take that factor as given; but in any case, according to Clausewitz, one should take to the field with as much force as possible as quickly as possible. Bringing force to bear in an encounter was the special capability of the military man's skill, and for this reason great emphasis was placed both on maneuver and on what would today be termed "strategic mobility."

This emphasis on maneuver runs like a central strand throughout Clausewitz's work. The outcome even in the seemingly static defense and assault of mountain lines was seen as a matter of relative mobility,[10] and for this reason, the German force design placed emphasis on maneuver and mobility. The latter permitted a concentration of force for a decisive engagement and it was facilitated by minimizing the amount of artillery and related logistic apparatus in the force structure. Maneuverability permitted the achievement of a decisive outcome in an engagement and enabled the victors to follow a defeated and retreating enemy so as to carry out the real destruction of his force. It was the application of these principles that explains the strong emphasis placed on cavalry in the German army.

The engagement therefore becomes the focal point of the business of war, and this is a straightforward expenditure or exchange process. "Now it is known from experience that the losses in physical forces in the course of an engagement seldom show a great difference between the victor and vanquished."[11] For the vanquished, the decisive loss takes the form of prisoners and abandoned materiel, the quantities of both being greatly enlarged by cavalry as it cuts up the retreating battalions. The relevant count, therefore, is prisoners and captured guns[12] (not bodies). More important, behind this capture of prisoners and guns is the shattered morale of the enemy troops and the corrosion of their will to fight.

But be that as it may, land war still demands its underlying ante, which comprises the casualties of the engagement, or of what today is more accurately described as the complex of small-unit fire fights that constitute a major battle or a campaign. Clausewitz's oft-quoted dictum that "war is a mere continuation of policy by other means"[13] may indeed be correct, but it is seldom stated in accompaniment with his earlier remark that war "is a serious means to a serious end."[14] After all, the "serious means" are the casualties.

The programming of naval forces for a major naval power was straightforward, and in many ways it was simpler than for land warfare.[15] The object was to control the sea—or more accurately, some portion of it—for some period of time. The primary focal point of programming was the "ship of the line" or a ship that could function in the "line of battle," the kind of ship that in the later age of steam and steel came to be called the "capital ship."

Toward the end of the seventeenth century, both ship design and the general outline of tactical doctrine had settled down,[16] their forms destined to remain unchallenged until the advent of steam and iron. Muzzle-loading cannon capable of firing 24-or 32-pound shot became of practicable use as ship-killers, to be substituted for the lighter and less efficient breech-loading and people-killing weapons that were used as ship armament in the age of galleons and caravelles. Square-rigged ships of deeper draft than the older, round-bottomed ships, provided better handling characteristics. Longer hulls (roughly, three beam lengths) provided room for more guns, and cargo holds were transformed into gun galleries through the construction of gun ports. Forecastles and aftcastles gave way to flush decks.

Ship size was basically constrained by nature, through the limited sizes of trees. Rib timbers, rudder posts, and "knees," by which decks were affixed to hulls, had to be of a single piece and of oak (or similar wood). Gnarled oak, such as that grown in southeast England, was ideal for the purpose.[17] Ships that could carry more than one hundred guns were built. But the line tactics of maneuver and engagement meant that some of the firepower embedded in a ship that was "too large" would be wasted. On the other hand, a ship that was "too small" would not make a contribution commensurate with its space in the line.[18] And so, by the late eighteenth century, the British fleet contained a preponderance of 74-gun ships.

The driving force of such fleet planning was to preserve maritime power: a fleet having enough capital ships to deter an enemy's fleet from venturing from its ports, under pain of destruction, was prerequisite to a nation's free use of the sea. Such dominance would also permit one's own smaller ships to blockade the enemy's ports, harass his commerce, and, in time, eliminate the enemy's raiders of one's own mercantile activity.

Naval power also permitted the (seldom decisive) harassing kind of land operations engaged in by England and character-

ized by General Sir John Moore, one of its successful practitioners during the Napoleonic wars, as "our old style of expedition
—a landing, a short march, and a good fight, and then a lounge
home again."[19] With these methods, one could acquire relatively small pieces of real estate, like Louisbourg or Havana, that
could be useful pawns in postwar negotiations. But not all such
operations were so sparkling, as was illustrated by the abortive
attempt to take Rochfort during the Seven Years' War and by
Cornwallis' fate at Yorktown or the attempt to take New Orleans. Serious problems often arose because of failure to achieve
effective command relationships among the divergent military
subcultures within a setting that permitted the Army and Navy
components to "cooperate."

Nevertheless, a rare combination of sailor and soldier, as was
that of Admiral Saunders and General Wolfe, could pull off an
amphibious operation like the one that led to the fall of Quebec
in 1759,[20] the level of competence of which was not to be
matched until World War II. One lesson learned by the British
from amphibious operations during the eighteenth century was
that naval firepower itself could not eliminate shore opposition
—rather, it was best used in support of assaulting troops. This
lesson was to be ignored, at high cost, in the World War I
Gallipoli operation. And it was to be confirmed repeatedly during World War II.

Naval power was highly profitable to England during the period prior to 1814, when it was used to enhance Britain's seaborne commerce and colonial holdings. "To secure one's own
people a disproportionate share of such benefits" was the payoff
from seapower, as Mahan points out.[21] Most of its naval operations, however, were adjuncts to major continental wars, like the
War of Spanish Succession, the Seven Years' War, and the Napoleonic wars. The heavy killing was done, and experienced, by
others.

The logic of naval force planning around the ship of the line
did not change with the advent of steam, steel, and advanced
ordnance. The written works and the experiments of Henri Joseph Paixhains, a French army artillery officer of the early nineteenth century, suggested a series of revolutions in materiel,
centering around the hollow explosive shell, and small, ironclad
ships, signaling a possible reversal in the scenarios of British-
French naval action.[22] The period from about 1830 to 1905 was
fraught with anxiety for British naval force planners, inasmuch

as it presented existing and potential naval rivals—French, Russian, Italian, Germans, and even Turks—opportunities to achieve parity or near parity of force through technical development. The French were generally in the lead in the various initial technical developments, and the French Navy acquired a "Young School" of thinkers who advanced the idea that technology could permit a revival of *guerre de course* techniques by placing emphasis on cruisers and torpedo boats that could destroy big ships and provide maritime dominance. However, the British development and procurement strategy was calculated to acquire at least "one of the kind" of whatever new combination of hull, propulsion, and weapon systems Britain's rivals (usually the French) might field. Some have described the Admiralty's policy as "conservative,"[23] and it was conservative, in that it brought the British new knowledge at low cost.

The major anxieties involved in the technical transformation to steel and steam were finally resolved by Sir John Fisher's H.M.S. *Dreadnaught,* an "all big gun," heavily armored, capital ship commissioned in 1906. Its main armament consisted of turret-mounted 12-inch guns plus quick-firing secondary armament to take care of any attempt to implement the theory of the Young School. Such a ship was the optimum scale of "plant" or "facility" that could carry guns; that is, it could produce the most firepower for a given cost. Since the object of a naval engagement was to subject enemy ships to a maximum amount of destructive fire, longer-range, heavier guns were preferred. And since maintaining a rate of fire had worth, one wanted to preserve one's guns by reducing the likelihood of having one's ship sunk; hence, armor protection was a critical design feature. A heavily armored and gunned ship therefore stood an even chance to beat any ship it could not run away from. The key to programming, therefore, was to have more capital ships than the potential enemy or combination of enemies. Consequently, British programming and naval appropriations during the nineteenth century were based on the combined capital-ship programs of the two largest European powers that could be allied against Britain.

Speed was a desirable attribute for capital ships. But large power plants necessitated much larger ships, which in turn posed problems of cost and limitations as to the ports at which ships might be stationed and consequently, the areas in which they might operate. There was a notable departure in the tradeoffs among guns, armor, and speed when the British fleet experimented with Fisher's conception of a thin-skinned, but fast and heavily gunned, "battle cruiser." The results of the first experiment with these were spectacular. Admiral Beatty, who commanded six of them in the Battle of Jutland and saw two blown up shortly after being taken under German fire, is reported to have remarked, "There seems to be something wrong with our bloody ships today."[24]

The underlying logic of naval force programming, centering as it did around the capital ship, did not change when the aircraft carrier supplanted the big-gun ship. An air battle, with its initial and primary objective being that of destroying the enemy's carriers and perhaps preserving some of one's own, merely supplanted the exchange of rifled-gun shells. The dive bomber was traded for guns, and airplanes were expended instead of shells. Pre–World War II naval doctrine (and the initial strategy of the wartime aviation force) also contemplated the use of torpedo bombers, to be coordinated in fleet actions with a dive-bombing attack. History is generally silent on this part of the endeavor, except for the well-publicized fate of the torpedo bombers employed at the Battle of Midway.

That potential adversaries of the United States have chosen not to acquire capital ships during the post–World War II era has posed difficulties for decision makers and the resulting questions have not yet been entirely resolved. The carrier remains a "capital ship" of sorts. Its main product is a tactical fighter-bomber capability, which has its primary use as support for ground operations. This subject will be treated at greater length in later chapters.

The logic of sizing and determining the mix of the elements composing the force structure appears to have been sustained more or less independently of the choice of selection of weapons per se—at least prior to the advent of aircraft, the impact of which we shall discuss later at greater length. This is not to say, however, that weapons and technological changes affecting the performance of weapons or other systems have not had an impact on military organizations or perhaps even on the outcomes of battles and wars.

The subject of the effect of changes in weapons technology upon the effectiveness of military organizations and their ability to conduct military operations, however, contains an element of complexity. A new development in weapon technology, in which the performance of the weapon itself is improved, seldom exerts its influence independently of other complex changes that must occur within a military organization. The totality of these changes and the process by which they are made are what can be described as "innovation."[25] An innovation should be sharply contrasted with a technological change, or "invention," per se. Since the nature of the relationships between innovations and inventions require elaboration, an analogy to the civilian economy may be of some use.

An invention is the creation of a new contrivance that can perform a given task more efficiently; or it may be the discovery of a new product or productive process—thus, the steam engine, the Bessemer process, and the hybrid seed corn were inventions. As such, inventions reduce or mitigate physical constraints that men encounter.

An innovation, on the other hand, results from a more subtle and complicated process. The reduction of physical constraints, as conceived by the engineer, is not sufficient to take the fullest advantage of technical improvements. Often, if not generally, other constraining factors in the social system may prevent full exploitation of a technical improvement, and these constraints must be eliminated or coped with.

The innovating function is primarily an organizational or entrepreneurial endeavor. For example, the invention of the flying shuttle for mechanical weaving could not be made "operational" until someone also assembled workers and trained them, built a factory near a power source, and arranged to assemble raw materials and distribute the product. The weaving industry was revolutionized in the process. The overall process is an innovation. In the business world, such innovations are the work of entrepreneurs or organizations that possess the facility to coordinate the innovative process. The drive to make the profits afforded by a successful innovation provides a spontaneous motive for assuming the risks associated with the activity.

An important characteristic of the innovative process is that the technical developments that catalyze a major innovation may often constitute minor events when viewed in their narrower and earlier context. A technical development designed to cope with a problem in one application may eventually have a profound impact on activities that are far removed from the initial one. The Watt steam engine, for example, was designed to pump water from coal mines more efficiently, but it also revolutionized land and water transport by facilitating the "invention" of the steam locomotive and the steam boat. This application of technical developments to areas other than those with which they were initially concerned requires a combination of imagination and organizational skill, the essence of which resides in the innovator. In the adaptation to such new applications, the constraining factor that delays the taking of the fullest advantage of a technical development may simply be the lack of knowledge itself, and so innovation is thus a creative activity. But it is creative endeavor applied in a purposeful way that simultaneously discards the elements of the old arrangements and supplants them with the new.[26]

Military management's counterpart to the nontechnical elements of innovation in civilian affairs resides in military tactics and organization. Changes in tactics constitute a critical link between technological inventions and innovations, whereby it is the innovation that permits a marked improvement in military effectiveness. The precise nature of the innovative process is imperfectly understood in military affairs, just as in civilian society, but the following general characteristics can be discerned.

First, an innovation is often made possible by some technological improvement, although the improvement itself may have resulted from some random event or purposeful action that was directed to a problem other than the one stimulating the innovation. Second, an innovation often requires organizational changes, which may involve either different supporting activities or communications and command systems or both. Third, innovations can often entail a change in the status quo among specialized subgroups within the larger organization. For this reason, innovations are apt to be resisted, for they involve struggle among the interested subgroups comprised by the larger organization. Fourth, innovations are most likely to occur after an organization has experienced some external force or shock, or at least it might be more susceptible to them under such circumstances. Fifth, although most military innovations have a technological foundation, this need not be exclusively the case, since changes in the social environment also may provide the foundation for innovation.

The character of military innovation can be illustrated by the changes that endowed France with the military machine that served Napoleon so well. Napoleon was no doubt a military genius, but it is an open question whether or not he could have gone as far as he did were it not for two major innovations. The first was facilitated by the political revolution, which provided a soldiery that was differently motivated; this in turn permitting an important change in infantry tactics. The groundwork for the other, laid by Napoleon's predecessors in the service of Louis XVI, permitted a revolution in strategic mobility and artillery tactics.

During most of the eighteenth century, infantry tactics were constrained by the requirement to maintain rigid lines and the discipline of infantrymen under fire. Such tactics achieved their highest form among the Prussians under Frederick the Great. With these tactics, large bodies of infantry could be closely controlled, and they could maneuver quickly on the battlefield and fire rapidly with the inaccurate smooth-bores muzzle-loaders of the day. (It was this type of infantry tactics that was met by the colonial troops in their encounters with the British regulars during the American Revolution.) The result was to impress the shock of concentrated fire upon the enemy and maintain the disciplined steadiness of the friendly soldiers themselves. This capability was well suited for fighting in open country, and it provided the ability to withstand cavalry attacks.

But there was also an underlying social foundation for these eighteenth-century heavy-infantry tactics: close-order formations and tight discipline were necessary for reasons that were quite remote from the possible effects of enemy fire. Professional soldiers in the enlisted ranks of Europe's armies were usually men who had been rejected by European society in general. And besides, in Frederick the Great's army between 30 and 40 per cent of his infantry soldiers were foreigners, many of whom had deserted from other armies. The advantage to Frederick of recruiting such individuals was that it permitted a larger number of the peasants of Pomerania and Brandenburg to remain on the farms, thereby enchancing the Prussian gross national product, as well as the nation's tax base. But such soldiers were unreliable, and they deserted at the slightest opportunity, particularly during the rigors of a campaign. It was unwise to permit a victorious army to follow a defeated and retreating army too vigorously in efforts to destroy it, since such an operation requires initiative at the small-unit level. Given such freedom of initiative, the professionals of the day were likely to desert and melt into the countryside. Hence eighteenth-century European land warfare characteristically was not decisive on a large scale and it was conducted for limited objectives.

Although heavy infantry was the hard core of military force, its tactics embodied disadvantages that prevented their use under all conditions, and even as the sole form for allocating one's infantry resources. Good use could always be made of light infantry using skirmish tactics that could harass an opponent's heavy columns and screen one's own movement, especially in broken country. On rare occasions and under the right conditions of terrain, light infantry could destroy heavy infantry, especially if the latter was afflicted with command problems such as those General Braddock experienced near Pittsburgh.

The Austrians taught the Prussians many lessons in light-infantry tactics during the Seven Years' War, when in her armies Maria Theresa used Croatian tribesmen who had developed guerrilla tactics to a high art by practicing them on the Turks. To employ such uncouth fellows in Western Europe was regarded with dismay, since they indulged heavily in looting and rape. But Maria Theresa was not inclined to be ladylike toward Frederick after he had so ungallantly siezed Silesia during the early and tenuous period of her reign. Moreover, her nobility were poor taxpayers, and the fiscal squeeze necessitated some winking at the more primitive forms of troop motivation. (In the same spirit, Hungarian light cavalry raided and sacked Berlin.) Therefore, even by the time of the American Revolution, most European army officers, including the French and British, knew all there was to know about light infantry and skirmish tactics.[27] But the raw material—the regular soldier—was not reliable enough to be used in such a fashion.

The French Revolution saw the rise of the national armies and conscription, and for the first time and on a large scale, the average soldier was motivated to identify simultaneously with an ideological cause, the national state, and his own role in the army. The result was an amalgamation of the classical ability to maneuver large bodies of infantry with the individual soldier's ability to use skirmish tactics when appropriate. The line partially gave way to the column as the principal infantry formation. Such tactics, combined with a willingness to take casualties, produced infantry capabilities for the French that few other European armies could withstand. This innovation in tactics had no technical foundation whatsoever; rather, it was made possible by deeper social and political forces that provided a motivational quality that had previously been lacking.

The second major innovation that enhanced the capabilities of the French armies was technical and organizational and had to do with artillery. A lighter artillery tube developed in a French arsenal permitted the use of a lighter carriage, which Jean B. Grebeauval designed, along with a harness system that enabled gunners to handle an artillery piece more effectively on the battlefield. And by the time France was raising its large armies, the idea of using horses to pull the lighter field pieces had been conceived. Prior to this development, most field artillery was ponderous and had to be drawn by bullocks; but the lighter, horse-drawn artillery could move as quickly as infantry and cavalry under normal marching conditions.[28] This possibility permitted the invention (or perhaps the reinvention of something that had not been seen since Roman times) of the army division as an administrative organization. The "division" literally *was* a division of a much larger army, it combined in a single administrative unit the three principal arms of the army, and it was capable of fighting on its own for a limited period of time.

The concept of a division as an organizational device had two distinct and somewhat revolutionary qualities. First, increased emphasis was placed on the tactical use of the three major military arms in combination. Second, the national army, consisting of divisible administrative units, could be deployed more rapidly over long distances, a capability that served France well, in view of the fact that she was subjected to attacks over widely separated points along her frontiers. The horse-drawn artillery also provided a marked advantage in tactical mobility, with the result that Napoleon, the artilleryman, could show the highest tactical virtuosity in moving and concentrating guns at key points on the battlefield.[29]

The accomplishments of the French Revolutionary/Napoleonic military machine illustrated two points. The first was the major military innovations can result from purely tactical and organizational changes—for example, they need not have a technical "cause" or foundation. But in such instances some external factor (for example, different troop motivation afforded by changes in the social system) must normally be the means of effecting the innovation, as was illustrated by the change in infantry tactics. The second point it illustrated was that technological changes often become manifest in unpredictable ways: what may seem a "small" technical change can often have a major impact in terms of military effectiveness. (The converse of this point—that seemingly major technological changes may have only a minor impact on military effectiveness—is a hypothesis that warrants further exploration, particularly in the contemporary American setting.) This unpredictability lies in the fact that a technical improvement almost invariably necessitates a change either in tactics or organization, usually in both. And it is precisely in these departments—tactics and organization—that military professionals exert primacy. The relevance of this point is that, although civilian policy makers, technologists, and scientists may propose innovative changes, little can come from their suggestions if the military professionals cannot or will not implement the change.

That major military innovations can derive their foundation from a number of technical developments initially designed to cope with problems unrelated to the innovation, but that necessitate extensive modification of tactics if not development of new tactics and organization, is a point that is no less cogent in modern times than it appears to have been in the distant past. For example, the combination of the parachute, the conventional air transport, and the infantryman led to parachute infantry in World War II. Credit for the conception, however, should go to Gen. William Mitchell, who contemplated using it during World War I. But making the concept operational required numerous and complex changes in tactics, training, troop indoctrination, and countless other details, both technical and administrative.

A more striking example of this kind of interplay was that of the fast carrier strike force developed by Navy airmen during World War II. Although numerous pioneering developments occurred prior to World War II that led to fleet carriers, the idea that carrier forces conduct ongoing, deep-water operations independently of battle lines composed of big-gun ships was not part of accepted navy doctrine in any Navy. Carriers were vulnerable, as the Japanese fate at Midway demonstrated. Yet U. S. naval airmen advanced the idea that if carrier task forces could be composed of several or more carriers, they could mutually protect each other.[30] Their fast speed and mobility would reduce the likelihood of a force being located and fixed by the enemy. Implementation of this doctrine was facilitated by radar, which permitted maintenance of optimum defensive formations in foul and night weather, and identification of friendly-versus-enemy aircraft. Beefed up antiaircraft defenses, composed mainly of Bofors and Oerlikon quick-firing guns, and the proximity fuse adopted to 5-inch guns, enhanced the carrier air defenses.[31] Finally, the administrative innovation of mobile logistics fleets and resupply during operations provided a further basis for the enhanced effectiveness of the fast carrier force.[32] Without these developments, carriers would have concentrated on providing air support for amphibious and land operations, and playing a secondary role in fleet operations as a scouting force. The drive to defeat Japan would have been much more drawn out and costly. These tactics were first employed on an experimental basis during the Gilberts campaign in late 1943; however, they were not fully hammered out and vindicated to the satisfaction of nonair admirals until the Marianas campaign of June–July 1944.[33] In the process, fleet doctrine was transformed, and with it the relative power status of airmen and the alumni of the Gun Club. The transformation process also had its counterpart in the form of bureaucratic warfare that occurred in Washington and in the headquarters of the Pacific theater of operations.

Although the innovative function is critical to military affairs, the subject should be placed in proper perspective by emphasizing the extent to which it is possible to counter a major innovation, often by purely tactical means. The examples from the French military revolution that were cited above illustrate the point. Military historians have observed that Napoleon's victories became increasingly sanguinary and costly as time went on. His Italian campaign is judged to have been a model of adroitness and tactical skill, as was also the battle of Ulm. But his later campaigns and battles, like Wagram, Friedland, and Borodino, were slugging matches, and the social institution of manpower conscription increasingly became the basis for his victories. Some military historians suggest that Napoleon lost his touch as he became older, a view that might be questioned, since the record suggests that it was merely that his opponents became adroit at countering and imitating the tactics and organization Napoleon employed with such initial success.

Increased emphasis upon technical means in warfare may operate to place even more reliance on tactical skill and, in particular, on qualities of command. Wellington demonstrated this point in that he invariably very carefully chose his terrain and employed his forces (which were equipped and organized in the more "classical" eighteenth century fashion) in ways that would take maximum advantage of his most valuable resource: the steadiness of British infantry. The principal quality of command exercised by Wellington was restraint. It is critically important to know the shortcomings of one's systems and to avoid using them in ways that would permit an opponent to exploit those shortcomings. Thus, General Chennault employed the P-40 (which was not one of the great fighter planes of World War II) in innovative tactics that exploited its strong features and avoided its weaknesses, and he trained his pilots to adhere rigorously to those tactics. The result was a kill ratio over the Japanese of 15 to 1.

Military professionals as a group seem capable of producing or absorbing innovations and inventions about as rapidly as any other of society's closed groups. Compared to medical doctors and central bankers, for example, the military segment of society might merit rather high marks for its ability to progress in thinking. Indeed, for hundreds of years central bankers engaged in operations that expanded and reduced the money supply in ways that intensified the instability of economic systems. For much of that period, they may not even have known as a group what effects their activities had on the economy. By the turn of the century, some insight into the process had been gained, but it was not sufficiently absorbed by bankers and treasury officials (this was true in all Western nations) to avert the great depression of the 1930s. In the same vein, it has been suggested that the "cross-over point" at which doctors saved as many people as they killed in their medical practice occurred around the turn of the present century.

If the point is not belabored, it is at least frequently asserted that military bureaucracies are "conservative." The observation is a truism: a nonconservative, or "radical," social institution cannot continue to exist as an institution is also a truism. The substantive force of such observations appears to be that military professionals are not innovative[34] or (as the "Colonel Blimp" image suggests) perhaps not even very bright. But such a conclusion is either unfair or inaccurate or incomplete—incomplete because most wartime problems of military tactics and force allocation are really terribly complex when they are actually encountered.

The World War I experiences of Allied and especially British

decision makers of the Western front have been used to illustrate a wide variety of views on military decision making, including the one that military professionals, at best, are not very
bright. As an officer, Sir Douglas Haig may not have been brilliant,[35] but he was the victim of a dilemma, born of a unique and
unhappy combination of weapons technology, geography, and
political forces arising from that geography. The politicians of
his time could not face up to hard political and strategic, decisions: the soldiers could not, by tactical means, surmount the
problems posed by the particular combination of weaponry and
geography in time. The result was the worst possible combination of strategy and tactics.

The tactical problem resulted from the machinegun and the
troop densities (including artillery) on the Western front, both
of which were necessary conditions. The troop densities resulted from both the small frontal distances of available terrain in
which armies could maneuver and the scale of the war effort by
both sides. A flankless line ran from Switzerland to the sea. It
is true that flanks can be produced by punching holes in the line,
but the large forces on both sides made the lines very deep, and
any attempt to produce a hole could only produce a salient,
which in turn would later become a meat grinder at the hands
of the defender. The infantry exchange ratio decidedly favored
the tactical defensive, given the prevailing infantry tactical doctrine, organizational structure, and force densities. The Germans learned the lesson at Verdun, and they did not repeat the
experiment until the 1918 spring offensive, at which time they
came forth with new infantry tactics that nearly worked (Ludendorff, gambler that he may have been, did not gamble blindly).
For more than two years, the Germans remained on the tactical
defensive and reaped the benefits of a favorable infantry exchange rate, turning at the same time to other pastures. The
troop densities were less on the Eastern front despite the large
Russian manpower, because the terrain available for maneuver
was proportionately greater. Flanks were either available or
easily made. And Russia was knocked out of the war. (Here,
horse cavalry could still be put to good use.)

The dilemma confronting the Allies on the western front was
therefore not a purely tactical one. Rather, it was primarily a
product of political-military strategy—a political decision by
civilian policy makers to conduct a strategic offensive necessitat-
ing large-scale tactical offensives for its implementation. This

political decision undoubtedly had strong support from France, in view of the large amount of French territory occupied by the Germans. The British policy makers may have been inclined to go along with the French because of their regard for the latter's feelings about the occupation; and also, they may have felt that large-scale operations could be better supported (and controlled) across the Channel. Sir Douglas Haig therefore did what he understood was expected of him. Moreover, as time went on, he would have had to be remarkably devoid of human frailty to admit that the initial decision and expenditures for which he was the responsible military agent might have been unsound. And in the meantime, the ambitious French General, Robert Neville, who advocated and commanded the massive offensive that nearly destroyed the French army, had told the civilian policy makers only what the latter wanted to hear, a propensity that is not rare. Whatever else the Western front may have taught, it did hold an important lesson for civilian-military relationships: Soldiers can render a valuable service by raising questions about strategy, at least occasionally; and in their turn, civilian policy makers might have an obligation to question the tactics of the military.

There is a final lesson to be derived from an experience, which, while it might have been but a tactical footnote in World War I, was to loom large in the main text of the following war. When the Germans finally turned to the offensive in the West, they again displayed their military professionalism, revealing new and highly effective infantry tactics that were exclusively organizational and doctrinal in nature. In their impact, these new tactics could be compared with the French innovation of the division, the difference being that this time the focus was on the smallest of army units—the infantry squad.

The new departure was an attack based on small quasi-autonomous units of about sixteen men, a "semiplatoon," each reinforced with automatic weapons, grenadiers, and heavy weapons—a veritable miniature combined-arms team. Maximum reliance was placed on the individual initiative of the unit commanders, with the general doctrine being to probe the enemy's defenses and seek out his weak points. The heavier firepower that was available permitted more effective close work at such points. When a weak point was discovered, an elaborate system of flare signals conveyed the information to higher command, who then sent strong forces to converge on the weak point. The 1918 spring offensive gave the Allies some anxious moments, for the territory and prisoners taken were impressive. But the main thrust of the offensive fell on the British, and Sir Douglas kept his nerve. The Germans simply ran out of resources, and the discipline of assaulting infantry declined as they fell upon abundant British stores and food stuffs in the British rear areas. The German panzer tactics of World War II were merely an extension of the 1918 innovation, greatly enhanced by employment of the tank and field-radio communications and by the partial substitution of dive bombers for artillery.[36]

During most of the modern period the rationale for programming military forces was fairly simple and easily understood by civilian policy makers. Technological change could be absorbed and countered, either by new tactics or by quickly adapting and fielding new weapons as they became available. Although military bureaucracies may be "conservative," they are also motivated to survive, and this appears to have stimulated tactical improvements and the organizational changes necessary to implement tactical change.

The military innovative process, however imperfectly it may be understood, appears to be the focal point of the actions of military professionals and of their adaptation to and use of technical change. Moreover, it is difficult to find instances where technical change in the form of a new weapon has of itself been decisive in the outcome of a war for the side that initially possessed it, at least in cases where the antagonists have similar degrees of organizing skill and tactical sophistication. Startling changes have sometimes occurred when one side was innovative, as were the French Revolutionary army and the pre-World War II German army, and the elements of some of the innovations had a technical foundation. But the transformation from technical change to innovation is complex, and probably the only clear aspect of the transformation process is that it must be carried out by the military professionals. Thus, a critical phase of military management appears to center around the innovative process and the creation of an institutional environment to nurture it. Civilian leadership can play a critical role in its respect, and at a minimum it should be sensitive to innovative forces that might be stirring within the officer corps, but which might otherwise remain suppressed due to dominance of established sub-groups.

There is nothing to suggest any correlation between this innovative process and generous spending either for materiel or for research and development. Indeed, the quest for technological solutions to tactical problems might even stifle military professionalism in its more fundamental workings. A related hypothesis states that military professionals might do their best in force development and its associated innovative process if they have to operate under some kind of broad budgetary and manpower constraints. Given such constraints, they might concentrate on getting the most military effectiveness per dollar or per man, or both.

Concentration on such an effort might be facilitated by a freedom of the military services from the external political/-budgetary process, with its pork-barrel manifestations. Such was the status apparently enjoyed by the military services of European powers during the eighteenth and nineteenth centuries. In imperial Germany, for example, military appropriations were made for five- or seven-year periods, a practice motivated by Bismarck's desire to minimize control by the government's legislative branch. The chiefs of the armed services reported to the Kaiser and were accountable only to him. The system contained flaws growing out of its broader politics, but it did shelter the officer corps from the necessity of participating in frequent, fine-grained external politico-budgetary deliberations.

5

THE UNKNOWN IMPACT OF THE AIRPLANE

> The weapon may have been double-edged in another respect: the forward elements of the Allied infantry were only 1,000 yards from the town during the bombardment and some bombs fell among them; it may have been that this circumstance had something to do with the slowness with which the infantry moved to the attack.
>
> Wesley Craven and James Cate, *The Army Air Forces in World War II*, vol. 3, p. 370.

The airplane is viewed as having had a revolutionary effect on military affairs. Indeed, the airplane had a number of effects, any of which alone would have been startling. But in combination, they have posed problems in politics and management that have never been resolved.

The airplane injected a much greater technical content into military decision making and sharply accentuated a trend that had been in evidence since the rise of artillery. This broad technological channel provided much greater opportunity than was previously available for civilians to become intimately involved in military decision making, an area that previously had been the special domain of the military officer corps. Furthermore, aircraft became the basis for the promulgation of a modern version of "strategic war." This concept is not new, but it was novel to men whose intellectual orientation was founded on modern European precedents. Relative to strategic war, the airplane became the focal point for the espousal of centralized management, pushed to its most extreme form. And finally the airplane importantly changed the conduct of conventional land and naval operations.[1]

The Wright Brothers flew the first airplane in 1903, and within twelve years a member of an advisory committee to the British military air establishment was able to publish a treatise entitled *Aircraft in Warfare: The Dawn of the Fourth Arm*.[2] The author, F. W. Lanchester, has been memorialized in the literature on operational research as the discoverer of the "n-square law" of combat, which was a formal and elegant presentation of the age-old military axiom known as the "principle of concentration of force." The real significance of Lanchester's endeavor, however, lies not in his mathematical model, but rather in the way his effort illustrates how engineering expertise applied in a systematic way could provide much useful information for military planners and tacticians. At the time of his writing (1915), airplanes and their power plants were most rudimentary and unspecialized in their functions. Much could be gained by applying the technical knowledge of terminal ballistics, machinegun design, and communications, for example, to aircraft in ways that would enhance their performance in military missions.

All of these technicalities plus the possible military applications of aircraft, including strategic air raids and the defense of London and the more subtle aspects of the application of the rules of warfare to aircraft operations, are treated in Lanchester's work. That a civilian with technical competence could approach the subject of warfare in such an imaginative way must have given the professional military caste two points to ponder. First, it surely must have become obvious that here was something to stimulate the imagination in a most lively fashion. Second, it must have been equally obvious that if imaginative applications of aircraft to military endeavors were to be made, then the physical laws of aerodynamics, ballistics, and thermodynamics, as well as other engineering applications of science, must provide insight into the tactical possibilities. The airplane therefore could not help but stimulate those of the military officer corps who possessed both technological competence and tactical imagination.

Interestingly enough, Lanchester viewed aircraft as a possible "fourth arm" of the military organization. Although he considered raids on "civilian" targets, his examples focused on the government command-and-control apparatus.[3] His orientation viewed the airplane as an adjunct of conventional land and naval-force operations. For land operations, aircraft had great potential for fulfilling the classical roles of cavalry—reconnaissance and interdiction of an enemy's supply installations and troop concentrations. For naval applications the emphasis was on reconnaissance and, by implication, the direction and control of gunfire.

There is also an extensive treatment of air-to-air engagements, which would deny the enemy full and effective use of his own aircraft. Lanchester pushed the cavalry analogy so strongly as to suggest that the number of aircraft employed for land warfare should equal the number of horses traditionally used in land forces. In this, Lanchester appears to have disregarded cost effectiveness; but the preface to the book, written by his military mentor, informs the reader that it requires twelve men to support an aircraft, while the man-horse ratio is roughly one to one.[4]

World War I saw the limited, but highly publicized, use of aircraft in a strategic role, with England experiencing 51 Zeppelin and 29 Gotha bomber raids and suffering nearly 3,000 casualties as a result.[5] The Zeppelins, destined to go out of business because of their vulnerability, need not be discussed further. Of 376 Gotha sorties against England, the Germans lost 63 aircraft, 30 of them to the British fighter and air-defense effort and the remainder to landing accidents.[6] Bombing of Germany by the Allies prior to June 1918 was mainly confined to attacks by the Royal Naval Air Service on Zeppelin bases. By June, a small, Independent Bombing Force, consisting of five squadrons operating out of Nancy, France, commenced bombing of German targets; and by the end of the war it had delivered 550 tons of bombs, half of which were expended on Rhineland industrial centers.[7] By the end of the war, the force had been built up to nine squadrons. Ninety-nine aircraft were lost in operations, about half of which were in accidents.[8]

By later standards, the World War I strategic air campaigns were not striking for either their military or economic consequences. But the experiences did make a strong impression on the residents of London, some of whom in the post-World War I years became increasingly important policy makers. Nor was the impact of these initial experiences lost upon some military men who possessed both imagination and expository skills and who were to become evangelists of strategic air power. This concept of strategic air warfare, however, contains elements of ambiguity.[9]

Strategic air warfare can be viewed essentially as an amalgamation of two doctrines. One of these, implicit in the naval blockades imposed by both the British and Germans during World War I, is concerned with the strangulation of the enemy's industrial potential for waging war. The other concentrates on terrorizing the enemy's civilian population. Implicit in the latter is the possibility that the threat of terror can itself be an instrument of foreign policy, and thus that it can be a partial, if not complete, substitute for the employment of organized military force. Such was the thrust of Giulio Douhet's written works.[10]

Terrorizing a civilian population as an adjunct to military operations has a firm historical foundation. The technique was brought to its greatest refinement by the Ottoman Turks, whose dual military organization was a product of the nation's social system and was excellently designed for offensive operations.[11] On one hand, the Sultan possessed household troops, such as the well-trained Janissary infantry, heavy cavalry, and assorted specialists, engineers, and artillerymen. On the other hand, there were feudal fiefdoms and nomadic quasi-autonomous tribal groups in the frontier territories, against which the Sultan could exercise a feudal claim. These feudal levies came in the form of light horsemen, who were self-sustaining and self-financing in their operations, in contrast to the household troops, who were financed through taxes and whose operations entailed commissariats and logistics supply trains.

Major military operations of the Sultan typically were two pronged. Simultaneous with the departure of the main household army, the light cavalry would fan out over the enemy's countryside. The professional army was employed for cracking the tough obstacles, particularly such hard targets as key fortified cities. The technique used in laying siege on such strong points involved the calculated use of a sliding scale that afforded the defending commander the options of exchanging the casualties he could impose on the attacker in a successful defense for an increasing probability that his garrison and the town's population would be slaughtered if the defense were unsuccessful. The besiegers would normally provide the defender an opportunity to satisfy his military honor by putting on an attack that could be repulsed with minimum casualties for all parties. But often, after these preliminaries, the defender had to get down to the serious business of making the awesome choice in which no quarter on the part of the attackers was an alternative to complete surrender. A large number of valuable possessions were acquired and many taxpayers were added to the lists at low cost to the Sultan through the use of such techniques.

During a siege there was always the possibility that a relieving army might be raised to rescue the sieged city, but this was difficult in the European feudal system, since local nobility, minor kings, and Electors owned most of the military resources. By a combination of bribes, possible postwar redistributions of territory and spheres of influence, and exhortation and even financial aid from the Pope, the Holy Roman Emperor (usually a Hapsburg, during the period of interest) could raise an army. But raising an army from among the various sovereigns was difficult, because the territories held by many of them were threatened by the light troops romping over the countryside. Many of the latter had nomadic and Tartar antecedents, and they tended to be insensitive to the preservation of property values and civilian lives. A local lord or a king of Poland thus faced a hard choice as to whether or not he should rally to the support of a centrally directed defense of Christendom. (In the east, the Shah of Persia and his feudal satraps faced a similar problem.)

Thus, there is precedent for the purposeful use of terror and real property damage as an aspect of military operations and an instrument of foreign policy. The system of the Ottoman Turks also illustrates how the techniques are conditioned by the military instruments that are available. The preponderance of light, generally undisciplined horsemen in the empire's forces was directed toward a diffusion of the resources of the defenders, who were only loosely allied, at best. Yet the use of military resources was constrained. The conquest of territory and people was the primary objective; there was a willingness to spare the lives of civilians because, even if they did not choose to adopt the Moslem faith, they could at least pay taxes to the Sultan. Thus, the social system permitted a measure of ideological tolerance that was not achieved in the Christian domain.

There is no evidence that the modern concept of the strategic war, which entails widespread application of military force to the opponent's territory, is as well conceived as the Turkish system. In the British setting, the use of the airplane for such a purpose rapidly led to a question as to whether or not aircraft forces should be organized and operated as a service independent of the Army and Navy.

The Royal Air Force was the creation of wartime British civilian leaders who were reacting politically to the air raids Britain experienced and were seeking a technical solution to the tactical-strategic dilemma encountered on the Western front. The answer finally came about through what was effectively a carrot-and-stick situation. The reaction of the British leaders to the air raids came in response to the stick of public opinion that demanded that Germany be bombed. Their quest for a technical solution to the problem of the Western front was the carrot. Strategic bombing of the German homeland seemed to satisfy both forces.

The airplane and in particular its use for the strategic bombing of a continental adversary was thus viewed as a panacea for the frustrations of a real land war,[12] of which World War I was Britain's first experience as a major, rather than peripheral, participant. Heavy infantry casualties produced a trauma among the British, who had never experienced them before. Also, deeply embedded in British tradition was a predilection for the destruction of real estate (as our own national capital became aware in the War of 1812). Before the Elizabethan period, the British and French engaged extensively in "cross ravaging,"[13] the practice of conducting coastal raids and destroying port towns that was an instrument of foreign policy. Only upon the advent of the rich maritime trade with the new world were the talents of seafaring men like Drake and Hawkins diverted from the calling of their predecessors. The airplane thus had great potential in the view of many British civilian leaders. With insight about bureaucratic organizations, they reasoned that its potential might not be fully exploited if it were left up to the Army and Navy. The continued existence of the Royal Air Force was thereby assured.

As an instrument of strategic war, the evolution of Royal Air Force doctrine during World War II was dictated by a combination of operational capability and civilian policy requirements. Initially, the RAF Bomber Command sought by accurate bombing to destroy targets thought to make a critical contribution to the war effort. Daylight operations, however, proved too costly given the technical means and the in-depth defense system the Germans enjoyed. Hence, night operations became the preferred mode. But at night, navigation and target-identification errors made precision bombing impossible. Hence, a surgical destruction of critical target systems was unfeasible.

For nearly two years, after the Battle of Britain, policy makers and military men wrestled with formulating an appropriate bombing policy, including the question of how much resources to allocate to it. By May 1942, an operational doctrine and implementing techniques were worked out by Sir Arthur Harris, commander of the RAF Bomber Command, and his staff. The first application was the one-thousand-plane night raid against Cologne. The aiming point was the center of the city, which also contained marshaling yards and a famous Gothic cathedral. The experiment was an operational success. It and subsequent similar operations also served several political and doctrinal objectives. Those who adhered to moral scruples about bombing civilians could rationalize that military targets were the objective; bombs that missed, however, could destroy other property, including housing, which could possibly sap civilian morale, and thus satisfy those who believed in Douhet's version of employing airpower; finally, politicians, like Churchill, who were reluctant to embark on a major land war until the Americans could participate, could satisfy the requirement to do something, and cater to popular sentiment to repay German raids on England.[14]

The emergence of an independent air force in the United States and the associated doctrine of strategic air war was a tortuous development. Army airmen, such as William Mitchell and his successors, had to thread their way through a maze of domestic political sentiments, intrabranch constraints, and interservice rivalries to sustain their advocacy of air power. However, as testimony to the latent force that resided in the popular appeal of the airplane and the hypothesis that aircraft could save lives and defeat Germany quickly, we note that Congress in July 1917 called for a $640 million aviation appropriation,[15] without a roll call and without the concurrence of the Army. But long procurement-lead times and a shortened war effort provided only enough operational experience to generate expectations that neither the Army nor the country itself could accommodate during the postwar period.

During World War I, Army aviation was removed from its status as a branch of the Signal Corps by a series of steps. The first occurred in France, when General Pershing, exercising an organizational autonomy that was continually to dismay the military headquarters in Washington, created an Air Service, AEF, in June 1917. Back in the United States, with a civilian leader and composed of civilians and military officers (both Army and Navy), a statutory aircraft board was created in October 1917 to spend the $640 million allocation mentioned earlier. The Army's Chief Signal Officer retained the responsibility of procuring and training pilots,[16] but the production and procurement of aircraft in the United States did not go well. Nevertheless, the AEF managed to get aircraft from the British and French, and by November 11, 1918, "of 2,925 planes reaching the AEF's Zone of Advance . . . only 696 were of American make."[17] By May 1918, the administrative apparatus was created in the United States for what came to be known as the Army's "Air Service," which had the primary effect of removing Army Aviation from the jurisdiction of the Signal Corps.[18] However, it consisted of two components, representing procurement and operating (or "user") elements, both of which reported separately to the Secretary of War.

The immediate postwar period was one during which numerous organizational alternatives were considered, one of which was structured on the British Royal Air Force model (with a Secretary of State for Air) and which was popular with airmen. The debate was caught up in the larger context of Army politics, however, an arena that General Pershing dominated; and in the broader perspective, the Army's organization, especially its Headquarters Staff—was to be modeled along the lines of the AEF (which, in turn, was adapted to the French system, with its familiar numerical staff section designations, such as G-1 through G-4). This organization was given statutory effectiveness by the Army Reorganization Act of June 1920, which also formally recognized the Air Service as a combat arm of the Army, authorized a total Air Service strength of 20,000 (including officers, flying cadets, and enlisted men) in a 280,000 man army, and specified an additional flight pay "which amounted to 50 percent of base pay for flyers."[19] The airmen were disappointed, and the stage was set for the political and doctrinal war to be launched by General Mitchell.

Although the Army airmen lacked both physical resources and organizational strength, they were not deficient in producing a military doctrine. The striking quality of Army air doctrine of the 1920's and 1930's was the way it was adapted to both internal Army politics and the external politics of the budgetary arena, which in turn were affected by deeper political sentiments prevailing in the country. By the middle 1930's, this doctrinal product was to influence the choice of equipment and the decisions on force planning that ultimately determined the character of Army Air Force operations during World War II.

There were two major facets of Mitchell's, and subsequently the Air Corps', pre-World War II doctrine. One, which grew out of Mitchell's (and the Army's) World War I experience, provided for the use of aircraft as an integral part of a combined-arms ground operation. The St. Mihiel and Meuse-Argonne offensives and the contemplated 1919 spring offensive, in each of which Mitchell played the dominant planning role, could have been models for the Germans' successful application of air power in World War II. The approach entailed gaining and maintaining air superiority over the area in which the offensive occurs, so as to protect friendly ground elements in maneuver and hamper or eliminate enemy air reconnaissance. Simultaneously, bombing attacks were to be carried out against any of the enemy's command posts, supply depots, and troop movements that were uncovered in the course of the action. (For the 1919 offensive, Mitchell also proposed the use of parachute infantry to enhance these disruptive tactics.)

The word "interdiction" can be used to describe critical parts of the operation. However, there is a vital distinction between the kind of interdiction unsuccessfully attempted by the Air Force on a number of occasions, that seeks to choke off the supplies of an enemy army over a long period and across an entire theater, as opposed to the tactical interdiction permitted by the dynamics of a rapidly moving but localized ground offensive. In the latter case, the movement of friendly ground forces requires the enemy to move his forces, especially his reserves. It is in such a situation, particularly if the enemy is compelled to move during daylight, that one's air forces can inflict decisive damage. The ground operation *creates* the lucrative targets for the airborne firepower (similarly, it creates the rich targets for conventional artillery or offshore naval-fire support). From the planned course and timing of the friendly ground operation and with prior intelligence about the general location of enemy reserves, the friendly commander can also make reasonable predictions about the location and the time availability of the lucrative targets. The problems of target location and identification and the timing of how one should schedule his bomber sorties are not as vexing in this context as they are when aircraft are employed to win ground wars by themselves.

To employ aircraft in this kind of operation, however, requires that they be under the command of the officer who is also responsible for the ground operation. It is inconsequential whether that officer be an airman who controls the ground forces or vice versa,[20] just as it apparently does not matter whether a division, corps, or field-army commander's early experience was in artillery, tanks, or infantry.

Although the door was never completely closed on this approach, neither the Army nor the Air Corps during the period between the two world wars appears to have developed clear doctrine on these issues as, for example, did the Germans during the same time period. The entire subject was shrouded in ambiguity,[21] and moreover it was likely kept ambiguous so as to spare senior army officers the pain of making hard decisions. Civilian leaders were probably either ignorant of or insensitive about the Army's internal doctrinal problems, or they found it convenient to ignore them by focusing on the housekeeping functions that traditionally occupied civilian secretariats. Nevertheless, the seeds of a way to work out the "airplane problem" coherently was present both in U.S. Army experience and in Mitchell's thinking.

The concept of tactical interdiction provides a doctrinal bridge between the integrated use of aircraft with the traditional combat arms and the concept of a strategic air war that involves attacks on civilian targets. The latter could have effects that range between two theoretical extremes. One of these might be described as the "Douhet effect," which postulates that air attacks on civilian centers evokes panic and a breakdown of the social and economic structure. The other, not insignificant, extreme might be described as an effect similar to that achieved by the Ottoman Turk's use of light cavalry. The enemy is compelled to allocate resources to air defense—guns, troops, shelters, construction, and so forth—which then are unavailable for the support of conventional operations. The magnitude of such a diversion of arms and men can be significant, as was illustrated by the German defense of the Ploesti oil fields during World War II. Toward the end of 1942, the Germans had committed 50,000 troops, 70,000 Slav prisoners, and 237 heavy flak guns to a defense of the fields. Up to 200 fighter planes were also tied down with the defense task, and additional resources were called for and provided.[22] Overall, it has been estimated that about one-third of German production allocated to its war effort in 1942–44 were tied up in air defense.[23]

There is no evidence that the thinking of Army airmen during the interwar period had hardened into dogma with respect to any of the uses of aircraft. Although Mitchell's World War I efforts provided a model for the use of aircraft to be integrated with other combat arms in a land camapign, his postwar writings also draw upon the effects that bombing might inflict upon the civilian sector of an enemy.[24] In Mitchell's thinking there was the idea that a violent tactical offensive directed against an opponent's armies could engulf an enemy's civilian sector as a by-product of extending an interdiction campaign to strangle opposing ground forces. In such a fashion the unfavorable casualty exchange rate for the tactical offensive that characterized World War I might be reversed.[25] However, some of the deliberations within the Air Corps staff indicated skepticism about the value of bombing civilians.[26] For a period, serious consideration was given to the twin concepts of a light bomber for the support of ground operations and a heavy night bomber for the strategic role.[27] The relevant doctrinal, tactical, and organizational options appears to have been left open up to, and even beyond, the beginning of World War II.

The factors that caused a hardening of the positions actually taken appear to have been external to the Army. During the critical period when the subject was being viewed professionally within the Army, the underlying concept of a World War I type of expeditionary force and its associated land war was becoming unpopular in the environment of American political isolationism, and continental defense increasingly became the focus of the underlying congressional sentiment. In that period, continental defense comprised a coastal defense against ships, particularly against aircraft carriers. This provided an alternative strategy for the Army airmen, and the issue became land-based air against offensive naval forces, with the case for land-based air force consisting of the benefits of lower cost. The local defense for key strategic points was to be provided by pursuit aircraft, and land-based bombers were to be used to destroy enemy ships. Thus, the issue of the bomber versus the battleship became the focal point of the controversy.[28]

The promotion of land-based bombers as a coastal defense weapon had merit in the bureaucratic/political context. From the Army's viewpoint, it held a prospect for obtaining part of the Navy's budget; and should such a happy outcome materialize, the Army would be spared the disruption of its internal status quo, particularly with regard to the field artillery, whose relative share of the Army budget might warrant reexamination, given the ability of aircraft to perform a fire support role (a reexamination that has not taken place to this day). The most likely to have its funds reallocated within the Army budget, however, was the coast artillery, which had maintained installations and payrolls for decades in such settings as San Francisco's Presidio and Boston. But this kind of reallocation could raise delicate problems of congressional liaison. Consequently, the Navy's battleships and associated budget, which most Army generals would have relished seeing carved up, became fair game. In the eyes of the Army chiefs of staff, General Mitchell would be an ideal instrument, given his popular appeal among potentially influential civilians, for implementing the tactic of placing the question squarely before Congress. The Army had nothing to lose in such a venture, however poor the odds, and yet there was much to gain. The Chiefs of Staff could remain aloof from the fight. Then, if the Army did not win and the game became too rough, Mitchell could be sacrificed in the interest of maintaining smooth Army-Navy relationships.

Very likely, Mitchell himself understood the game and its possible punishments and rewards; and the feeling that he played it precisely according to the Army's rules is supported by a lack of any strong evidence of his directing intense fire toward the Army's artillery.[29] Nor should he be criticized for not raising questions about the Army's own management that he might have raised, for if he had, he would have been cut down quickly and perhaps even more severely than he ultimately was. Mitchell may have been a zealot, but he was not bureaucratically naive, nor could his political naivete be assumed. He simply played a very serious game, in which the percentages were quite sporting.

General Mitchell and the Army lost the fight, but the effort was not a complete loss for the airmen, or for the country either for that matter. In fact, it produced concrete results that carried over into World War II, and Mitchell's biggest contribution may indirectly have redounded to naval aviation, inasmuch as the Navy, as a minimum, had to demonstrate that it was in the air age. Having very little operational experience with the airplane, the Navy conferred upon its aviation community the standing of a statutory bureau, which in the Navy setting perhaps gave its flyers more autonomy than their Army counterparts were to enjoy during the early years. In 1935, the Army created a "General Headquarters Air Force," which involved the assignment of a substantial portion of the operating force directly to the Chief of Staff or to his operational control, which meant, really, that the Chief of the Air Corps in fact had operational control. The rationale for this move was a facilitation of the continental coastal defense (internally, it also denied the commanders of the Army corps areas any control over the air arm).

This focus on coastal defense and the concomitant mission of bombing approaching enemy ships also determined the military characteristics of what came to be the principal offensive air-weapon system in World War II, as well as of the basic American World War II bombing tactics. Ships—moving ships in particular—are difficult targets to hit. It is necessary to see them, which means engaging in daylight operations. For a long range—and therefore, big airplane that would be vulnerable to shipborne antiaircraft guns—the bombing had to be carried out from high altitudes and had to be accurate; and for this, the existing bombsights were the limiting factor.

A gyro-stabilized bombsight combining a drift meter and mechanical analog computer that could simultaneously compute aircraft ground speed and bomb-dropping angle was designed by a Navy civilian consultant, C. L. Norden. (With such a sight, a ship's movement merely changed the wind vector.) Norden's creations were quickly acquired and adapted to the needs of the Air Corps.[30] The B-17, another Navy development, was "optimized" for a daylight bombing role. Thus, the commitment of American airmen to the concept of "daylight precision bombing" in World War II had its deep origins in the American tradition of military management.

The evolution of the airplane and the many technical features associated with it (for example, electronics) in World War II and Korea have added a new dimension to military literature. In a past era, historians and writers refought battles (and, by implication, wrote speculative social history) by posing such questions as these: "What if Longstreet had moved more promptly on that fateful day at Gettysburg?" or "What if Nelson had lost at Trafalgar?" Since World War II, air battles and air campaigns are recounted in similar fashion, and the historian can now pose such questions as "What if Britain had had no radar in 1940?" Within limits, such questions and their associated intellectual exercises provide insight, and if the accounts are well written they also provide worthwhile entertainment. Many lessons may be learned; but a major difficulty is that of determining which lessons are the most useful.

A continuing thread that runs throughout the weave of advocacy and decision making as it bears upon the airplane is the idea that aircraft afford a means of breaking a tactical deadlock in land warfare or perhaps even of eliminating the need for conventional land warfare. More specifically, it could be a way of substituting machines for men, particularly for infantrymen. It was this potential payoff that led British policy makers to create the RAF. The hope was offered by Mitchell; and apparently the idea is believed by American policy makers, if postwar development and procurement practices are any indication.

Yet the expectation has not been consistently achieved; or, at best, the evidence cast up by World War II and subsequent wars does not clearly support the hypothesis that resources, embedded in equipment and aircraft in particular, can be extensively substituted for fighting manpower in war. Germany's defeat in World War II can be accounted for by its large manpower losses in the relevant age groups, with most of these casualties occurring on the eastern front. Even so, the land fighting in Western Europe and Italy, in which Americans and British participated, acquired a sharp flavor of being a straightforward exchange of manpower. Korea revealed a similar pattern, although the exchange rate favored the United Nations by a ratio of perhaps two to one—in large part owing to materiel superiority in both air and, especially, artillery (indeed, the terrain and other features of the Korean War, in retrospect, appears to have been an artilleryman's ideal setting). Finally, American operations in South Vietnam suggest that high airplane and artillery densities cannot extensively substitute for combat infantrymen, some of whom are destined to be expended in the manner suggested by Clausewitz. The airplane, including its associated technical derivatives like electronics and guided missiles, appears to have exerted its revolutionary impact by way of greatly complicating military management and, for a wealthy nation like the United States, significantly increasing the money and resource cost of possessing and employing military force.

These observations are not offered to deprecate the role that technical developments have played or might play in future wars. The fact is that little has been attempted in assessing how equipment, tactical changes, and other forces interact in ways that affect casualties, and the subject is still very poorly understood, despite the enormous intellectual effort expended during the past twenty years or so on the study of "war."[31] Whatever revolution has been provoked by the airplane and its associated technology, it has not greatly changed things with regard to the focal point of the political forces stimulating advanced technology and creating independent air forces.

Nor is this to dismiss the important role of the airplane in World War II, especially its critical place in the American effort. In Europe and especially in the Pacific, amphibious operations were necessary first steps. Amphibious landings are perhaps the most lucrative target systems ever created, and might be considered ideal for airplanes to attack. Thus, air superiority for the attacker, in the local area, is a minimum condition for a successful landing, as well as for sustaining the operation once the assaulting elements are ashore. This capability was provided most of the time; and when the air support was thin or tenuous —as it was at critical stages of the Guadalcanal and Salerno operations—the ground troops and supporting ships were in jeopardy.

Perhaps one of the reasons air forces did not drastically change the conduct of ground war was institutional considerations. (The early World War II German experience may have been a major and perhaps transitory exception.) Whenever a major new item of military equipment emerges, a justification exists to create a specialist organization to operate and employ it. Its technicalities alone may warrant the organizational specialization. The specialists, in turn, become dedicated to their equipment, if not advocates about its potential. They also enjoy a degree of autonomy owing to their specialist organization. The existence of the equipment justifies the organization, and there is an understandable motive to see the organization grow. Those who identify with such an equipment-dominated organization, therefore, seek to conserve their equipment. They are apt to insist on managing their equipment in operations, or to push for a high degree of central management. Yet if equipment is to substitute for the expenditure of people in war, it too may literally have to be expended—just as troops are expended. Herein lies a source of difficulty between different military subgroups.

Most social institutions develop management philosophy that facilitates the performance of their functions. Through analysis and experience, they evolve rules for making decisions, make internal organizational changes, and promulgate procedures that, it is hoped, will serve the organizational objectives. An air force as an independent military organization, however, turns this normal pattern upside down, simply because an air force is the institutionalization of a management philosophy. It can be argued that, among the vast variety of social contrivances, air forces are perhaps unique in this regard. The management philosophy of which an independent air force is the institutional embodiment is that of central management, with particular reference to the conduct of its operating missions. Herein lies a source of instability in military decision making and budgeting. This management philosophy combines with the doctrine of strategic war to create forces that have greatly complicated the military decision-making process, the resulting problems of which the United States has not resolved. This management syndrome warrants elaboration.

A consequence of the increasing diversity and complexity of skills (as illustrated by the application of the principle of the division of labor) is that closed organizations like military services, police departments, and universities find it necessary to accommodate specialized suborganizations. But this creates a major management problem. The outputs of the suborganizations are inputs for a larger endeavor, and the different inputs must be blended and combined in a way that facilitates the performance of its social function by the larger organization. Invariably, that larger social function is best performed by an integration and combining of the diverse inputs.

Military organizations, especially armies, have resolved this issue in perhaps the only practical way. On one hand, they recognize the need for specialized suborganizations, such as engineering and artillery branches, so as to provide specialized training, develop expertise, and even provide special administrative services that an artillery organization, for example, would require. Therefore, the "artillery community" is permitted to exercise control over those of its activities that provide for technical excellence in the performance of its special function. On the other hand, in an operational and field context, artillery units are subordinate to commanders who are responsible also for the command of other specially trained and skilled capabilities—infantry, armor, engineers, and so forth. Furthermore, in armies exhibiting a high degree of professionalism, great emphasis is placed upon combining the activities of the diverse branches, since, as Clausewitz points out, these diverse capabilities are complementary insofar as the conduct of effective operations is concerned.

To recognize the need for combining different specialties does not necessarily solve the centralized management issue. The more costly or specialized a resource is, or the greater the extent to which it possesses physical attributes such as speed and long range, the more likely it is to be managed centrally, even in the context of a combined arms organization. The facts of high costs and extreme specialization suggest that the capability be used economically, which in turn implies that it should not be expended in activities that can be performed with less specialized or less valuable resources. For example, although combat engineers can function as ordinary infantry (because they are trained to perform special assault operations), they will not normally be so employed because their ability to perform their specialized functions such as demolition work or constructing field fortifications, will have been degraded. Other troops can also do these jobs, of course, but certainly not as well. Well-trained commanders of combined-arms operations fully understand these relationships, and they therefore husband their specialized and more valuable resources. Conversely, however, the commanders of combat engineer units understand that when their superiors do order the employment of their specialized resources for tasks other than their primary mission, they most likely do so under conditions of extreme emergency.

Weapons which have high speed or long range are also properly susceptible to being centrally managed, since either quality enables decision makers to concentrate their capability at a particular point. To the extent that the range of cannon can be extended, it is possible for more guns to be brought to bear on a single target. Thus, the extent to which weapons should be purposefully designed to possess long range and the amount of resources they should absorb, as well as judgments regarding the worth of this ability to concentrate fire power relative to other capabilities, become part of an intertwined whole.

These problems associated with specialized and costly resources have cropped up in armies in many forms. Should the cavalry be organized in separate divisions or even entire corps, or should it be dispersed and operated with smaller units? When rifled small arms came to be employed in armies around the turn of the nineteenth century, when smooth-bore muskets were still the dominant weapon, the question was concerned with whether riflemen should be organized in separate regiments or should be interspersed in individual companies attached to battalions. Should machineguns be organized in separate battalions or regiments, or should they be interspersed throughout the regular infantry battalions? Should tanks be organized in separate armored divisions, or should they be interspersed among infantry units? The problem of centralized versus decentralized management is therefore not new.

The resolution of this problem as a managerial philosophy, however, has usually been highly pragmatic. When a specialized capability is very scarce and costly, it is usually centrally managed with regard to its training and, especially, with regard to its operational use. However, as it becomes less costly or proves to be highly efficacious, it will be dispersed. For example, as rifles became less expensive, more efficient, and more reliable (in contrast to smooth-bore muskets), all infantrymen were equipped with rifles, and the old distinction between light and heavy infantry disappeared. During World War II, the U.S. Army first concentrated its tanks in armored divisions, along the lines of the German model. But as the war went on and tanks proved useful for infantry support, they became more abundant and were assigned to regular infantry divisions. In this case, both centralized and decentralized management and use were employed. Thus, even though doctrine may suggest central management of a specialized resource, it has never been allowed to persist as dogma for too long with regard to most experiences with specialized capability or equipment. Such has not been the case, however, with independent air forces.

The institution of an air force, in contrast to that of an air service, derives its rationale from the philosophy of central management, which also serves the quest of the force's members for autonomy. The institution and its philosophy also sustains and nurtures a "bias" in favor of high performance, multipurpose use, and hence, costly equipment. Finally, with regard to nonstrategic war, where an independent air force is at least obliged to cooperate with the other services, particularly with the army, air-force doctrine tends to reflect its special "scenario" of military operations, which sustains its claim for central management and independence.

The air-force scenario of joint operations, with particular reference to the use of aircraft, is sequential, as follows: (1) An air battle is fought with enemy aircraft, presumably over one's own territory; (2) the air battle is continued by bombing the enemy's air bases, so as to destroy his remaining aircraft on the ground; (3) to assist one's ground forces, an interdiction campaign is conducted so as to deny the enemy's supply to his ground forces; (4) finally, close air support will be provided to one's own ground forces. It may also be implicit in air-force thinking that the above sequential order is the same as the relative ranking of the missions. That is, even if the scenario should not in fact proceed in the above order, the priorities of resource allocation should be in that order. Such priorities mean, for example, that aircraft will not be used to provide close support for ground troops if there are enemy airfields that might profitably be attacked.

Since numbers figure importantly in war, one should have a maximum number of aircraft to perform any mission. Thus, the aircraft should be of the multipurpose type, not specialized in performing a single mission. But this is costly, a factor that in turn supports the case for central management. It is also anathema to air-force managers to "hand off" aircraft to the army or other commanders for, say, close-support missions. To use aircraft exclusively for that purpose may suggest designs, tactics, and special pilot training that are especially adapted to the single mission, which then opens the door for the consuming service itself to own the aircraft. Such a trend reduces the air force's size. Moreover, army generals and navy admirals are willing to expend items like airplanes in warfare. For, while army generals must normally plan on expending troops as a matter of course, the fact remains that if equipment can be sacrificed in place of troops, an army commander will not hesitate in making such a sacrifice. But while admirals, for example, are willing to expend many aircraft in destroying an enemy's capital ships (at Midway, the U.S. Navy lost 60 of 300 aircraft), such losses in an air-force bombing mission portend institutional disaster. So aircraft expenditure for purposes other than air battles tends to be regarded with dismay by air-force leaders.

One of the consequences of air-force doctrine is that land-force commanders do not trust the air force, and they are unwilling to take account of the capabilities of the air force for close air support in the programming and design of land forces. And their reasoning is sound, however unpleasant it may be for dollar budgeting. Ground operations require reliable support. When an attack is made against a major objective, the working over of key points with fire power, including close air support, is important to the success of the attacking infantry. But if the air commander discovers some operational enemy airfields, he might prefer to attack them, and raise questions about changing the timing of the ground operation. Such prospects hound ground commanders, and for this reason many may be inclined to prefer artillery for fire support, if only because it is definitely at their disposal or, over the long term, army-force planners might contrive to get their own air force.

Thus, the airplane epitomizes management problems that are perennial. And yet, the institution of an independent air force and the high cost of the technicalities that airplanes embody have institutionalized the problems themselves and, hence, arrested any of the forces that would normally stabilize or balance diverse management philosophies. The problems that can occur have important budgeting and resource-allocation implications. They can often raise difficulties in operational settings that may not be adequately surfaced, with the resulting compromise not providing the best, overall solution.[32] These are problem areas to which civilian leaders should be continually attuned.

6

THE RISE OF THE AMATEUR ANALYSTS: OPERATIONAL RESEARCH AND COST-EFFECTIVENESS ANALYSIS

> 'The Services,' said Iles. 'The Navy's demands occasionally have some relation to the facts. The R.A.F.'s and the Army's never.' He closed his eyes wearily and said, 'It's a thousand pities that the Services are allowed to interfere in matters they don't understand. If they would concentrate on their fighting and leave the thinking to us, we should get on a good deal quicker.'
>
> Nigel Balchin, *The Small Back Room*, p. 37.

The previous chapter pointed out that the airplane stimulated civilian technologists to think about broader aspects of military affairs. It, through its technicalities, also created channels that permitted civilian scientists and analysts to become involved with many fine-grained decisions that had traditionally been the primary preserve of the professional bureaucrats. This trend was reinforced by other factors which, in England, gave rise to operational research and the beginnings of cost-effectiveness analysis. These developments were deeply intertwined with Winston Churchill's style of personal leadership and the concept of an independent air force, as was the Royal Air Force. Through the interaction of the RAF and the U.S. Army Air Force and such American happenings as the development of nuclear weapons, there emerged in the United States a community of "defense intellectuals" and their associated institutions, which were to become a force in contemporary American defense decision-making. An understanding of these developments is useful for three reasons. First, they are intertwined with and had an impact upon the management innovations in the Defense Department that were instituted by Robert McNamara. Second, it is possible that operational research and cost-effectiveness analysis contain much potential for enabling men to cope with the "bureaucracy" problem, which is the major subject of this inquiry. Finally, these phenomena importantly impact upon the scientific and intellectual community insofar as large elements of it became dependent upon government spending. The background and origin of these developments are the subject of this chapter.

With the rise of Hitler and the advent of German rearmament, British policy makers and military-force planners began to face up to the prospect of England being bombed in the event of war. Air defense, particularly with respect to better ways for detecting attacking aircraft, became a matter of high priority; and to cope with the detection problem, the government and the RAF turned to the scientific community.[1]

Through the administrative device of advisory committees, the British had, during World War I, experience with employing scientists to address technical problems that related to war. By 1918, in acknowledgment of the point that Germany managed to make great technical progress in weaponry with the aid of scientific endeavor, a Department of Scientific and Industrial Research was formed, which had a charter to operate in both civil and military fields. In 1919, the Air Ministry created an aeronautical research committee to advise the Secretary of State for Air upon "higher matters of research."[2] Until 1935, this committee was mainly composed of members of the aircraft industry. A reorganization in 1935, however, changed its main composition to that of scientists from government departments and universities. Nevertheless, throughout the entire period, prominent academic scientists—including F. A. Lindemann and H. T. Tizard—were affiliated with the committee.[3]

Through the mechanism of the Air Ministry's Advisory Committee and at the suggestion of the Air Ministry's Director of Scientific Research, H. E. Wimperis, an ad hoc committee was set up toward the end of 1934 "to consider how far recent advances in scientific and technical knowledge can be used to strengthen the present methods of defense against hostile aircraft."[4] Its chairman was H. T. Tizard. Hard upon the formation of the Air Ministry's committee, Parliament set up an Air Defense subcommittee of the Committee of Imperial Defense, to be chaired by the Secretary of State for Air[5] and with a function to coordinate interservice and interdepartmental activities bearing upon air defense. Tizard was made a member of this latter committee.[6] Under Winston Churchill's auspices, F. A. Lindemann was made a member of the Tizard Committee. (Churchill was a minority member of Parliament at the time.) The stage was set for a bitter struggle between Tizard and Lindemann that subsequently evoked, if nothing else, much acrimonious comment on personalities, intertwined with philosophy on the use of a role of scientists and intellectuals in government.[7]

Despite (or perhaps because of) an untidy administrative apparatus inhabited by strong-minded and mutually suspicious personalities, resources were made available to pursue the development of radar. Robert Watson-Watt (later Sir Robert), who had been doing research on radio communications, was installed at a government-provided facility to develop a new means of detection. Progress was rapid, and in 1935 a workable radio-ranging and detection device was invented. The next problem was how to use it most effectively. The RAF obtained for Watson-Watt and his colleagues a larger facility and began to lay on field-type experiments—employing aircraft, to simulate operations—in order to gain data on the operational behavior of the new equipment. The civilians participated in the design of the experiments, reduced and interpreted the data, and offered recommendations on how to use and deploy radar. In the process, the scientists and technicians obtained further insight on how to modify and improve the equipment so as to enhance its operational effectiveness. This phase of the activity was a joint affair, or an operating partnership, between military-operations officers and the civilian scientists. The scientists became privy to knowledge about operations; the military officers acquired increasing expertise about the technical aspects of the equipment. Hence, operational research was born. Further products of this seminal effort was the deployment, by the outbreak of the war, of twenty radar stations in Great Britain and three stations overseas, that could detect aircraft flying at medium altitudes at a range of 100 miles.[8]

Critical to the "invention" of operational analysis was the idea that scientists work closely with the operators. For achieving this objective, credit is due to Lord Swinton, who became Secretary of State for Air and who indicated to the Chief of the Air Staff, "I want no secrets from these men; they will be as much a part of the Operational Staff as you and your staff are."[9] As Watson-Watt explained, "The length of the arm which formerly held the staff user, and even the field user at a distance from the technical developer" had not only been "bent to a shorter effective length . . . ," but had "been curved into a cordial embrace."[10] It was, indeed, something new. That civilians came to have access to the workings of one portion of a military bureaucracy was due to high-level, civilian policy makers who were greatly worried about the air-defense problem. Note that it was the RAF Fighter Command, not the dominating Bomber Command, that was the object of the initial effort. The Fighter Command did not enjoy the favored budget position within the RAF. It was consequently somewhat "hungry" and was therefore apt to be more receptive to getting help from whatever quarter it might come, including question-raising and often vexing civilian scientist-analysts.

Perhaps of equal importance to high-level interest and a desperate Fighter Command was the personal role played by H. T. Tizard. "Tizzy," as he was called, had been involved in aircraft design during World War I. As part of carrying out his job, he learned to fly. A vexing problem at that time was to bring under control an aircraft in a spin. To test and refine his theories on the subject, Tizard deliberately put an aircraft into a spin (an unheard of thing at that time) and recovered. Subsequently, he toured air bases and taught young pilots the proper technique. Since many of those pilots were high-ranking RAF officers by the 1930's, Tizard enjoyed a confidence and respect far beyond what would normally be accorded a scientist. He was therefore ideally equipped to function as a bridge between the military and scientific "subcultures," which is precisely what he did during those short, desperate years before the outbreak of World War II. Such a role is usually best performed in subtle and quiet ways, partly to permit credit for success to fall to others. Tizard may therefore be regarded as one of those rare men who really got something important done in the bureaucratic/political context.

After the Battle of Britain, the integration of civilian scientists with military-operations officers in teams, functioning in a military staff apparatus, extended rapidly throughout the British military establishment, and especially the RAF. Radar and derivative electronics items were the initial and principal focus of these efforts. Successively, the RAF coastal command and the Navy employed such teams to address antisubmarine warfare problems. The RAF Bomber Command acquired operational research staffs for assistance in navigational and bombing problems.[11] Overseas commands acquired operational research sections. The scope of the intellectual efforts also broadened to encompass such subjects as fuse settings for ordnance, bomb loads and bombing patterns, targeting doctrine, shipping and submarine search problems, and—as applied to naval operations—convoy design. Thus, the civilian scientists became privy to an ever-expanding portion of the sphere of the operations section of the military staff system. Operational research analysis sections also began to filter downward in the military hierarchy and appear in the headquarters staffs of subordinate commands.

Extension of operational analysis from the RAF to the British Army and Navy followed after the outbreak of war. In 1940, Gen. Sir Frederick Pile, commander of the antiaircraft command, appointed P. M. S. Blackett as his scientific adviser. (Blackett was a charter member of the original Tizard Committee.) He formed a mixed team of scientists that addressed aircraft acquisition, employment of gun-laying radars, gun-site location, and related antiaircraft problems. Under the War Office, elements of this group severed their association with the air defense "establishment," and expanded its scope and created sections to treat the entire range of land-warfare problems, to include infantry, artillery, and antitank gunnery. During 1942 and 1943, sections worked in the field with land forces operating in the Middle East, Italy, and India.[12] The pattern of field work was repeated on an extensive and highly professional scale with the British (and in some instances American) land forces in Northwest Europe. The report of the 2nd Operational Research Section with the British 21st Army Group, covering the period of June 1944 to July 1945, contains a number of gems bearing upon combined-arms operations, as well as some studies that shed light on Air Force claims regarding the efficacy of tactical air, that could be profitable reading for both contemporary policy makers and military analysts. In the land-warfare business, operational research was not as clean cut as it was (or is) with air or naval war. The method of inquiry is similar to that of a criminal investigation. The researchers follow closely the scene of an action, drawing upon operations orders, and commanders' after-action reports as much as possible. But the main effort consists of examining scars upon tanks or vehicle carcasses to determine what actually made the kill; the counting of spent cartridge cases and hastily dug graves; the interrogation of prisoners, farmers, and one's own soldiers; and from these and other sources gathering enough statistics to learn what happened and to verify or refute hypotheses.

In early 1942, the Admiralty established a Department of Operational Research, which was headed and formed by Blackett. (He had also played a similar role for the RAF Coastal Command.) The main effort of the Navy's group was antisubmarine work. Unlike operational research activities of the RAF and the Army, the Admiralty's endeavors did not extend to field commands, but were centered in the headquarters.[13]

Operational research extended to the American war endeavor mainly through the Air Force, or airplane-oriented operations. First was the British precedent in the use of operational research, and its relationship to the need for the U.S. Army Air Force to interact with the RAF in English-based offensive operations. In the early part of 1942, General Spaatz requested General Arnold to provide the Eighth Bomber Command "a group similar to those attached to elements of the RAF."[14] One suspects that the motivation of senior U.S. air officers to acquire the capability was in part stimulated by bureaucratic requirements vis-à-vis their RAF counterparts. It is known that American and British air doctrine differed in important respects with regard to tactics, including targeting. One can picture a meeting between senior officers of the two air forces. The British have with them their "scientist" (who, of course, sits quietly against the wall, along with other staff seconds—not at the table at which sit the principals). Straightaway, one side has gained an element of "one upmanship" which is intolerable to the opposite side. For this reason alone, irrespective of any real regard that General Spaatz may have had for civilian scientists, his request to General Arnold no doubt contained a strong element of urgency. By October 1942, General Arnold recommended to all Air Force commands that they acquire the capability of operational research.[15] The quasi-official Air Force history notes that Arnold "became fond of admonishing his staff that 'the long haired boys' could help."[16] The scope and scale of employment of analysts to address operational problems proceeded rapidly. As the air offensive in Europe got underway, including the U.S. daylight bombing effort, a joint Anglo-American team emerged (which administratively was under the British Air Ministry), that primarily focused on targeting and bomb-damage assessment. One of the members of this team was Charles Hitch, who was destined to play an important future role in military decision making. This section was also to provide the nuclei of teams that were to conduct the postwar Strategic Bombing Survey.[17]

Like the British antecedents of operational analysis, the wartime evolution of the American counterpart had a strong foundation in the employment of civilian scientists and engineers to address the purely technical aspects of war. Although a sharp distinction exists between operational analysis on one hand and technical research and development on the other, there is an important common ground with regard to the two activities. Some attention to these points is relevant to the understanding of differences between British and American developments in the use of scientists and intellectuals.

As part of the effort to prepare for war and the specific product of the belief that the United States might be technically lagging in the field of weaponry, the National Defense Research Committee was created in June 1940. There were two institutional or administrative underpinnings for this act. First, there was the National Academy of Sciences, created by Congress in 1863, which by Executive Order in 1918 was empowered to create a National Research Council. The Academy was composed of prominent physical and life scientists, elected by the professionals themselves. Second, there was the Council of National Defense, created in 1916 and composed of the Secretaries of War, Navy, Interior, Agriculture, Commerce, and Labor. As a government instrument, it was authorized to create committees of "specially qualified persons." The National Defense Research Committee was its creation. Initially, it was composed of eight members—two to be selected by the Secretaries of Navy and War, respectively, the president of the National Academy of Sciences (who was also president of Bell Telephone Laboratories), the Patent Commissioner, and four members at large, who included Vannevar Bush and James Conant.[18] The committee promptly created five divisions, containing numerous sections, to treat the many aspects of the interaction between technology and war. That it intended to get down to specifics, as contrasted to high-level considerations, is suggested by the listing of sections on "paint removers" and "pyrotechnics" as well as "propulsion" and "proximity fuzes for shells."[19] The divisions and sections were chaired by individuals drawn from both universities and industrial firms. The Committee also had authority and funds to undertake research contracts.

A year after the establishment of the National Defense Research Committee, the President, by Executive Order, established the Office of Scientific Research and Development (OSRD). It was placed in the Office of Emergency Management of the Executive Office of the President. The primary function of OSRD was to stress the development phase of research and development, to ensure coordination with regard to some government scientific activities over which the National Defense Research Committee had no cognizance, and to stimulate research in military medicine.[20] Although officially and formally it operated in a staff capacity by virtue of being in the President's Executive Office, the frequent use of the verbs "initiate" and "support" in the Executive Order suggests that it was intended at the outset that the OSRD play an activist, if not a line, role. Subsequent Executive Orders allowing OSRD to acquire and dispose of property and to function under the same legislation that governed the Army and Navy with regard to contracting reinforced this indicator.[21] Vannevar Bush was made Director of OSRD. The National Defense Research Committee was designated to function in an advisory capacity to OSRD. Thus, within a year, two important and mutually supporting steps were taken. First, a mechanism was created to establish communication channels between academic and industrial scientists on one hand and the government on the other. Second, the bureaucratic apparatus was created that had the power both to implement the advice of the scientists and, equally important, to exert a force that could cut across and through the diverse bureaucratic fiefdoms. The means was available to "open up" the closed system.

Through the mechanism of OSRD, scientists and engineers fanned out throughout the military services to work in the laboratories and arsenals. The emphasis was on developing weapons and quickly getting them into operating units. Such items as the bazooka (and its associated combination of a rocket and shaped or hollow charge), aircraft rockets, the proximity fuse, radar-bombing techniques, and specialized amphibious vehicles were some of the instruments fielded. To expedite the deployment process and to obtain fast remedies for flaws that appear whenever new systems are operated in the field, OSRD created in November 1943 an Office of Field Service. The Administrative Order establishing the Office emphasized the need "to make the most effective possible use of developments . . . and minimize the effectiveness of any such developments made by the enemy, especially those in combat use."[22] Operational research was listed first as one of the services to be provided. The Director of the office was also authorized to employ and train personnel for the activities. Since the function was both delicate and important, Karl T. Compton, president of the Massachusetts Institute of Technology (M.I.T.) and a member of the National Defense Research Committee, was named director of the Office of Field Services.[23]

The objective of employing scientists in the field was delicate, because it entailed mixing individuals of different backgrounds who had different responsibilities. Military officers were mainly worried about conducting operations; scientists and engineers in the field, on the other hand, would view operations as a means to an end. The question-raising and probing necessary for the scientist to perform his task, if not put tactfully, could easily be construed by the military operator as an implicit criticism of the latter's decisions or performance of his own craft. Moreover, especially in time of war, the uniformed military, no doubt manifesting attitudes of the ancient warrior cult, feel superior, if not contemptuous, of civilians, even though the latter may wear fatigues and combat boots in the field. Finally, civilian scientists, through their attachment to a higher headquarters or through their spontaneous and informal information channels, can cause information regarding activities in the local setting to be made known in higher quarters (often in mysterious and roundabout ways), so they they are likely to do a local commander more harm than good. For these reasons, the injection of "combat scientists" into operations commands was difficult.[24] Karl Compton had to be a missionary as well as a scientist.[25] It is significant that his missionary effort was primarily directed to the Pacific theater of operations. In that theater there was no British counterpart to provide the American military either an example or a bureaucratic incentive to acquire operational-research capability.

For these reasons, operational research did not become as extensive throughout the American World War II military establishment as it did in the British. "Combat scientists," on the other hand, were nevertheless used extensively in all theaters to perform "field engineering" (which was also part of the Field Service's charter) and to address highly technical problems, such as coping with fungi in the South Pacific, which affected such diverse equipment as combat boots and radio sets. With respect to these kinds of problems, both because of their immediacy and their neutrality with regard to operations, even the most encrusted military officer could be expected to welcome the scientist (although he would prefer to see him arrive in uniform, to be under military command). For these reasons, the main accomplishments of the American operational-research endeavor centered on Atlantic convoy operations and strategic bombardment. In these areas there was either a requirement to deal with the British or the precedents established by the USAAF or both. This was no small achievement: apart from the substantive contribution, a large number of civilian scientists and intellectuals (many in their impressionable and formative years) acquired a feeling for and interest in military operations and planning. The monopoly of knowledge that a closed community normally maintains was shattered. It remained to find ways to harness and redeploy that additional capability that posed new challenges and actions in the post-World War II period.

Although it is something of a postcript, it is interesting to note that in the American idiom "operational" research became "operations" research. It is unknown why and how the adjective became an attributive noun. There are two plausible explanations. One is simply that Americans are careless about the "King's English." The other, which we find more suggestive, is offered by Watson-Watt:[26] The "s" instead of the "al" implies clearly that the activity is part (and only a part) of a traditional military-operations staff section. In such a setting civilians are clearly subordinate to the military. Some way had to be found to arrest the growing influence of civilians in a traditional preserve of the professionals or, perhaps, to mollify the military caste by suggesting or signaling that the activity would be under its control.

The rise of operational research is now recounted by some historians of the phenomenon as being a consequence of the payoff provided by radar in the Battle of Britain. Although it is true that nothing succeeds like success, the question should be raised as to why the accomplishments of Watson-Watt and his group, who were oriented to the air-defense problem, did not remain a "one-shot" event? Given the fact that operators jealously preserve the secrecy of their expertise and further that civilian scientists question and sometimes exhibit a disdain for military customs in ways that can be irritating, if not infuriating, we must conclude that success in coping with one technical-operational problem is not sufficient to transform precedent into an institution. Rather, the stress that is inherent in mingling military and civilian personalities and the potential of such a situation for destroying the secrecy a bureau seeks to maintain could have caused the relationship to be terminated after the air-defense problem was treated (with appropriate military citations awarded, of course, to Watson-Watt and his civilian colleagues). But such a disengagement did not occur. Instead, the use of mixed teams of civilian scientists, civilian analysts, and military officers to address operational problems spread throughout all parts of the British military establishment.

The question is not an academic one. It is highly relevant to military decision making in the contemporary United States setting. There exists in the United States a large community comprising both individuals and organizations, a learned society and its journal, university departments offering a curriculum on the subject, and staff sections in military organizations, all of which in one way or another employ the appellation "operations research." Yet very little operational research of the type conducted during World War II is in fact performed today. The difference between the World War II endeavor and the contemporary activity is one of methodology, with the former being heavily empirical and experimental. Contemporary military operational research in the United States consists overwhelmingly of theoretical model building, with an emphasis on mathematical techniques. Indeed, the reading of standard works on operations research would suggest that the subject is nothing but applied mathematics: inventory theory, queueing theory, linear programming, simulation, gaming, and other techniques appear to dominate the subject.[27]

It is true that operational research is a scientific approach to problem solving and that the essential quality of a scientific approach is to formulate the solutions to problems in the form of mathematical models and try to deduce relationships among observable phenomena that are tied to simple first principles. But it is equally true that the scientific approach necessitates that deductions flowing from the models be checked against reality, either by experimentation or experience. Moreover, it is important that the basic quantitative data fed into a model have some foundation in reality. The extent of model building in contemporary military-operational research, however, is exceeded only by an absence of the empirical data and related experimentation necessary for the theoretical endeavor to be considered part of a scientific activity. The difference between the World War II operational research and its present descendant is profound: it is a difference between science on the one hand and speculative philosophy on the other.

This methodological problem and its implications will be treated at greater length in a later chapter. But for immediate purposes it is sufficient to note that operational research literally means the researching of operations. To gather information about operations requires that the researchers be privy to operational decisions or, better, that the operators themselves or individuals having operational experience assist the analysts by actively participating in the gathering of data and, where it is possible to experiment, the design of experiments. Thus, the formation of scientist/military teams was central to both the style and spirit of World War II operational research. The relationship, to be fruitful, has to be one between equals, not one between subordinate and superior. (It was for this reason that the task of Karl Compton, in his endeavor to inject "combat scientists" into the field environment was "delicate.") Yet full exposure of a bureau's operations to outsiders destroys the bureau's secrecy and clashes with the strong political and bureaucratic forces that require secrecy for their sustenance.

For these reasons, World War II operational research was an institutional, if not a cultural, phenomenon of major magnitude. Because it is confronted by strong forces that operate against openness and clarification, one must look beyond the single event of the invention of radar as an operational system. Other conditions and circumstances must have been prevalent for operational research to emerge as an extensive activity. These circumstances were the product of characteristics of the British setting and the personal leadership qualities of Winston Churchill, factors that generated the precedent for modern cost-effectiveness analysis.

To appreciate the wartime leadership technique of Winston Churchill, it is perhaps necessary to reconstruct the possible impact that World War I might have had on him. World War I had a singular quality with regard to the relationship between military bureaucrats and constituted policy makers, which developed in both Germany and Great Britain.

As the war dragged on, the policy makers increasingly became captives of the professional military bureaucrats. In Germany, the officer corps—through the General-Staff system—had achieved the highest degree of professionalism in their operations and especially in their administrative expertise. Its administrative expertise permitted it to take over functions such as economic mobilization, manpower allocation, propaganda, and the administration of occupied territories that were necessitated as the war began to require complete mobilization. Such a takeover may have been necessitated by the fact that the Empire had no bureaucratic apparatus other than the foreign service, post office, navy, and army, which performed government functions cutting across the three separate kingdoms (Prussia, Württemberg, and Bavaria) that made up the Empire. What basis there may have been for civilian policy-making was lacking because the Kaiser was not capable of it, nor were there any vigorous parliamentarians to make policy in his stead. The military takeover was therefore inadvertent; but it was no less complete. Thus Ludendorff ("whose almost brutal powers of work and quite extraordinary organizing ability subserved a mind that was essentially one-sided"[28]) could try to seek a military solution to the war through a major offensive as late as the spring of 1918. That offensive—although it exhibited brilliant innovations in infantry tactics—squandered whatever military resources that may have remained for facilitating a negotiation that would be fruitful for Germany.[29]

In Britain, the setting differed in significant ways, inasmuch as the British military bureaucracy had not achieved the same high degree of professionalism as was possessed by their German counterparts. The Army reforms instituted by Haldane in 1906–07, although serving mightily to enhance Britain's capability for waging land war in 1914, did not have sufficient time to offset the older customs fully. Tactical, and especially strategic, imagination may have been lacking in the higher reaches of the military hierarchy, but its lack may not have made too much difference relative to the tactical-strategic dilemma that frustrated British political leaders.

The British nevertheless did make some effort to cope with the World War I strategic-tactical dilemma, and Churchill had a hand in both a strategic and tactical approach. The amphibious Gallipoli operation was advocated by Churchill to break the deadlock. Unfortunately, the operation was bedeviled by faulty staff work related to intelligence, an unwarranted faith in naval firepower, and failure in such mundane matters as the loading of ships in a way that would facilitate smooth amphibious operations.[30] Indeed, it can even be argued that "foot-dragging" at high levels of the British military hierarchy may have been the basic cause of the operation's failure. By the time it was being discussed, the high-level military staffs had come to be dominated by "Westerners," or individuals who viewed the Western front as the decisive theater of operations. Partly, this kind of bias arises from loyally carrying out of the normal tasks of supporting the field troops and their commanders. But whatever the motivation, implementation of the plan did not sparkle. The major losers of the Gallipoli campaign were the Australians and New Zealanders, who took the brunt of the infantry casualties. The only gainer appears to have been the United States, inasmuch as the Marine Corps took to heart the lesson that was revealed on how not to conduct an amphibious operation and developed the doctrine that was to serve so well in World War II.

Back in England, a new mechanical contrivance termed the "tank" (the word was chosen for intelligence purposes to mask what was being developed) appeared to have some tactical promise; and as with the Gallipoli campaign, Churchill had an association with the tank program. It was during his tenure as First Lord of the Admiralty that the Naval Air Service undertook the development and procurement of armored vehicles for providing perimeter security at naval airfields located in Belgium.[31] It was felt by many that Haig lacked imagination in its use, however, and its potential was not fully exploited.

These must have been experiences that gave Churchill considerable cause to brood during those interwar years when he was absent from active government life. If they were not the basis for his concern, then they at least must have reinforced his professed distrust of "the bureacracy."

When Churchill entered the wartime Chamberlain government as First Lord of the Admiralty, he brought with him his

personal scientific adviser, F. A. Lindemann, an Oxford physi-
cist for whom he had developed a sense of personal esteem and
trust during the prewar years. One of Lindemann's first items of
business, undertaken at least with Churchill's blessing if not by
his instruction, was to create a small staff that came to be named
the S Branch ("S" for Statistics). The function and character of
this group is central to our story.[32]

The purpose of the S Branch was to treat questions addressing the entire range of issues related to resource allocation in
wartime with, as much of the section's subsequent work revealed, particular reference to interaction between military and
civilian "requirements." (The record shows that Lindemann,
the scientific adviser, spent about one-third of his time on technical and scientific problems, with the remainder devoted to
economic/resource allocation.)[33] His staff numbered about
twenty, including clerks and typists, and its heart comprised
about half a dozen economists, plus "one established civil servant (with economic training) to help keep the amateurs on the
rails."[34] The economists, who were young, were recruited by R.
F. Harrod, an Oxford economist colleague of Lindemann.

The motive for creating such a staff was twofold. The ostensi-
ble reason was to enable Churchill to discharge his function in
the cabinet on matters that the cabinet as a whole had to treat.
This required a knowledge of the reports of other ministries,
particularly of critical knowledge that might be useful in any
interministry struggle. The second reason, used by Lindemann
in recruiting his staff, was the hope that Churchill would become
prime minister. Knowledge of the entire range of government
resource-using programs could serve Churchill both in attaining
the number one position and in discharging its functions more
fully and quickly should it be attained.[35]

It was unclear, at least for all the concerned parties such as
Harrod, whether or not, as a prime minister, Churchill would
"wish to have around him a band of critics, who, precisely because they were not fully merged into the general machinery of
government, would give him an independent judgement."[36]
Whatever doubts there may have been on this point (and whatever understanding there may have been between Churchill and
Lindemann) were resolved when Churchill retained his "band of
critics" upon becoming prime minister.

The reason Churchill, as the leader or "sovereign," could
create (or retain) an independent staff to perform critical analy-

sis lies in the dynamics of bureaucratic behavior, and it is revealed by descriptions of some of the problems the Statistics Branch addressed. Each bureau or ministry is a fiefdom, which struggles with every other bureau for scarce resources, and in time of war each bureau tends to take a pessimistic view of the problems or threat it must cope with, so as to lay claim to resources.

Thus, the Air Ministry in 1940–41 estimated the German air order of battle to be about 50 per cent greater than it actually was. The major technique by which this alchemy was achieved was to compare the number of RAF aircraft in *operational* squadrons with the total number of aircraft that intelligence sources had detected on the German side. The latter's resources therefore included first-line aircraft used for operational training, aircraft under repair, and other leakages. The discrepancy suggested either that one side was very inefficient in terms of the number of battle-ready aircraft it could squeeze from a given production (less attrition) or that the other side was very efficient. The issue was apparently finally resolved by Lindemann when he personally interrogated some German prisoners on the relevant points. Upon his clarification of what the numbers meant, which was a bureaucratic defeat for the Air Ministry professionals, additional aircraft were transferred from the defense of England to a role in the North African campaign in Egypt in 1941.[37] In such fashion, the experts were to be confounded, exasperated, and infuriated many times. How could the Army, which with other ministries was strongly advocating increased austerity for the civilian sector, justify both its stocks of ten pair of trousers per man and an increased rate of production?[38] Did it make sense to procure antiaircraft munitions in quantities whose cost would exceed the damages an unopposed German air force could inflict?

In response to the Army's request for conscription of additional manpower, Churchill in a two-page memorandum to his Secretary of State for War summarized the essential bureaucratic principles of land-force organization that led to great discrepancies between "what used to be called bayonet or rifle strength . . . 'the staple of the Army,' " and total manpower; and closed by suggesting that at least a million be "combed out of the fluff and flummery behind the fighting troops, and be made to serve effective military purposes."[39] Numerous questions impacting on the use of shipping, encompassing everything from turnaround times at docks to alternative back haul routes and cargos, were raised.[40]

While he and his staff were infuriating most, if not all, of the ministries on resource allocation issues, Lindemann was also exasperating everyone else, including military officers and some of his scientific peers in operational analysis, on narrower operational and equipment issues. One of these concerned the development of the "sticky bomb," of which an Army major Jefferies was the proponent. This was a plastic charge contained in a case that would stick to a tank until detonation. It was hand thrown and was therefore a weapon of desperation; it was to be issued to the home guard and other interested citizens for their use in greeting the possible arrival of German Panzers in England. During the difficult period of its development, the sticky bomb was resisted in certain military quarters, a response that caused Churchill, in a memorandum to General Ismay, to close with "any chortling by officials, who have been slothful in pushing this bomb, over the fact that at present it has not succeeded will be viewed with great disfavour by me."[41]

In the same manner, Lindemann was to become involved in other technical-operational issues, such as the allocation of heavy-bomber resources to targets and the intelligence appraisals of and countermeasures against such mysterious German activities as the development and deployment of the V-1 and V-2 missiles. These endeavors, too, were charged with controversy, which has waned only slightly with the passage of time.

Churchill and Lindemann may deserve credit for being the "inventors" of cost-effectiveness analysis as an integral part of the government decision-making process. The problems addressed were clearly those of seeking to get the most efficient use of resources. They also ensured that operational research was institutionalized in the military services.

It is likely that the activity that spontaneously grew out of Watson-Watt's endeavor would have withered away because of the incentives the bureaus have for preserving secrecy and the natural inclination of operators to resist any question-raising tendency by outsiders. However, Churchill vigorously and extensively used the offerings of his personal staff to "shake up" the bureaucracy. The emphasis was on quantitative relationships, and often the arguments implicit in the question raising were based on a mastery of highly technical considerations. The bureaus and ministries, therefore, had a strong incentive to acquire their own expertise, if only for bureaucratic self-defense —much in the same manner our own military services followed the pattern established in the Office of the Secretary of Defense. To the degree that the RAF had the basic elements of operational capability, it therefore had a ready-made instrument for communicating (and in some instances, trying to counter) the Prime Minister's arguments. In the ongoing bureaucratic struggles, the other military services were thus well advised to acquire insurance in the form of their own operational analysis capability, much in the same fashion that the USAAF felt motivated to follow the RAF's lead.

7

POST-WORLD WAR II MILITARY DECISION-MAKING IN THE UNITED STATES

> It is beginning to look to me that the war after the war
> will be more bitter than the actual war.
>
> Admiral John S. McCain to Secretary Forrestal, Quoted in Albion
> and Connery, *Forrestal and the Navy*, p. 260.

The end of World War II confronted the United States with the need to maintain a large peacetime military organization. Whatever forces may have been underway to revert to a low-budget military establishment were shattered by the invasion of South Korea and the Soviet acquisition of nuclear weapons. In turn, the possession of nuclear weapons created two strong developments in this country. First, it provided an increased impetus for civilian specialists—both technicians and those who inherited the mantle of the World War II operational analysts—to exert an influence on decision making with respect to defense operations. Second, it may be that without the possibility of having a national arsenal that would include nuclear weapons, the best we could have hoped for was a very unstable relationship among the three military services; but the advent of such a possibility transformed even this less-than-desirable state of affairs to one characterized by very sharp interservice rivalry. The struggle centering around the creation of the Department of Defense was only slightly mitigated by its actual establishment: the form of its management became the object of repeated organizational soul-searching and occasional legislation affecting the relationships among interested parties, including the Secretary of Defense, Robert McNamara.

Secretary McNamara made a major effort to change the decision-making process "from within." A significant aspect of McNamara's system was the extent to which it drew upon the

124

updated tools of cost-effectiveness analysis and operational research—both of which were products of the community of defense intellectuals and of the RAND Corporation in particular.
In this chapter, we seek to draw the loose strands of the characteristics of this system together.

   Nuclear weapons greatly enhanced the status and prestige of
the scientific community in the views of both the policy makers
and the general public. Had there been any doubt about the
potential contributions of scientists and analysts in the improvement of military capabilities on the basis of their experience with
radar, electronics, operational analysis, and other endeavors—
or had there been any bureaucratic inclinations to forget the
accomplishments of these professionals—such doubts and inclinations were dissipated to a large extent by the unknown technical and operational prospects implied by the use of nuclear
weapons. During the first few years following the end of the war,
a variety of organizational contrivances were established in
efforts to continue that which NSRD and OSRD had started
under their wartime emergency and ad hoc commissions. With
the creation of the Atomic Energy Commission, and at the same
time that Congress was deliberating at length Vannevar Bush's
recommendation that the National Science Foundation be the
principal instrument for governmental support of basic military
research, the military services proceeded to strengthen their use
of scientific endeavor.
   The Navy set up its Office of Naval Research (ONR) in 1946
and placed it on a bureacratic par with its statutory bureaus.
ONR's principal research resource was to be the nation's universities, operating with grants monitored by this office. Also in
1946, the Navy transformed its wartime Operations Research
Group into the Operations Evaluation Group, which was to
serve the Chief of Naval Operations and the field commands and
which would have a mechanism linking it to the Office of Naval
Research. The Air Force created its Air Research and Development Command, established a Deputy Chief of Staff for Development, and continued to maintain an operational-analysis division within the Office of the Deputy Chief of Staff for
Operations. In 1946, Gen. H. H. Arnold got Douglas Aircraft
Corporation to manage the Air Force's Project RAND (Research
and Development); and two years later the project was spun off

and, with the aid of Ford Foundation funds, reorganized as the RAND Corporation.[1] And still in that same year, the Army created its Operations Research Office (ORO), administered by the Johns Hopkins University and headed by Dr. Ellis Johnson, whose career pattern in some ways resembled that of England's Blackett. Initially, Dr. Johnson had worked for the Navy on mine warfare problems, and then he shifted to the Air Force to focus both on the operational problems of the 20th Air Force and on its strategic operations against Japan.

This flurry of acquisitions and reorganizations was capped by the Joint Chiefs of Staff's acquisition of its Weapons Systems Evaluation Group (WSEG) for providing "rigorous unprejudiced analyses and evaluations."[2] And to provide WSEG with an adequate civilian scientific technical capability, the Institute for Defense Analyses (IDA) was set up in 1956. The latter's sphere of operations was subsequently expanded so as to serve the Office of the Secretary of Defense.

A complete, comparative history of these intellectual endeavors remains to be written. The differences among them are marked, and they greatly reflect the personalities within the organizations, geography, and attitudes of their sponsoring agencies. For example, The RAND Corporation benefited from the wisdom of General Arnold, who was responsible for locating the operation 3,000 miles from the Pentagon and establishing the procedure of funding the corporation by a single line item labeled "Project RAND." The geographical decision provided the insulation of distance from Air Force staff politics, and the budgetary device provided the RAND management with a maximum amount of intellectual freedom. And the company was further insulated during its formative years by an Air Force regulation that no officers could visit its facilities without approval of the Deputy Chief of Staff for Research and Development. But on the other hand, a vigorous (perhaps imprudent, in the eyes of some) practice of intellectual freedom on the part of Dr. Johnson impelled the Army to "disestablish" the Operations Research Office, sever its relationship with Johns Hopkins, and create a new organization called Research Analysis Corporation (RAC), which continued to serve the Army in somewhat less risky ways.

The product of this postwar defense research community began to emerge in the 1950's. The community had two arresting characteristics, of which the RAND Corporation is viewed as providing the leading examples, if not the models. First, there was a major focus on nuclear weapons and strategic war,[3] including continental defense. Second, the spirit, but not the methods, of World War II operational research was applied to strategic war in the process becoming contemporary cost-effectiveness analysis. Nuclear weapons as instruments for implementing the Air Force's doctrine of strategic war provided ample opportunity for civilian amateurs to penetrate an area in which the professional officer corps could normally claim a monopoly of operational expertise. The subject necessarily had an extremely high technical content, partly because of the power of the weapons themselves; that is, knowledge deduced from the physics of nuclear weapons appeared to govern the behavior of nuclear-weapon systems and their employment as military forces. Furthermore, there was no experience in the details of strategic nuclear war upon whose basis the professionals could seriously question rigorous analyses stemming from the inputs derived from physical equations. Hence, a Ph.D. degree in physics was often regarded to be as good a qualification for addressing the subject of strategic-weapon-system selection and force planning as was experience in commanding bombers and long-range artillery. The initial product of these intellectual endeavors was "systems analysis," which was "invented" by physical scientists and engineers. But in the RAND environment, largely due to the influence of Charles J. Hitch, who headed RAND's Economics Division, economists came to play an increasing role in the analytical process. The primary reason for the transformation that led to economists frequently becoming project leaders of studies was that the question of effectiveness criteria, or the specification of the utility of systems, became an increasingly critical part of analyzing problems. Clarification of criteria was one area where the intellectual discipline of economics appeared to provide insight. Moreover, the cost of nuclear-weapon systems and their targeting in terms of economic variables were subjects that the economists could not ignore. Perhaps the union between economists and physical scientists was inevitable. But, be that as it may, contemporary military cost-effectiveness analysis was the result.[4]

Such analysis has two important characteristics. First, the performance of a strategic-force structure is dominated by a few weapon systems; and the individual performance of these is in turn dominated by technical-performance characteristics, such

as warhead yield, accuracy, system reliability, and the hard-
nesses of one's own systems and the enemy targets. Second, the
effectiveness criteria are relatively simple, if not monistic. The
primary effectiveness criteria are those relating to deterrence of
a potential enemy. Specifically, they add up to assured destruction in terms of enemy casualties having a high economic content, such as population or manufacturing value added, and the
end product of such analysis consists of estimated exchange
ratios of damage or casualties or both.

The analysis becomes complicated when consideration is
given to damage limitation on one's own side, which extends to
counterforce options and active and passive defense. Further
complications arise if it is considered how different offensive
weapons, such as bombers, airborne missiles, and long-range
surface-to-surface missiles, can be employed jointly and in complementary ways against varied defensive and offensive systems
and tactics employed by the opponent. The subject of strategic-
force structure design (embracing all systems) thus lends itself
nicely to modeling and the associated computer simulations,
and the models thus developed can easily be employed for tactics, targeting, and contingency planning. Strategic war perhaps
must necessarily be treated in such a theoretical fashion, because there is no body of human experience to permit verification or refutation of the findings of the strategic war models. At
best, one can only apply scientific methodology to strategic systems by verifying and ensuring through operational testing that
such inputs as the CEP and reliability used in the modeling are
in fact the relevant ones. Beyond this, the justification for the
theoretical approach rests on the belief that the modeling ensures that decisions will be internally consistent.

The empirical methods of World War II operational research
are therefore impossible to apply to strategic war. The strategic
war analyses conducted in the 1950's addressed primarily (but
not solely) the efficacy of prospective systems, whereas the older
operational analysis primarily addressed how to use existing
systems. In the first case, dollars and prospective budgets are
the constraints, while in the second the constraints were physical. For these reasons the focus was increasingly (and properly)
on dollar cost, and thus change in analytical emphasis resulted
in what came to be termed cost-effectiveness analysis.[5]

One implicit distinction between operational research and
cost-effectiveness analysis is the idea that the latter would be

used to formulate and evaluate weapon concepts. Then a preferred concept could become the object of engineering development and, eventually, a procurement program. One of the striking points that became apparent during and immediately after World War II was that a rapidly unfolding technology in electronics, nuclear weapons, propulsion systems, and other fields provided a very wide range of options with respect to the precise performance characteristics that future systems might have. By analyzing the military missions in the context of foreign policy and perhaps other broad constraints, and by relating those missions to a wide range of technical options and their associated program costs, a basis for making rational choices would be provided. It was hoped that sound (that is, efficient) weapon-system concepts would result from good cost-effectiveness analysis. The method of analysis was thus in principle a way of guiding the development and engineering strategy. And the development and engineering program would eventually drive the weapon-system procurement programs.

Operational research, on the other hand, occurred within the constraints of given systems (for example, Spitfire fighters and radar systems), ships of certain types, and so forth, and the operators had options as to how such systems could be used in combat. Operational research was therefore a way of addressing the old-fashioned field of applied tactics. The operators and higher policy makers also had many choices as to the combinations of systems that could be used for a broadly defined mission, such as convoy protection.

There is no impenetrable barrier between operational research on one hand and cost-effectiveness analysis on the other. But there are two differences between the disciplines, one of them conceptual and the other historical, that figured importantly in subsequent developments.

The conceptual difference lies in the fact that in conducting cost-effectiveness analysis, the decision options are more numerous; and dollars and such aggregates as manpower are homogeneous. In an operational research problem, the analysts and operators may be asking what the best way is to deploy and use antiaircraft guns in an air-defense problem. In a cost-effectiveness approach to the same problem, one can ask why there need be guns at all. Perhaps surface-to-air missiles can do the job better. To fail to ask the guns-versus-missile question is to run the grave risk of committing the error ("crime" is the impression one gets upon reading some offerings on the subject) of "suboptimizing." A cousin, if not indeed an ill-bred brother, of the suboptimizing error is the error of focusing on the wrong criterion of effectiveness. For example, is it the function of an air-defense system to shoot down attacking aircraft, is it to reduce the damage they can inflict by their bombing raids, or is it something else?[6]

The historical factor bearing upon military cost-effectiveness analysis is the timing of its appearance relative to concern with strategic nuclear-weapon systems, a coincidence which meant that analysts could "think big" and imaginatively. Since the technical performance of the weapons and their delivery systems (or more specifically, the *theoretical physical* performance of the conceptual systems) governed the *estimated operational* performance of the conceptual weapon systems, the analysis perforce was highly theoretical. And it could not be any other way in the area of strategic weapon and force planning.

One consequence of this conjuncture of method and application of the analytical technique, however, was to cause a break between the older kind of operational research that emerged in World War II and what is now considered cost-effectiveness analysis. Unfortunately, this break has been responsible for a certain amount of dilettantism, and moreover, it has promoted a tendency to focus on improved technical performance and sophistication in equipment as the way to solve so many of the difficult problems associated with war. The injuction to avoid errors of suboptimizing and faulty choice of criteria is the soundest of advice. But it is often applied in such a way as to avoid addressing hard, current problems at all or to address them in a simple way.

Very little of the kind of operational research conducted during World War II is in fact done today. As a result, the empirical foundation of military intellectual endeavor has been eroded; and moreover, many critical questions are either ignored or poorly treated. For example, much talent and effort is devoted to "optimizing" the load-carrying capability of a fighter-bomber aircraft, but little talent has been devoted to providing infantrymen with good weapons or equipment. One reason for this may be that talent is usually allocated to the activity where the procurement dollars are likely to be. Other forces are operative. Intellectually, problems having a seemingly high technical content are more tractable by theoretical methods, while other problems having a high organizational and doctrinal content become tractable only after much grubby work.

It is not surprising, then, that a concern with strategic and nuclear-weapon systems tended during the 1950's to dominate the analytical effort sponsored by each of the military services. The Army, which (following the British pattern) would not normally hasten to employ critical civilians for addressing operational problems, was greatly concerned about the use of nuclear weapons in land warfare. This, along with an interest in and responsibility for continental defense, no doubt led to the Army's sponsorship of its Operations Research Office, a point that is confirmed by an examination of ORO publications during the 1950's. Then came the Korean War, presenting ORO with the opportunity to conduct the World War II kind of operational research. Consequently, it sent teams of analysts, some comprising both civilians and active military officers, to Korea, and these addressed a variety of subjects, such as the employment of indigenous manpower, the use of tactical air, the role of armor, and relative merits of different infantry weapons. Experience with the old-fashioned kind of war stimulated a branching out in the post-Korean period to treatment of a wide variety of subjects by novel methods, including experiments in the field to measure critical variables.

Similarly, organizations like RAND did not concentrate exclusively on nuclear war. A large effort was made in logistics, which included not only attempts to formulate models of such theoretically tractable subjects as inventory management and transportation systems, but also extended to working at air bases with supply sergeants and maintenance personnel to obtain data and understand how the logistic system worked. Thus, the RAND effort was neither purely theoretical nor entirely directed to strategic nuclear war. But strategic war was most amenable to purely theoretical and technical treatment to say nothing of being the most "glamorous" subject and the one in which the civilian amateurs were destined to make their mark. And finally, strategic war and nuclear weapons were also the precursors of a decade of anguish that centered around the organization and management of the Department of Defense.

World War II not only stimulated a strong sentiment that the nation's postwar defense establishment should be organized differently than it had been on the eve of that war; it actually presented the fact of a different organization. What could not be ignored was the quasi-autonomous status of the Army Air Force, a product of both the political advocacy of Air officers and General George Marshall's resolution of the problems posed by the advocacy, as well as of other problems that were inherent in the Army's organization. Marshall solved these many difficulties in a series of steps that culminated in his March 1942 reorganization of the Army.[7] But there were also other wartime organizational developments. The Joint Chiefs of Staff was established, for example, and so were numerous ad hoc committees designed to coordinate service, civilian, and joint Allied war endeavors.

Wartime military operations were placed under joint commanders whose authority purportedly cut across traditional service lines. These arrangements worked well enough to spare the Republic such fiascos as the Gallipoli operation and the Spanish-American War's Cuban campaigns. Yet enough manifestations of interservice rivalry and rigid adherence to service doctrine occurred during the war to cause thoughtful men to hope that the organizational apparatus for facilitating joint operations could be improved. Among such events were the Navy's successful effort to change an agreed-to demarcation of theater zones of primacy in order to place the Guadalcanal operation under Navy control instead of General MacArthur's,[8] and General Claire Chennault's successful efforts to gain a larger share of the supply capacity available for China in order to try to show (unsuccessfully, as it turned out) that air power could do what land forces and General Joe Stilwell seemed unable to do.[9] In sum, more than being a good thing, joint operations were a necessity. But joint operations require joint strategy; and joint strategy suggested to many persons—among them, President Truman—that budgeting and administration also be unified. And so support for the idea of a "unified" peacetime military establishment gained momentum.

The Army, and especially the Air Force, favored unification. Others, including the Navy and some members of Congress, did not. It is of some relevance to examine why, at that particular time, the principal military services held these different views.

The Navy faced a somber dilemma posed by a future in which the most likely adversary was a continental land power. While joint Navy, Army, and Air Force operations would still be possible in such a setting, any joint operation involving ships and troops would have to be under a single commander if it were not to run grave risks. Thus, a critical question arose: Was the operation to be commanded by an admiral or a general? Now, a strong case can usually be made for the operation being under a general's command, at least from the time the troops board the landing craft, since the primary objective from that point on is to get the troops ashore and support them once they are ashore. In such a situation, a soldier is likely to consider ships expendable if necessary to ensure the success of the land fighting. But such an expenditure of ships is of course painful to Navy officers, and their threshold of value for an outlay of these proportions can very well be higher than that of a general.[10]

The Navy avoided the dilemma that was inherent in these conflicting values on doctrines by a simple expedient: it expanded its Marine Corps into an army consisting of six specialized infantry divisions. It also had its own air force (Navy and Marine Corps). It thus became, in effect, a unified service unto itself, and in such fashion was able to attain primacy of command in the wartime Central Pacific theater. The Navy therefore had nothing to gain from any unification of the services that extended to budgeting. It had much, perhaps almost everything, to lose; and it probably *would* lose in a defense establishment that was dominated by either the Army or Air Force or by a coalition of these. For example, the Army, since it would reckon land war as being its primary business, would exert its influence in budgetary deliberations in such a way as to cut back the Marine organization to a corps that would provide small shipboard detachments, and perhaps a few regiments and embassy guards.[11] The Air Force would seek to restrict Navy air power.

Therefore, the Army and Air Force could advocate unification, both having a sincere concern that overall defense decision making be coherent and both exhibiting a degree of self-interest. The Army, for its part, had been and still is the most advanced in its thinking on matters of joint doctrine, if only because day-to-day experience in managing such diverse military resources as infantry, cavalry, and artillery requires solution of the inherent management problems. The Army might have had reservations about how it would work things out with the Air Force; but even kiloton atomic weapons did not render future land warfare unlikely, and in such a war a land-force commander would rate a primacy of command. Moreover, the Army saw the intriguing prospect (as did the German technicians who could possibly bring about a realization of that prospect) that missiles might replace aircraft at least in land battle, if not in strategic war; and hundreds of years of experience embedded in army culture by way of developing and implementing artillery doctrine prepared one's organization well for that eventuality. The Air Force, on the other hand, was dedicated to strategic war. Whatever cold water may have been cast upon the concept by findings of the World War II Strategic Bombing Survey was overlooked, because of the prospects afforded by nuclear weapons. The missile-airplane problem could be resolved later.

It can be seen, then, that the Navy was fighting for its institutional survival. And in this it was able to muster strong support for its cause—in Congress and in the Eastern community of influential, service-rendering civilian leaders. That James Forrestal was Secretary of the Navy was fortuitous for the Navy's cause: his prestige and skill was a key element that enabled the admirals to wage adroit political war in the Capitol. The result was the compromise National Security Act of 1947, which "established not a unified department or even a federation, but a confederation of three military departments presided over by a Secretary of Defense with carefully enumerated powers."[12]

The next ten years or so were hectic, in terms of both managing the Department of Defense and the substantive defense issues the country had to resolve, the latter centering around the interservice struggle for dollars. The instruments of struggle were weapon systems conceived to enhance the sponsors' claims to defense missions that civilian policy makers deemed worthy of funding. The Navy acquired nuclear weapons, which, to the Air Force's dismay, put the Navy in the strategic war business.[13] The resulting carrier/B-36 controversy crossed the Potomac, to be aired in Congress and, of course, the press. Temporarily, the main fighting was directed against the North Koreans and Chinese. But the Korean War, with its large number of infantry casualties, led to a new defense policy, which conceived strategic war and nuclear weapons as the major military instruments. The Air Force benefited most from the change, but the Navy and Army sought to gain a large share of the strategic missions, and in this the Navy developed the Polaris system and successfully gained its larger share. The Army was unsuccessful. Long-range artillery in the form of its Jupiter missile did not win for it a part of the strategic offensive role. It did retain and strengthen its air-defense function, as surface-to-air missiles, on paper at least, offered impressive prospects of disposing of high-flying aircraft. The Air Force countered, with limited success, with its Bomarc missile and a renewal of the doctrinal controversy on area-versus-point air defense. And yet, the Air Force was not consistent in its doctrine of area defense when it proposed to deploy the Navy-developed Talos missile to provide point defense for its air bases.

When the military services were not contesting roles and missions issues, they were, through the mechanism of the Joint Chiefs of Staff, presenting the Secretary of Defense with statements of requirements. But the funding of these was more than the President considered prudent, for fiscal policy (or political) reasons, and in any case it was more than Congress would appropriate. Civil/military relationships, as well as consciences and the officers' ability to execute adroit intellectual footwork, were often subject to severe strain. Civilian secretariats occasionally would resort to such techniques as classifying Army training divisions or combinations of garrison troops as "divisions," so as to support public statements that budget cuts involved no reduction of military capability. Some military men, after retiring from active service, commented on the "deception and duplicity" that characterized defense management.[14] Other ambiguous aspects of civilian guidance prevailed on such matters, particularly in the NATO context, as when and under what ground rules tactical nuclear weapons would be used.

The mechanism and manner in which the professional military were cast to play a role in the dollar-budgeting process warrants examination. Strictly speaking, the Joint Chiefs of Staff had no legal responsibility to recommend a dollar or total manpower budget.[15] Rather, their role in the budgetary process came about indirectly, when they were asked to provide a statement of the force level and its composition that would implement national-security objectives. The statement of national security objectives, in turn was the product of the National Security Council, although the document, being the product of several major bureaucracies, was a compromise and, hence ambiguous.[16] From this ambiguous guidance, the Joint Chiefs of Staff prepared their Joint Strategic Objectives Plan (JSOP), the end product of which was a tabulation of the military forces ("force tabs") that would implement the national security objectives, as the Chiefs in their corporate deliberation understood them from the vague guidance of the National Security Council.

A critical part of the Chiefs' endeavor was estimating or, more accurately, appraising the military capabilites of possible adversaries, which is at best a highly uncertain intellectual venture. Military men, as bureaucrats, will tend to overestimate the military capabilities of likely adversaries. The more powerful the opponents may be, the larger are the friendly forces (and budgets) called for. Equally, if not more, important is the point that military men are indoctrinated to be winners not losers; and, of course, possessing a preponderance of force enhances the probability of winning. For this and other reasons, the JSOP force level, when costed out, entailed a dollar and manpower budget that civilian policy makers deemed excessive.

A case can be made that the post-World War II practice of involving the uniformed military, in the persons of the Chiefs, in the dollar-budgeting process—however indirect their participation was by means of the JSOP exercise—was an abrogation of civilian responsibility, but not authority. Determination of the total defense budget and even its allocation as between major mission categories must be and is performed by civil authority. These functions, in fact, are performed by civilian policy makers, including Congress. Performance of these functions by this group is central to the concept of civilian control of the military, and necessarily must be exercised by civilians. To ask the military bureaucrat (or for that matter, any bureaucrat who pursues a special callling) how much of the nation's resources should be spent on his activity, will consistently evoke a recommendation that cannot or will not be met. It is somewhat like a private individual asking a car salesman how much one should spend on a new or used car. In the same way, the recommendations of the bureaucrat will consistently be rejected. It is not clear what good purpose is served by the dialogue. In military affairs, the dialogue provides at best only an indirect appraisal of the threat and how to meet it. However, information on the threat can be directly sought.

Similarly, the allocation of the total military budget between major military missions is a civilian responsibility. There are two reasons for this.

First, for the same reason that military leaders cannot offer useful advice on the total budget, they cannot offer it on its allocation as between major departments or missions. Either offerings will be the result of a compromise developed to maintain an amicable status quo between advocates of particular departments or mission functions, or the advocates for each activity will recommend amounts that in the aggregate will exceed the total that civilians want to spend. In either case, the advice will not be very helpful. The second reason the major mission allocation decisions must be made by civilian authority is that the composition of military capability as between major functions is an important determinant of foreign policy, and foreign-policy formulation is a civilian responsibility. For example, small land forces affect the kind of commitment we can make to NATO; assured second-strike strategic capability will affect Soviet attitudes differently than will a powerful but vulnerable first-strike capability.

Involvement of the uniformed military in these aggregative budgetary deliberations becomes a way by which civilian authorities may unconsciously try to evade the awesome responsibility that is inherent in determining the size and major composition of the military forces. Civilian authorities would like to be assured that the means available to meet the threat are "adequate." But the military realize that war is a highly uncertain enterprise, and can only offer the prospect that the means might be reasonably adequate if one's side has an apparently large margin of superiority. The margin, however, will almost invariably require more resources than the country is willing to spend.There is no solution for the dilemma because there is no certainty in these matters.About the only practical advice that can be drawn from the situation is that foreign policy must be conducted carefully, and that one should not go to war lightly. And conduct of business in both of these areas is a civilian responsibility that cannot be avoided.

During the postwar period, the Joint Chiefs were nevertheless called upon to support the administration's budget before Congress, because they were considered to be part of the administration's "team." This management philosophy was introduced by James Forrestal, the first Secretary of Defense, and was a derivative of his idea that the newly created office should play a coordinating rather than decision-making role. With the exception of Louis Johnson, who operated under a strong directive from President Truman to make sharp cutbacks in defense

spending durng 1949–50, subsequent Secretaries of Defense in
the Eisenhower administration adhered to the scenario established by Forrestal. Since that same period, from 1946 to about
1958, was characterized by major swings in the substance of
national security policy and in thoughts on how the changing
policy might be implemented by military means, enormous uncertainty surrounded the military roles and missions. There was
little historical precedent for American policy makers. The military decision-making apparatus, which evolved out of a hundred
or so years of accommodation to unstable relationships between
the executive and legislative branches of government and between military "line" and technical specialists, was ill-adapted to
the times. But it, too, was modified by a series of legislative
changes that focused on the Joint Chiefs of Staff and especially
on the Office of the Secretary of Defense.[17]

A consequence of this tumultuous period was a series of
investigations and reviews of the decision-making process.
These reviews ranged from that of the Hoover Commission
through that of the Rockefeller Committee to those of congressional subcommittees. The inquiries were accompanied by
recommendations from the Secretaries of Defense—including
Forrestal, who as Secretary of the Navy was instrumental in
bringing about the confederation created by the 1947 legislation—that the Office of the Secretary of Defense (and occasionally, the JCS) be strengthened. Legislation to achieve that end
was enacted in 1949 and 1958. In addition, a major internal
reorganization occurred in 1953 within statutory constraints.
The Office of the Secretary of Defense and the JCS grew in
numbers, and the statutory power of the civilian secretariat increased, while that of the military departments decreased.

One concern that emerged in the postwar evaluations of Defense Department management involved the lack of any mechanism by which materiel requirements, fiscal controls, and
policy objectives could be related. The term "programming,"
with particular reference to materiel requirements, came to describe what was felt to be a critical deficiency of the decision-
making process. The second Hoover Commission of 1955 emphasized the need[18] and recommended that a new post be
established in the Office of the Secretary of Defense, to relate
National Security Council endeavors to those of the Joint Chiefs
of Staff "and would supervise the requirements review process."[19] One of the criticisms of the Hoover Commission's

recommendatons was that the commission's concept involved an "incorrect" assumption that there was a way to relate coherently the factors of "national policy, strategy, industrial and fiscal considerations, and service functions."[20] However, armed with the power that accrued to the Office of the Secretary of Defense through the legislative steps culminating in the 1958 Act, this is precisely what Secretary McNamara undertook to do.

A most significant change was embodied in the 1958 Act. The Assistant Secretary of Defense for Research and Development was redesignated the Director of Defense Research and Engineering, "with 'precedence' before the Assistant Secretaries of Defense."[21] The statute also authorized him to "direct and control . . . research and engineering activities that the Secretary of Defense deems to require centralized management."[22] Early in 1958, the Secretary also set up in OSD the Advanced Research Projects Agency (ARPA), with line responsibilities for handling research projects assigned by the Secretary of Defense. This activity was also placed under the Director of Research and Engineering by the 1958 Act. Several reasons could be offered for strengthening civilian control over the Research and Development process. An immediate one, at the time, was the advent of Sputnik in 1957, which gave enhanced status to scientific accomplishment. Another factor was the desire to control what appeared to be a haphazard aggrandizement on the part of the services of each other's missions by means of new weapons developments. There were also memories of experiences in World War II, when, despite the position of OSRD, it seemed that too often civilian scientists were roughly treated or inhibited by military supervisors.

Finally, the division of labor between civilians and military during the prewar period, whereby civilians purportedly focused on procurement and the military upon strategy and tactics, was fragile at best, if not illusory. As illustrated by War Department experience in World War II, and to a lesser extent World War I, once a war began and the major priorities and strategy were determined, the military and its technical services could and did take over the details of logistic administration and procurement. Strategy and procurement have a higher programmatic content, once it is clear who the real enemies are. From that point, it takes a large degree of administrative and bureaucratic expertise to do the programming, and in these qualities the professional military normally have skills that few

civilians possess. The technical services, whatever may have
been their faults in protecting their arsenals and fiefdoms in
peacetime, were superb in moving the materiel during wartime.
Research and development, however, had none of this history.
Consequently, civilian executives may have regarded research
and development as a functional area where they could possibly
make their mark.[23]

It was Secretary McNamara's intention to play an active leadership role in the Defense Department. The negative implication of his approach was a rejection of the management philosophy characterizing the administrations of most of his
predecessors (including the Secretaries of War and the Navy),
whereby the civilian secretariat concentrated on housekeeping
and the mechanics of procurement, while the military dominated the decision-making processes affecting force structure
and weapon selection. Rather, under the new approach the elements of the force structure had to be related to policy and
strategy, and both had to be adjusted to fiscal constraints. In
addition to this, there was a prevalent feeling that the approach
characterized by the rough-and-tumble process of interservice
rivalry led haphazardly to an unbalanced force structure. Control was thus deemed necessary, and that control could be exercised through the financial and funding mechanism. Accordingly, the Comptroller's Office of the OSD became the focal
point for key elements of the decision-making process. It fell to
Charles Hitch, former head of the Economics Division of the
RAND Corporation, newly appointed Assistant Secretary, and
senior author of the book *The Economics of Defense in the Nuclear
Age* (published in 1960), to implement the suggestions contained in that book. Two changes were instituted: First, a formal
Planning-Programming-Budgeting System (PPBS) was established; and second, a staff—labeled a Systems Analysis Directorate—was acquired for doing cost-effectiveness analysis. A description of each of these endeavors is warranted.
     Financial and cost data presented in terms of such categories
as research and development, personnel, procurement, operation and maintenance, and installations were deficient in their
applicability to broader policy deliberations. The focus would
have to be on strategic bombers, Polaris submarines, land
forces, tactical Air Force squadrons, and naval-carrier strike

forces. It was desirable to make the force structure more visible and to relate its elements more systematically to cost. The traditional budgeting format of personnel, procurement, and so forth was also inadequate for providing decision makers with a clear idea of what a new system or program would cost. The acquisition of a new bomber force, for example, requires not only procuring airplanes, but also acquiring and training personnel, operating the airplanes over a number of years, and possibly constructing new base facilities. Accordingly, some 1,000 program elements, which were also deemed to correspond to "systems," were identified and costed for a period of five years (later, and currently, an eight-year period was specified). Thus, the Polaris submarine force, consisting of its boats, personnel, and operating and maintenance requirements, is viewed as a program element, and its estimated costs are projected. Program elements, in turn, are grouped into major programs. Currently, ten major programs are employed: (1) Strategic Forces (including offensive and defensive), (2) General Purpose Forces, (3) Intelligence and Communications, (4) Airlift and Sealift, (5) Guard and Reserve Forces, (6) Research and Development, (7) Central Supply and Maintenance, (8) Training, Medical, and Other General Personnel Activities, (9) Administration and Associated Activities, and (10) Support of Other Nations.[24]

The program's format was the skeleton of the new management system, but its heart was the use of cost-effectiveness analysis, combined with Secretary McNamara's management philosophy.[25] Initially, the Systems Analysis Directorate consisted of about a dozen or so civilian analysts, to be augmented later by five or six military officers. Its director was Alain Enthoven, a RAND protégé of Hitch. That the endeavors of the group were appreciated by McNamara is attested by its growth and the fact that, with Hitch's departure in the summer of 1965, the systems-analysis function was separated from the Comptroller's Office and established under an Assistant Secretary, who turned out to be Enthoven.

The function of the systems-analysis staff was to assist the Secretary, through cost-effectiveness analyses, in making decisions on force structure and weapon selection. Since the military services and the JCS, through the JSOP, almost invariably requested resources (dollars and manpower) exceeding the amounts that were fiscally or politically possible, their requests had to be cut back or rejected. Such cuts could be made by applying either of two principles, both amounting to rejections of the JCS requests. The differences between them, however, had important implications for internal management.

One principle was merely that of requiring the services to live within a given budget ceiling and of maintaining a budgetary status quo among the services. But such a gross approach to the budgeting process contained the seeds of future instability and surprise, particularly with regard to military programs. For example, the expectation that the strategic mission, say, would claim an increasing share of the defense budget served to create an incentive for each service to deploy its talent and resources in such a way as to lay claim to the future strategic mission. Conversely, the missions judged to be vulnerable to future budget cuts would suffer, inasmuch as resources and talent would be diverted from those missions to the ones judged to have a better future. Thus, the conventional, as contrasted to strategic, forces appeared to suffer far more than might have been intended. It was observed, for example, that the Navy during the 1950's gave short shrift to the programming of support for the Marine Corps through the development and procurement of amphibious ships and offshore fire-support capability; that the Air Force was not concerned with its mission of providing the Army with tactical air support, including airlift; and that even the Army was concentrating unduly upon nuclear and strategic systems, to the detriment of its infantry in getting the tools that an improved, although less esoteric, technology could provide.

Concern with this problem suggests an alternative management philosophy: that higher authority should examine the content of the service programs more closely, particulary their research and development activities. The power given to the Office of the Secretary of Defense under the 1958 legislation through the establishment of a Director of Research and Development reflected the concern with this problem. It was implicit in the legislation that the Secretary would be able to control the orce structure itself more precisely. That is, service-program proposals could be rejected or cut back piecemeal, or the Secretary could augment some programs or even propose programs of his own. The research and, especially, development processes tended explicitly, if not increasingly, to drive the decision-making process. The PPBS format was designed to make the elements of the force structure more visible to senior decision makers, and the Systems-Analysis staff existed to enable the

Secretary to make specific decisions for controlling the force structure by providing analyses relating system cost to system effectiveness. Rather then imposing gross dollar and manpower ceilings on the services it was possible to constrain or expand specific functional elements or weapon systems, and in this fashion to befable to relate military capability to both fiscal constraints and national-security objectives more coherently.

The precise mechanism by which this coherence was to be achieved was embodied in the concept of Presidential memoranda, which were instituted in 1961. These were based upon a Tentative Force Guidance promulgated by the Secretary and laid out the principle issues and alternatives in major program categories like strategic forces, airlift/sealift forces, research and development, and other critical areas. They contained suggested force levels and funding. Drafts of these memoranda were sent to the services and the JCS, who would submit their criticism and thereby surface major issues to be resolved by the Secretary. Most of the Draft Presidential Memoranda (DPM)were prepared in the Systems Analysis Office, although some were prepared in offices that had special cognizance over an activity. For example, the one on R&D was prepared in the Defense Department Research and Engineering office. By 1964, the DPM had become a major vehicle for implementing exchanges among the Secretary and the services, including the JCS, and had settled down to playing a key role in the decision-making process.[26] In the aggregate, the DPMs supplanted the Joint Chiefs' JSOP. Thus by consistently recommending force levels and, hence, implicitly recommending budgets that exceeded the levels deemed financially feasible by the senior policy makers in the executive branch, the military services (through the JCS mechanism) effectively priced themselves out of a critical phase of the decision-making process. It should be emphasized, however, that McNamara did not institute this relationship with the military. Rather, it began in the 1950's. By means of the programming format, however cuts were made by the Secretary in terms of identifiable military outputs, as measured by program elements. Previously, the cuts were either made in terms of inputs like dollars or manpower, or both; or, in some cases, military departments were simply told, by informal means, not to request funds for particular programs. If nothing, the McNamara system at least made explicit a dialogue that had gone on for some time.

Cost-effectiveness analysis was the calculus that provided a rationale through which competing claims on behalf of diverse elements of the overall force structure were to be reconciled. In principle, cost-effectiveness analysis might be viewed as doing for the complex process of national security decision making what double-entry bookkeeping did for the less complex problem of managing business organizations some five or six hundred years ago. However, the application of these tools got underway promptly, before the above-described DPM process was fully implemented.

Thus, the decision to cancel the Skybolt program drew its rationale from a cost-effectiveness study that suggested that a combination of alternative systems—for example, Minuteman and air-breathing, airplane-launched Hounddog missiles— could do the same job for less cost. The proposed B-70 bomber procurement was denied by the Secretary on the ground that missiles were less costly for killing targets, particularly when account was taken of aircraft vulnerability to both missile attacks on their bases and to missile air defense.[27]

This approach to decision making was regarded with apprehension by the military services. However, their initial anxieties were partially assuaged by increased spending, particularly in the critical research and development and procurement categories. Estimated fiscal-year 1962 expenditures for these items, under the last budget submitted by President Eisenhower, were $18.3 billion. Actual 1962 expenditures were $21.2 billion. For fiscal year 1963, which reflects almost the full 1961 calendar-year deliberations of the new administration, the total R&D and procurement expenditures were $21.6 billion, an increase of 18 per cent over what would have been the 1962 Eisenhower budget. The comparable increase in total defense spending—for example, between the fiscal-year 1962 estimated expenditures under the Eisenhower budget and the actual fiscal-year 1963 expenditures—was about 10 per cent.

The activist approach of the Systems-Analysis staff (and the Secretary) especially extended to programs that were to benefit from the increases in expenditure. The airlift-sealift program witnessed the injection of forward-floating depots of Victory ships containing stocks of Army equipment, a concept that was to spawn the Fast Deployment Logistics (FDL) ship. Further analysis of airlift rapid deployment played a role in stimulating the design efforts that led to the C–5A.[28] Although the Air Force was encouraged to acquire more tactical aircraft, its preferred model, the F–105, which was optimized for the delivery of tactical nuclear weapons, was vetoed by OSD.[29] Rather, the Navy's F–4 was acquired by the Air Force, but only with mixed feelings on the part of the Air staff. The F–4 was designed for fleet air defense and relied on the Sidewinder heat-seeking missile. Some Air Force personnel had a strong preference for guns as an air-to-air combat weapon. Moreover, some Air Force proponents pointed out that the F–4 lacked air-to-ground electronics to facilitate delivery of ordnance; however, this point could not carry much weight since such electronics gear as has been developed has yet to demonstrate much utility in tactical air missions. But since an airplane like the F–4 evokes enthusiasm among pilots, the mixed feelings rapidly faded away. It was a different matter, however, to induce the Air Force to acquire conventional ordnance. There apparently still prevailed an institutional bias that disposed the Air Force to favor nuclear weapons, which was tantamount to making foreign policy by procurement decisions. The Secretary therefore caused a series of studies to be undertaken, in which many hundreds of man-hours were spent working through air-battle scenarios in an effort to get better estimates of ordnance requirements.

Army programs also received Systems Analysis Office scrutiny. The Army was invited to look afresh at its aviation requirements,[30] with the result that a faction of Army officers who had been waging a campaign to increase the Army's aircraft resources had the opportunity to give full expression to their views. One of the favorable consequences of this development was that the Air Force took a renewed and more lively interest in its mission responsibilities of providing close air support and tactical airlift for the Army. Forward air controllers who had been scarce during the 1950's began to appear at Army divisions and even battalions; C–130's which were designed to operate on unsophisticated landing fields but seldom did in order to avoid the risk of occasionally busting a landing gear, began to make occasional landings on dirt strips.

Although the coffers were opened to the Army, some of its programs experienced deaths ranging in character from sudden to agonizing. Among those in the former category was the Mauler air-defense missile, while the M–14 rifle was one of the latter. The first, if not fatal, blow was "a report prepared by the Comptroller of the Department of Defense in September 1962 (that) concluded that the M–14 was almost completely inferior to a rifle known as the AR–15, now designated the M–16. "[31] The Army was also encouraged to examine its artillery requirements comprehensively, and a series of studies and computer simulations that are still being debated was set in motion. As a result of the initial study, however, decisions were made to convert all armored and mechanized division artillery to 155–mm. self-propelled howitzers.

These and other dialogues between the Office of the Secretary of Defense and the military services became increasingly frequent, with the procedures relating to the systems-analysis endeavor initially being rather rough-and-tumble. During the period that the Systems Analysis Directorate was part of the Comptroller's Office, broad areas were assigned to individual analysts or, at most, a team of two or three individuals, with only general guidance being suggested by Hitch and Enthoven. Beyond that, the analysts followed their own instincts. Initially, specific and critical areas were singled out for analysis, but with the passage of time, the military services were requested to justify more and more of their proposals by means of cost-effectiveness analysis techniques. In 1965, the directorate was separated from the Comptroller's Office and elevated to the status of an office headed by an Assistant Secretary. The staff greatly increased in size, and became more "structured," bureaucratically speaking. The demand that the military services do cost-effectiveness studies, and that they employ even more sophisticated analytical techniques, increased correspondingly. The services, of course, responded.

Some of these service studies were conducted in the headquarters' staffs or the JCS. Others, increasingly as time went on, were farmed out to the various commands or were done by ad hoc boards or study groups, which in turn engaged the services of contract research firms. Subordinate commands, which did not have them, acquired scientific advisers and operational research staffs, and extensive contract study work was stimulated. The military services, for their part, also greatly increased the number of officers who were to receive formal training in operational research and cost-effectiveness analysis, through a variety of newly created courses and through programs offered in service schools, and also by sending officers to universities to get formal degrees in operational research and related disciplines. Although the services had incentives for acquiring such expertise, if only in bureaucratic self-defense, they were strongly encouraged and supported in this endeavor by OSD. Enthoven, in particular, gave generously of his time and energy to advance the objective of strengthening the analytical capability of the military services.[32]

One reason for the increased demand for cost-effectiveness studies was that, after the services absorbed the initial increment of defense spending that accompanied the advent of the new administration, they began to advocate new procurement programs that were products of previous research and development programs. Since most of these systems embodied elements of newer and advancing technology, they were more costly. More sophisticated weapon concepts, some of which had been stimulated by the immediate post-Sputnik excitement, were nearing the end of their development gestation period. There had also been an increase of research and development funding with the advent of the McNamara period, which strengthened a trend started much earlier and this, too, was bound to produce its progeny.

A critical feature of the new Defense Department management system was that the method of cost-effectiveness analysis was not rigorously applied (in most cases, not applied at all) to proposed new weapon concepts. For example, the TFX concept (presently the F-111), formulated in 1960, was never subjected to a rigorous systems analysis, and it was accepted uncritically by the new administration with the provision that it be a joint Air Force–Navy program.[33] During the early years of the McNamara system, a practice emerged in which the Director of Research and Engineering and the Comptroller kept out of each other's territory: the Directorate of Systems Analysis concetrated on procurement and force-structure issues, while the Director of Research and Engineering concentrated on future programs. This division of labor was rationalized on the ground that current procurement and force-structure funding involved the largest resource outlays and, hence, provided an ample vent for the efforts of a rather small systems-analysis staff.

But as the systems-analysis endeavor grew, limited efforts were made to extend critical analysis to conceptual programs. A formal mechanism for achieving this end was the Development Concept Paper (DCP), which was to be prepared in the Office of the Director of Research and Engineering, but which was to be jointly endorsed by the Director and other Assistant Secretaries, including the Assistant Secretary for Systems Analysis, prior to submittal for the Secretary's approval. This system scarcely got off the ground, however, inasmuch as the older division of labor continued to dominate the way in which business was done. At stake in the DCP mechanism and its entailment of dual concurrence or perhaps split positions between a Director of Research and Engineering and an Assistant Secretary for Systems Analysis was a potential power struggle between two staff sections (one of which enjoyed statutory primacy) that could only be resolved by the Secretary himself. This power struggle could easily acquire some of the manifestations of the older struggle (which existed at the service level) between users and technical services (or bureaus), but with an important difference. The struggles of past eras occurred in settings of parsimonious budgets, but their current counterparts could take place under conditions of more lavish spending.

The Development Concept Paper as a control of the engineering-development program did not have full opportunity to become operational. Rather, the 1961–62 substance of the agreement to divide the territory between the two staff sections remained effective, its enforcement meaning, for example, that although a Skybolt program might be cancelled, several other similar systems could nevertheless be conceived and even enter into a development phase.

The substance of the agreement would hold if only because in the bureaucracy the staff section that has the charter to prepare a paper has the opportunity to write the final paper that goes to the decision maker. That the conception phase of the weapon-system selection process was not subjected to rigorous cost-effectiveness analysis (or systems analysis) is paradoxical. Recall that what differentiated systems analysis (as it was originally fostered at the RAND Corporation and elsewhere) from the older operational research was the point that dollar constraints, rather than numerous specific materiel and personnel constraints, permitted taking a broader view of the world, simultaneously permitting more rational choices in a setting where an unfolding and advancing technology provided many more options. The consequences of this omission and the problems that must be surmounted if those consequences are to be coped with will be the subject of our remaining chapters. It should be fairly clear that the problems are too complex to be resolved simply by altering the relative power of staff sections within the Office of the Secretary of Defense, or by the mere writing of position papers in that office.

8

SYMPTOMS OF THE TECHNOLOGICAL SYNDROME

> It was amazing how many trained people made suggestions which were quite all right from an engineering point of view, but just didn't make sense from any other—you could do it, but why should you? We called them the tame dog ideas. The wild-cats were things that needed perpetual motion, or a barrel two hundred yards long.
>
> Nigel Balchin, *The Small Back Room,* p. 84.

By the late 1950's, an approach to developing and procuring weapons had evolved that possessed two striking characteristics and was primarily encountered with aircraft and missile systems. First, an emphasis was placed on a "weapon system," which was composed of a complex of interrelated subsystems like an airframe, engine, electronics fire control and navigation equipment, and other elements, to include specially designed ground-support equipment and facilities. The concept of a weapon system entailed an engineering development philosophy that implied developing each of the major subsystems in a way that conformed to an overall set of design objectives that described the weapon system itself.

A second characteristic of this process was to adopt a strategy of "concurrent" development and procurement, and an associated high degree of programming the dates on which a new system would be developed, procured, and phased into the field. One of the motives for this element of the development and procurement philosophy was to reduce the time between conception of a weapon and its availability for possible "use," including deterrence.

It is possible that many decision makers pondered this question: What if during World War II the Germans had developed nuclear weapons before we did? World War II also witnessed

150

many less spectacular efforts to achieve technical developments, and higher-performance characteristics of existing weapons, on a "crash" basis in order to overcome some superior feature of an enemy's system. For example, during the early phase of the Pacific war, the Japanese Zero fighter outclassed the U.S. Navy's F4F Wildcat fighter in speed and maneuverability. This was not fatal, however, because Navy fliers adopted tactics and disciplined adherence to those tactics that helped reduce the combat effectiveness of the Zero's strong points. But the situation was nevertheless uncomfortable, and a higher-performance fighter was desirable. Hence, within three months of its conception, the first F6F Hellcat flew. This airplane was more than a match for the Zero, and came to be the mainstay of the carrier forces. The history of World War II technical development and procurement is replete with numerous tales of measures and countermeasures, and an associated race to counter by technical means either new tactics or new weapons developed by an enemy. American, British, and German technologists made a mark in this contest, and generated for their fraternity a measure of prestige that has scarcely abated with time.

But it also became apparent by the end of the 1950's that the postwar weapon-system approach to development and procurement contained flaws. The Air Force, if only because it was the the biggest spender, was the major proponent of the weapon-system philosophy, including the emphasis on concurrency of development and production. The process and some of its shortcomings became the object of a major study effort at the RAND Corporation.[1]

One striking feature of the development philosophy was the consistent manner by which cost, performance, and time predictions have failed to materialize. For a total of 22 programs, mostly Air Force, consummated in the postwar period prior to 1960, actual costs exceeded predictions by an average of from 4.1 to 6.5 times (the higher, 6.5, factor follows if one missile program that exceeded cost expectations by 57 times is included);[2] predictions on time availability were off on the average by a factor of 1.5;[3] that is, it took about 50 per cent longer to develop the average system than was the program objective; and most systems failed to meet performance objectives.[4] Performance shortcomings were not as prounounced as cost or time-availability shortcomings, primarily because the performance specifications are taken very seriously, and program slippage and especially cost overruns are incurred to attain performance objectives. This behavior is simply a recognition of the fact that if enough resources are spent, a technical objective can often be attained.

Inaccurate estimates can be explained by the fact that technical development is a highly uncertain business, and little is understood about how to cope with uncertainty. But the optimistic bias of estimates is not hard to explain. The incentive to make optimistic estimates is strong, and it has a bureaucratic—budgetary—political foundation. During the postwar period, new weapon concepts were devices by which military services could aggrandize each other's missions. They were and are still means to the end obtaining dollars through the budgetary process. For contractors, optimism is both natural and self-serving. Technologists also wish to do their thing, and it cannot be done unless there is funding.

Little has changed since the 1950's by way of the basic behavior that characterizes the weapons-acquisition process. The behavior, however, has become more widespread. The Air Force "model" also seems to characterize the procurement practices of the other services. Perhaps this was in the cards as the Army and Navy came to enjoy more funding during the McNamara period. It is also possible that with the directive control on the part of OSD of research and development provided by the 1958 legislation, and with that directorate dominated by people drawn from the aerospace industry, or with a background in aircraft and missiles, standardization would come about. But whatever the reasons, the present approach still has the shortcomings that were well established by the late 1950's. It also has a shortcoming that has not been as well publicized as the more obvious ones of interrelated cost overruns, slippages in time availability, and failure to meet technical-performance objectives. That shortcoming is the possible limited usefulness of the proposed systems *even if they met their technical-performance characteristics.* To develop this point in connection with the overall behavior of the weapons-procurement process is the purpose of this and the following chapter.

The problem begins with the evaluation process that leads to formulating the concept of a weapon or system. Formulation of a weapon concept is necessary in specifying the characteristics that a new weapon should have. Specifications may be explicit or implicit, and they can be treated in a testing process. For example, Gen. Sir Archibald Wavell recounts the practice of weapon testing and evaluation during a bygone era: When a new mountain gun was presented to the Artillery Committee, it was first taken to the top of a high tower and dropped. If it survived that test, further evaluation was conducted.[5] The story illustrates that users of mountain guns had certain views, as well as a hierarchial ranking of those views, regarding the performance characteristics of mountain guns. Similarly, for hundreds of years soldiers have been dragging new small arms through dirt, soaking them in mud, weighing them on scales, and timing how quickly a Redcoat or Pomeranian Grenadier could fire and reload. The British Admiralty developed a strict list of specifications for ship timber, which, although biased in favor of oak grown in Southeast England, were only occasionally bent in response to the pervasive corruption that ruled the day.

Where and when the requirements concept originated is unknown. But its basis derives from the point that those who must use a thing will have ideas about what contributes to or detracts from its utility. The military consumer is called the "user." The instrument by which a dialogue occurs between the military user and producer may be termed generically the list of military "requirements,"[6] consisting of a list of performance characteristics and physical attributes for a new system that the users think the weapon should possess. Physical attributes take such forms as weight or dimensional constraints; for example, a rifle's weight should not exceeed 9 pounds, or the length an airplane to be operated off a carrier should not exceed 50 feet, or the width of a tank should not exceed 11 feet. These kinds of physical constraints are often well founded: the limitation on tank width, for example, may be dictated by the load width that rail systems can handle, combined with the strategic requirement for moving tanks by the railroad system.

Performance characteristics are stated in engineering terms. Speed, range-payload, cyclic rate of fire, service ceiling for aircraft, takeoff or landing distance, range and accuracy of a gun, degree of resolution for radar, penetration of some specified material at a specified range for an antitank device, and mean time to failure for a guidance system or an engine are a few of the attributes that illustrate the concept. Performance characteristics are critically constrained by the specified physical attributes, and it is at this point that the laws of nature or physics exert their force. The military services have an extensive engineering and laboratory-testing system for conducting such measurements, thereby determining whether or not the system's developer does in fact meet the original specifications. Military characteristics for a future weapon system are therefore the primary focus of different groups in the military community: the user and the technician.

The formulation of military requirements can be a highly political process, in which the diverse interests of various users are reconciled. For example, all soldiers and marines are equipped with small arms. Within the army, the infantry community exerts primacy with regard to the user interest in small arms. But within the infantry community there are subcommunities: foot, mechanized, airborne, marine, special forces, and in some countries, mountain, all of whom can have divergent views on small arms. Broader intrabranch and interservice politics can come to a focus in weapon concepts. For example, artillerymen will watch any effort to specify that the range of infantry mortars be increased, or they may attempt to take control of mortars that have increased ranges. (The Air Force does not have a monopoly on the central management argument.) The Air Force keeps a careful eye on the Army's specification of the characteristics for a new helicopter gunship. Intraservice and interservice doctrinal and organizational issues are often inseparably bound to the specification of performance characteristics for new equipment and weapons. Problems that are ignored at the time performance characteristics are specified may erupt later in a seemingly purely organizational and tactical context; or seemingly technical issues may be overwhelmingly doctrinal or tactical. The process of formulating military requirements is therefore seldom devoid of political considerations.

Nor need the specification process necessarily be devoid of crass external politics. For example, a private firm might develop a new gun that promises to meet a broadly stated military need. The weapon may have a barrel length of 36 inches. But if an "in-house" arsenal is in need of work to stay in business, it may turn out that the specific military characteristics stipulate a barrel length not exceeding 34 inches. In this way the final selection can be kept open for a period during which the arsenal's designers or more favored contractors scramble to formulate their alternative weapon concept.

The performance and physical characteristics of systems are not measures of the operational effectiveness—or measures of utility in combat—of a weapon, either singly or in combination. They are no more measures of system-combat effectiveness than are brake horsepower, wheelbase, and similar characteristics measures of the utility a passenger car will provide for a consumer. Rather, there is only a presumption that some combination of improved performance characteristics will enhance effectiveness. But just how it does so, in what way relative to tactical and organizational factors that also influence combat effectiveness, and by how much relative to the cost of the new system— these are questions to which answers are seldom clear or readily forthcoming.

It is also generally true that an enhanced attribute of an item entails a technical tradeoff cost, in terms of another performance atribute—most car owners are familir with this point, and so are the military consumers of military weapons. However, basic research, or the transfer of technological improvement in one area to another area, offers the prospect that the enhanced performance of one characteristic may not incur the cost of less performance in some other respect. For example, higher speed normally involves a higher-powered and heavier engine. The greater engine weight reduces the payload to gross weight ratio —thereby either the vehicle's range or payload—and the military user faces the difficult problem of having to trade off speed for range-payload. But if there is any prospect of increasing engine power without increasing weight, say, because of a new principle of fuel combustion or a new lightweight metal, then the user is spared that difficult decision. Indeed, in the hope that he will get more effectiveness if the technical improvement is attained, he does not have to think hard about effectiveness.

The equipment designers and the engineers and scientists whose expertise enables them to conceive and develop new fuel systems or metals, for their part, are optimists and advocates by nature. They are not normally concerned with military effectiveness per se, because that is the province of the military operators. Should a technologist raise probing questions about effectiveness, it is often of no avail. The operators generally prefer that the technicians should not raise questions about operational use, especially if the latter are civilians, because these questions are pregnant with doctrinal and internal political considerations. The concept of the military requirement for a new system therefore becomes a device whereby members of diverse cultures can have an ongoing relationship with each other, while yet ensuring that the relationship has an arm's-length quality. The designers and developers are happy to concentrate on their efforts, not only because it is profitable for the firms that employ them, but also—and this is more important—it is inherent in the nature of their calling to try to achieve the technological improvement. The operators can often avoid addressing hard doctrinal questions; they can adhere to the faith whose tenet is that higher technical performance provides better weapons. Although arm's-length relationships among different groups with possible conflicting interests are sound, the present approach to formulating military characteristics achieves that result at the price of too much irrelevance, self-deception, and high costs for the taxpayer.

For these reasons, contemporary lists of military requirements for new systems resemble the maximum performance that users would like to have, constrained only by what engineers and scientists convey to be theoretically infeasible. Our military services have not been concerned with military effectiveness despite possible protests to the contrary, because they indulge in the intellectual alchemy in which higher technical performance itself constitutes improved effectiveness. They conduct little or no operational testing; they are not organizationally set up to do so. And even if they were, the interservice or interbranch rivalries and the politics of the budgetary process would operate to degrade the testing endeavor.

In a previous chapter, it was shown how relationships between the military and the advocates of technical improvement were often dominated by footdragging and conservation on the part of the military. Even the newly emerging military technical services, as illustrated by the nineteenth-century U.S. Army Ordnance Bureau with regard to small arms, could be highly negative to technical improvements, especially if the new offerings had not been invented or developed in the government arsenals. The post-World War II period in the United States, however, saw a sharp reversal in this older pattern. No longer can the military be accused of being laggard in its willingness to embrace new technicalities; indeed, it eagerly seeks them out and spends large amounts to promote them. As part of the process, the uniformed military technician (as compared to the combat-oriented user) has become more powerful within the military hierarchy; and simultaneously the officer corps as a whole has become more caught up in "technicism," with the older distinction between military user and military producer becoming less clear and even downright fuzzy in many military functional areas.

Although the older form of conservatism had many bad consequences, it had one positive feature: there was a heavy "burden of proof," so to speak, upon the adoption of weapons embodying new technical improvements. That it was often overdone was a consequence of a system of "checks and balances" peculiar to the then prevailing internal sociology of military organizations. The external political process may have contributed to this internal condition insofar as it reflected a general reluctance on the part of citizens and their political representtives regarding government spending in any form. Whatever the merits of these previous constraints, there was nevertheless a check on the advocacy of new weapons. In the post-World War II American setting, however, this check was shattered. Nothing has been developed to perform, at least partially and hopefully in constructive ways, what the older conservatism did, although often in wasteful and crude ways. There has thus emerged what we label a "technological syndrome" as it applied to weapon development and procurement. The recently invented tools of operational research and cost-effectiveness analysis not only failed to cope with it but also have contributed to it. We will try to illustrate these points by a case study that focuses upon the Army's combat vehicle and antitank programs.

Ground-combat vehicles and ways of defeating them loom importantly in the composition of European land forces. Soviet-bloc armies exhibit a high density of tanks and other combat vehicles; and conversely, coping with tanks is a critical part of the NATO defense posture, which bears importantly on the United States commitment to NATO. This problem acquires even greater significance, inasmuch as NATO seeks to rely on conventional (nonnuclear) forces to avoid early use of nuclear weapons in the defense of Western Europe. Since offensive armored operations can stake out large tracts of real estate in a matter of days, arguments to the effect that NATO forces in the aggregate may have as many troops under arms as does the Soviet European bloc may not mean much. If it is also recog-

nized that a "full option" policy on NATO's part might lead the
opponent to think that he can play the same game, the tactical-
technical problem of stopping offensive armor in Western
Europe acquires critical importance for fundamental national-
security policy making.[7]

The materiel programs involved are extensive and costly.
They range from "main battle tanks," which are multipurpose
vehicles possessing heavy armor and powerful main guns (and
their associated bridging and retrieval vehicles) through self-
propelled artillery and specialized-assault vehicles to armored
personnel carriers and scout vehicles. To counter these vehicles,
there is a large variety of infantry antitank weapons such as
recoilless rifles and wire-guided missiles—descendants of the
World War II bazooka and *Panzerfaust.* Finally, extensive consideration has been given to airborne tank-defeating systems, including helicopters. The Army's proposed Cheyenne helicopter
derived much of its rationale from its potential as a tank killer.
The Air Force, by means of its Maverick missile and a new
proposed close-support aircraft, also hopes to acquire an important part in this mission. Currently, the U.S. Army is seeking to
replace its existing generation of equipment with entirely new
and more sophisticated systems that would draw extensively
upon the technology pioneered in the aerospace sector. The
complete transformation, by way of equipping NATO-oriented
forces with all the contemplated vehicle and antitank systems,
could increase land-force costs (both investment and annual
operating) substantially.[8]

As in most specialized military fields, the interaction among
technological change, organization, and tactics in the field of
armored warfare has been complex and controversial. A key
issue is that of specialized versus "all purpose" vehicles; and if
all-purpose vehicles, precisely what should be their performance and design characteristics? Prior to, and particularly during, World War II, specialized vehicles tended to dominate.[9]
The main armament, initially relatively light or low-powered,
was sufficiently effective against targets like trucks and enemy
infantry. Great emphasis was placed on agility and, later, on
protection against enemy antitank capability. The tanks that
sustained the early German success in World War II, including
the initial phases of the Russian campaign, were based on equipment of this variety. As opposing tanks acquired heavier armor,
there were two ways of countering the development, one of
which was to develop special antitank, or "tank destroyer,"

weapons. The Germans pioneered this approach, effectively adapting their 88-mm. antiaircraft gun to the needs. They also developed special vehicles like the Ferdinand, which was a turretless, armored tank destroyer; and the United States Army followed the same approach with its "tank-destroyer" concept, which included special battalion units, special equipment, and school for training the units.

World War II also saw the beginnings of the general-purpose or main-battle tank, and the principal catalyst for this was probably the Soviet T-34, of which the Germans did not become aware until they invaded Russia.[10] The Germans apparently had received no knowledge through their technical intelligence channels that the Soviets had even developed, let alone fielded (albeit in limited numbers) a 32-ton tank mounting a 76-mm. gun. The mainstay of the German armored forces was the MK-IV Panzer, which was lightly armored and armed with a low-powered 75-mm. gun. Promptly, the Germans wrote the "military requirements" that led to the Panther and Tiger tanks, and the Soviets responded with their T-34/85 tank, which had an 85-mm. gun. Finally, toward the end of the war, the Soviet Union fielded the Stalin tank with its 122-mm. gun. This trend continued after the war.

The United States Army's tank-destroyer community was quietly liquidated during the 1950's for some obscure reason that is perhaps embedded in the internal army decision-making process. It is likely that the tank-destroyer concept had powerful opponents and no devout advocates within the Army. After all, they did exert a claim against scarce resources and they were competitive with the armored community, whose members, by inclination, selection, and combat doctrine, are aggressive (a characteristic that undoubtedly surfaces during budgetary deliberations). On the other hand, the tank-destroyer segment of the Army was part of the larger infantry community; and although infantrymen will fight for what they own (usually in more devious ways than do other military subcultures), they apparently did not feel strongly enough about this question to fight very hard. The infantry's attitude was perhaps characterized in World War II by a certain amount of muttering by infantrymen to the effect that the tank destroyers did not fight very well, although the criterion for forming such an opinion was probably that the tank destroyers did not take as many casualties as did riflemen and machinegunners. Among the military subcultures, it is of course characteristic to have contempt for groups experiencing a lower rate of casualties than one's own. The tank-destroyer segment of the Army no doubt labored under this handicap. That they generally gave a good account of themselves as tank killers in World War II seems to have been overlooked in postwar decision making. For these and perhaps other reasons the doctrine that "the best tank destroyer is a tank" came to prevail.[11]

During the 1950's, forces were operating in the technical and systems-analysis communities to cause the subject of tank and antitank warfare to be placed in a different perspective and to set the stage for an attempted basic change in tank weaponry. Guided missiles appeared to afford a capability to hit vehicle targets at long ranges. By that time, high-velocity tank guns had been fully developed and their tactical potential exploited. At ranges up to 1,500 yards, the high-velocity gun possesses a combination of accuracy and rapid rate of fire which makes it the best antitank weapon.[12] The guided missile, however, "at ranges of 2500 meters or more . . . has advantages in the chance of a first round hit which the gun is never likely to match."[13] There was accordingly a push to develop long-range, antitank guided missiles. This line of thinking was a product of the same decade (the 1950's) that produced the widely held belief that the guided missile would relegate the airplane to extinction.

Interest in the guided missile also raised the question regarding a vehicle from which it would be launched, and so the project was coupled with a new tank program. Now one of the features of a missile is that its launching produces little recoil, which obviates the need for a vehicle that is heavy enough to absorb the recoil of a high-powered gun. This prospect of a light vehicle apparently offered other advantages, among them being that it could be amphibious, air-transportable, and even air-droppable. Such qualities combined in a single vehicle might simultaneously serve more than one of the Army's subcommunities and thereby ease the political problems associated with the budgetary process. As it turned out, the two Army communities that were to benefit from the program were the armored cavalry and the airborne infantry.

Although the horse cavalry has disappeared, the classical cavalry functions of screening and reconnaissance must still be performed in a land war, and for these purposes the Army has armored cavalry squadrons and regiments—the former of which are organic to divisions and the latter of which are assigned to corps.[14] The desirable performance attributes of a vehicle that would perform these functions can be deduced from the nature of the missions. It should provide good mobility, preferably greater than that of a heavy tank, and it must also be a good fighting vehicle. The reconnaissance function requires poking into places where heavy strength might be encountered; so as a minimum, some elements of the scouting unit should be able to report back to headquarters, which requires that the unit have adequate firepower (and that the vehicles have adequate armor protection) for fighting its way out of a sticky situation or at least to cover the withdrawal of the lucky elements designated to report back. On other occasions, enemy roadblocks will be encountered, and here, doctrine and intelligence needs require that the cavalry test how well defended the obstacles are, which involves a quick charge and perhaps a fight. What is called for is a vehicle that enables a reconnaissance unit, on one hand, to stomp over minor roadblocks or obstacles and continue its mission, and on the other hand to extricate itself should an obstacle turn out to be heavily defended. By the late 1950's, the Army had just bought the M41 light tank (26 tons), which mounts a 76-mm. gun and has a maximum speed of 40 miles per hour, for the tank sections of its armored cavalry units.[15] By any criterion, the M41 tank appears in a careful analysis of the missions to have been a good substitute for the horse.

Insofar as the airborne community of the Army was concerned, it also had problems. Whatever merit the doctrine that "the best antitank weapon is a tank" may have had, the limits on aircraft capability meant that armored units equipped with 26- to 50-ton tanks could not accompany airborne divisions in an airborne operation. The union could be made only by the airborne unit and the friendly tanks fighting their way toward each other. Should enemy tanks in the meantime be encountered (which can happen as a result of faulty intelligence or air navigation), the going would be difficult. During the 1950's, a turretless, self-propelled 90-mm. gun, weighing about 15,000 pounds, which made it air-droppable, was the main antitank capability for airborne divisions. The troopers were seeking something better.[16] What they wanted would have better armor-defeating capability, without a commensurate increase in weight. For this reason, the Army developed the ONTOS, a tracked vehicle that mounts six 106-mm. recoilless rifles. It lost interest in the ONTOS for cogent tactical reasons, but the Marines found it attractive and it became the mainstay of the Marine Corps' antitank capability.[17] Meanwhile, the Army's airborne community focused on a new light tank mounting a new missile concept: the Shillelagh.

Since the Army had just bought the M41 light tank and was also pushing its M60 medium tank, there was sensitivity about using the term "tank" for still another new system. It was therefore referred to during its development phase as the Armored Reconnaissance Airborne Assault Vehicle. (The acronym, ARAAV, was pronounced in rhyme with a Texan's rendition of "Arab"). But as the time for procurement approached, the Army followed its practice of naming its tanks after its past generals, this time bestowing the honor on General Sheridan by designating the system the Sheridan /Shillelagh. There are some who label the honor a dubious one, in view of General Sheridan's reputation as a great fighter. Rightly or wrongly, these cynics appear to doubt the ability of the namesake to achieve a comparable distinction.

Whatever the merits of Sheridan/Shillelagh as ordnance, it does represent an interesting example of the technological syndrome in the military's procurement process. Its development[18] was initiated in September 1959, and its scheduled deployment was to be early 1964.[19] In the effort to maintain this schedule, the development and procurement, as with most contemporary programs, were carried out concurrently. Table 8.1 shows some of the sought-for military characteristics, which are those of a "light tank" or a general-pupose fighting vehicle: The turret with the 360° traverse, and the coaxially mounted 7.62-mm. machine gun are attributes of such a vehicle. The principal justification for developing the system, however, was the Shillelagh missile concept, which afforded the prospect of high-hit probabilities at "long" range. In and of itself, a guided missile might be viewed as a way of implementing a pure tank destroyer concept; that is, the missile launcher could be mounted on an agile vehicle for employment in a tactical defensive mode. The quest for a general-purpose combat vehicle also led to the idea that the system should be able to use conventional ammunition; thus, the missile launcher was also to be a "gun-launcher," for which a new family of ammunition had to be designed. The more elaborate weapon system and its rationale warrant explanation.

Table 8.1 Selected Military Characteristics as Development
Objectives of the Sheridan/Shillelagh Weapon System

VEHICLE

Weight, Combat Loaded	33,500 pounds
Length	20 feet
Width	9 feet
Height	10 feet
Power Plant	300-hp Turbo-charge Diesel
Top Speed	45 mph
Climbing Ability	50% Grade
Crew	4
Swim Capability	Yes, 4 mph
Air Droppable	Yes

MAIN ARMAMENT

Mount	Turret, 360° traverse
Weapon	Gun-launcher, 152 mm.

MISSILE

Guidance System	Infrared command, mounted in vehicle
1st-Round-Hit Probability, 7.5′ x 7.5′ target	.95 @ classified* (but "long") range
Rate of Fire	6/ minute*

CONVENTIONAL AMMUNITION

	six types, with combustible case
Rate of Fire	6/ minute*

SECONDARY ARMAMENT

	7.62-mm. machinegun, coaxially mounted with gun-launcher .50-caliber machinegun, commander's cupola

Tank-gunnery doctrine involves the use of a variety of ammunition with the main-tank armament so as to cope with a wide

* *Source:* All data, except footnote items, are from *Army, 1967, Green Book* (Washington,
D.C., Association of the United States Army, October 1967), pp. 146, 156, and 158;
other data are from *Review of Army Tank Program: Report, op. cit.,* p. 25.

spectrum of targets in different tactical situations.[20] A major distinction among the various kinds of targets is that of armored versus "soft" targets, the latter including personnel. Armor-defeating ammunition, in turn, can be classified in two broad categories, in accordance with the physical principle they employ: chemical-energy rounds and kinetic-energy rounds. The Shillelagh missile, with its shaped-charge warhead, utilizes the chemical principle. For a general-purpose fighting vehicle, the placing of sole reliance on only one armor-pentrating technique, as well as on a specialized delivery system, may not have seemed wise. Conventional tank guns also employ high-explosive, phosphorus, and canister ammunition for use against softer targets, purposes for which the missile was unattractive, because of the costs involved. Each guided missile, which contains some fourteen hundred parts, could cost more than several thousand dollars, in contrast to conventional ammunition, which costs only a small fraction (as low as 1–3 per cent) of that amount. This was why the missile launcher was called upon to function as a gun. And so it was that the development of a new family of conventional ammunition also became part of the Sheridan/Shillelagh program.

A conventional-ammunition 152-mm. cartridge, a size dictated by a gun launcher whose size in turn was determined by the missile's size, posed a weight problem. Its weight would exceed 50 pounds, which would limit a man's ability to handle the ammunition within the constrained space of a tank in any way that would facilitate rapid firing and reloading. To reduce the cartridge weight, a concept that had been around for some time was adopted. The traditional brass cartridge case would be supplanted by a combustible case and primer possessing the chemical qualities of the propellant itself, so that it would be consumed upon ignition of the propellant. Thus, a technological breakthrough in conventional ammunition and guns was programmed to accompany the missile and vehicle development.

During the period that the Sheridan/Shillelagh system was being developed, additional thought was given to improving our capability of coping with the armored threat. The mainstay of U.S. armored forces is the M60 tank, which mounts a British-designed 105-mm. gun, but there has been some question as to what the follow-on main battle tank should look like. In the meantime, the apparently high performance of the Shillelagh missile was sufficiently tantalizing to planners and decision makers that they sought to improve the capability of the existing M60 tank by adapting the Shillelagh weapon system to the vehicle. The same system was proposed as the main armament for a new tank.

The proposed weapon was designated the "Main Battle Tank-70" (MBT-70), to suggest the date upon which procurement and deployment would commence. Now the decision to develop the MBT-70 was made in 1963; and in 1964 "a plan to apply the system of combined missile and a 152-mm. combustible cartridge to M60 tanks on a 'crash basis' " was adopted.[21] During this period, only a limited number of Shillelagh prototype missiles became available, and moreover, test results regarding their performance were meager. Nevertheless, concurrency of development and production was extended to turrets that would accomodate the Shillelagh gun-launcher and that could be mounted on M60 tanks, both those in inventory and those to be produced.

The MBT-70 incorporated a number of other advanced technical features in addition to the Shillelagh weapon. A lower silhouette was to be provided through a design that made the traditional tank turret more nearly flush with the body of the vehicle. This feature was to be facilitated by reducing the required interior space, which in turn was to be permitted by a reduction of the crew size from four to three. The latter was to be accomplished by eliminating the gun loader and replacing him with an automatic mechanical loader. Lowering the vehicle silhouette would be aided further by the use of a hydropneumatic suspension system that could permit varying the height of the tank body above the ground. This capability could enhance its speed over rough terrain, a feature that in theory might reduce the probability of being hit. There was to be a stabilized sight-and-turret system so weapons could fire accurately while the vehicle was moving.[22] Weight was to be saved while improving the horsepower-to-weight ratio, and fuel economy was to be improved through the use of advanced engine-design concepts, such as a variable compression-ratio engine. The tank would therefore have better acceleration, which could further reduce the probability of being hit; and better fuel economy would enhance the operating range. Finally, in the interest of good relationships with a major NATO partner and perhaps for economy, as well as objectives associated with balance of payments, the MBT-70 was to be a joint development by the United States and the Federal Republic of Germany.[23]

The Shillelagh missile program, with its associated conventional ammunition, had one unique distinction: it was the main armament of a system currently under development and shortly to be issued to troops. The Shillelagh was adapted to a system developed in the past (the M60 tank), and it was the key element in the development of a future system(the MBT-70). Past, present, and future were thus bound up in a weapon concept that combines the elements of a guided antitank missile and combustible-case conventional ammunition.

Ten years after the initiation of the Sheridan/Shillelagh program, a House Armed Services Subcommittee Report issued in the summer of 1969 noted that, although $1.2 billion had been committed to Sheridan/Shillelagh, there was no convincing evidence that the system provided an improvement that was worth the cost.[24] As of spring 1969, the Army had three hundred M60 tanks worth $200 million and equipped with the Shillelagh gun launcher, and 243 gun-launcher turrets worth $70 million and all unusable because of turret stabilization deficiencies. As someone expressed it at the 1969 Congressional hearing, the Army and the taxpayers supporting it were confronted with the dilemma of "tanks but no tanks."[25] The Committee report suggested that the spirit, if not the letter, of Army regulations governing acceptability standards for procurement of new equipment had been treated casually[26] and that "misleading reports . . . also influenced the decisions to produce" the system.[27] It was suggested that the production decisions were made so "that the appearance of satisfactory program progress would lessen the chance for searching and critical reviews by 'those who control funds.' "[28] The observation was also made that the commitment of the developers to the programs increased as the expenditure of time and money increased and that the project manager "became more of a captive rather than a manager of his project."[29] These are not findings of a muck-raking journalist or an antimilitary liberal raging about the military-industrial complex. They come from a source with a well-established record of good will toward the military services. The happenings that evoked such commentary from such a sympathetic quarter warrant elaboration.

Major problems can be addressed in terms of three categories: the Shillelagh missile, the caseless ammunition, and the Sheridan vehicle itself.

The most serious shortcoming that has appeared in the Shillelagh missile is its failure to achieve the very high, 0.95 hit probability at long ranges—the performance specification whose attainment was the principal consideration driving the development program. In tests conducted in Panama, the missile failed to find the target eleven out of thirteen times.[30] The firing of conventional ammunition displaces the vehicle from its position,[31] which suggests that the lightweight vehicle may be poorly matched to the ammunition. One of the advantages viewed by the advocates as a major asset of the guided missile is its ability to fire while on the move, a capability that might be facilitated by a gunner being able to make course corrections after launch. But the Sheridan/Shillelagh has not yet demonstrated this capability,[32] nor can the missile be employed effectively in darkness or conditions of limited visibility.[33] One of the problems largely responsible for this difficulty seems to be that the glow of the missile's jet after launch degrades the gunner's ability to keep his crosshairs on the target. But even without this difficulty, a target has to be visible for the entire period of the missile's flight, whereas with a gun the initial sighting and aim of the gunner prior to firing is sufficient for providing a hit. This is one of the reasons why reliance solely on a guided missile as a major antitank weapon is very risky. The risk gives added urgency to a gun capability, and this in turn was where the caseless ammunition part of the program entered the picture.

The night-firing capability appears to be further degraded by other similar distractions that might come into the gunner's field of view, including tracers from the vehicle's own .50-caliber machinegun, which might be fired at the same time by the vehicle's commander.[34] This possibility is important in combat situations wherein the vehicle is confronted by combined tank and infantry attacks, as typified by sophisticated armor tactics.[35] There were also hints that the use of the missile might be affected adversely by electronic countermeasures.[36]

Upon conditionally releasing the weapon for troop issue, the Army's Testing and Evaluation Command (TECOM) suggested that "Shillelagh missiles should not be fired over friendly troops in training due to the hazard from early ground impact."[37] The basis for this instruction and its implications are not spelled out in detail; but the following is of disturbing relevance. A missile is launched from a gun tube at a relatively low muzzle velocity, compared to the muzzle velocity of a conventional tank round. It then picks up velocity as its propellant is expended, reaching a maximum somewhere downrange, after which momentum carries it to the target. Initially, after launch, deviations from a straight path to the target occur while the guidance system "hunts" for the path; hence, the suggestion that no firing take place over the troops' heads, to avoid the consequence of premature impacts. These characteristics also suggest that whatever the potential of the missile for high accuracy at long ranges, it may show a highly degraded accuracy at shorter ranges, which incidentally are those wherein most tank engagements occur. This feature of the missile has other very important tactical implications. In a tactical defensive role against attacking tanks, defending vehicles are placed in a hull defilade, or "hull down," position so as to minimize the frontal target area available to the attacker's antitank weapons.[38] But if the missile has a high probability of impacting the ground when launched from the normal height of the launcher, then so much the greater is this risk when the vehicle is in the hull-down position. Greater vulnerability in at least one important phase of combat operations therefore results. Finally, the specification of six-rounds-per-minute rate of fire has not been realized either for the missile or for conventional ammunition. It appears that placing a missile in the tube while a previously fired missile is being tracked degrades the functioning of the guidance system.[39]

The combustible-cartridge caseless ammunition has presented serious problems. The combustible-case compound was susceptible to cracking during handling and was affected by humidity. The latter difficulty was in turn responsible for burning residues remaining in the gun-launcher chamber after firing.[40] Such residues, if located in the chamber, could prematurely ignite a newly chambered round, and moreover, if they should enter the interior of the tank, there is a danger of igniting the stowed ammunition. Working in the presence of the latter possibility might be likened to that of requiring the vehicle crew to function in an environment where they are knee-deep in kerosene. To cope with these problems, various expedients and crash minor developments were undertaken. Neoprene plastic bags were acquired for containing the cartridges as a protection against humidity, and efforts to develop alternative case compositions were undertaken. A scavenger system was developed for the gun-launcher, to blow the residue out of the launcher after firing. It was "an open-breech scavenger," which blew air into the gun tube by means of a jet of carbon dioxide after the breech was reopened, so as to clear the tube of residue. But this increased the smoke inside the tank, to the crew's discomfort, impairing the crew's visibility, and hence, its target-acquisition capability. The scavenger system also blew "flaming residue into the turret instead of out of the barrel, settling alongside highly combustible ammunition stored within the vehicle."[41] To cope with this problem, a closed-breech scavenger system was developed. This system involved the use of a mechanical air compressor located inside the tank, and of course, one of the by-products of an air compressor is heat energy, which greatly increases crew discomfort. The Congressional report refers to this series of efforts as "the $10 million scavenger hunt."[42]

Despite these deficiencies, a number of the original requirements (including some shown in Table 8.1 such as the rate of fire of six per minute), were waived and the Sheridan/Shillelagh was issued to troops in the field, including South Vietnam. But in South Vietnam the Shillelagh and its guidance system were not included, both for security reasons and because there was no tank threat. The $1.2 billion tank-killing system was employed as an antipersonnel weapon, with conventional ammunition being the mainstay. There, the cartridge was subject to "breakage, misfires, and extraction problems."[43] The shock of mine explosions and vehicle vibration caused the projectile to split from the case,[44] and ammunition stowed in the racks would dump powder on the vehicle's floor.

One of the functions of the old-fashioned brass cartridge case is that the rim of its metal base permits easy extraction should a round not fire. The new ammunition does not possess this facility, and the only reliable way to extract misfired ammunition from the tube is for one of the crewmen to ram it from the muzzle end. This is not healthy work in the middle of a firefight.[45] Another function performed by a brass cartridge is that of absorbing heat from the firing, thus reducing the heating of the gun's breech, an excessive amount of which can cause premature ignition (or a "cookoff") of a newly chambered round. Obviously, this danger can be avoided by not loading the gun until a target is acquired. But understandably enough, the idea of operating in a combat environment with an empty weapon is unappealing to fighting men.

The Sheridan vehicle itself has disappointed the expectations of those who wrote its military characteristics. Its swimming capability is 3.8 mph instead of the marginal 4 mph that was originally sought despite the feeling of some potential users that even the 4 mph swimming speed is not useful in tactical situations requiring the crossing of a flowing river. The system's weight has increased to the point where, if it is to be air-dropped from a C-130 aircraft, it could not be combat-loaded. Consequently, these elements of the load would have to be dropped from an accompanying aircraft, causing a great deal of scurrying by the paratroopers to find their ammunition (and perhaps fuel) and load it onto the vehicle—and all of this possibly at night and under fire—before they could start their business. In acceleration, the engine produced a distinctive and high whine that was recorded in Panama tests as being heard at a distance of three miles on a quiet night. This sound is due to the turbocharger, the function of which is to squeeze more horsepower from a lightweight engine. In daylight, the engine's exhaust produced a distinctive "rooster's tail," which was observable at great distances.[46] None of these qualities are well suited for a reconnaissance vehicle.

At the time of the 1969 Congressional hearings the status of the Main Battle Tank development was unclear, somewhat shrouded in the obfuscation permitted by security classification.[47] A strong case could be made, however, that the conceptual shortcomings of the Shillelagh missile and combustible ammunition that have been revealed in the Sheridan program apply with even greater force to the MBT-70 program. That the original conception of the MBT-70 might cost as much as $1.2 million per unit[48] (about four times greater than the per-unit cost of the standard M60) added a further disconcerting element to the program. There were indications that the automatic loader, which is the key to eliminating the fourth crewman, and hence, achieving the changed vehicle silhouette, encountered severe difficulties.[49] It is likely that the delicate handling characteristics of the combustible-case ammunition (if not of the missile itself) posed problems in this category.

All this suggests that ten years of development effort produced little. Many of the "bugs" that afflicted the Shillelagh missile may eventually be corrected—it is a matter of spending enough money. However, the Sheridan would still remain a dubious scout vehicle because its design was compromised to take advantage of the weight-saving afforded from launching a missile, and other features. As for the Main Battle Tank program, the Germans dropped out of the joint-development project in January 1970. Meanwhile, they have consummated development of their Leopard family of combat vehicles, which includes a more conventional battle tank and which has been enjoying brisk sales in Europe. Since the 1969 congressional investigation, congressional Armed Services and Appropriations subcommittees exhibited increasing skepticism of the Main Battle Tank program, although they continued to fund it at rates somewhat lower than the Defense Department requested. Apparently, the "get-well" efforts did not satisfy elements of Congress, since the program was terminated as a result of Committee action impacting on the fiscal-year-1972 budget in the House of Representatives in December 1971.

9

THE LIMITS
OF TECHNOLOGY

> Moreover, technology works best on things nobody
> really needs, such as collecting moon rocks or building
> supersonic transport planes. Whenever we try to apply
> it to something serious, it usually falls on its face.
>
> John Fischer, "The Easy Chair," *Harper's*, April 1970, p. 28.

The Sheridan/Shillelagh story is encountered too frequently in
the weapon-system development process: cost overruns, failure
to meet scheduled deployment dates, and failure to meet technical-performance specifications are the dominant characteristics.
Perhaps a unique quality of the program was the way the dominant but untested-weapon concept (the Shillelagh missile) was
extended to two other programs, and jeopardized them as well.
Indeed, it is hard to find any development program instituted by
the Army within the past ten or twelve years that has not exhibited some element of sourness, regardless of whether it be concerned with small arms or the latest jeep, with conventional
artillery pieces or sophisticated surface-to-air missiles.

Even as mundane an item as the jeep is not unaffected. The
latest model of this vehicle, the M151, was designed with more
horsepower and a stronger suspension system to permit carrying a heavier load (a 106-mm. recoiless rifle and six rounds of
ammunition) under off-the-road conditions. On ordinary roads,
the higher horsepower also permits faster speeds. But because
of the suspension system, the new model jeep "corners" differently from a conventional automobile, and the driver's normal
reaction to this characteristic is such as to increase the possibility
of a roll-over. The accident rates with the new jeep greatly
exceeded what had been the norm for this important killer and
incapacitator of soldiers.[1] The Army now requires a special one-
week course of driving instruction for proposed drivers of the
vehicle. Here is a good example of failure to ask a question of

172

relevance to the user: There is much support for the assertion that driving safety is of importance to the consumer. Some might defend the Army from criticism on this score by pointing out that unsafe new model automobiles occasionally enter the civilian market. But in the civilian sector, the individual consumer at least has a choice of different brands to purchase. The eschewal or lack of similar options by a military service provides all the more reason for it to undertake careful testing of a new model before major procurement.

Occasionally, a private firm will develop a weapon independently of the official R&D apparatus, as the AR15 rifle, for example. The Army adopted this weapon after much political tugging and pulling and redesignated it the M16. The initial procurement of the M16 was delayed by some technical changes made, in the original AR15, including the addition of a bolt-closure device that had limited, or even negative, utility but that increased cost, a change in barrel twist that reduced the system's lethality, and a change in the ammunition propellant that reduced the weapon's reliability. These problems of reliability produced difficulties in the field that threatened to undermine the troops' confidence in the weapon. Subsequently, a number of complicated and interrelated changes were urgently implemented, and these may have served to cope with the problem.[2] But all this effort was unnecessary, since there was evidence that the original configuration of the system—including the weapon itself and the ammunition propellant—was better suited for operational requirements than the technical contributions of the in-house system.

Intertwined with the tactics that delayed procurement of the M16 rifle was an effort made by the Army to promote a weapon of its own conception. This came into being in 1963 and was designated the Special Purpose Infantry Weapon (SPIW). The technology was exotic, in comparison to established small-arms technology.[3] But the SPIW program, unfortunately, was not a weapon; it was a political tactic. It was a political tactic in the sense that Army thinkers quickly conceived the program as a way of heading off a possible major purchase of M16's or similar systems involving conventional technology, but a markedly different concept of small-arms design. The innovative potentialities that are implicit in going from a .30- to a .22-caliber basic-concept infantry weapon are numerous. But instead of exploring these potentialities, the Army chose to expend resources on a technical approach that might possibly produce a new weapon a decade from now, which would cost several times as much as existing systems, and which would likely produce no improvement—or indeed, might induce a regression—in combat effectiveness.[4]

The reasons for this behavior were political. It was galling to the Army to have a program that it had promulgated—the M14 —terminated by a Secretary of Defense, and it was even more galling to be forced to procure the M16, which the Army had neither conceived nor developed. These bruised feelings may have been compounded by the fact that a company that had never dealt with the Army-ordnance system had developed the weapon on its own. There were technical specialists in the Army who had been seeking over the years to do basic research on new principles that might be applicable to small arms. Given "the requirement" for a "major breakthrough" in small arms and because of political factors, the advocates of the more exotic technical approaches were given the most attentive hearing. They also got the money, partly because the exotic nature of the technology appealed to those who directed the R&D process. In exchange for their new-found riches, they were required to come up with a system within three years that could be issued to the troops. Predictably, the new system was not available at the end of three years, and indeed, it may not be available even ten years after the promised date. Given such management and motivation, charges of inadequate funding of research, development, and engineering egregiously miss the mark. Indeed, even what is meant by "the state of the art" in technology is a moot question. The term perhaps best describes the result of a pursuit of technical hobbies combined with the pursuit of budgetary objectives.

Nor are the Air Force and the Navy without their problems. If these services do not have as many as the Army does, it is because they do not procure as wide a variety of systems. However, on the average their programs are individually more costly, and the Air Force and Navy can produce systems that generate monumental cost overruns or failures to perform. Thus in the 1950's there was conceived, produced, and deployed the "Sage" system, which was a complex of sensors, a communications network to control systems containing digital computers, plus communications links to air-defense weapons, which was to permit an optimum employment of fighter interceptors and missiles against a bomber attack. By the early 1960's nothing like the planned capability was attained. "Time scales stretched out, subsystems failed to attain their planned capabilities and cost increased."[5]

The Navy experienced large cost overruns trying to develop its Mark-48 torpedo,[6] and its promised availability for fleet use is long overdue relative to earlier plans and promises. During the 1950's and early 1960's, the Navy's Talos, Terrier, and Tartar missile systems absorbed resources to develop and make them operational, which caused much budgetary anguish, which only matched the apprehensions that centered around the question of whether those systems might provide fleet air defense. Apparently, these systems still contain deficiencies.[7]

Generally, airborne and seaborne weapon systems, if they fly and float, can give taxpayers the warm feeling that something was obtained for the resources spent. However, the Air Force's F111 (formerly the TFX) has not clearly provided this psychological benefit. Despite the large amounts spent on aircraft to support land forces, it appears that the costly and sophisticated avionics crammed into modern fighter bombers do not provide bombing accuracy adequate for the task.[8] And since most of the aircraft types possess such high speed, or poor turning characteristics, close air support carried out by visual bombing may not be as good today as it was with the Douglas A1, or the Stuka. Nor are the problems confined to weapons developed for the conventional forces. The Air Force's B-47 bomber, as a system, was hastily deployed into the field; but a large portion of that force for a long time was plagued by operational failures, most of which centered around the bombing-navigation system.[9] The present mainstay of the Strategic Air Command—the Minuteman missile—also has exhibited symptoms that suggest poor reliability in its normal operational setting. Attempts were made to launch four "shortburn" missiles from their operational silos in the Dakotas. One launch from South Dakota was successful; three attempted from North Dakota were failures, for different technical reasons.[10] The Minuteman system has cost much more than originally contemplated, although it is impossible to separate cost overruns from modifications in the system, some of which were warranted to cope with revised technical-performance objectives, which, in turn, were deemed necessary to cope with a new threat.[11] Finally, the Navy has been experiencing a rash of higher costs in ship development and construction that afflicts aircraft carriers,[12] destroyers,[13] destroyer escorts,[14] attack submarines,[15] and amphibious assault ships.[16] So serious are these developments that the future of the Navy itself may be grim.

The major conceptual shortcoming of the present approach to procuring weapons is that it forecloses the options that an unfolding advancing technology may have yet to provide. At the initial stage of writing the specifications, the theoretical limits of performance within the state of the technological and engineering art constitute the upper limit on the critical performance characteristics to be attained. Such theoretical limits are those that seem most feasible of attainment through the embodiment of new technical developments in operating equipment, given the knowledge available to scientists, engineers, and designers at the time the specifications are written. For example, at the time the Shillelagh specifications were written in 1959, it seemed that an infrared tracking approach was the best technical solution for guiding a tank-launched missile. Similarly, a number of other highly specific technical approaches were conceived as best ways of attaining other performance characteristics. Wrapped in one package, they require a highly programmed development effort in each of a number of technically complex areas. And to specify, in addition, a definite time within which the item is to be produced and issued to the troops requires an even higher degree of sophistication in the programming.

An important consequence of this approach is that, for some period during which the initial conception is being pursued, alternative technical ways of coping with the same problem are neither pursued nor considered. For example, it is possible, given the advances that have occurred in technology, that better antitank missiles could be conceived today and fielded within a year or two than will result from the approach characterizing the Shillelagh program. These advances have occurred for a variety of reasons, of which the need for guiding antitank missiles is not a major one.

Since the development of a weapon system is theoretically feasible within the state of the technical knowledge prevailing at the time of its conception, any manufacturing firm possessing a group of engineers and designers with expertise in each of the several technical areas can, in perfectly good conscience, seek the job of transforming the concept into hardware. Everyone, including the military customer, also knows that the endeavor will require pushing the state of the arts. It is also well known that when such endeavors are undertaken some unanticipated design and production engineering problems will have to be overcome; and it is equally well known that such unforeseen obstacles can be overcome, simply as a matter of cost and effort. With some luck, the extra costs may be "low," and each potential developer/manufacturer has as much right as any other to entertain the faith that he will be lucky in keeping his extra costs at a minimum if problems are encountered. Similarly, the military and civil advocates of any given program are justified in hoping that their project will experience good fortune.

A prominent characteristic of this approach to weapon-system concepts is that it results in *overspecified* systems. Technical research takes place at the conceptual phase, but the research effort is simply a series of paper studies addressing the engineering feasibility of translating *known* technical possibilities (slightly stretched to reflect recent trends in the specific areas of applied metallurgy, chemistry, and electronics) into application for a generally stated military "requirement"—for example, how to stop tanks when outnumbered. From these paper studies, a specific concept like the Sheridan/Shillelagh system is formulated, and the concept becomes fixed. The development effort then commences, and any efforts undertaken afterward are programmed to translate the particular combination of concepts into an item that will meet the performance specifications, or they are initiated on an ad hoc crash basis to cope with problems that inevitably arise during the course of the development. These are admixtures of production engineering and exercises in trial and error, aimed at solving particular problems.

This research that takes place at the conceptual phase of the process warrants scrutiny. Its focus is technical, but its foundation is theoretical. It is theoretical in the sense that existing knowledge in the technical arts, including trends based on that knowledge projected into the future, is translated into a conceptual weapon, to determine whether it is feasible and to determine what combinations of enhanced technical performance attributes such a future weapon might possess. From the extensive list of such combinations, the military users select one that seems most useful to them.

The process as described has some interesting and paradoxi-

cal qualities. It can be characterized as one wherein large
amounts of money are spent in such a way as to reduce the
number of options with the passage of time. In terms of research
philosophy or strategy as these relate to design problems, it is
a curiously unscientific process, inasmuch as it commits technicians and designers to specific technical solutions for operational problems. Such prior commitments in themselves involve
an eschewal of the idea that there may be a variety of solutions
to a given problem, one of which may be superior to the others,
and that the only way to determine which is best is to experiment. Failure to experiment is a failure to buy knowledge. For
this reason the great emphasis on development in the "research
and development" means that very little operational evaluation
is undertaken.

Because everyone—designers, engineers, and users—
becomes committed to a specific concept at a very early time, the
concept that becomes a program is transformed into an end
itself. Reputations—both of the scientists who successfully advocated a particular technical approach to a problem and of
military officers who approved the military characteristics describing the concept in physical terms—are laid on the line.
Technicians and operators end up by mutually supporting and
protecting each other. The operators, or line-officer users, are
compelled to adhere to the notion that the military specifications originally chosen for the system were the "right ones,"
while the technicians are motivated to cover up revelations that
certain technical approaches may not be working out. Standard
and well-founded regulations on quality control and materiel
acceptability are waived, in the hope that engineering changes
will eventually achieve "fixes," and so the development process
continues far into the procurement process, to an extent that
renders the budgetary distinction between development and
procurement nebulous, if not totally meaningless.

The contractors, who become the developers upon getting
the contract, obtain a license to spend large amounts of money
to protect those reputations. Seldom are all the original performance specifications met; but this should not be surprising,
given the fact that the original list represents what is only
theoretically possible. Even so, failure of a system to meet all
specifications is not considered a reason to forego procurement
of the new system. With some superficial justification, it is argued that the relevant comparison is not the degree to which the

new system meets its specifications, but how the new system compares with its predecessor. For example, the requirement for a new vehicle's speed may be 60 mph, while in its tests it only goes 50 mph. The program is not then judged to be a failure, because the present generation (in the inventory) of vehicles perhaps goes only 40 mph. The product of the most recent R&D cycle is thus "technically superior" to the current model, and on this basis its procurement is advocated.

There is a very serious flaw in this approach and its rationale, which becomes even more serious as successive cycles of weapon research, development, and procurement are consummated. Recall that the newly developed 50-mph vehicle is advocated for procurement because it is "better" than the 40-mph vehicle currently in the inventory. But what is the meaning of 40 versus 50 mph? It's quite likely that the 40-mph vehicle derived its justification on a similar rationale; namely, it was superior to a 30-mph vehicle. And yet, for all one knows, the 30-mph speed may have been quite satisfactory for performing the mission all along. The fallacy in assuming that enhanced technical performance provides a better system springs from the possible irrelevance of the initial reference point. There can be no rational end to a process for which there is no rational beginning. Thus, the contemporary weapon-system development process is caught in a dilemma of its own making. The dilemma is not exposed, however, because operational tests for the comparison of the old and the new systems under conditions similar to those that would prevail in the field are seldom, if ever, undertaken. This is because modern operational research as applied to weapons and, hence, cost-effectiveness analysis, is bankrupt.

Little careful thought is given to the subject of effectiveness; nor is any effort expended in measuring effectiveness. Instead, greater technical performance is assumed to be equated with enhanced combat effectiveness. But whether a transformation from technical performance to combat effectiveness can in fact take place, how it might occur, and whether a possible resulting increase in operational effectiveness is worth the additional cost —these are all questions that remain unanswered throughout the decision-making cycle. It was questions like these that World War II operational research addressed; but today such questions are begged or avoided. Paradoxically, the begging and avoidance of such questions is in a large measure achieved by using those techniques and efforts of the intellectual community that purport to do operational research and cost-effectiveness analysis. This curious inversion of intellectual endeavor requires examination, because it is an instrument for promulgating the present approach to development and procurement.

Figure 9.1 depicts a likely initial focal point that might be of interest to users and technicians with regard to the possible development of a new antitank guided missile. The solid curve shows the single-round hit probability of an existing tank gun as a function of range, while the same capability for a yet-to-be-developed guided missile is portrayed by the dashed curve, labeled the "conceptual system."

The relationships represented by both curves can be deduced from physical equations. With the tank gun, for example, a knowledge about the projectile's weight and cross-section and about the muzzle velocity of the projectile (which can be deduced from the projectile-to-propellant weight ratio and knowledge about the propellant's burning characteristics) permits a calculation of the time of flight to the target and of the operation of such forces as wind on the projectile during the flight. These performance characteristics are further affected by errors bearing upon optical sighting of the gun (parallax) and the error factor caused by the gun platform (for example, the tank) not being perfectly level or in line with the target (cant). But complete reliance on such *a priori* forecasts is neither desirable nor necessary. One would like to see experiments conducted. And a great deal of such engineering testing is done.

The nature of the engineering testing is to shoot at a target on an actual range. A 7.5' x 7.5' target panel may be used, because those dimensions are similar to those of tanks. Since the

Figure 9.1

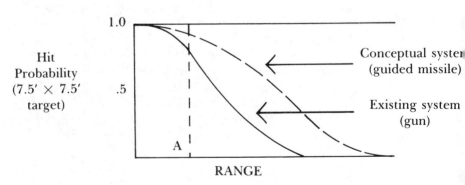

object of the engineering tests is to verify the equations (or the behavior of the tank gun relative to the predictions that follow from well-established physical equations), a number of very special conditions are satisfied when such tests are undertaken. The gunner himself is a technician employed by the proving ground or test range, the target is fully visible to the gunner, and the range at which he is firing is known to the gunner. Finally, the gun will have been accurately boresighted for proper alignment to the sighting instruments, and the instruments themselves will have been checked for proper functioning.

That such conditions should prevail for the conduct of test firings is quite proper for the narrow, but vital, purposes of engineering testing itself. Such testing is designed to measure the physical performance of the equipment—and only of the equipment. For this purpose, maximum effort should be made to separate from the measurements the effect of, say, whether gunner/technician Jones is better than Smith in estimating range, wind angle, and velocity. Since one of the functions of engineering tests is to compare unlike physical systems (including ammunition) in ways that will be objective, the impact of other diverse influences should also be eliminated. Finally, there is the need to specify performance objectives for the contractors who develop and produce the weapons, for both initial acceptance and ongoing quality control. For these purposes, the measuring processes must also be highly objective.

Thus, the solid curve shown in Figure 9.1 can accurately describe a part of the real world. As applied to tank guns, the solid curve suggests that accuracy does fall off sharply with range. To the users, the point is well known. But now something happens: a curve such as the dashed one, labeled "guided missile," is drawn. How does this happen and what is behind it?

A curve like the dashed one in Figure 9.1 comes into being through the application of the standard physical equations describing ballistics and other phenomena, supported by bits of evidence from the latest developments in the application of those fields to other problems. Because of these varied developments, it is technically feasible to develop an antitank guided missile that would provide hit probabilities as shown by the dashed line. Thus, at distance A, the missile has a hit probability of .95, whereas that of the tank gun is only .5. The .95 hit probability at range A becomes one of the "military characteristics" of the new system that is to be developed. In the case of the tank program, it becomes a major factor that governs, if not drives, the entire development process.

Other considerations may nevertheless have impact on the forming of the concept of a new weapon, and they will evolve in a way that is similar to the specification of hit probability. For example, it may be decided that the new weapon should be mounted on a tank. Such a decision, of itself, is a major doctrinal one, because the vehicle, as a tank, must perform other functions. To perform those functions it must, for one thing, possess a turret to permit rapid slewing of the main armament. It may also seem desirable that a tank possess a low silhouette, to reduce the target cross section available to enemy gunners. (The payoff from this characteristic can be demonstrated by applying in reverse the kind of analysis and experiments by which hit probabilities against the 7.5' x 7.5' target were deduced.) Such an objective entails allowing less interior space for the vehicle. Perhaps a smaller crew will permit such a reduction. One crew member that could be dispensed with is the loader, if a mechanized loader could load the gun.[17] Greater acceleration of the vehicle seems like a desirable attribute, since it can confound the enemy gunners. But this requires a higher horsepower-to-weight ratio, and the more powerful engine that will be needed imposes a cost in weight and consumes more fuel, which in turn will reduce the vehicle's cruising range. But regardless, if it is possible to develop an entirely new engine that incorporates some new principle of fuel combustion, then this objective will also be sought. Through such a chain of reasoning did it come about that the Army's new Main Battle Tank was to have a three-man crew, an automatic gun loader, and a lower silouette, and was to incorporate an engine having a variable compression ratio.[18] Now each of these attainments is technically practicable, so the performance specifications derived from the theoretical capability of the combined highly specified subsystems (each with its unique technical solution) become the military characteristics of the new system. A formidable weapon is created—on paper.

But some critical questions were not asked before formulating this concept of the new weapon, and each of them can be illustrated by one major question: *How relevant are the hit-probability performance estimates, like those depicted in Figure 9.1, to the conduct of tank gunnery under actual combat conditions?* One answer, of course, is that they may not be relevant at all; and to the extent that they can be correlated with combat effectiveness, the relationship is at best very indirect and murky. Before any correlation can be made, a great many other questions must be asked and answered, it is to be hoped, in some quantitative way.

As for the worth of the long-range accuracy of antitank weapons, the first question that must be asked is: How great is the opportunity to engage targets at long ranges? Terrain intervisibilities—for example, the distances one can see when at vehicle height level—as determined by the geography of areas likely to be contested, provide the outer limit for such opportunities. It may be that over the relevant "tank courses"—for example, routes that tanks can follow in their operations—the opportunities to utilize a long-range weapon are very few. If so, then it may not be wise to buy so many of the weapons at all, let alone make them the main armament on the standard combat vehicle. Gathering information on terrain intervisibilities is a straightforward process, involving the use of standard surveying instruments, although it is time-consuming, and does incur a cost. Nevertheless, it is critical information for addressing the question of operational relevance.

The information is also critical for cost-effectiveness reasons that bear upon the design of the force structure. A long-range weapon may be costly. Even if it is effective on a per-unit basis, it may nevertheless be more efficient from the standpoint of overall force design to have a larger number of less costly weapons. Furthermore, if it turns out that the type of terrain where the more costly long-range systems can be employed effectively is limited, then the case for large numbers of less sophisticated systems that are effective at short range is even more powerful. For example, the Shillelagh missile is designed and optimized to kill tanks at long ranges by means of a large warhead capable of penetrating the thick frontal armor of tanks. But in most combat situations, tanks as targets are acquired at ranges of less than 1,000 meters, because tankers sneak up draws, avail themselves of other terrain-masking features, and often employ smoke to conceal their deployment. Combat experience also suggests that the majority of hits taken by tanks are on the side or rear, where the armor is not so thick. Thus, in defending against attacking tanks one is apt to encounter large numbers of them at short distances. A good defensive system would be one with larger numbers of weapons, that can do quick but effective work at short ranges. Thus, even if the Shillelagh system does achieve its design objectives, it would probably be a poor investment, because its underlying concept is unsound for the relevant terrain conditions and the operational threat.

Another complex set of questions centers around the relevance of such measures as hit probability, which are written into the performance characteristics—for example, the .95 hit probability at very long range, against a fully visible 7.5' x 7.5' target. Recall that in the tests the gunner is expert, the distance is known, and the target is fully visible. Measuring the gun performance under such conditions is useful for limited engineering purposes, including the determination of whether the manufacturer of a new system meets certain engineering specifications. But the meaning of the measure is suspect and can even be downright irrelevant as a measure of combat effectiveness, the reason, of course, being that operational conditions differ greatly from those encountered on the engineering test range.

Under operational conditions the targets are seldom highly visible to gunners. What gunners generally see at long ranges (and even at short ranges) are glimpses of targets, which are shrouded by combinations of smoke, dust, shadows, and camouflage. They may also see target signatures, like gun flashes and dust trails. At long ranges, targets either move at speeds that are difficult to estimate precisely or they are carefully concealed so they cannot be seen at all. When they move, they take advantage of terrain masking and are visible only intermittently. The precise ranges are unknown and variable, and they must be estimated. The operational situation is generally one in which "the target" is the complex of an enemy unit, containing several or more tanks plus other vehicles such as personnel carriers, and often accompanied by dismounted infantry. If the target is in a defensive mode, then infantry crew-served antitank weapons may also be deployed in positions that are favorable for their use. In brief, the targets, or even elements of the target, do not remotely resemble the 7.5' x 7.5' highly visible panel employed for providing estimates of hit probabilities. The friendly individual tank gunner, and crew, usually operates as part of a group, normally a platoon or section of tanks, to which friendly infantry and other support are attached. Any engagement involves the employment of procedures by which enemy targets are selected, one's own type of ammunition is selected, and related decisions are made.

Tank gunners, for their part, are not technicians like those who fire on the test ranges, nor do they operate under conditions that resemble test-range conditions. Their own immediate visibility is generally impaired by dust and smoke from friendly, as well as unfriendly, sources. They are often fatigued as a result of operating in the constrained space of a tank, which also vibrates and provides a rough ride, and because of lack of sleep in the field. They are under stress, not only because of combat, but also because they must operate as part of a crew and must be attuned to commands and the behavior of fellow crewmen. In combat, they are additionally stressed because they are scared. They are scared because they face the prospects of high-velocity metal fragments bouncing around inside their tank, of their tank being turned into a container of burning fuel, and of being shot at by unfriendly infantry should they manage to bail out of such a tank. Because they are required in large numbers, they cannot be as carefully selected and trained as can astronauts or even bomber and fighter pilots.

Engagements involving armored vehicles can be viewed as consisting of three major types: offensive, defensive, and meeting. When one is on the offensive, one is up against enemy weapons that are in a defensive mode. If the defense consists of tanks, then these fire from hull-down positions, and if possible they will change positions frequently so as to deny the attacker the advantages to be gained from fixing their position. The defenders generally hold their fire to avoid prematurely revealing their position. In the tactical defensive mode, the enemy attackers employ terrain to minimize their own exposure to fire, and they utilize smoke and the time of the day to hinder the defenders' view. In a meeting engagement, a unit stumbles onto enemy forces which may or may not have had adequate warning to take positions that will permit an ambush. The engagement ranges are generally short, and the contest resembles a melee.

How much is known about the anatomy of tank/antitank operations? Or, perhaps more to the point, how much operational evaluation has been conducted to provide insights or knowledge about the complex and interacting forces that would determine or influence combat effectiveness? British Operational Research Sections during World War II conducted extensive research on the subject, including an analysis of a large number of engagements in the Ardennes battle between tank-destroyer units (self-propelled and towed, with and without infantry support), and they generated evidence suggesting that specialized tank-destroyer capability has much merit. The U.S. Army's Operational Research Office did extensive field work in Korea on tank employment in that war. But in the post-Korea period, little effort has been made to determine and measure the characteristics of tank and antitank behavior under field conditions that might approximate those encountered in actual operations. There were a few such instances, however, and these were notable for the questions they raised; but the questions were left unanswered.

In the early 1950's, tests with regular tank crews showing varied proficiencies, with a variety of tank-fire control systems, and in tactical contests simulating offensive, defensive, and meeting engagements, suggested that neither training (as measured by crew proficiency) nor different combinations of equipment revealed any effectiveness differences as measured by hit probabilities, which were also a function of crew reaction times. These tests results were the object of subsequent controversy centering around the test design. The controversy was not resolved, however, by more pointed testing. In the late 1950's, a less well-designed test suggested that tank sections and platoons badly distribute their fire against enemy tanks. More than one tank fires at a single opposing tank, and that fire continues to be directed at a tank that is hit. This behavior operates to degrade the effectiveness of the equipment. Moreover, it suggests that people do not always do what doctrine tells them to do.

One field test was designed to measure the ability of tank crews (in an overwatching position) to acquire targets by means of target weapon signatures, and, for example, to identify enemy tanks as contrasted with recoilless-rifle infantry antitank weapons. The test suggested that this kind of identification was not performed very well. This deficiency suggests that crews should obtain training on the subject, which, if applied, could lead both to a better distribution of fire and to a more rational selection of the ammunition to be used. From the viewpoint of equipment effectiveness, the problem of target identification constitutes another factor that can degrade the effective application of technical sophistication.

Finally, in 1963 a field experiment was conducted in rolling terrain that is suitable for armored operations to determine the length of time moving tanks at different ranges would be visible to defending antitank weapons.[19] The tank courses were selected by armored officers, and the positions for the antitank weapons were selected by infantry officers. The exposure times of moving tanks were shown to be drastically less than commonly believed, and this leads one to believe that the efficacy of guided, low-velocity weapons at long ranges could be considerably less than initially expected.

In varying degrees, these field tests suggest that the technical performance of equipment—in an operational tactical context—might be greatly degraded, or dominated by the complexities of operational considerations. That these complexities exist should not be construed as meaning no effort should be made to develop new equipment. They do suggest, however, that the route from enhanced equipment performance to improved operational performance is not a direct one. The operational constraints, including the tactical skill of those seeking to counter the higher-performance equipment, greatly degrades the performance of all equipment. Nor is there any basis to assume *a priori* that the operational factors will degrade different types of equipment by the same proportions. For example, on the engineering test range, items A and B may have hit probabilities of .95 and .5, respectively. But under one set of tactical conditions, at a similar distance, they may be .2 and .1, respectively, while under another they may be .02 and .05, which would be an inversion of the relative effectivensss of the systems. But no one can know this unless the measurement of operational effectiveness is addressed directly.

The measurement of operational effectiveness, along with the issues of what should be measured, constitutes a difficult conceptual problem. For example, single-round hit probability—a concept that is useful and relevant for engineering testing—is not a measure of operational effectiveness, if only because no one encounters rectangular panels as targets in war and, conversely, because real targets are seldom encountered under conditions similar to those on the proving-ground test range. A more relevant measure of tank-gunnery effectiveness might be the time it takes for, say, a section of five friendly tanks to dispatch some number of simulated enemy targets that have been realistically programmed to behave and appear like their counterparts in actual combat under different conditions of terrain and movement, with different scenarios resembling different tactical situations, and with different conditions of visibility. One should employ regular GI tank crews for the exercises, trained either in official doctrine or alternative experimental doctrines, or both. Or the measure might be the number of enemy targets dispatched within a given time.

To conduct such tests would require construction of a "shooting-gallery" set of tank courses, along with related instrumentation and target-control systems that permit scenario replication and accurate real-time measurements of hits, positions, and other critical variables. Such a laboratory might cost $5 million to $10 million and a few million dollars a year to operate. Since regular crews could be cycled through the system, there should be no troop costs. Upon the building up of a body of data from such field experiments, such information could be related to the technical performance data generated in engineering tests, so as to discover any correlations. After a few years of such activity, it should be possible to acquire not only knowledge about design parameters for new equipment but also insights about training and how to formulate the tactics for getting the most effectiveness from existing equipment. In the process, a lot of military officers and operational analysts could also learn much about system behavior and operational analysis.

The amount of this type of field testing and operational evaluation undertaken in the U.S. defense community is meager. The effectiveness of the little that is done is plagued, if not vitiated, by a combination of factors. But it would be incorrect to suggest that systems and operational analysts merely focus on some one measure like single-round hit probability and directly equate it with effectiveness. Such an approach would be very naive. This is an age in which analytical methods possess a sophistication that matches the sophistication of our technology, and sophistication is the essence of contemporary operational research and cost-effectiveness analysis. The next chapter examines how it is applied to actual problems.

10

COST-EFFECTIVENESS
ANALYSIS AND
THE *A PRIORI* METHOD

> To attempt an a priori solution of this problem is
> clearly absurd.
>
> P. M. S Blackett, *Studies of War,* p. 188.

It has been suggested that perhaps the major contributions that
World War II operational analysis made to the Allied and, especially, the British war effort were of two kinds. First, it provided
insights on how to make the best use of available weapons or
systems. Second, it performed a negative function of aiding
decision makers to avoid technical developments that potentially could absorb large amounts of resources but that would
provide limited or meager contributions to effectiveness. There
is much evidence suggesting that the German scientific and
technical community of World War II was not inferior to those
of the Allied countries, and that the German capacity to develop
new weapons was extremely great. Accordingly, it might be
asserted that the net contribution the Allied scientific community provided the Allied war effort flowed from the ability and
opportunity to extend the critical and question-raising spirit of
the scientific approach into operations, and thereby avoid some
of the waste of a haphazard or unstructured pursuit of weapons
developments.[1]

Thus the Allies were able to allocate their resources more
efficiently by virtue of a willingness and ability to raise and
address questions about the relative worth and cost of different
systems. Cost-effectiveness analysis is nothing more than the
formal attempt to bring about these results in a systematic way.
Since the specific *operation* is critical to attaining any objective
requiring the use of scarce resources, understanding the operation is a necessary part of making cost-effectiveness analysis
itself operational.

It is therefore relevant to ask what is the role that operational research plays in the present weapon-system development and acquisition process. Recall, as pointed out in a previous chapter, that there is now a large operations-research community in the United States, much of which is supported by the Defense Department and the taxpayer. As a result of the power attained by the Systems Analysis Directorate under Secretary McNamara, the military departments were encouraged and instructed to examine and justify programs by means of cost-effectiveness analysis. One would think, therefore, that use of these analytical techniques would reduce the frequency of happenings like the Army tank program. But this is not the case. Rather, systems analysis and related intellectual tools are used to rationalize, justify, and advocate programs like the Shillelagh, the Main Battle Tank, sophisticated aircraft, and similar developments.

An important approach, if not the principal one, employed in contemporary operational research is that of building analytical models and conducting computer simulations of two-sided combat actions. Such models take the general form of the earlier "war gaming," as developed by the Germans during the nineteenth century.[2] The models come in a large variety, the different ones treating air-to-air, air-to-ground, ground-to-air, and ground-to-ground combat situations. Some are "mixed" air-battle models, in which surface-to-air weapons and air-defense fighters are simulated as coping with an air-offensive operation. Ground-to-ground models simulate infantry small-arms fire fights, tanks versus tanks, tanks versus antitank weapons, and other combinations. Finally, there are models that treat submarine and antisubmarine warfare.

The purpose of this chapter is to show how model-building designed to treat combat and evaluate existing and, especially, conceptual weapon systems is used (or more accurately, abused) in the bureaucratic setting. This abuse occurs because models and model building tend to become equated with the scientific method itself. But scientific endeavor also requires that models (or theories) be validated, which necessitates recourse to empirical methods. It is this latter part of the scientific method that is largely absent in the existing military study and evaluation system.

Thus, a curious situation exists. People who are trained in such fields as physics and economics, which have a long tradition of emphasizing that theories be validated by some independent intellectual process such as experiment or historical statistical study, also function as weapon-system analysts or operational researchers. And yet, the hard and demanding standards regarding evidence and relevance, as applied to these people's basic disciplines, are not carried over to the military-oriented endeavors. Little of the World War II type of operational research is done. The reasons for, and consequences of, this situation will be the principal focus of this and the following chapters.

Many of the models employed in weapon-system evaluation have the following major characteristics. First, they are two-sided simulations of combat. Second, the performance characteristics of weapons (as they are specified for engineering and procurement purposes) are the principal numerical inputs for weapon and system performance. Finally, the two-sided quality of the simulation lends itself to specifying kill ratios or derivations of kill ratios as the principal effectiveness criteria. In this fashion, the exercise has much in common with simulations of strategic war. With the kill ratios and a differential advantage for Blue's (our side's) new system over Red's system being given, the cost-per-kill advantage or similar cost ratio can also be estimated.[3] The computer-simulated war gaming is thus adapted to playing the cost-effectiveness game.

The basic logic of such two-sided simulation of combat is very simple, although the numerical computational techniques have become very sophisticated, involving the use of high-speed computers. Essentially, tactical scenarios are postulated. Weapon systems, assumed to behave in accordance with their specified performance characteristics, then engage in simulated actions, in accordance with the various tactical scenarios. Many such models are stochastic or "probabalistic," which is why the activity consumes large amounts of computer time.

This stochastic quality of the key variables is important, and has subtle implications. For example, let us take a .5 hit probability for an air-defense missile launched against a flying airplane at a specified slant range. Such a number implies a rather complicated set of phenomena, in the statistical sense. It may mean that a hit consists of only one fragment of the missile striking the aircraft or of a large number of fragments, perhaps of varying size, striking it. The distribution of fragment attributes—size, velocity, and density—will itself exhibit certain statistical properties, either randomly or in a way that is affected by the warhead design and the fusing, the special characteristics of which will also display some random characteristics. It is possible to play the behavior of missile fragments in ways that are "realistic"—as contrasted to a simple deterministic application of the .5 hit probability—against different types of aircraft, which in turn possess different structural and, hence, vulnerability characteristics. By relating hit probabilities and the varying degrees of difference regarding the nature of a "hit" to the characteristics of the aircraft, it is possible to estimate the probability of getting a "kill." From just this one type of missile at one slant range (however, slant range is itself a variable that is a function of tactics), with a specified, but random-normal, hit probably distribution characterized by the average of .5 against different sections of different types of aircraft, a large number of combinations can be played in estimating the effect of the missile on an aircraft.

The scenario form of the analysis means that events are played sequentially, and in a way that represents combat actions. Conditional orders are often part of the scenario, and simulated systems are "directed" to do certain things only after other events occur—e.g., if a target is acquired, commence tracking; then, upon estimating range and finding that the range is less than 10,000 meters, fire. These sequences, too, can be treated stochastically by means of the statistical technique of queuing theory. These kinds of simulations become increasingly complex as account is taken of variable flight patterns, varying times during which the target is in view to the missile acquisition and range-estimating radars, system reliability, different degrees of clutter and error affecting radar behavior, and, finally, multiple aircraft penetrations and missile launchers, with the associated different firing doctrine and penetration tactics.

It was stated at the end of the last chapter that no one takes a single number or set of numbers treating a characteristic like single-round hit probability and advocates a costly new system on this basis alone. Rather, what is actually done is that numbers representing the performance and physical characteristics are fed into a computer model. After the simulations and replications are carried through, the kill ratios or similar effectiveness criteria come out. They can almost invariably favor Blue's conceptual system, and it would be astonishing if they did not. For the principal data inputs for the proposed new system consist of the technical and physical-performance characteristics, like the high first-round hit probability of the Shillelagh missile, which were specified when the "requirement" was written. And since those specifications are superior in all respects to those of Blue's or Red's existing system, the kill ratios derived from the computer simulations cannot possibly come out any other way. Indeed, failure to achieve such an outcome is usually a clear signal that something was wrong with the computer program itself.

The output of such models are numerical estimates of some criterion of effectiveness. In the antiaircraft/aircraft penetration simulation, probability of penetrating an air-defense system may be the effectiveness criterion. Another model may be employed to treat the likelihood of finding and hitting a target, or destroying some portion of the target. Often, two-sided actions are treated. In such fashion, tank-antitank duels will be fought, for example. The duels will be replicated in accordance with good statistical sampling theory to permit the assignment of confidence levels to the outcomes, with the latter taking the form of kill ratios for different tactical situations. Thus, one may deduce that Blue's systems relative to Red's for some weighted average of scenarios are as follows:

Blue's existing versus Red's existing   1.2: 1
Blue's conceptual versus Red's Existing   6.3: 1

Hence, it is asserted that Blue's conceptual system is more than five times better than Red's. Even though Blue's conceptual system (which is probably already under development) is three times costlier than the items presently in the inventory, it is highly "cost effective." In such fashion is the case made for a new system. The case also has an aura of science because the model employed the sophisticated mathematical and, especially, statistical techniques.

Cost-effectiveness analysis, then, is largely based on model-building. It is important to examine how such models are put together, and on what basis they derive their credibility.

First, the model builders make a list of variables presumed to be relevant to the operation. These lists are generally compiled as a result of research by teams of analysts, who often consult extensively with military officers. In some instances, military officers and civilian analysts may participate jointly in this effort. When a study is done by a contractor for particular military subagencies, the agency usually has a military Study Project Officer, whose job is to "monitor" the study and assist the contractor's analysts in contacting military people who can provide useful suggestions.

Next, the model begins to take form. Simultaneously, the data are gathered, where obtainable. With regard to variables for which data are not available, estimates are made, often on the basis of "judgment." The structural relationships or the theorectical underpinnings of the model are also discussed with military officers. Sometimes these are presented in formal program-report briefings to higher commanders, especially if the project is treating some critical program. Sometimes the military customer has a civilian "scientific adviser," who is a civil servant, who offers his guidance or suggestions. Progress reports on some service-sponsored efforts are occasionally presented to OSD analysts and officials because, more often than not, the service was directed to conduct the cost-effectiveness study or it is hoped the study will validate some request it plans to make to the higher authority.

In some projects and in the course of briefings and consultations a more or less standard scenario emerges. The contractor (specifically, the contractor's project leader) knows that often he is in a sensitive position, because usually the study either addresses a controversial problem or is being conducted to justify some particular development or procurement program or both. The military-study process and its associated model-building may be involved either with intraservice doctrinal political issues or the higher-level service/OSD budgetary struggle. Occasionally, when the study treats aircraft or antiaircraft systems or strategic deployment problems, interservice politics is at least a latent issue. Many who attend the briefings or who are interviewed have a strong and sometimes vested interest in the subject that is being "modeled." Military officers often have strong views on doctrinal matters and, very frequently, on equipment design. Scientific advisers sometimes have a vested intellectual interest in a particular technical approach to a problem. The contractor's study-project manager, therefore, is confronted by a difficult task. For this reason he is often selected, wisely enough, because he can quickly perceive complexes of political and bureaucratic nuances, give good briefings, and, especially, be quick on his feet in both briefings and meetings.

Through the interactions between the military (and sometimes civilian) customers who buy operations and cost-effectiveness analysis and the study teams employed by the contractors (profit and nonprofit) who sell them, "realism" is injected into the model-building. Realism of the models, including the credibility of the end results, has become the hallmark of acceptability. However, because it is a theory, no model can be realistic. It must necessarily depart from reality to some extent. Herein lies a dilemma that besets much military analysis, intensified by the bureaucratic/political forces. It also exacerbates the political problems. A dilemma exists because "realism" of a theory involves a contradiction, and, clearly, it is not the hallmark to evaluate the worth of a theory or model.

Two criteria are used for evaluating computer simulations: credibility and realism. Credibility describes the judgments of either the analysts who construct the model or the customer who may or may not like the model's end results. When the customer does not like the end results, he generally falls back upon the argument that the model is "unrealistic."

With many simulations, aggregations must be made, because it is mechanically impossible to design a model or a computer program that can accommodate the fine-grain detail that in fact may be needed to describe a combat situation. For example, in an infantry fire fight, very small gradations in terrain and foliage conditions play an important role in tactics, the choice of position (location of foxholes), and even the terminal ballistics of bullets. Yet in one model designed to treat small-arms and infantry operations terrain gradations were incorporated by grids measuring 50 meters square. Vegetation was not simulated, and all elements of units played in the simulation were assumed to be located in the center of a grid square. In a tank-antitank simulation, the defenders did not move; so no tactical flexibility was incorporated in the model. Deficiencies like these can be termed structural shortcomings of the models and simulations.

Such structural shortcomings need not be serious if it is in fact generally believed or demonstrated that the abstraction that is implicit in a particular structural feature of the model is of no importance. For example, most analysts and operators would agree that it is of no moment whether riflemen are blond or dark haired and that to depart from that element of reality is appropriate, in the interest of economical analysis. On the other hand, the abstraction that infantry fire fights take place on flat pieces of terrain will cause some, especially experienced, soldiers to have severe reservations about the analytical results. The only way to resolve the issue of whether the particular abstraction is appropriate is to make some effort independently to verify or refute the hypotheses that flow from the model that contains the contested abstractions. This independent effort may consist of purposefully designed field tests, historical-statistical research, or operational research carried out in conjunction with actual operations. But if no empirical endeavor is undertaken, there is no way of knowing whether the seemingly important structural deficiencies are serious. For this reason, a model can also lack credibility in the eyes of some, especially among operators whose intuition or prior experience causes them to believe that the elements ignored by a model are in fact important.

Computer simulations are also plagued by a second serious shortcoming. As suggested by the previous discussion of tank gunnery, the performance of weapons can be seriously degraded by such factors as crew fatigue. The list of variables of aircraft and antisubmarine encounters contains such "human factors" as well, but in some models no such degradation factors are introduced. This is often the case because there are no quantitative data to suggest what those factors might be, with respect to different systems or under different operational conditions. For example, the recoil of a .30-caliber rifle is greater than that of a .22-caliber rifle, and the muzzle blast of the larger system will have a different distracting effect upon one's companion in a rifle squad than will the blast of smaller systems. But if data or knowledge about the impact of such degradation is not available, what is done? Either it can be ignored or a factor based on judgment may be used. But, then, *whose* judgment should be employed? This problem can be approached by voting or interview techniques.

There are also large uncertainties about the terminal effects and dispersion behavior of different types of ordnance under different terrain and vegetation conditions and as a function, in the case of air-delivered ordnance, of an aircraft's speed and glide angle at the time of release. These behavior characteristics are purely physical, and they can be addressed with straightforward methods, including experimentation. But surprisingly, there are large unknowns in this area, and estimates must be made by theoretical or *a priori* methods.

These kinds of deficiencies can be described as operational-data shortcomings, and they are to be sharply contrasted with the structural deficiencies that bedevil much of the model-building. Between the structural and operational-data deficiencies, many studies based on computer simulations become a shambles. The two types of deficiencies create an unfortunate situation, which detracts from the contribution that analysis and scientific endeavor can make to decision making. It is also a situation that few in the military-study community are happy about.

Computer simulations are merely replications of models, and models are nothing but theories.[4] There is nothing wrong with theory. But until a theory (or model) is verified by some independent process (field experimentation or an empirical evaluation relating it to past experience), it is *only* a theory and is thus subject to a higher court of empiricism, which is common sense. Military judgment is one variety of common sense. But the military has been denied the opportunity to make its requests in terms of judgment. Rather, it has been required to justify its requests for new systems, and in many cases the force-level elements, in terms of operational analysis and its related cost-effectiveness calculus. But military people have often found themselves playing a "heads you win, tails I lose" kind of game. When the computer simulation shows or suggests a highly favorable ratio of cost to effectiveness, analysts in a higher headquarters can easily dismiss the findings, either because the model was "unrealistic" or because there were serious operational-data deficiencies bearing upon operational constraints that could render the system less effective than the analysis "proved." An analyst who makes such a point—and it is fairly easy to do—obtains favorable recognition from his superior because he has "saved" money, or at least he has provided a rationale that enables his boss to refute a claim.

On the other hand, should an analysis show that the substitution of a less costly system for some elements of a more costly system might provide more capability for a given total cost (some A7's and some F111's and, hence, more total aircraft are more effective than all F111's for the same amount of money), analysts can urge a reduction in the total outlay on the ground that the same level of capability can be maintained. One also suspects that in such a case they do not examine the analysis (and the data deficiencies) with the same jaundiced eye as when the total cost of the advocated program is higher.

For these reasons, many military people bitterly came to feel that civilian judgment was substituted for military judgment, an opinion that is not without foundation: The cost-effectiveness game resembled the older budgetary game. The systems analysts could achieve exactly what the older-fashioned budgeteers did; only the dialogue was performed in a newer esoteric language. However, to the even greater chagrin of the military services, the Comptroller's Office of the Office of the Secretary of Defense also continued to play its old budgetary game.

Much military cost-effectiveness work has therefore taken on the form of advocacy proceedings. One uses a cost-effectiveness study to prove one's case. Analysts working in the Office of the Secretary of Defense use their talent to refute claims. The military services can be criticized for not conducting detached, scientific analytical work. The OSD analysts can be criticized for not vigorously addressing both methodological and data deficiencies that plague analytical endeavor. Moreover, their position in a higher headquarters, plus preaching about putting the decision-making process on a higher level, might suggest that they give particular attention to the quality of the analytical endeavor. For these reasons, incidentally, it is not true that "computers" took over the decision process, as some critics of Mr. McNamara have asserted or have seemed to suspect. Judgment was indeed still a very large part of the evaluation process, but it was no longer revealed as the explicit preference of the senior decision makers. Rather, the judgment and subjective factors are injected by way of assumptions concerning many variables for which there are no objective data and by the way the theoretical models are structured. Since many of the computer simulations are structured primarily to accommodate engineering or performance data, the technically superior (and more costly) system will invariably appear to be the more effective system. Hence, there was no rigorous check on the claims of technologists or the political efforts of military advocates who seek funds for new systems. Operational research, therefore, does not perform in the American decision-making process the hard-nosed evaluation function that it purportedly did for its British inventors. Rather, the American rendition has transformed it into a pseudoscientific activity that enriches the old-fashioned budgetary struggle.

The reasons for this unfortunate state are to be found in both the incentive within the existing system and the lack of independent testing and evaluation of the theories. The lack of independent testing is also responsible for the use of poor data as inputs for the models. In turn, there is little independent testing and data gathering, because of the incentive system.

Few analysts, civilian or military, are happy about the poor state of operational data and the structural deficiencies of the models that underlie most of the computer simulations. Two major approaches to improving the situation are generally advocated, focusing on the structural and operational-data problems. They are not mutually exclusive or even necessarily incompatible. But at their roots exists a basic philosophical difference.

The structuralists generally focus on the lack of "realism" in the models. If the ground-combat simulation model does not take account of trees or finer terrain gradations, the answer is to design finer-grained models. This quest for "realism" entails more intricate computer programs and will consume larger amounts of computer time (however, advances in computer technology are the technical solution to the latter problem). It is also likely that computer programmers, rather than analysts, would increasingly come to formulate the detailed structural aspects of the operations—the theory—as the computer program debugging problems become more severe with the finer-grained models. This focus on structural problems or the quest for realism in the computer simulations is essentially a rationalist approach to looking at the world and coping with reality. Theory and pure reason are the guiding and driving forces of the effort. It has great appeal for those mathematicians who think that pure reason, logic, and mathematics generate knowledge. This orientation appears to be the one that prevails in "operations research," as it is taught in universities (where, more accurately, it is applied mathematics), as generally practiced in the military community, and even as pursued by those who seek to sell their wares to business firms. One practitioner has characterized the emphasis on large-scale model-building as "Sonking," the acronym being derived from "*Scientification of Non-Knowledge*."[5]

The plea for more realism in computer simulations and mathematical models (or theories) misses the mark, and the quest for it leads to a blind alley. But more than that, the notion of a "realistic theory" is a contradiction. The purpose of theory is to distill from the mass of data that constitutes "reality" the facts and variables that are relevant. The criterion for evaluating theory is relevance, and the hallmark of relevance is predictive value. Without independently derived evidence to support the assertion that follows from theory, the most sophisticated theory (or model) will still be judged against common sense. Thus, there can be no end to the laments already voiced. The net result can only be that of creating computer simulations in which the quest for "realism" could encompass the most irrelevant factors, resulting in little or no useful knowledge for decision making. In rigorous scientific fields, testing and experimentation provide the evidence that refutes or verifies the assertions or predictions following from a theory or model. In operational research (of the older variety), it was the detailed probing of actual operations to obtain data for verifying and refuting hypotheses and to experiment by varying the aspects of the operations themselves. For the initial British success with radar, it was a field exercise that simulated operations.

Without independent tests—or good data treating the constraints that are often operative within the confusing complexities of operations—simulation of operations and associated paper studies have an *a priori* or synthetic quality. The data inputs for conceptual systems are mainly synthetic, deduced from engineering equations. Often, even the data for existing weapon behavior are deduced from engineering equations, with limited test firing under laboratory conditions providing a basis for estimating some of the coefficients used in the equations. Most of these performance measures are optimistic. Often they are misleading.

In studies that evaluate new or conceptual systems, the engineering performance characteristics are the principal numerical inputs. Since performance specifications are the only "numbers" available to the model-builders, the theory (or model) of the military operation must necessarily be structured to accommodate those numbers. The process of specifying and defining relevant operational criteria of combat effectiveness is done poorly. Thus, model-building is constrained to the world of military specifications and their associated technical "inputs." Yet a vital and necessary objective of studies and analysis should be to improve the process of specifying military characteristics and to determine whether the technically advanced system is worth its cost. There is an inherent fallacy in the approach that uses performance characteristics as inputs for a model or theory to evaluate a system, if there is no *independent* test or check of the theory. Even if someone should develop a good model, how would anyone know?

There is also a frustrating state of affairs caused by an unwillingness of anyone in the military study and evaluation system to take responsibility for the unsatisfactory results of the study system. The military commands and the contractors who produce the computer simulations will readily agree that the conclusions of a study are dubious, because the input data are inadequate; but they add that "it represents the best data available." The military-engineering test laboratories, which are the principal sources for most of the real numbers on weapons behavior, when confronted with the complaint that the studies are unsatisfactory because the data inputs may not be relevant, will acknowledge the point. But they disclaim responsibility by correctly pointing out that their data are generated for engineering design and test purposes, not for operational evaluation. The professional analysts are split. Those who have an empirical bent feel very uneasy, although they continue to take their salary checks, rationalizing their behavior by correctly pointing out that they cannot get data in the field unless the military participates in the endeavor, because the military controls the resources that must be employed to generate the data. An empirically oriented analyst can also in good conscience maintain that his awareness of the data shortcomings can enable him to point out more clearly the limits of a study. Analysts who accept the ancient idea that the exercise of pure reason generates knowledge have no problems, although some may grant that better data would do no harm.

But even though there is a great deal of muttering, overall, about the sad state of the military study and intellectual effort, the buck can be passed conveniently. It will continue to be passed until fundamental changes are made in organizational arrangements, roles and missions, and attitudes of the principals involved. One change that must be made is to do more operational testing and improve its quality. That will be the subject of the next three chapters.

11

OPERATIONAL TESTING AND EVALUATION

> The calling seemed to interest him and, as he said in
> later years, he "was not so young as not to know that
> since I had undertaken a profession I had better try to
> understand it." His curiosity . . . began to move; and
> in a laudible pursuit of knowledge he had a Highland
> private weighed in full marching-order.
>
> Philip Guedalla, *Wellington*, p. 27.

Very little operational testing is done by the military services; and what little *is* done is often poorly conceived or structured, poorly managed, and subject to political pressures that degrade the objectivity of the testing or cause it to avoid addressing critical questions directly. This dismal situation results in inadequate operational data for analytical models and computer simulations, and there is no way of checking the hypotheses that follow from many models by an independent test. There is no way of checking the assertions of individuals who advocate particular systems or specific technical approaches in the design of systems. Nor is there any assurance that the doctrine and rules of decision embodied in field manuals and troop or crew training are those that will provide the best use of systems in combat.

Because of this lack of operational testing, the major inputs to the military decision-making process by the intellectual and scientific communities are made through the *a priori* method described in the previous chapter. The principal data inputs are those treating technical performance, and much of these data are derived by *a priori* methods. Because there is no vigorous effort to understand how systems perform in an operational context, great expense can be incurred in endowing systems with performance qualities that may have little operational worth. A lack of operational testing also means that there is no assurance of our knowing how to use existing systems most

202

effectively. In this case, and in time of war, the nation incurs a cost of having to overcome a loss of effectiveness by expending more resources. Hence, the country pays a twofold price for poor testing and evaluation of its military systems: First, it has no way of controlling the military application of technological improvement to new weapons. And second, it foregoes obtaining knowledge that would improve the effectiveness of existing systems. To develop these assertions and their implications is the object of this chapter.

Evaluation and testing fall short in three critical respects: (1) Failure to test theoretical models empirically; (2) failure to obtain adequate data on critical operational factors; (3) failure to test doctrine (and its associated troop and crew training) under which weapon systems are to be employed; and (4) failure to determine the best mix of weapons.

1. *The Testing of Models.* This requirement is most demanding, and yet model testing is the hallmark of the scientific method; that is, one conceives a theory and a model for that theory, and certain hypotheses follow from the theory in the form of quantitative statements that are susceptible to measurement. Next, an experiment is conducted to verify or refute the theoretical findings. The experiment must be conducted and reported in such a way that others may be able to repeat the experiment. In the physical sciences, a laboratory test or systematic observations (often facilitated by instruments that are specially designed to measure the phenomena suggested by the theory) of natural phenomena constitute the testing. In the social sciences, statistical methods in application to demographic, economic, and other social data are employed.

To test theoretical models of war by such empirical methods is difficult. Indeed, it is unthinkable in the case of strategic nuclear war or even nonstrategic war involving nuclear weapons. There has been no human experience with mass nuclear phenomena. Recognition of this point merely means that the modeling ensures that in some way there is internal consistency, given the inputs governing the behavior of the different systems and assumptions made about the reactions of Blue and Red to each other's behavior. Such models are useful for force planning, since they can expose major inconsistencies and the implications of many assumptions. But, as with any application of the method of pure reason, such models can be "wrong" in a very critical way. Although they are effective tools for exposing the effects of many small errors, they can lead to monumental mistakes, particularly when a subject such as strategic nuclear war is being analyzed. However, as long as the effectiveness criteria in strategic war models are casualties and heavy property damage, which is a simple concept but which is hoped will achieve deterrence, the worth of the modeling may be preserved by the power of the weapons themselves. It is only when people start thinking of more subtle variations of strategic war, involving damage limitation and counterforce, that the fascination with an *a priori* method might give some reason for concern.

Recognition of the difficulties of testing combat models in a rigorous and independent way suggests that when one turns from strategic weapons to land and tactical air forces, it might be advisable to scale down the scope of the model-building itself. The treatment of land and tactical air operations is not susceptible to large-scale, fine-grained, computer simulations. For aggregations of such forces, no single system or small group of systems dominate the large-system performance, since the constituent parts of suborganizations are highly interdependent. The performance of equipment (and in turn, the impact of technology) is especially sensitive to the limitations and strength of men—particularly large numbers of men—and the organizing capacity of planners and decision makers that permits the development of new tactics.

Model-building for large, complex ground-force systems is questionable on further methodological grounds. Ground forces are composed of highly interdependent subsystems, and they are highly organized. A mathematical characteristic of very highly interdependent systems is that there is *a priori* no distinction between independent and dependent variables. Yet decision making (and the concept of causation) implies that there are independent variables that, when manipulated, will produce the desired effects on dependent variables. The analytical task becomes one of identifying self-contained subsets of relationships that can be treated independently of the larger interdependent system. If in fact there is some degree of sparseness in the interdependence of elements composing the larger system, it is possible to identify meaningful cause-and-effect relationships.[1] Thus, for example, the effectiveness of armor is critically dependent upon infantry, if only to protect the tanks from enemy infantry employing shaped or plastic charges or gasoline-filled pop bottles. In turn, the effectiveness of infantry depends critically on the quality of its small arms. Thus, the effectiveness of tanks may also depend on the effectiveness of small arms. However, it does not follow that a model (and an experiment) that simultaneously treats small arms and tanks must be developed. Tanks and small arms can be evaluated separately. Moreover, unambiguous and economical field experimentation designed to test the models will likely require that they be treated separately.

This point is recognized, of course, in much current model-building that does isolate major systems for analytical scrutiny —for example, tank versus tank or antitank. However, the two-sided quality of such simulations and the focus on kill ratios serve to couch the model in terms of a combined-arms operation. Other important contributing combined-arms elements are either ignored or aggregated, and the effectiveness criteria as expressed in terms of kill ratios cannot themselves be directly verified or measured by independent tests. Such efforts are thus poor forms of "partial-equilibrium" analysis. They may have a facade of generality (or "realism"), but they are incapable of being subjected to the gamut of scientific rigor, including independent tests.

What is the alternative? The answer lies in taking seriously the idea that ground forces are combined-arms organizations and taking intellectual advantage of that fact. Moreover, it is vital to recognize the additional fact that a man's performance dominates the performance of equipment rather than the other way around. These two facts lend themselves to the notion that purposeful, controlled-field experimentation provides a means of evaluating systems one at a time. Such experimentation is also similar to experimentation designed to measure critical variables.

2. *Obtaining Better Data on Critical Operational Factors.* In the analysis of many critical force-structure issues, and in the effort to analyze what the performance characteristics of new systems should be, it often becomes apparent that great uncertainty exists concerning the critical variables. Indeed, there is controversy about which variables are the critical ones. These are interrelated issues that can rapidly become political.

One of the principal contributions that model-building and simulation of combat can make to decision making is that they can provide a "sensitivity analysis." For example, if it is known that strategic targets cannot actually be located within an average of two miles because of imprecise data concerning target coordinates, there is a highly limited payoff in designing missiles with an accuracy of less than two miles. More precise target location should proceed, at least simultaneously, with attempts to develop more accurate missiles (or perhaps manned bombers do have a place in the force?). Such an example may strike one as being obvious common sense—and it is. But there are many more subtle interactions, many of which may be unknown, that are not systematically developed, let alone measured. Building a model is a way of discovering how important some of the variables are or how "sensitive" the system performance may be to certain unknown variables. But after many combat models are designed, the analytical use to which they are put reveals that the outcomes are highly sensitive to factors about which empirical evidence is lacking over a wide range. To narrow the bands of uncertainty with regard to such critical determinants of operational effectiveness requires a purposeful experimental and measurement process.

As another example, it is costly to endow a new tank with a lower silhouette (by means of a three-man crew, an automatic loader, and a complicated suspension system) or to increase its rate of acceleration. Intuitively, these features would seem to improve its survivability. But by just how much these more demanding performance characteristics might actually do so is uncertain. Estimates that have been made were derived from computer simulations like those described in the previous chapter. Similarly, it may be desirable to stabilize a tank's main armament system so that it can fire while the tank is moving (currently, the British Centurion tank has such a stabilized system, whereas the U.S. M60 does not). But this, too, is costly, and its combat worth is unknown. These kinds of questions can be tested systematically and rigorously under conditions that realistically correspond to actual operational conditions.

Similar uncertainties center around the performance of countless other systems in an operational environment. This is particularly true with regard to tactical air and antiaircraft systems, including air-defense acquisition and range-estimating radars at low altitude. In the same fashion, the ability of low-flying aircraft to avoid detection by air-defense systems, including the optimum tactics for achieving the avoidance, is a further unknown, the resolution of which could have important implications for aircraft-design objectives. Nor is much known about the details of how pilots identify and find targets, particularly in the performance of a close air-support role, and hitting those targets when they are identified. This phase of operations is importantly affected by the tactics pilots employ to avoid being acquired and hit by opposing air-defense weapons.

There is often a need for better, well-founded empirical estimates of critical variables that might be viewed as being highly technical. It is desirable, if not necessary, that the numbers employed in strategic war models for reliability and accuracy should have some resemblance to the likely performance of those weapons in silos or submarines. Frequently it is found that there are large uncertainties concerning the terminal effects of various kinds of conventional ordnance and the ways in which those effects may vary because of terrain, the angle and speed of delivery, and other influences.

3. *Testing of Doctrine.* Current U.S. Army infantry machinegun doctrine suggests that gunners fire 8- or 9-round bursts. For tank-mounted coaxial 7.62-mm. or .30-caliber machineguns in an anti-infantry role, a 25- to 30-round burst is recommended. The empirical basis for such a doctrine is unknown or unclear, or perhaps nonexistent.

In the case of infantry machinegun tactics, it is likely that the 8- or 9-round-burst figure has its origin in World War I machinegun tactics, when a heavy, tripod-mounted machine gun was the standard weapon and when it was fashionable to use machineguns for long range (1000 yards or so) grazing and plunging fire. The current standard machinegun, however, is a light weapon that can be fired in either a tripod or bipod mode. The 8- or 9-round burst may be appropriate in the tripod mode in certain tactical situations. But an 8-round burst in bipod mode may be poor firing doctrine, given the gun's recoil and the lack of stability. Issues like these are wide open, however, since no systematic testing against a variety of target systems has been undertaken.

What limited field testing has been done (directed to different questions) suggests that the current doctrine in this area is very deficient. One suspects that the doctrine governing the use of vehicle-mounted weapons (including those mounted on helicopters) is also deficient. One compensating feature is that troops in the field often evolve their own practices, which may be more appropriate to tactical conditions. However, there is no way of knowing whether these *ad hoc* tactics themselves are optimal. Because of the lack of adequate operational testing, there is no way of knowing whether or not maximum effectiveness is obtained from existing systems or troops receive the best possible training in their use.

4. *Mixes of Weapons.* In U.S. infantry squads (both Army and Marine Corps) there is a mixture of riflemen and grenadiers. Grenadiers employ an M79 launcher, a short-barreled weapon that fires at low velocity a 40-mm. fragmenting grenade that weighs 8 ounces. The launcher is a single-shot weapon with a maximum range of about 400 meters. In the 10-man Army infantry squad there are two grenadiers—20 per cent of the unit's strength. In the 14-man Marine Corps squad there is one grenadier—slightly more than 7 per cent of squad strength.

There is no necessary reason, of course, why both the Marines and the Army should have identical proportions of identical weapons in their organizations. They specialize in somewhat different missions, and they also have different mixes of support weapons at the platoon, company, and battalion levels. Yet the factor of 3 difference by which the "staple" of an army and of a marine corps is armed is striking. However, it should not be surprising, in view of the fact that such weapon-mix decisions are generally based on judgment and intuition.

The question concerning the mix of grenadier and rifleman, however, merges into another set of questions related to technical developments. With the advent of modern grenades during World War I, attachments were developed for launching grenades from rifles. However, rifle-launched grenades posed difficulties. They were heavy, weighing one and a half pounds. A launching device had to be affixed to the rifle's muzzle, and soldiers would often misplace or lose the device. There was a loss of flexibility because of the fixing and removal of the devices. The launching of heavy grenades from rifles also developed heavy chamber pressures and frequently broke the rifle stock when the butt was placed against the ground to achieve high-trajectory fire. Rifles for grenade launching therefore had to be ruggedly built.

In recent years, advances in grenade technology, as illustrated by the 40-mm. grenade, have permitted the use of lighter grenades. In its M14 rifle development, however, the U.S. Army sought to reduce the weapon's weight by finer machining and by thinning out certain parts of the weapon; and so the idea of using the rifle as a grenade launcher was not pursued, despite the availability of lighter grenades. Instead, grenade launching came to be focused on the development of the M79 system. Thus, riflemen and grenadiers came to be specialists as a result of development decisions, not because of decisions based on operational effectiveness.

Lightweight-grenade technology makes feasible a grenade that can be launched easily from the muzzle of a rifle, with the rifle's flash hider functioning as a grenade launcher, as on the M16 and Stoner rifles. Grenades can thus be launched without the aid of the old-fashioned attachments. Technically, it is therefore possible for all men in the rifle squad to be both riflemen and grenadiers, making possible a wide mix of bullet and grenade fire, as warranted by a given tactical situation. But what the mixes and firing doctrines should be has not yet been addressed.

It is possible to go through the entire organizational structure and equipage of Army and Marine Corps infantry units, including the battalion, to determine the best mix of equipment and how to employ it most effectively. It may be that the existing mixes and doctrines are optimal. But if so, no one *knows* that it is, and it results purely from chance. On the other hand, it is plausible that the combat effectiveness of the U.S. infantry might be improved substantially merely by using different mixes of equipment and more effective doctrines.

Ample precedents exist for the operational testing of military systems. The Romans drew upon findings from gladiator contests to develop tactics and select weapons for its legions.[2] Maneuvers and field exercises have been used to test new organizational concepts and doctrine. Significant occasions of such practices were the U.S. Army field exercises of 1937 and 1939, from which the triangular-army-division concept was evolved,[3] and the 1939 maneuvers also provided important knowledge for air-ground relationships.[4] During the 1920's and early 1930's, the British operated an Experimental Tank Brigade, the intellectual harvest of which appears to have been reaped mainly by the Germans. There have also been dramatic "one-shot" experiments, like General Mitchell's bombing and sinking of the *Ostfriesland* in Chesapeake Bay. Some years later it was demonstrated that an Air Corps navigator could locate ships at sea when a B-17 intercepted the Italian liner *Rex.* After the acquisition of the carriers *Lexington* and *Saratoga*, U.S. Naval aviators participating in regular exercises during the late 1920's and 1930's developed many of the tactics and doctrine that served the nation so well during World War II.[5]

Maneuvers and exercises are often useful in demonstrating the administrative feasibility of new organizations. They can surface possible logistic constraints that might afflict new organizational concepts or new types of equipment. However, they do hold serious disadvantages for testing and evaluation. For one thing, commanders in maneuvers are primarily interested in the training of troops and, especially, of staff, and they regard with dismay any attempt to restructure an exercise so as to test a particular idea. A more serious disadvantage of using maneuvers as a laboratory is common to the "one-shot" demonstrations like those the Air Corps conducted in the prewar period: only one sample point is provided. Such single events, particularly when they are part of a highly complex activity like a maneuver or major exercise, can be interpreted in many ways. For example, in 1936 at Fort Benning, truck-mounted infantry and horse-mounted cavalry commenced an exercise. The trucks permitted the infantry to get into a position from which they laid an "ambush." As the cavalry troopers entered the objective area, camouflaged soldiers rose from their positions, shouting and waving bed sheets. The effect on the horses was dramatic. Because of the experiment, the infantrymen were convinced that trucks enabled them to outmaneuver cavalry, while the outraged horsemen concluded that the infantrymen were practical jokers.[6]

The principal shortcoming of maneuvers or similar "two-sided" field exercises as devices for conducting operational tests is that they seldom provide numerical data that are usable for operational evaluation or for estimating weapon effectiveness. Most of the information is gathered from the reports of referees and headquarters' staff observers, who wander among the maneuvering elements and register their impressions on forms attached to clipboards. Such evaluations have all the characteristics of a tribal ritual, and as such, they serve the function of sprinkling holy water on a new organizational proposal or principle that is favored at the higher levels of the hierarchy.

Operational testing requires the measurement and replication of activities or scenarios. Both are necessary to provide knowledge that minimizes the role of impressionism. Such knowledge is quantitative, and it measures the physical behavior of systems in an operational context. This emphasis on measurement also suggests the need for appropriate instrumentation. The replication of a part of a system's behavior is necessary for minimizing the possible error that is inherent in the "one-shot" experiment, wherein chance can play an inordinate role in affecting the observed outcome. In addition, operational testing must be carefully designed and controlled, so that measures of critical variables can be taken. This description of operational testing entails several important considerations.

Operational testing is not engineering testing, nor is it testing to determine whether the requirements of physical performance and characteristics are met. Consequently, the engineering laboratory or the proving ground are not suitable environments in which to conduct operational testing. But neither are operational tests substitutes for engineering tests, which must perform a special function that is vital to conducting the technical research and development process and which are also necessary for production quality control.

Operational tests can generally be broken down into two major types: (1) those that take a specific operation and measure system performance directly in terms of criteria that are judged to be either the effectiveness criteria or a good proxy for effectiveness, or both; and (2) those designed to measure variables, the behaviors of which are critical to a system's operational performance.

Live-fire tests are examples of the kind of test that focuses directly on an operation in its entirety. It is possible to construct a target system, for example, composed of elements that can be made to behave like the targets encountered in actual combat, such as infantry or ground vehicles. By means of instrumentation, a given scenario can be replicated. An experimental matrix, balanced with regard to the time of day, troop proficiency, and other factors can be "played" against such a target system by actually using groups of friendly firers, such as an infantry squad or tank section, to fire at the system. Hits and near misses can be recorded in real time (the latter by the use of acoustic or camouflaged panel sensors). Thus, it is possible to compare an M16 rifle with an M14 or AK47 rifle, for example, or rifles with machineguns, under conditions that more closely resemble combat than do the Olympic-style target-shooting matches.

Similarly, such live-fire tests can be made against vehicle targets by crew-served antitank and antiaircraft weapons to test for the effectiveness of changes in such design characteristics as speed and silhouette of vehicles, as well as the effectiveness of the weapons and alternative firing doctrines. Performance in other operations can also be measured. For example, search patterns employed by small patrols under darkness might be tracked, to determine how the patrols can detect targets or how they themselves might be detected. The processing and filtering of information from modern sensors like side-looking airborne radars (SLARS) by headquarters staff personnel can be an object of experimentation, to determine whether or not the information can be employed and, if so, how.

Tests that focus on critical variables are undertaken either because it is impossible (or highly impractical) to treat an operation as a whole or because it may be undesirable to do so. For example, with aircraft and antiaircraft systems, actual combat engagements are out of the question in peacetime. Moreover, actual combat operations are generally so confusing that, literally, there may be too much to measure. Even the conduct of wartime operational research focuses on attempting to measure, at most, only a few variables that prior analysis suggests to be critical. For this reason, purposeful field testing can in some cases be an even better "laboratory" than actual warfare.

For example, in the study of antiaircraft systems, the elements of behavior can be broken down into two major parts. First is the ability of a weapon's sensing system (men or radar, or a combination of both) to detect, acquire, and track hostile aircraft. There is also an identification problem, if one operates a friendly air force. Upon completion of these tasks and the order to fire, there is the question of hitting the target, which involves another complex set of interactions. In the case of air defense, not only is it impractical to try to shoot down friendly aircraft, it probably would also be undesirable to do so even if it were "practical." The two sets of operations, or the two equipment subsystems—the detection, acquisition, and tracking and the firing—each warrant operational evaluation and a system design based on careful evaluation.

Thus, for many purposes, the most useful operational testing involves isolating critical suboperations of complex tasks. The measurements derived therefrom can then be used as inputs to computer simulations and combined with relevant technical performance data.

Operational testing, as an experimental process, requires interdependent and simultaneous consideration of a model or theory and of instrumentation, as well as the specification of effectiveness criteria or of the critical variables to be measured.

Instrumentation, including target systems, is a key element. Modern technology provides much scope for imaginative development of instrumentation systems adaptable to conducting field experiments. For live-fire experiments, it is possible to construct target systems that not only record hits in real time but also miss distances, which provide indications of fire distribution. Target behavior can be controlled, and thus replicated, and event behavior can be recorded in real time. Most progress in this area has been made with infantry targets. Little has been done to design and develop vehicular targets, despite the large amounts that have been spent on ground-combat vehicles and systems to defeat such vehicles.

Aircraft drones have been developed to facilitate the firing of guns and, especially, missiles for training purposes. Unfortunately, the available target drones behave like friendly airliners, and thousands of air-defense missiles have been fired at them. Such firings serve to verify empirically the hit probabilities that missile manufacturers promise the government, to impress VIP's (including visiting science boards) who visit places like Fort Bliss or who are guests at fleet exercises, and to buttress the morale of the troops manning the missile systems. But attacking and penetrating aircraft do not behave like friendly airliners. Little effort has been expended in trying to develop drones that can maneuver evasively.

For many kinds of experiments, the instrumentation for position location and event recording is critical. Several approaches, some of which draw upon aircraft navigation systems, are employed and are capable of further development. But generally, the instrumentation must be configured, adapted, and in some cases specifically designed for the needs of a particular experiment. This is also fairly standard practice for experimentation applied to basic research in the physical sciences. A very important implication of this point is that instrumentation engineers must be part of the team that designs the experiment. The analytical members of the team, for their part, must formulate the model that identifies the critical variables to be measured. Such model formulation, of course, need not be a *de novo* development of a theory. It can be an adaptation of someone else's theoretical findings. But the model employed by the operational-analysis team must be tailored to the capability of its instrumentation systems. The instrumentation systems, in turn, must be calibrated or attuned, with respect to accuracy, to the critical questions of the experiment. For example, it makes little sense to try to achieve a resolution of six inches in miss-distance measurements if the critical operational questions revolve around a less refined estimate of, say, two or three feet. The error tolerances in instrumentation will also constitute an important determinant of the number of replications required for an experiment. The mathematicians and statisticians who lay out the experimentation matrix must therefore be able to communicate and work with the instrumentation engineers and vice versa. Analysts identifying and specifying effectiveness criteria or variables to be measured must also be cognizant of instrumentation capability. It is of little use to say that a certain variable is critical and should be measured, if in fact it is technically unfeasible to make the measurement.

Thus, modeling, instrumentation, and measurement must be treated simultaneously and must be mutually adapted to each other in the design of an operational experiment. A recognition of this point could meet the objection that experimentation is "antitheoretical" or that the advocacy of operational testing implies a rejection of prior analysis. Good experimentation requires good theory or a good model. Without these ingredients, experimentation is pointless measurement or random data-grubbing. On the other hand, model-building and theory without good data and testing are empty endeavors. Disguised versions of the age-old philosophical issue regarding the roles of pure reason as opposed to practical reason, or of deduction as opposed to induction, as analytical methods need not be an overwhelming consideration bearing upon military research.

Analysts, mathematical statisticians, and instrumentation engineers must work as a team in conducting operational experiments. Military officers must also be part of the team, since operational testing focuses on system behavior in an operational context. Military professionals usually possess the best understanding of what is tactically relevant, and thus their knowledge is essential in placing the experiment in the proper operational context. Moreover, they possess a knowledge about terrain and operational procedure that most civilian analysts lack. The effort must therefore be a joint scientific-military one. Such was also the characteristic of the pioneering World War II operational research. But putting together such teams, with their diversified mixture of technical, analytical, and operational skills, is difficult. The actual conduct of operational experimentation is stressful and exasperating, even under ideal circumstances. Attention therefore must be given to the character of the military-testing process, and the broader institutional environment in which it currently functions.

12
ORGANIZING THE TACTICAL TEST

> The Minuteman may be a thing of beauty and a bull's-eye forever at Vandenberg, but back in North Dakota it acts more like a reluctant dragon that refuses to come out of its hole.
>
> Richard Pollack, "Missileland," *Harper's,* October 1969, p. 86.

Military testing and evaluation necessarily take place in an organizational setting, and the various military services and departments possess markedly different and changing formal organizational structures, which reflect their different missions and past histories. Testing, evaluation, weapon development, and related decision making, in turn, impact upon tactical and doctrinal matters, and vice versa. It is useful to relate these characteristics.

Chart 12.1 is a diagram of a hypothetical organization, show-

Chart 12.1

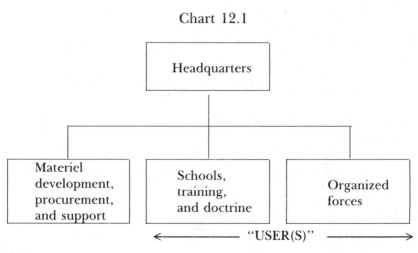

ing the major functional activities of a military service that impact upon weapon and force structure decision-making. The depicted organizational structure is hypothetical in that it is not representative of any of the three services in all its particulars. However, it does seek to identify the principal kinds of suborganizations around whose interests the testing, evaluation, and doctrine-formulation endeavors revolve.

Materiel development, procurement, and logistic support are performed by organizations like the Air Force's and Navy's Systems Commands and the Army's Materiel Command, some of which retain vestiges of the older technical services and bureaus. These organizations operate the technical laboratories, supply depots, arsenals, and shipyards, and they interact with industry in the private sector. They constitute the "producer" side of the weapon's development and procurement process.

The box labeled "organized forces" also describes the "user." For the Navy, it is the "Fleet" or identified fleet organizations, such as the Pacific and Atlantic Fleets. In the Air Force the users' community consists of the functional commands, such as SAC, TAC, and so forth. Such elements, in turn, are under the operational control of joint commanders for military operations.

The school and training systems are also shown in Chart 12.1 for completeness and to illustrate some differences between land forces and other forces. With armies, the "school system" has always figured importantly in the critical aspects of higher-level decision making. It is here that one can identify the subcommunities of infantry, artillery, armor, and so forth, which, in their specialized schools, train and qualify both enlisted men and officers. The school system also contains the command and staff college, which trains people to handle the subgroups that possess diverse skills. Army forces, in turn, are organized in combinations of the specialists and special equipment, in the form of battalions, divisions, and other units. Because armies do consist of such "combined arms and service" aggregations, there is nothing in their makeup that is comparable to the Air Force's functional commands, like SAC or TAC. Hence, the elements of the school system that specialize in infantry and so forth play a critical role in doctrine and the use of weapons. Such schools or service "centers" have traditionally exerted an important, if not key, role in representing the "user." But this role has often been a source of difficulty.

In the Air Force and Navy, however, the functional commands or specialties that compose the fleet (for example, destroyers, aircraft, and submarines) play a prime role, in both doctrine and training that is directly related to the performance of their functional missions. Thus, although there is an Air Force Training Command, which produces pilots and navigators, it is the SAC that controls and specifies the training of air crews that will man the SAC bombers and tankers. The two Navy fleets contain training components and facilities that train and certify crews for performing their respective special operations in the context of the fleet. These training elements also possess "development groups," whose functions are to address questions of tactics and doctrine and express the views of the user on matters of new equipment design.

The principal difficulty identified with the school and training system of the Army—with its traditional "centers," like Fort Benning for infantry, Fort Sill for artillery, and so forth—being the fountain of doctrine and user interest for the specialized arms and services was that it tended to be too tradition-oriented and conservative. Training, especially of officers, requires imparting the traditions of the particular service in which they are trained, among other things. Instructors are well advised not to be skeptical of either tactics or the equipment that the students will use in the field. War requires that people make the best use of whatever is at hand; but it also requires that tactical procedures and practices be standardized, for the essential reason that standardization preserves the organizational integrity of combat units, even when its members are subjected to fatigue, stress, and the shock of battle. Furthermore, a unit commander should have some idea of what the commanders of units on his flanks may do when he and they jointly confront the enemy under conditions where communication among them is difficult, if not impossible, and this is another reason for standardization.

Thus, indoctrination is a proper and necessary part of military training for combat operations; and indoctrination cannot easily be performed by skeptics. The instructors, at least while instructing, must comport themselves in such a way as to ensure that, from the Army's viewpoint, what they teach is the best doctrine, which means they must teach that the Sheridan/Shillelagh system—or whatever system may be issued to the troops—is the best weapon that the best talents of the Army and the country can provide. In the process, if they happen to be teaching the infantry, for example, they must teach that, while the artillerymen and tankers may be good fellows, they are not of quite the same stuff that infantrymen are—and so, too, with teachers in the other service specialties.

This sort of indoctrination is not unique to the Army, although it is probably more intense than in the other services. Nevertheless, it is carried out in all the services. A notable example in Air Force experience involved the Martin B-26 medium bomber in World War II. Although that airplane was not quite a lemon, it certainly would not have come out on top in any cost-effectiveness analysis. It was costly, compared to the B-25 medium bomber, and it was tricky to fly—many crews died while training with it. But Air Force commanders nurtured the idea that crews of that aircraft had to have special qualities. This psychology worked to such a degree that, after some fitful starts by the first units deployed in North Africa, the B-26 units turned in the most consistently accurate bombing record of any of the units later employed in Europe.

So it can be seen that critical thoughts about tactics, organization, and equipment are not likely to flow freely in a military school system, particularly in one that is organized around a specialized branch or service structure. Nor, for that matter, is the "user" community of any military service likely to be composed of free thinkers in any great number. Herein lies one reason why the military services (or at least, important elements of them) are conservative—a point that is frequently observed, although not fully appreciated by civilian students of bureaucracy—that at least some aspects of "conservatism" are very necessary if there is to be any kind of military organization at all. That military organizations do progress is an indication of a sophistication perhaps matching that of, say, the academic community.

For these reasons the Army, in a major reorganization in 1962, set up its Combat Developments Command on a par with the Army Materiel and Continental Army Commands. The latter formerly performed the "combat developments" function as a part of its school and training system, while the Army Materiel Command, created in the same 1962 reorganization, swept together the older "Technical Services" (the Engineer Corps being a major exception).

The major function of the Combat Developments Command was to formulate concepts for the future Army. In this capacity, it also exerted primacy in initiating and specifying the requirements for new equipment. Theoretically it was free of the conservatism of the "school system." It represented the "user" and could deal at "arm's length" with the "producer," the Army Materiel Command, organizationally speaking.

These points should serve to emphasize the difficulty of clearly identifying the military user in ways that facilitate forward-looking and critical operational evaluation. Probably the only firm statement that can be made regarding the military-user concept is that it does *not* comprise the development, technical, procurement, and support elements of the military community. It is also important to recognize that the user community has responsibilities and problems other than the conduct of critical operational evaluation to absorb its energy. Training, which includes maneuvers and exercises, is demanding. The maintenance of unit and organizational readiness, which necessitates that the attention be given to countless details of materiel and personnel, is another major absorber of energy and talent. Currently, in the U.S. military establishment, each field unit is attached to a specific commander whose major responsibility is to develop and implement contingency plans. These requirements are most demanding on organizations like SAC. Overseas units and commanders are also confronted by problems that are unique to the local setting (for example, border patrolling and skirmishes in Korea) and by the demands of functioning in countries that have vibrant domestic activity and their own military organizations (for example, West Germany). For all of these reasons, operational testing and evaluation entails the expenditures of scarce currency of different kinds.

Finally, and of critical importance, elements of the user community may be parochial and unduly conservative in their views. In some matters in a given functional area, the user community as a whole may be temperamentally incapable of objective evaluation. For example, neither the Air Force's Tactical Air Command nor the Army's new air force—composed mainly of helicopters, many of which perform a "gunship" mission—can be expected to approach in a detached way the many thorny questions regarding the nature of close air-support, the kind of equipment that should be designed to perform the close air-support mission, and the command relations that should be established to govern its use. If operational testing is to be done, careful attention must be given to how it should be organized and to assurances that it is rigorously and honestly conducted.

It was stated earlier in this text that the military services do little operational testing and that even that little suffers from a variety of difficulties. Yet the military services do a great deal of testing and similar physical activity, such as engineering and acceptability testing, that assume a quasi-operational quality. It is from those activities that much of the real data employed in analytical and staff studies come. There is thus a testing tradition of sorts, as well as varied experiences, that are unique to each service. The purpose of this section is to describe the main features of each system.

The Air Force has perhaps the simplest approach to testing, although it is the most difficult to implement because of the complicated systems the Air Force develops. Three formal categories of testing make up its process. Categories I and II relate to materials, components, subsystems, and early prototypes. These tests are part of the R&D process, and they are under the control of the Air Force Systems Command, administered by the System Program Director, and conducted both in the Command's laboratories and at contractors' facilities. The tests are also monitored by other agencies, including the user who will eventually operate the equipment.

Category III tests are conducted by the operational command, and they involve complete weapon systems that are newly off the production line. These essentially are system checkouts. They provide the operating command with some information on what it must do to achieve its initial operating capability with the new system, usually specified by a date and a programmed deployment. Often the Category III tests reveal that expensive retrofits must be made on initial production units and that modifications in the remaining production is necessary. Occasionally, an initial operating capability date is slipped, which of course entails numerous reprogramming actions throughout the system—for example, crew training, phase-out of old systems, and so forth. Seldom, however, is system procurement terminated as a result of Category III tests, because by the time they are completed procurement decisions have already been made, production is underway, and contracts and subcontracts for long-lead-time items have been let. Also, payrolls in many parts of the country are already being sustained, and Air Force operating units have commenced receiving the new equipment. As a result, in the cases of many systems, the commanders and personnel of the first units implementing the "phase-in" must struggle to learn how to operate and maintain the new system so as to be in a posture to satisfy a state of operational readiness dictated by contingency plans or mission assignments.

Since the Air Force's Category III tests relate to the phasing of new systems into operating commands, the testing process is relatively unstructured and of an ad hoc nature. Moreover, this testing is performed by each of the separate operating commands, according to which command is to operate the new system. For these reasons, strong tradition for operational testing or a strong body of expertise in operational test design, evaluation, and instrumentation has not emerged. Whatever instrumentation capability the Air Force has acquired for the operational evaluation of aircraft and related systems has been the responsibility of the Systems Command for the Air Force Weapons Evaluation Testing System, located at Eglin Field. And there appears to be no strong user input into the design of this instrumentation system.[1]

As for the Navy, the equivalents of the Air Force Category III tests for addressing operational suitability are conducted by two major instruments that report directly to the Chief of Naval Operations. For aircraft, a Board of Inspection and Survey has been established, and this is composed of officers from the development and operating agencies. Its task is to evaluate aircraft, their support systems, and the compatibility that exists between the aircraft and their weapons, so as to determine their acceptability for fleet use. The tests are extensive, rigorous, and objective. That they should be follows from the fact that the operation of aircraft on carriers is a very demanding undertaking, even in peacetime. The Board of Inspection and Survey also evaluates ships or, more specifically, the shipboard equipment other than weapons, to determine whether the equipment functions satisfactorily. In this, its evaluations appear to be based mainly on the results of contractors' demonstrations.

The Navy's other instrument for addressing operational suitability—its principal operational testing agency—is an organization called Operational Test and Evaluation Force (OPTEVFOR). The charter of this group directs it to conduct technical evaluations (including those needed to assist the developers) and operational evaluations, including "the determination and promulgation of such tactics as are naturally incident to the conduct of the investigation,"[2] and to conduct fleet research investigations, which focus on "natural or special phenomena in an operational environment."[3]

This Force consists of a headquarters staff and working detachments located at various shore facilities and specializing in particular functional areas—for example, submarines at New London and surface antisubmarine forces at Key West. The Commander of the Force and his staff are located in the headquarters of the Atlantic Fleet, and he reports to the Chief of Naval Operations through the Fleet Commander. The Deputy Commander of the Force is located with the Pacific Fleet at San Diego. Evaluation tasks are assigned by the Chief of Naval Operations, whose Operations staff section evaluates various requests in their relationships to the Force's capability. Requests for evaluations come from both the developers and users. A decision to undertake any evaluation also entails the assignment of fleet resources, particularly ships and aircraft, to the endeavor, as well as charging the relevant Systems Command with the responsibility for providing certain forms of technical support, including instrumentation.

The Operational Test and Evaluation Force, because its reports go to the Chief of Naval Operations, is in a position to conduct objective tests without institutional pressure from the developer or the user. Its specialized Evaluation Detachments enjoy opportunities of having officers assigned to them for three-year tours, many of these officers having advanced degrees in fields such as operational research. The Operational Test and Evaluation Force, although representing the user, does not play any role in writing the specific operational requirements for systems. That task is done in the headquarters. A question can be raised whether an organization whose business is testing the operational worth of systems might not have something worthwhile to contribute by way of recommendations affecting the technical performance requirements of new systems. Nevertheless the reports that arrive in the CNO's office should therefore be unbiased and detached. How seriously the reports are studied is another matter affected by higher-level considerations.

One disadvantage that may adversely affect the operations of the Evaluation Force is its dependence on the Fleet for experimental assets and, more importantly, its dependence on the Systems Command for technical assistance, particularly instrumentation. But to draw upon the Fleet for ships and aircraft is economical, and it should not pose problems if the CNO makes clear that such assignments are intended to support the evaluation process.

Instrumentation support, on the other hand, poses subtler

problems. Technical developers have no self-serving interest to promote and develop instrumentation for operational evaluation, which, by its nature, is critical of new systems. They may not have enough knowledge of operational problems or evaluation to be able to inform the Test and Evaluation Force of new instrumentation developments that might facilitate the latter's efforts. This may be one of the reasons the reports often place too much reliance on subjective evaluation. It is unfortunately true that the Navy's study and evaluation system, despite having a well-conceived and well-structured empirical evaluation apparatus, places too much reliance on study processes that may not have resolved critical uncertainties, particularly with regard to aircraft and air-defense systems.

The Army's testing and evaluation system has a strong historical foundation of emotionalism and of controversy among different elements of the user community, as well as between users and producers. Civilian decision makers, including on occasion Presidents, have dabbled in the evaluation process. Testing methods themselves often have a form that would not pass muster if they were subjected to a critical review by, say, a visiting board of examiners sponsored by the National Academy of Sciences. There was even one recent occasion when a Secretary of the Army felt compelled to institute an Inspector General's investigation of some test proceedings.

Army testing is dominated by the developer, which is the Army's Materiel Command. The equivalent of Air Force Category I and II testing is performed by, or under the supervision of, such elements of the Materiel Command as the Munitions Command or Weapons Command, which have primacy for the development of a system or subsystem. The equivalents of the Category II tests are conducted by the Testing and Evaluation Command, which is a subordinate agency of the Materiel Command. Thus, one subordinate agency of the developer passes on the "user acceptability" of equipment that has been produced by other subordinate agencies of the same developer.

This apparent conflict of interest suggested by the formal relationship between the Testing and Evaluation Command and its peer development agencies is mitigated by both historical background and the lack of relevancy of the Army's form of user-acceptability testing. This same lack of relevancy may also afflict the user-acceptability tests conducted by the other services in varying degrees.

The principal instruments for conducting the Army's Testing and Evaluation Command's user tests are a number of "test boards," whose history goes back to the 1940's. These Boards are organized around branch or service lines, such as infantry, artillery, aviation, armor, air defense and electronics, transportation, and special warfare. They are physically located at places like Fort Benning (infantry), Fort Sill (artillery), and so forth. When originally created, they were assigned to the Command that was responsible for training—to the "school system" —and were thus part of the service community. Finally, the boards were mainly composed of, and presided over by, officers specializing in the particular Service arm or branch with which they were associated, with a sprinkling of technical service officers. The test boards thus had a strong user interest and orientation, and, indeed, they worked for the user. They were acquired by the Materiel Command as part of the 1962 Army's reorganization.

The test boards have had a long tradition of testing. It was they who soaked the rifles in the mud, fired at pine boards at ranges up to and beyond 1,000 meters, observed the fatigue of crews, kicked the tank treads, measured the displacement of artillery pieces upon firing, and engaged in similar activities related to the equipment and the requirement traditions of the particular service. Overall, however, the testing processes conducted by the Boards were nevertheless of a highly impressionistic nature. Instrumentation, careful planning of experimental procedures relative to sample size and control, and application of related sophisticated testing procedures were generally lacking. There was also a tendency, which has now become most pronounced, to focus on the measurement of technical-performance characteristics specified in the statement of military requirements. As development-and-procurement programs became more nearly concurrent, the tendency to focus on technical performance and to conduct the "user tests" concurrently with technical tests became even more pronounced.

Army Test Board findings have also had to go through at least two, if not three, command echelons before reaching Army headquarters. When the Boards were part of the school system, the reports went through the local center (for example, the commander at Fort Benning) to Continental Army Command and thence to the Headquarters. Today they go through the

Testing and Evaluation Command to Headquarters, Army
Materiel Command, and on into the Pentagon.

With the possible exception of the Navy, the user-testing
processes of each of the services contain serious deficiencies,
being afflicted as they are with organizational, conceptual, and
technical shortcomings. The Navy's system has the best organizational arrangement, wherein test reports go directly to the
Chief of Naval Operations. Of the three services, only the Navy
explicitly recognizes that its Operational Test and Evaluation
Force has a responsibility to perform operational and tactical
evaluations of systems in their natural environment.

The Army has the worst situation. On one hand, the user tests
are performed by a subordinate agency of the Command that
developed the item. On the other hand, the test boards have
traditions and physical locations identifying them with the conservative, parochial elements of the user community. Although
the test boards have a long tradition of testing, their methods
have been unsophisticated. Finally, the focus of the test boards
is placed essentially upon technical-performance characteristics.

This focus on technical-performance characteristics, which
also characterizes Air Force Category III user testing, contains
both an inescapable potential for conflict of interest and large
elements of irrelevance. On one hand, the user specifies the
technical-performance characteristics. When a new system
meets those characteristics, the user conducting the test asserts
that the "requirements are met," and it will have no incentive
to question whether or not the requirements were relevant in
the first place. Certainly the advocate of the system will naturally
not question the worth of the systems he advocates. On the
other hand, the attitude of the developer toward the user is "tell
us what you want, and we will develop it for you." Upon completion of the system to the user's specifications, the developer can
then claim that the "right" system was developed and that "it
works well." For the developer to say it was not the right system
is to preempt the user's role as a sovereign consumer. For the
user to conduct tests focusing on technical performance is for
him to duplicate the developer's expertise in the testing department and, often, to do so maladroitly. There is a circularity in
the testing process that causes it to resemble the *a priori* method
employed in the study process. The critical questions centering

around whether enhanced technical performance provides combat utility and which combination of technical performance may in fact provide the best weapon are simply not addressed empirically. Instead, there is a recourse to the *a priori* study method. Finally, the users, to the extent that they focus on technical performance in whatever maladroit testing they do carry out, do not undertake rigorous operational testing that focuses on tactics and organizational considerations. Attention must be given to other ways of coping with the problem of conducting operational testing and evaluation.

13

FIELD EXPERIMENTATION: TWO EXPERIENCES

"As technology, modes of warfare, and fighting environments continue to expand, it is becoming increasingly difficult to determine in peacetime the effectiveness of some offensive and defensive weapons systems and tactics. Although field exercises can contribute to our general understanding of the merits of various existing force structures the lack of quantiative data on the relative effectiveness of specific weapon elements makes it difficult to assign meaningful figures of merit to the contribution derived from each."

Dr. Harold Brown, statement before Subcommittee on Appropriations, House of Representatives, 89th Congress, Hearings, Part 5, p. 28.

Neither technical-engineering tests nor military maneuvers and exercises provide useful data for evaluating weapons and tactics. Engineering test data might constitute a proxy for certain operational qualities, provided sufficient operational data and experience that can be correlated with technical performance are generated. Such a correlation process requires operational evaluation as an independent process, but very little empirical operational research is done. Maneuvers and military field exercises lack adequate control, structuring, and measurement of performance; and for these reasons, they are poor activities for evaluation, although they are useful for providing information on administration and logistics.

Deficiencies of these information sources led to the World War II type of military operational research. The actual operations were approached experimentally, or quantitative data were gathered from a large number of similar operations to provide experimental evidence. Also, as is illustrated by the prewar development of radar and its application to the air-defense problem as an operational system, field experiments were conducted. Such experimentation may be viewed as a way of avoiding sole reliance on a purely *a priori* method; it is a means of obtaining the operational type of data that are unobtainable from actual warfare.

Although the Army has the worst organizational structure for testing and evaluation, it has had the most experience with field experimentation. This chapter recounts some of that experience, with particular regard to the problems the activity leads to in terms of present organizational relationships, incentives, and differing views on the methods of conducting inquiry. It also examines the experience with a multiservice test of air-defense and aircraft systems.

In 1956 the Army created a Combat Development Experimentation Center to provide a "field laboratory where . . . theories could be proven, disproved, or modified as a result of actual field experimentation."[1] This new organization was a result of Project Vista, undertaken in 1950 by the California Institute of Technology. Project Vista led to the Chief of Staff to direct the establishment of a Combat Developments Group. As a follow-up to the Vista project, a committee headed by Dr. Leland Haworth recommended the establishment of the field laboratory so as to strengthen the Combat Development function.

The Combat Development function and its field laboratory, being a part of the Continental Army Command, was included in the Army's school system. In 1962, as part of the reorganization that created the Army Materiel Command (and ostensibly disestablished the old Technical Services), a Combat Developments Command was created as a "coequal" to the Continental Army Command and the Army Materiel Command. The Combat Developments Command retained the Experimentation Center. In late 1972 the Combat Developments Command was dismantled, with most of its functions turned over to a reorganized Continental Army Command. The net effect of this change was to restore the pre-1962 status whereby the Combat Developments function reverted to the training and school system.

The Combat Developments Command represented the "user," in a way. That qualification, "in a way," is added because in armies all of the officer members of the combat branches and services are users, and it ill befits a neophyte not to understand that. The Combat Developments Command was also explicitly charged with formulating new doctrine and promulgating it. Hence, it was responsible for preparing army field manuals, and it also wrote the Tables of Organization and Equipment for the Army field units. It initiated the technical-performance specifications and physical characteristics for new weapons and major equipment items. And finally, with the advent of the McNamara system, Combat Developments Command undertook the production of cost-effectiveness paper studies and computer simulations.

The Combat Developments Command had its headquarters at Fort Belvoir, a half-hour drive from the Pentagon. The actual fulfillment of the Command's business, however, was performed by a number of "agencies," each representing a functional combat or service arm of the Army—for example, an Artillery Agency, Infantry Agency, Signal Agency, and so forth. An agency consists of thirty to fifty officers, mainly of field grade, and it is physically located at the traditional school center of the service of which it is a counterpart. For example, the Infantry Agency is at Fort Benning, Artillery is at Fort Sill, and so forth. The agencies are counterparts of and are generally colocated with the Army Materiel Command's test boards, which also specialize in a functional area. Thus, places like Fort Benning, Fort Knox, and so forth have become close-knit communities, or "service centers." A major general usually commands the center, and he reports to, and is part of, the Continental Army Command's "family." The test boards and agencies are commanded by colonels. Legally, these boards and agencies were "tenants" at their respective Continental Army Command "centers." Whatever may be the advantages of the Service Center concept, it is not a setting guaranteed to promote critical question raising on the part of the tenant Combat Development agencies.

To complete our picture of the organizational structure of the Combat Developments Command, it should be pointed out that the individual agencies are organized in groupings that have broad functional orientations. For example, Infantry, Artillery, and Armor are part of a "Combined Arms Group" and are subordinate to an agency headed by a brigadier general (with an agency staff) located at Fort Leavenworth, which is the home of the Command and General Staff School. There is also a Combat

Service Support Group at Fort Lee, which embraces the Engineer, Signal, and Aviation agencies; and there are other major groupings. The heads of these groups reported to the commanding general of the Combat Developments Command, while the heads of the agencies reported to the heads of the groups. The commander of the Experimentation Command, at Fort Ord, also reported to the commanding general of the Combat Developments Command.

The Experimentation Command has the physical capability of testing weapons, doctrine, and organizational concepts in a field environment. It has promoted the development of instrumentation systems and procured them to faciliate field experimentation. It possessed a brigade of troops, composed of armored infantry, tanks, artillery, and a detachment of combat engineers. It has access to the Hunter-Liggett Military Reservation, which provides a variety of terrain for conducting tests. It engages civilian expertise in such fields as operational analysis, computer programming, and instrumentation engineering through contracts with private-research organizations, to implement the concept of military-civilian teams jointly participating in an operational evaluation. But despite these resources, this Command has not produced any product that is worth its cost, let alone any output approximating its potential. The reasons for this lie both in the organizational setting in which the center is required to function and in an unclear conception of the role of experimentation in the overall study process. The root of these difficulties were found in the Combat Developments Command itself.

The Combat Developments Command had a disdain for what was termed "hardware testing," and so it deferred to the Materiel Command and its Test Boards in the matttter of working with equipment and testing it. This attitude appeared to spring from a literal interpretation of its charter, which directed it to formulate the concepts, doctrine, policy on materiel, and organization of the future Army. Such a forward-looking view provided a rationale not to test existing tactics with existing equipment, a rationale that also spared the agencies located at the school centers the embarrassment of questioning what was being taught in the school system.

Such a policy not withstanding, existing tactics and orgnization, implemented with existing materiel, constitute a beginning for any intellectual effort that is to have an empirical foundation.

For example, machinegun doctrine exists only if the machinegun exists. The relevant and interesting doctrinal questions center around such matters as whether a 3- to 4-round burst or an 8- to 9-round burst is the most effective mode of fire, what the ratio of ball to tracer ammunition should be, the relative merits of the tripod and bipod firing modes, and so forth. In other words, given the machinegun, what is the most efficient way to use it? Usually this question cannot be addressed in a satisfactory way independently of the organizational context in which the equipment is used. Should machineguns be used in specialized battalions (as they were, albeit not exclusively so, in World War I) or should they be organic to rifle squads—or should there be some other combination? It is only in the organizational and doctrinal context that decision makers can choose from among an extensive array of mechanical tradeoffs in technical machinegun design to ensure that the machineguns are used "optimally." But in making that determination, the "optimal" doctrinal and organizational factors are simultaneously specified. Thus, the precise specification of machingun design (for example the technical-performance specifications), as well as the doctrine, organization, and use, must be treated in an interrelated way.

To address these questions requires thinking, or better, a theory or model. But it also requires operational data and a mechanism that permits an independent verification of the assertions derived from the theory or model. In short an experimentation process is necessary, and the process of theorizing and experimentation must be closely related. Such interaction between theory and testing did not occur within the Combat Developments Command. The agencies had prime responsibility for the intellectual effort in a particular service or branch area. They formulated the theories, specified the effectiveness measures, and caused the models (computer simulations) to be designed (usually by private-study contractors). They had no resources for experimentation, nor did they have any obligation to ensure that their data inputs were either valid or meaningful or that the results of their models be verified or refuted by independent test. One of the consequences of the absence of this responsibility is that effectiveness criteria are specified neither rigorously nor meaningfully.

On the other hand, the Experimentation Command had a responsibility to "measure." It was generally expected to defer to the agencies on matters of doctrine and the kinds of questions that might be raised. As such a system actually works, however, the model-builders or thinkers do not gracefully accede to having their pet doctrines subjected to tests that might reveal their assertions to be wrong. With a premium on maintaining harmony within the command (if not the Army), it required a degree of recklessness on the part of the Experimentation Command to propose and stage a tough-minded experiment. (Occasionally it did pull one off.) But all too often scarce experimentation resources were dissipated because experiments tended to be designed by committee, with a heavy input by people who had neither a knowledge of nor a responsibility for the conduct of experimentation. Hence, there was an abundance of model-building without related measurement—often because the models were structured by the agencies and their contractors in a way that precluded independent testing. Thus the *a priori* and experimental worlds existed within the Combat Developments Command, but there was little effective interaction between them. For this reason, little useful knowledge came from either effort.

When the Experimentation Command did conduct an unambiguous experiment, it was often possible to draw upon a computer simulation conducted elsewhere in the Army to support whatever position is deemed appropriate to pursue budgetary objectives.

About 75 per cent of the defense budget is allocated to general purpose, or nonstrategic, forces. Of this amount over one-half is spent on aircraft and antiaircraft systems. Tactical air defense includes such systems as the Navy's shipborne Terrier and Tartar surface-to-air missiles and the Army's Hawk missile, which the Marine Corps also operates. Currently, the Army is developing a new field army air-defense missile, SAM-D. In addition, the Army has air-defense battalions assigned to divisions and these battalions are equipped with mixes of fast-firing 20-mm. guns (the Vulcan) and the Chaparral missile, a land-based version of the Navy's heat-seeking Sidewinder missile. Finally, the Redeye, a small heat-seeking missile that can be fired by an individual soldier, is available for forward-area air defense.

The other side of the subject of air defense deals with the

aircraft, including their survivability in a battlefield environment and issues regarding the utility they provide relative to their cost. Tactical air missions include the range of activities from the defense of one's own operating area against enemy aircraft (a function that some extremists contend can be performed by Army-operated missiles and guns), through the interdiction of the opponent's supply lines, to close air support for one's ground forces. The latter function can be performed also by such systems as artillery (guns and missiles) and infantry mortars.

The role and record of aircraft in performing each of these functions are controversial and mixed. Our World War II and Korean War experiences suggest that the interdiction of land-communications routes is a questionable endeavor, especially if the opposing ground forces do not require heavy tonnages of materiel and supplies, as does the artillery and vehicle-intensive U.S. Army. The close-air-support function presents difficult operational problems, including those of target identification and communication with ground units, and a requirement for close cooperation with, if not actual control by, the ground forces. These considerations pose command and control problems, which rapidly become issues concerned with roles, missions, and joint doctrine. Yet airplane capability can effectively and profitably be traded for conventional artillery capability, as the Germans demonstrated during the early and successful phases of their World War II operations.

These ever-present controversial problems promise to become more severe in the United States setting as aviation and air-defense technology advances. Already the Army has acquired a substantial aviation capability which will not be surrendered graciously. Moreover, it has been pursuing the development of more sophisticated helicopters that can carry heavy ordnance loads for accurate delivery. Other services have countered with proposals for new fixed-wing aircraft that would specialize in ground-support missions; but even if they are developed, they could just as well be operated by the Army.

The future of both the airplane and the antiairplane business is therefore very cloudy, and the controversy that has long shrouded the subject should become more intense in the future. Finally, there is the problem of the airplane's future role in the strategic mission, which depends critically on the ability of aircraft to penetrate air defenses at low altitude. But just what performance attributes such airplanes should have are themselves uncertain. Thus, substantial elements of the force structure—including Navy carriers, tactical Air Force fighter-bomber and reconnaissance wings. Army aviation programs, the Strategic Air Command, and air-defense systems—and their respective military communities are tied in with the problematic future of the airplane.

Although modern air-defense missiles do not destroy aircraft at the rates that the advocates of such systems envisaged during the 1950's, it should be borne in mind that during the 1950's it was anticipated that aircraft would fly as high as nuclear weapons carriers. It was also intended that air-defense missiles would employ nuclear warheads against attacking aircraft. For a short period, thought could be given to the defender's dream of a "leak proof" defense. But a reorientation of aircraft to nonnuclear war as part of a changed national policy drastically altered the "model" of the 1950's. Surface-to-air missiles may not shoot down large numbers of aircraft, because the aircraft will fly low. Low-level flight brings them within range of old-fashioned guns, which have been improved by means of aids like range-estimating radars. At lower altitude, the mission effectiveness is degraded because of navigation, and especially because of target-identification problems. Airplane operators can and do control their losses by selecting targets and varying their tactics—at an extreme, the tactics can resemble those of the bombardier Yossarian in Joseph Heller's novel, *Catch-22*. The unknown variable is still the same one that has been unknown ever since the invention of military aircraft—mission effectiveness.

An unfolding technology provides a wider range of options in aircraft design and performance attributes, bombing and navigation systems, air-delivered ordnance, and mixes and types of air-defense weapons. Since the most critical problems regarding the effectiveness of these systems come to a focus in operations at low altitude, present and future air operations may increasingly have many of the characteristics of land warfare. Terrain and proximity to terrain degrades and distorts the operation of equipment, including radar, and the man-equipment combinations, including the training of air crews and air-defense systems operators, become vital considerations. The activity becomes less dominated by purely technical performance, and tactics and organization become more, rather than less, important.

An awareness of some of these problems in the early 1960's

led to an extensive study in the Defense Department, conducted by the Weapons Systems Evaluation Group of the Joint Chiefs of Staff at the request of the Deputy Secretary of Defense, and after the study results were in, one conclusion stood out: the uncertainty caused by a lack of empirical operational data regarding the performance of both air-defense systems and aircraft operating at low altitude was extreme. The recommendation was made to conduct an extended program of operational testing with the use of instrumentation and valid statistical techniques; and it was also recommended that the testing be a joint effort of the different services. Accordingly, Joint Task Force Two was established in August 1964.

Joint Task Force Two was designed to be a joint agency, composed only of a headquarters staff that received its directions from the Joint Chiefs of Staff.[2] It was "authorized 106 officers from all the military services and 29 professional civilians,"[3] plus supporting enlisted and civilian personnel, and its function was to plan, design, and analyze the results of operational tests. The military services were to provide units, weapons, and crews "as needed and when directed by the Joint Chiefs of Staff."[4] Technical assistance and staff review were also to be "provided by the Director of Defense Research and Engineering through the Weapons Systems Evaluation Group (WSEG)."[5]

In January 1965, JTF–2 moved to the Sandia Base in Albuquerque, partly because the Sandia Laboratories (a subsidiary of the Bell Laboratories), which works for the Atomic Energy Commission and possesses civilian technical and scientific capability that could support the task force, was located there. The financial mechanism for extending this support was one wherein the Defense Department reimbursed the Atomic Energy Commission, which in turn paid Sandia Corporation.[6] The level of the Sandia effort was such as to require 97 full-time personnel in FY 1966, with a budget of $2.6 million.[7] The FY 1967 proposed level of effort included about 20 additional people, or a total of about 115, at a cost of $3.5 million.[8]

The JTF–2 test program was extremely ambitious. It was focused upon the mesurement of critical variables by means of instrumentation and upon replication of activities. In this fashion, it was responsive to the needs for data that the initial WSEG study had found to be lacking in the many facets of low-altitude penetration. The ambitiousness of the test plans also reflected the urgency apparently signaled by those studies and the impact of the high-level Department of Defense support for the program. The first test was conducted during the late spring and early summer of 1965 over the Nevada desert. It consisted of a series of flights by different types of aircraft over a planned "racetrack" course, designed to measure low-altitude flying capability and the relationships between speed and low altitude.[9] Moreover, it was simple and it provided the task force and the Sandia technicians with experience on how to conduct operational tests. But a major level of effort was planned for FY 1967, and funds were requested for the conduct, the monitoring, or the planning and preplanning of thirteen different tests.[10] That this was far too ambitious is suggested by the fact that, in response to a congressional subcommittee inquiry during the appropriations hearings for the FY 1968 budget, the task force reported an effort centering on only eight tests for FY 1967.[11]

In spring 1967, the deputy commander of the task force reported that a phase of a test had been conducted in the summer of 1966 in the Louisiana-Arkansas-Oklahoma area, over rolling terrain, to treat navigation at low altitude and to simulate an attack on a target. In fall 1966, a nonfiring test was carried out by the Army's Combat Development Command Experimentation Center at Hunter-Liggett Military Reservation to "obtain information on aircraft vulnerability to ground weapons and the effectiveness of ground weapons against simulated enemy attack."[12] A previously planned test on the Hawk missile had been canceled. Monitorship of the first phase of some Navy tests of the Terrier and Tartar missile systems had also been conducted. Activities for fiscal year 1968 have not been recounted to Congress. Although a $15.0 million funding for 1969 was proposed in the Department's budget submitted in February, the need to defend it did not arise. In April 1966, the Joint Chiefs of Staff recommended to the Secretary of Defense that Joint Task Force Two be disestablished, and the Secretary of Defense approved the recommendation in the same month.

Joint Task Force Two cost between $50 million and $100 million, depending on how the cost of military resources expended on it, including aircraft sorties, would be allocated. Overall, it appears to have been a failure. The 1965 Nevada low-altitude tests were a learning process. The antiaircraft/aircraft vulnerability tests run in 1966 in conjunction with the

Army's Experimentation Center at Hunter-Liggett, became a shambles because of changes in the instrumentation plan and the test's measurement objectives that occurred right up to the field trials, and because the tests were run without adequately ascertained instrumentation errors. A major change in the instrumentation plan resulted from the task force's insistence on using modified Nike-Ajax radars for aircraft position location. Since uncertainties exist regarding the accuracy of radar at low altitudes, uncertainties that also degrade the operational effectiveness of air-defense missiles, the data from such a source are suspect unless careful prior testing of the instrumentation is carried out. Such testing was not done. Also, the task force decided to exclude the Army's Hawk missile from the test, on the ground that Hawk procurement had been completed. Results from the Louisiana-Arkansas-Oklahoma low-altitude navigation and target acquisition tests are not available in the unclassified literature. However, there is little basis for believing that the task force acquired sufficient expertise by the time the tests were completed to have produced useful information.

Among the reasons for the apparent failure was the fact that the original advocates of a testing program were naive regarding the scale and scope of the testing program that was implicit in their theoretical offerings. Although the deficiences in data bearing on the subjects of aircraft and antiaircraft systems are great and there is an urgent requirement for such data, the analysts pointing up the problem had little appreciation of the intricacies of field testing and especially of the instrumentation problems involved. The theorists shifted the problem to the experimentalists, but none of the military staff members that composed JTF–2 had experience with applied operational research or field testing. For scientific advice, they turned to the Sandia Corporation, which has many fine engineers, mathematicians, and statisticians. But their expertise was in testing atomic weapons, not in the theoretical analysis of tactical weapons or in instrumentation for field-type operations. Nevertheless, as time goes on, people can learn to do field testing.

Experience with the Army's Experimentation Center suggests that it takes two to three years to build up even a small civilian group consisting of operational analysts, mathematicians, and instrumentation engineers who can function effectively as a team. Such a buildup requires that the military component of a field-experimentation endeavor develop a capacity to work with civilians, so as to form a joint military-civilian team. The capability of the Joint Task Force's military component to function in this fashion was not apparent during its initial operation; and that it may never have acquired such a capability is suggested by the Sandia Corporation's stated intention to sever its relationship with the task force. But whether a capability to design, instrument, and analyze field experiments was in the process of emerging remains an academic question, in view of the disestablishment of the task force. In the meantime, a statement made by the task force's commander in 1966 that "no one really knows how effective they [aircraft] will be in low-level operations"[13] appears still to be valid.

To conduct useful operational testing requires three critical conditions. First is the creation of a group whose individual members have experience and specialized knowledge about military operations, analytical methods, and instrumentation, but where each specialist group has sufficient knowledge of the specialties of one's counterparts to work as a team. Second, it is necessary to avoid complicating an experiment with spurious realism or attempts to measure too many things at one time, so that it produces ambiguous results. Finally, an experiment must address relevant problems, including the measurement of effectiveness or critical variables.

The first requirement is achieved by careful management and the blending of individuals with diverse skills. Military professionals must actively participate in such a group, since they usually have the best knowledge of what is tactically relevant, a consideration that is critical in designing the experiment. Frequently, military officers can interpret the results of an experiment, to cast up new hypotheses in ways that civilians might miss. Civilians should provide the needed analytical and technical skills. One would expect them also to be more detached in their thinking than military officers might be, since the latter must function during their future careers in a hierarchial system that places little premium on critical ideas about the preferences of seniors. Thus, in those cases involving military officers who are critical and detached, the military-civilian team approach to operational testing provides a mechanism whereby the civilians can relieve the officers of the onus of being the critics. For this reason, non-civil-service civilian analysts and scientists can be especially useful in an experimentation process. Finally, the military side of such an operation under such conditions cannot be secretive, nor can it try to dominate the civilians.

The achievement of openness is difficult, if not impossible, in the present bureaucratic setting, and the avoidance of military dominance requires a sensitive touch in interpersonal relationships. Such sensitivity is not promoted if people are required to work under strong political pressures. Finally, experience on the part of the individuals and groups is necessary if the organization is to have the capability to conduct field evaluations in a mechanical sense. Joint Task Force Two did not have that experience, nor was it permitted to operate long enough to acquire it.

Avoidance of the possiblity of unnecessarily complicating an experiment by attempts to achieve spurious realism is in one sense a methodological problem; but in the world of military testing and evaluation it is primarily a political-bureaucratic problem. A field experiment must be sufficiently "realistic" that its results will be credible to decision makers, but the tough question to answer in complex organizations centers around *which* decision makers it must be credible to. For example, it is unlikely that any program of field testing would convince some advocates that long-range, high-powered small arms are *not* the best infantry weapons. But purposeful field testing or an agreement to experiment forces decision makers and other participants in the decision-making process to be more specific regarding a number of critical variables, including the specification of effectiveness criteria. To experiment requires that people be able to attach numbers to such adjectives as "long," "fast," "agile," and so forth. A careful survey of terrain intervisibilities and engagement ranges from past actions becomes an object of inquiry that must be undertaken *in the design* of an experiment.

The effectiveness-criteria problem often has to be addressed directly, and proxy measures may have to be agreed upon. In evaluating infantry small arms, for example, some professionals correctly point out that hits, or the needed time to get hits, are not the most important measure of combat utility. Rather, fire "suppresses" an enemy—for example, it causes him to duck or cower in his position—during which time friendly elements can maneuver, communicate, or do other things that provide a tactical advantage. The degree of suppression, however, is difficult to measure, since it is a function both of an enemy's qualities and of one's own weapons, although people might agree that "near misses" are a good proxy measure of the suppressive effects of weapons. It is next necessary to agree about the proper choice of miss distance as a criterion—for example, is it two feet, six feet, or ten feet? Either the boss can pick his number or near misses might be measured in terms of several distances.

Thus, the dialogue centering around the design of experiments becomes a social activity that begins to change the nature of the decision-making process itself. Once the ranges are selected and the effectiveness criteria (or their proxies) or critical variables are specified and agreed upon, most rational men are obligated to abide by the decisions suggested by the results of the experiment, in much the same way that gamblers agree to "rules of the game." The assertion that an experiment is not realistic is often a way of saying one does not like its results.

In the bureaucratic context, the quest for realism in the experimentation aspect of operational evaluation is a way of ensuring that an experiment will yield ambiguous results. And if the results are ambiguous, it is possible for the decision makers to keep their options open, or it enables analysts to avoid confronting senior officials with unpleasant findings.

"Keeping the options open" within the internal workings of the bureaucracy is another way of describing a condition in which the decision maker can do anything he wishes to serve his political objectives, which may be directed internally or externally at any given time. In some cases he may want to make a procurement choice that benefits the district of a particular Congressman; in another situation, he may make his choice so as to pacify a particular group or a powerful individual within his organization. The possession of options is therefore the possession of political power; and conversely, clear evidence that one system is superior to another erodes or destroys this kind of power. The old adage that "knowledge is power" is thus less than 100 per cent correct.

A more accurate view of the subject is that some optimum combination of knowledge and ignorance best serves decision makers in complex settings and that ambiguous experimental results are ideally suited for such situations. On one hand, these conditions present to outside observers the picture of an organization pursuing truth and objectivity, while on the other hand nothing dangerous need come of the endeavor. For many analysts, their own survival in such a situation, either by way of getting study contracts or in functioning in the staff hierarchy, means that the quality of work must be scaled down to meet the requirements.

The search for clear statements or relevant variables or effectiveness criteria therefore confronts senior officials with questions, the posing of which may implicitly or explicitly counter the assertions of seniors. The dialogue involved in such a search also requires that there be open communication channels between decision makers and analysts. For these reasons, the issue centering around realism in field testing is often a smoke screen. Strong bureaucratic and political forces drive the discussions and actions that center around realism in the design of military operational testing and instrumentation programs related to it. These forces have operated in such ways as to degrade the output of the Army's field-experimentation endeavor.

The requirement that relevant variables be measured may seem trivial, as may also a part of the idea that spurious realism be minimized. Nevertheless, it is possible to put together a good experimentation team that will avoid the errors following from spurious reality, but that will design or direct the experiment in such a way as to avoid addressing critical questions. Recently, the Army Experimentation Command ran some live-fire infantry experiments, in which each soldier, by means of a grenade-launching device attached to an M16 rifle, had the ability to fire bullets or grenades. Here was an excellent chance to address the grenadier-rifleman mix problem. However, the individual soldiers were permitted to choose their own firing doctrine—under which circumstances, it would be difficult, if not impossible, to determine from the experimental data the relative merits of different weapon mixes. Further, no effort was made to test 40-mm. grenades, which are available in Europe, launched from the muzzles of rifles. This manner of directing the experiment suggests that it was intended to avoid raising questions about existing doctrine and past-equipment decisions, because there is not an infantryman around who does not understand the relevance of the rifle-grenade question to infantry tactics and combat. Such behavior in experimentation may seem inexplicable in terms of rational decision making, but it makes sense when viewed in the totality of Army politics.

The direction of experiments in such a way as to address irrelevant measurements or objectives nevertheless serves political purposes, and it is not a way of operation that is exclusive to the military services. The Office of the Secretary of Defense itself has also demonstrated this capability in the case of a field experiment conducted in Panama during the early part of 1967 with modified M16 rifles and ammunition having alternative propellants. The Marines conducted the test under the supervision of the Joint Chiefs' WSEG. The directive to conduct the test came from the Office of the Secretary of Defense in response to a Special Subcommittee Investigation of the Committee on Armed Services, House of Representatives, which held hearings on the Army's M16 rifle program in September and October 1967.[14]

The M16 had exhibited serious malfunctions in Vietnam, which provoked the Congressional investigation, the latter in turn prodding the Office of the Secretary of Defense to do something about the situation. The cause of the M16's poor reliability was the Army's changing of the ammunition propellant, when it adopted the weapon, to a "ball propellant," so characterized because the propellant grains resemble small balls.[15] A number of subsequent changes were made in attempts to cope with the malfunctions, including the development of a new propellant in some ways resembling the original one but in other ways behaving like the one causing the difficulty.[16]

The Panama tests treated combinations of the modified weapons and the two propellants that the Army either had adopted for the M16 or had developed to cope with the problem caused by the ball propellant it specified when it procured the M16. (During much of this period, it continued to use the original propellant in acceptablility tests for newly produced weapons, because with the ball propellant the reliability standards specified in regulations governing quality control could not be met.)[17] No test of the original rifle configuration with the original propellant was made in the Panama test because the Office of the Secretary of Defense so directed. In that original combination, the system had shown no serious reliability problem, either in field tests or in Vietnam, where it was used on a trial basis by elements of the South Vietnamese forces during 1962 and 1963. As a result of the Panama tests, the use of the Army's newly developed propellant was suspended. One reason it did not look good in the test was that all the rifles that were used had been modified to perform with the ball propellant, which was responsible for the poor reliability that evoked the outcry. Thus, something was "done about" the problem, and that something was based on a test.[18] Congress may have been satisfied; but a test of the original weapon-propellant configuration, along with the Army's *ad hoc* combinations, might have been relevant both to getting better weapons in the hands of the troops and to revealing that serious mistakes were made when the M16 system was modified relative to the original AR-15 configuration. This line of inquiry was not pursued.

In the case of JTF-2, another force appears to have been operative. The future weapon-selection and force-structure issues within each of the services and especially among the services upon which the possible findings of JTF-2 might bear are major. The Joint Chiefs of Staff have never been able to resolve these kinds of questions in a decisive way when they make recommendations in the budgetary and programming deliberations. The members of the task force were confronted with a difficult technical and analytical task, even under the best of circumstances; but the bureaucratic setting confronted them with an almost impossible dilemma. Would the Army elements of JTF-2 press to show that Air Force pilots might not be able to identify targets in such a way as to suggest that the airplanes might be too fast or that the bombing navigation systems do not perform in a way that enhances effectiveness in proportion to their cost? Would the Air Force components of the task force push to demonstrate that aircraft could penetrate Army air-defense systems with impunity? Both sides may deeply suspect that such is the case and might welcome the opportunity to prove it. But the budgetary risks are extremely great in pursuing such a program. In view of the uncertainties, all parties may see that they might have much to lose relative to the established funding levels, with little to gain from unambiguous tests. Hence, there are strong budgetary incentives for having ambiguous test results or, better, no testing at all. One cannot yet say that all the tests carried out by JTF-2 were ambiguous, since the results of the analyses are not all in. But JTF-2 was terminated apparently without the slightest objection from anyone.

Some other means must be found to conduct joint operational testing. The incentives for doing it, as well as unilateral-service operational testing, must be strengthened. Yet the incentives are tied up with the financial and budgeting process, and this process and its relationship to intellectual and testing endeavors will be treated in the final chapter.

14

ARMS PROCUREMENT
AND DEFENSE POLICY

> What we have is technology, and administration out of
> control, running for their own sake, but at the same
> time subject to manipulation and profiteering by the
> power interests of our society for their own non-
> human ends.
>
> Charles A. Reich, *The Greening of America*, pp. 92–93.

Weapons procurement is only one phase of military management. Yet it is the key to peacetime military decision-making. It
drives the internal workings of the military services because it
determines the relative importance of the competing combat
specialities. New weapons impact upon tactics, training, and
organization. Through the formulation of new weapon concepts, the scientific, technological, and even the academic communities interact with the military. Finally, spending the dollars
for weapons affects payrolls and profits throughout the civilian
economy, and through this channel generates political interest.

Civilian "control" of military affairs in large part centers on
weapons procurement and, especially in the post-World War II
era, their development. Yet the activities of specifying the characteristics of weapons, the formulation of new tactics and troop
and crew training on how to use them in war, and making the
associated changes in organization like squadrons and battalions to accommodate new weapons, are necessarily interrelated
and interdependent activities. Each of these activities has a very
high if not overwhelming administrative and technical content,
which are the special domains of the military man or the technologist who should be responsive to valid military needs. Coordinating these activities, in turn, requires a sophisticated blending of administrative and technical skill. Because of the
necessary preponderance of administrative and technical decision-making in these matters, it is not clear just what is meant
by "civilian control" of them.

245

A more relevant question may be whether the present process is "controlled" by anyone. It could be contended that recent experience manifests signs of a mindless technology driving a mindless bureaucracy. Policy makers—in the persons of Congress and Presidentially appointed officials—appear unable to cope with it. The military "bureaucrats"—who it might be tempting to label as the "heavies" in the scenario—appear not to have much control over it either; and, paradoxically, the military may very well be major victims of the system's shortcomings. It is they who are charged with conducting effective military operations (including deterrence of war). Weapons of dubious combat utility do not facilitate performance of that responsibility. With the cost of weapons increasing many times with the completion of each development cycle, the country may be in serious trouble if their combat utility is of limited worth. Indeed, a form of unilateral disarmament may be taking place.[1]

Bringing the system under "control," however, casts up many questions. What is meant by "control"? Is it a matter of eliminating cost overruns on new weapon developments? If so, it might merely suffice to get "better" cost estimates, perhaps by finding cost estimators who are less susceptible to bureaucratic, advocacy pressures. Or is it, as some critics charge, that there is too much "control," which is responsible for costly delays and red tape in the decision-making processes. Should concurrency in weapons development and procurement be eliminated? Should operational and prototype testing be required? Should weapons development and manufacturing firms be nationalized, so as to eliminate the impact that private profit seeking might have upon administrative and, especially, political decision-making? Should the military services be given more autonomy in selecting and developing weapons? Or should the development process be operated by a separate and completely civilian-dominated Defense Agency? Should the system be more "centrally managed?" Or is "decentralized management" the thing? Is it mainly a matter of providing decision-makers with better information? And if it is, how is better information to be generated? Or is it sufficient simply to cut military budgets?

Peacetime military management in the United States has always been vexed by two major problems. One centers around the relationship between the military user and the technician. The other is that of determining the division of labor between the military and civilians. For a long period, it seemed that a resolution of these problems could be achieved by civilians focusing on the housekeeping or logistics functions, and leaving the military to concentrate on the operating (and fighting) side of the business.

This division of labor was not meaningful. Prior to World War II, it only provided a workable system because military technicians—who dominated the statutory Bureaus and Technical Services—handled day-to-day affairs, and in the process accommodated the War and Navy departments to congressional interests, usually at the price of getting less military effectiveness per dollar spent. Congress, in turn, exerted its influence on many fine-grained decisions made by the military departments, as the latter catered to Congressmen in order to get support for appropriations. If "centralized management" means control of many decisions by the highest authority, here was a high degree of centralized management that predated the present Defense Department. In this system, high civilian officials in the executive branch could play a variety of roles, from important to trivial. Yet the pre-World War II system did not provide a coherent relation between means and ends. Nor did it consistently provide the equipment or weapons worth the money spent, despite a technology and civilian industrial apparatus adequate to the task.

In the pre-World War II period the military services also exhibited a strong conservative streak toward new weapons and ideas. Part of this behavior was motivated by the military bureaus who had responsibility for wartime procurement and logistics, which tend to foster a preference for fewer systems and for systems whose supply and maintenance requirements were known and therefore predictable. Military users, for their part, were also inclined to be conservative in a setting of limited budgets because more costly weapons could mean fewer battalions and smaller fleets. Thus new ideas were reluctantly accepted; and usually only after they were demonstrated on foreign battlefields or through the occasional active prodding of a high official, such as the President.

World War II shattered this conservatism toward technical development. In the postwar period, there was instituted the process of seeking to get new weapons into the field as rapidly as possible, for which concurrency in development and procurement became an explicit strategy. Every kind of weapon, and every possible improvement in a given weapon, came to be treated as if it were a minor Manhattan Project. The purposeful devlopment of technology for weapons application also eliminated any vestige of the idea that procurement and housekeeping could be separated from tactics and military organization. As the problems of relating means and ends grew more complex, the organizational changes were designed to give civilian secretariats increasing authority. The advent, around 1950, of a fine-grained, input-oriented accounting system, contained within the broad budgetary groupings of "Operations and Maintenance," "Procurement," and so forth, was accompanied by the growth of staff sections in the Office of the Secretary that sought to exercise suzerainty over their respective areas that roughly corresponded to major funding categories. In this setting, budgeteers in the Comptroller's Office frequently exerted the last word. The directive control in the Office of the Secretary of Defense over research and development, however, was perhaps the penultimate step that could have been taken to provide the Secretary of Defense the maximum power in defense management consistent with the appropriations power of the Congress.

The transition from the pre- to the post-World War II "models" of military management was one that entailed a major shift of power from the congressional to the civilian executive branch, the culmination of which attained a peak during the McNamara period. The controversy over the pros and cons of this development has unfortunately masked a very important element of constancy in American peacetime military management during the entire history of the Republic. That element is the fact that the professional officer corps never had—during peactime—much opportunity to make resource-allocation decisions. Rather, such decision making was made in fine-grained ways by civilians through the budgetary process. The professional military, in turn, were cast in the role of advocates and, necessarily, they were compelled to advocate in a fine-grained way—whether it be for horse feed or fuel for jet engines. Because Congress or interested high-level policymakers in the executive branch were sensitive to where and for what the money was spent, the military administratiors were also obligated to spend the monies as designated.

Such a system, in effect, precludes the professional officer corps from directly allocating resources. The situation, in an important way, resembles that of an immature housewife who must justify in advance to her husband each outlay required for running the household, with the husband in turn doling out the money. A frequent consequence of this scenario is that the one who actually spends the money has little or no incentive to spend it carefully, and consequently little opportunity to acquire financial maturity. How can one have an incentive to economize on the use of resources if one has no freedom to make choices; or in a setting where, should a saving be uncovered by careful management, one simply receives less money as a result? In effect, because of fine-grained supervision of the many details of procurement and administration by high civilian authority, the American professional military have never had, during peace-time, either opportunity or incentive to spend resources in an efficient way.[2]

The introduction of the Planning, Programming, and Budgeting System by Robert McNamara did not alter this incentive structure. It introduced a force-accounting system, or a listing of force elements like battalions and missile wings, for which cost estimates (and in most instances not very good ones) were made and which, owing to a large "General Support category," was made approximately consistent with the older input-oriented budget categories. It did, however, provide a device by which inputs (means) and ends (force elements) could be related. That a Secretary of Defense such as McNamara may have made fine-grained decisions on the basis of a force-accounting (or programming) calculus was accidental. Such decisions on the Secretary's part were perhaps no more or less fine-grained than what his predecessors, including Congress during the pre-World War II period, had done in their way for some time.

What was unique about the McNamara system, however, was that the Systems Analysis Directorate (and later the Office of the Assistant Secretary for Systems Analysis) took on a role that was novel in American civilian management (whether Congressional or Executive) of military organizations. In a sense, it was "user-oriented," rather than "producer-oriented" in its outlook; whereas civilian secretariats up to that time focused mainly on imputs. The initial application of systems and cost-effectiveness analysis did expose many inconsistencies as between major force-structure elements within a given service and, especially, as between different services.

This development, by any appraisal of past struggles in the old War and Navy departments and the pre-McNamara Defense

Department, was badly needed and long overdue. Yet it was paradoxical that the rigorous approach to the user's problems, encompassing the formulation of weapons concepts and specifying military characteristics for new systems, was explicitly not carried over into the development process.[3] In retrospect this decision appears astonishing in view of the fact that systems and cost-effectiveness analysis, as promulgated at places like RAND during the 1950's, was differentiated from the older, World War II operational research precisely because conceptual and future systems were the objects of critical scrutiny. As time passed, cost-effectiveness analysis—by means of the *a priori* method described in a previous chapter—became perverted and extensively used to justify and advocate even more sophisticated weapon developments.

Thus, through the entire post-World War II period, the leverage of development funding dominated much of the decision-making. If one takes a long view of the history of American military management, little seems to have changed except the scale of spending. Prior to World War II, Technical Service and Bureau Chiefs, striving to preserve and enhance their fiefdoms and adapting their procurement action to their perception of signals emanating from Congress, dominated the way business was done. In the post-war period, civilian technologists—often pursuing technical hobbies and financially supported by policy-makers who seem to accept the idea that technical inventions can be directly equated with more effective fighting capability—exerted a dominating influence. This trend was well established during the 1950's. The McNamara system did not cope with it. Unless the system is changed in a much more fundamental way, other administrations will provide its followers a legacy of systems that will resemble the F-111, C-5A, and Shillelagh.

Under the present system of establishing and allocating defense budgets, the professional military labor under perverse incentives. Each service and each faction of a service is concerned with its relative share of the budget. Since Congress and the senior, civilian leaders of the executive branch insist that the budget be justified in terms of much fine-grained detail, the aggregate budget for a service is built up from a detailed list of weapon-development programs, procurements of developed weapons, and force-structure elements. The primary role of the services, and even major components of each service, in the resource-allocation process is that of justifying and advocating each of the items the aggregate of which comprises the proposed budget. Thus, each year, the civilian masters in the Pentagon and in Congress encounter the assertions of the "requirements." Since the aggregation of the requirements in peacetime is more than the country or the taxpayers is willing to provide, the civilian masters have opportunity to make detailed decisions by selecting the items and the respective amounts by which the service requests are reduced to accommodate a budgetary constraint dictated by other policy objectives. If the system is nothing, it is both centrally managed and under "civilian control."

Three closely interrelated effects, each of which can be dangerous if not potentially disastrous for the country's future national security, can follow from the way the present system operates.

The first effect impacts upon the quality of the officer corps. Survival and the future of a service depend on budgets. The advocacy that characterizes the budgetary process commences in subordinate commands, absorbs most the energy expended by the 25,000 persons who occupy the Pentagon, and extends across the Potomac to the Executive offices and, especially, the Capitol. Military officers who excel in the staff work that feeds this process capture the attention and gratitude of their military and, occasionally, civilian superiors. Whether the qualities that endow a man to perform this function well are positively correlated with the classical military skills of command in field operations (which entails making the most efficient and best use of the resources available), or of doing staff work in a field or operatonal context that must necessarily be objective and critical, is a question which is somber to contemplate.

It might be argued that the American budgeting process, with its emphasis on the pork barrel and the necessity of bureaucrats to lobby, has always presented this problem. However, the pre-World War II period was one in which the Technical Service and Bureau Chiefs took on the major burden of the "external political" activity for their services, while most of the line officers were able to avoid, if they were not prevented from, playing the budgetary game. A price was paid for this division of labor in the form of some waste in the peacetime military budgets. But in time of war, we could either procure most of our needed weapons from allies (World War I) or the Bureau Chiefs could be subordinated by a temporary reorganization (World War II). Simultaneously, officers oriented toward field operations could come forth and assume command. Although this split was not airtight in the past, it is virtually nonexistent today.

A second major consequence of the budget-maximizing incentive when it obligates military professionals to advocate in the budgetary process impacts upon military-threat assessment. The capabilities of opponents, including many of their individual systems, are exaggerated by the military. This can lead to major foreign-policy errors. For example, a case can be made that an overassessment of Soviet strength may have contributed to the "Cold War." In defense of the military, however, it can be argued that this tendency is in line with a sound, "conservative" attitude, coupled with an instinct to want to win in war. These appropriate motives, however, should not be combined or mixed with the self-serving motivation to maximize budgets in the context of rivalry with sister services or even branches within services. A better way to utilize the military man's threat-assessment capability is for the civilian leaders to ask, given the size and structure of armed forces, what the probablity of winning a particular, possible war will be. In this context, the reply of military men could have a healthy and sobering effect on the civilian leaders, especially those who might contemplate an activist foreign policy.[4]

A third major effect of the advocacy process and the incentive system responsible for it is upon the quality of information bearing upon the inner workings of the military services, including information that high-level policy makers must have to make decisions that only they can and should make. Students of management and organization place great emphasis upon the truth that management and resource allocation require information, and that an "information system" is a necessary part of a "management system." Yet little is understood about the critical and interdependent relationship between the incentive system that drives an organization and its information system.[5] However, it is unwise to assume that the information generated and processed through the hierarchy is "correct," or that the organization has the facility to determine what are the "relevant" information requirements for superiors. This assumption is generally true for a business firm, where it is possible to harness the motive of subordinate managers to maximize earnings to the profit-seeking motive of the company and its stockholders by means of sales commissions, profit sharing, and so on. Moreover, the occasional "salad oil" or Price-Waterhouse scandal notwithstanding, independent auditing procedures serve to keep people honest. Finally, double-entry bookkeeping was a brilliant invention because it doubles the effort necessary to manipulate the numbers. Similarly, a military organization will quickly develop a first-rate (although not necessarily formal) combat intelligence net in time of a major war. In this case national, to say nothing of institutional survival, provides the proper incentive.

For government bureaucracies, including military ones in peacetime, institutional survival is understandibly viewed by senior bureaucrats to be highly dependent on budgets. If an organization's budget must be justified and defended in terms of fine-grained detail—as for individual weapon developments and procurements—then the information bearing upon those individual systems is apt to be affected by the larger budgetary incentive. The finer the detailed justification, the further down the hierarchy incentive impacts, to afflict individual project officers in distant headquarters of subcommands. Thus there is the oft-told story of the project officer, responsible for the "management" of a new development, who is forced to become an advocate of "his" system, and is often constrained to discount or suppress information that the program may be running into difficulty. Similarly, people who call attention to those in high authority that something may be going wrong "too soon" have, on occasion, found their career prospects jeopardized. Indeed, a case can be made that there are few "numbers" in the Pentagon—from statements of quantitative requirements and asset holdings of major systems to those describing terminal ordnance effects—that are not tainted.[6] And when a particular number is "correct," the chances are very good that it is because either it is of no relevance to budgetary issues or its correctness serves an advocacy purpose.

The problems that afflict the bureaucratic information system also impact adversely upon testing and experimentation. This effect can be especially severe on field experimentation or operational testing, since these activities necessarily require involvement in all its phases of military officers who are oriented toward user or line command. It is a major contention of this book that the weapons-development process cannot be properly directed until the technical-performance specifications for new weapons can be laid down in an intelligent way. They cannot be so laid down until there is a purposeful, systematic effort to relate in a quantitative way technical performance with qualities that measure combat utility, or which are judged to be good proxy measures of utility. However, it is difficult if not impossible to initiate or conduct a tough-minded experiment, which might suggest, for example, that the high accuracy, fast speed, low visibility of the Belchfire-II currently under development, with a multi-billion-dollar procurement programmed after development, are characteristics that provide little, zero, or negative improvement in combat effectiveness. Reputations—of officers, scientists, and analysts—are at stake. Either the experiment will not be conducted, or the incentive to do it rigorously, should it be undertaken, will be blunted.

This dependency between budget incentives and the quality of a bureau's information output poses a severe dilemma for public administration. For one thing, it means that mere analysis of programs, through the use of cost-benefit or cost-effectiveness techniques, is not adequate, even if it is done by staffs that serve a hard-nosed cabinet official or a Congress that someday might decide that it wants critical, independent analysis. In government, the vast majority of data is produced by bureaus either as a by-product of their operations or in response to specific directives from higher authority.[7] Further, most data are literally produced at the "end of the line," by supply sergeants, maintenance personnel, crewmen, or statistical clerks at a laboratory. The data then go up the hierarchy, where at each level they are edited, aggregated, or manipulated in the statistical sense. There is ample opportunity to manipulate both data—and in many cases the experiment—to serve budgetary objectives. In addition, there is the opportunity, by mere omission, not to gather data judged to have a probability of revealing things that could be detrimental to budgetary objectives. For these reasons, the attempt to "revolutionize" management of the Defense Department by the techniques of the Planning, Programming, and Budgetary System employed by Secretary McNamara was unknowingly frustrated if not defeated by the military services. In the same vein, the civilian secretariat, through the instrument of more than a hundred analysts in the Systems Analysis Staff, unknowingly caused a sharp decline in the quality of the data produced by the military services as they sought to probe deeper and into an expanded number of subject areas.

It did begin to dawn on people at higher levels that something was amiss. As a result, more of the staff effort became focused on a glorified form of "bean counting," or conducting "audit trails," by checking last year's claim of a service with this year's. The amount of analysis did not increase in proportion to the growth in staff size; its quality decreased as the data sources either dried up or became degraded as a result of subordinate agency behavior. Parkinson could no doubt derive a new "law" from this experience.

Getting better information for high-level decision making and resource allocation is greatly complicated by the matter of determining just what kinds of information those policy makers should have. Large, complex organizations literally produce enormous amounts of data. Information available to senior policy makers must necessarily be filtered and aggregated, the outputs of prior analysis, and the result of past decisions and previously determined set of procedures, including an auditing or inspection process that specifies a bureau's information system. Many students of public administration recognize that analysis is no better than the empirical data upon which it is based, that decision makers and the public should be "better informed," and that much more program visibility is a desirable if not necessary condition for the operation of an open, democratic society. Hence, after either acknowledgment or exposure of the fact that management and decision making is going badly, a plea is made for better information and, incidentally, for higher-quality analysis.[8] But how to get these good things is seldom laid out.

Compounding the effect of self-serving bureaucratic incentives upon the quality and production of data is the difficulty of designing information systems to serve senior policy and decision makers. The problem can be illustrated by the following question: Precisely what information is to be available to these policy makers, to what degree of aggregation, and how timely should it be? In recent years, effort has been made to deal with this question, or more accurately to avoid addressing it, by devising Headquarters Information Systems employing large-scale electronic computers and extensive communications links capable of pouring enormous amounts of data into the headquarters. (Given the incentives impacting so adversely on the quality of the data, some of these kinds of systems have also been described as a "GIGO System"—the acronym representing "Garbage In, Garbage Out"). Even so, this brute force, technological means is unable to handle the amounts of information an energetic (to say nothing of a large and expanding) bureaucracy is capable of producing, and the senior people have inadequate time and energy to absorb it.[9]

The key to this information problem resides in the kinds of decisions senior people make. For example, if the husband and breadwinner of a family decides to entrust to his wife the purchase of groceries, he needs to concern himself only with the total monthly grocery outlay. He need not keep track of the cost of bread, beans, salt, and so on. Suggested in this domestic illustration is the idea of a divison of labor in management and decision making. How labor and responsibilities are divided in complex social arrangements also has an impact on incentives and, simultaneously, the kind of information the incentives produce. What follows relates these elements by means of a suggested strategy on how to improve Defense Department management.

Much interest has been expressed in decentralizing the management of the Defense Department. The objective has much to commend it. However, how to do it poses a difficult set of problems.

One way to address the subject is to ask "What are the minimum things that the Office of the Secretary of Defense *must* do (consistent with congressional powers) if only because they cannot be done or handled well by the military departments?" The following list is offered:

1. Determine Total Defense Budget
2. Allocate Budget Between
    a. Military Departments
    b. Major Defense Missions
3. Resolve Critical Roles and Missions Issues
4. Promote Innovations
5. Specify and Evaluate Combat Readiness and Sustainability
6. Overwatch Service Operational Testing, and Conduct Joint Operational Testing and Evaluation.

1. Determine Total Defense Budget. Strictly speaking, this and the second function—allocating the total budget as between major categories and services—is an activity in which the executive and legislative branch jointly participate and determine. They are functions that must be performed by the constituted civil authorities, are central to the very concept of civilian control of the military, and are, in fact, performed by civil authority. But not all civilian leaders have alway faced up to the full responsibility that goes with the power.

The negative implication of the civilian role in this process is that the military services cannot give civilian leaders very useful advice on what the total defense budget should be. The reason military advice is not useful is that it will almost always advocate amounts that greatly exceed what civilians are willing to spend. Hence, it remains that civilian leaders must and do determine the total budget. To ask the military for their recommendations is to reject them. It is not clear what purpose is served by the dialogue other than obtaining, in an indirect way, their exaggerated appraisal of the threat. However, information on the threat can be directly sought; and preferably organizations other than the military services should be prime producers in this business.[10]

2. Allocate Budget Between Military Departments and Major Missions. Civilians must make these decisions because of their impact upon foreign policy. For example, the type of strategic deterrence capability, or the principal regions toward which conventional forces are oriented, must be keyed to foreign-policy objectives. The opportunity of military services to intepret foreign policy should be minimized. The extent to which they interpret or are able to try to anticipate changes in foreign policy can be reflected in the force structure and impact upon the kind of military capability the country will have. In this fashion, the military bureaucracies implicitly influence foreign policy itself. Although such influence can never be entirely eliminated, given the fact that the distinction between means and ends is seldom airtight, its incidence can be minimized if civilians explicitly make the decisions on the major force-structure allocations, as between missions, and on the major ways of reforming a mission (e.g., land-based versus sea-based tactical air), rapid deployment capability, and so on.

3. Resolve Critical Roles and Missions Issues. Allocating the major missions between military departments through budgets solves a large part of the "roles and missions" problem. However, critical loose ends may be overlooked, or not squarely faced, by the military departments. Senior authorities must check to see that a military service fulfills the spirit of a decision that assigns it a particular mission. For example, it is possible that an air force, upon obtaining resources for tactical air lift and close air-support for the Army, may not give careful attention to training crews and providing other resources such as forward air controllers to perform those missions. The resources may become oriented to more favored air-force missions such as strategic deployment of its tactical air force or long-range interdiction missions. The resulting problems from these kinds of behavior should be explicitly surfaced and decisively resolved. Failure to do so can foster ill feeling on the part of the service that feels its needs are not properly served; it creates embarrassment in actual operations.

4. *Promote Innovations.* Major military innovations seldom occur unless either (1) a country has experienced a shock in the form of a military setback or defeat or (2) a superior authority prods the military hierarchy, often by encouraging and protecting the military advocates of new ideas. Raising questions about the old way of doing things also encourages a more explicit dialogue within a military service, which reduces the tendency to become hidebound and encrusted. Civilian authority should perform this role, but with tact and restraint, simply because there is no mechanism built into the services that guarantees it will occur.

5. *Specify and Evaluate Combat Readiness and Sustainability.* This subject is critical to both budgeting and foreign-policy objectives. Military units can be in different states of combat readiness, which has different cost implications. It is more costly to have a unit in a high state of readiness than one that requires intensive training or some reequipage before it can fight. Some units can be operated at reduced strength, to be brought up to full strength by calling up reservists, and these will be less costly to operate in peacetime. The extent to which reserves are to be activated in response to varying military needs is a high-level policy matter that civilian leaders must determine. The level of readiness demanded also determines training requirements, which importantly affects cost.

Readiness affects the time availabilty of combat capability, which must be linked to foreign-policy objectives, including the proportion of our military forces deployed overseas and the kind of military arrangements we have with allies. Since readiness has cost implications, military services might prefer to have more units at a low state of readiness than fewer units at a high state. Combat readiness and ability to sustain combat also depends upon the number and quality of support units or capability like maintenance organizations, as well as stocks of war consumables. Military services might prefer to spend less of their budget on these items in preference to the more visible combat units or more sophisticated equipment.

Readiness must be related to strategic deployment capability, and vice versa. It makes no sense to acquire strategic-airlift capacity if combat forces are not ready to be deployed. Readiness of tactical air and land units should correspond. Failure to pay careful attention to the complexities of readiness, training, mobilization, and the time dimension of military capability can lead to an unbalanced force structure, wasted peacetime spending, and foreign-policy embarrassment. Specification of these objectives—for both their budgetary foreign-policy content—must therefore come from civilian authority.

Evaluation of combat readiness is a subject that requires careful thought, to include specification of readiness criteria and ways to measure such criteria. Presently, there is a tendency to measure readiness in terms of the equipment, manpower, and spare parts that a unit may actually possess, as a percentage of its "authorized" allowances. This focus is on "inputs." A better way to evaluate readiness is to focus on "outputs," or ability to perform mission-like tasks. How quickly can a ship get underway, how accurately and quickly can a reconnaissance unit locate and report back the position of a target, how well can a fighter-bomber unit shoot? These are measures that convey something about "output" performance. Units should be required to do these things on a "no announcement" basis. Performance in this manner will reveal something about the abilities of commanders to manage resources and to train their men. Rewarding commanders, by promotion, and their troops by, say, extra leave, can also create healthy incentives.[11]

6. *Overwatch Service Operational Testing, and Conduct Joint Operational Testing and Evaluation.* With the right budgetary incentives, the military services would have a stronger incentive to do more operational testing. Yet there could still remain pressures within a service that could impact upon those who do the testing. Someone has to protect the testers. A reviewing and auditing function should therefore be performed to ensure that good experimental procedures are employed, and that test reports accurately reflect the experimental evidence. An organization

like the National Academy of Sciences could perform this function under the Office of the Secretary of Defense sponsorship.[12]

As for joint-service testing it might seem that the JCS could perform this function. However, the findings of such operational testing can often have roles and missions implications. For the same reasons that the JCS cannot resolve major budgetary issues, it cannot perform a monitor or testing function that impacts upon future procurement that could possibly change the relative shares of service budgets. It is also for this reason that testing involving the interaction between systems operated by different major services, like Army air defense and Air Force or Navy tactical air usage, cannot be conducted under JCS auspices. This critical joint testing, therefore, apparently must be supervised by OSD, and overwatched by an independent agency or instrument.

If senior policy makers decisively and clearly make the decisions listed above, the military departments could then obtain rather large but constrained aggregations of resources. In such a setting, a particular weapon (or proposed weapon) would no longer need to be a means to get dollars (or manpower authorizations). Hence, there would not be an incentive to advocate in a fine-grained way.

Professional military men do have a strong and instinctive incentive to possess effective fighting capability in the event of war. This is a desirable attribute and if it can be properly harnessed it should lead to greater efficiency. A secondary but important consideration to the uniformed military is a desire to maintain senior command positions. This is neither good nor bad in itself but it is a motive that should be kept in mind by senior authorities, and to the extent that it too can be harnessed in a constructive way it should be done. Yet it is the instinct to be able to win in war, or to be able to conduct military operations most effectively, that can potentially energize the professional military to attain efficient peacetime military management, *provided it has no incentive to do anything else.*

Giving the military services rather large aggregations of resources seems the only way to change incentives in this desirable way. However, to avoid the problems that existed before McNamara, budgets must also be specified in terms of *major mission categories* as well as military departments. Within such constraints a military service could be on notice that if it finds a more efficient way of doing a particular thing, it may employ the resulting cost saving in some other way that will benefit it. For example, if the Army develops a new, low-cost tank, either it can employ the savings to acquire other equipment in the same combat mission or, should a service find a more efficient way to manage its spare-parts inventory, it can use the savings to improve capability. On the other hand, if it undertakes a development that proves more costly than anticipated, it will have to either acquire fewer units or give up something else in the specific mission category. It would then have a much stronger incentive to give up "gold plating" of new weapons or to ask whether a costly performance feature is really worth it in terms of superior fighting capability.

If budgeting ground rules can be satisfactorily laid out that constrain service behavior in terms of broader aggregations, considerable reduction of making many fine-grained decisions in the Office of the Secretary of Defense could occur. Detailed regulation on the part of the Office of the Secretary, either by way of tight decision rules, or by way of low-decision thresholds, or by other controls, could be greatly reduced. Military services in turn could be free to make a wide range of "tradeoffs" as between different types of equipment, manpower and equipment, and other inputs.

Let us illustrate how such a system might work by means of an example applied to Army land forces. First, let it be decided how many land-forces divisions there should be, in both active and reserve status. Next, assume that a certain kind of division force has the following characteristics:

Size of division force (manpower)	50,000
Average equipment investment per man	$10,000

Total investment per divison would be $500 million. If it is decided to have 10 divisions, the equipment investment would be $5 billion. If it is also established that the equipment has an average weighted life of 10 years, an annual procurement budget of $500 million would be called for. This allowance could be budgeted to the Army as long as the 10-division force objective is in effect. Within very broad limits, the Army could be left free to program and spend this amount. The Army, in turn, should be constrained by that amount. Thus if it wishes to acquire a new, sophisticated helicopter, it will have to give up some other things. Conversely, if it develops more efficient ways of maintaining its trucks, so that the average life of trucks can be extended from say, five years to six years, the resulting cost savings could be kept to buy some of the more costly helicopters. Similarly it would have an incentive that is presently absent by way of getting rid of marginal or redundant items.

If this approach were employed to determine the materiel funding for units, the decision thresholds might be as follows: civilian policy makers would cut the procurement allowance only if they cut the force level, which presumably they would do on the basis of a revised appraisal of the threat or a changed foreign policy. In such an event, they explicitly take the responsibility for a reduced military capability. Conversely, the Army might argue that technical developments by opponents warrant a more costly family of weapons; but in this case there should be clear technical intelligence of the development as well as evidence generated from field tests that the new items provide enhanced capabilty before major procurement is undertaken.

The opportunity for the service to make changes need not be confined to the materiel area. For example, if the division force threshold is 50,000 men, the service might find more efficient ways to perform some of the support functions (perhaps by employing less complicated or more reliable systems). The manpower or its associated cost savings could be employed in other ways—say, to provide some extra battalions of tanks or infantry, or to acquire some preferred new sytem.

Such an approach can also be easily extended to the land forces component of the Marine Corps. Land forces perhaps pose the most difficult problems of force planning and programming because they contain so many details each of which impact upon their fighting capability. Higher authorities need not immerse themselves in these details if they focus on combat readiness and ways to measure it. This is why states of readiness for various units must be specified to make a more aggregative budgeting approach workable. If it is not, a service may tend to spend its resources on more units with a low state in preference to a smaller number in a high state of readiness.

These problems, which are most severe for land forces, should not be as serious for air and naval forces. For one thing, aircraft and ships normally operate in a hostile environment, which necessitates maintaining a measure of operating proficiency in peacetime that in many ways approximates wartime performance. With air units, exercises and associated tests in navigation, rapid deployment, air-to-air tactics, target identification, and bombing and gunnery can be conducted. Indeed, the Air Force Strategic Air Command developed an extensive system for maintaining, measuring, and providing incentives such as spot promotions that centered around readiness and simulated combat performance. Exercises can be conducted, on a spot check or unannounced basis, to determine crew proficiency, deployment, maintenance, and logistic performance by requiring, for example, a unit to run the 25 sorties per month per aircraft, if that is its readiness category. Similar exercises are presently conducted by Navy antisubmarine warfare forces.

The suggested budgetary approach could provide a way to harness interservice rivalry to serve a useful purpose. Presently, two or more services have a role in specialized functions that serve a major mission objective. (The only exception is the Navy, which currently has a monopoly in the antisubmarine warfare mission.) This situation contains the potential for a healthy competition over mission budgets. The competition can be healthy if civilian authority clearly resolves roles and missions issues, if it has a rational basis upon which to make budget reallocations as between services, and if it makes those reallocations in a decisive way. It can make the reallocations in a decisive way if it has a basis upon which to evaluate the performance. Operational testing and objective-evaluation procedures to treat combat readiness are critical if not necessary aids to perform this function.

Thus, if the Marine Corps shows it can produce combat units of equal proficiency at less cost than the Army, it could get some of the Army's budget, and vice versa. If Air Force can perform a close air-support mission better than the Marine or Navy Air (in exercises that test ability (1) to locate the area where a forward air controller says the target is, (2) to identify the target and (3) to hit it, and not simulated friendly ground elements), it should get more of the tactical air budget. Some of each service's budget (including savings generated) might be employed for research and development to discover ways to perform better another service's missions.

Only if the military services have a direct responsibility and the freedom necessary to carry out that responsibility will they have an incentive to attain efficiency, to do imaginative and rigorous operational testing,[13] and to create information systems that serve management and resource allocation purposes. In addition to the professional military, technologists, civilian secretariats, and Congress also have a need for the information that is produced; and the system should be "open" to them. Openness can also improve an information and evaluation system. When it is open, it benefits from criticism. Sloppy work is recognized more quickly. Conclusions improperly drawn from data will be flagged and contested. New hypotheses from evidence will be forthcoming more rapidly if more people have access to the evidence and knowledge about the process that generates it. An open-study and evaluation system protects those who do the work against themselves and others who might try to influence findings.

A necessary condition to achieve this result, however, is that specific testing and evaluation efforts be functionally divorced from board budgetary or manpower constraints. Unless this condition holds, the process will be turned on and off to serve political budgetary purposes. In such a case, it ceases to be an evaluation and testing process that can consistently achieve objectivity or scientific detachment. Restraint on the part of a higher authority is therefore necessary if a subordinate agency is to develop an information system that serves operational (as contrasted with budgetary-political) objectives. If that restraint is lacking, either on the part of Congress or the executive branch, the bureau will proceed to develop its mechanism to defeat, or cope with, the extensive intervention. Moreover, the higher authority, upon intervening, must make its decision or proposal on the basis of information. It cannot do this intelligently if it does not have access to a detached and open-study and evaluation system. Yet if it intervenes too much, or in the wrong ways, it destroys the information source needed to make wise decisions on those matters that must be made by higher or central authority. The power of the higher authority to intervene can only be effectively used if it is used sparingly. There is an element of paradox in this point. But it is not unfamiliar to most thoughtful people. The relationships between parent and maturing child provide ample basis for reflection on the use of authority, the fostering of candor, and development of a sense of responsibility on the part of the subordinate.

It seems reasonable and fair to assume that if an officer corps is professional and has good leadership, it has an instinctive desire to get the most effective capability from its resources.

Since overall budgeting policy is presently inserted at such a low organizational level, incentives operate to acquire the costly system, and to retain redundant systems. Eliminating these incentives is necessary if the instincts and aspirations toward professionalism are to have an opportunity to dominate the internal workings of military bureaucracy. There is little reason to expect that detailed weapon selection and decision making by civilian superiors, either in the executive or legislative branches, can compensate for a lack of detached professionalism within the military bureaucracy itself, and, certainly, civilians will not be the ones to handle the battalions, ships, or aircraft under fire.

Over the years, especially during the past four or five, many ideas have been advanced as ways to improve the Defense Department's management of weapon development and procurement. Important recommendations emerged from the year-long investigations and deliberations of the Blue Ribbon Defense Panel, appointed by President Nixon and Secretary of Defense Laird in July 1969, and which were made public in July 1970.[14] Earlier, the Joint Economic Committee (chaired by Senator Proxmire) held two major hearings on procurement;[15] recently, the Senate Armed Services Committee (chaired by Senator Stennis) conducted public hearings on the weapons-development and procurement process, with an emphasis on procedure.[16] Since the Congressional hearings afforded opportunity for individuals in the executive branch, from industrial and academic oranizations, and in the legislative branch to express their views, they are a rich source of information. All these endeavors taken together, along with numerous recent books and articles on the subject,[17] confront the interested citizen with a staggering array of proposals for improvement.

Recommendations range from highly general ones summarized by a slogan—such as "Fly Before You Buy"—to very specific and detailed lists of procedural changes that should be made in a functional area. This section attempts to identify the major kinds of suggestions, to examine interrelationships between some, the shortcomings of some, and their relation to our recommended approach.

The following list covers many, but not all, of the proposals. Nor is each item an airtight category, since some of them are closely interrelated:

1. Provide Better Information
2. Conduct More Operational Testing
3. Employ a "Fly Before You Buy" Weapons Acquisition Philosophy
4. Cease Concurrency of Weapon Development and Procurement; Contractually Separate Development from Production
5. Nationalize Weapons Development and Manufacturing Firms
6. Decentralize Defense Department Management
7. Employ Better Contracting Arrangements, a "Should Cost" Approach to Development and Acquisition, and Tighter (Including Standardized) Cost Accounting and Auditing Techniques.

1. Provide Better Information. This is usually a general recommendation that is difficult to object to. Yet, it is not of much help if it is silent on the matters of "what sort of information," "for whom," and, especially, the cost of obtaining better information. More important, the problem of the interrelationship between bureaucratic incentives affecting the quality of information is usually overlooked. Specific recent proposals, however, have urged that Congress strengthen its independent capabilty to conduct audits and critical analysis of Pentagon proposals and budgets, in the form of a General Accounting Office type of agency,[18] plus a demand for more up-to-date reporting by the Defense Department on a wide range of activities, to include employment by defense contractors of former military personnel and civil servants.[19] The purpose of these kinds of proposals appears mainly to provide congressional watchdogs better opportunity to detect "excessive" profits of defense contractors, cost overruns, possible conflict-of-interest situations, and so on. One cannot object to better exposure; however, without a coherent divison of labor between the executive and legislative branches, such information programs can easily be caught up in obfuscation that advocacy and counter-advocacy creates. If the purpose of eliciting more information is to facilitate fine-grained decision making by Congress (or more accurately, Congressional-Committee members or their staffs), much trouble could follow.

An alternative plea for better information is oriented toward providing better inputs for more extensive systems analysis, conducted by staffs serving senior decision makers in the executive branch.[20] To the extent that it implicitly advocates trying to improve if not extend the McNamara type of management system, it is naive unless something is done to change the incentives that such a centrally managed system has upon the military departments to influence the data-production process itself. The same criticism also applies to efforts to provide Congressional instruments with better information.

2. *Conduct More Operational Testing.* This is a version of providing more and better information. The Blue Ribbon Defense Panel strongly recommended an increased emphasis upon operational testing. It also urged that operational testing be under cognizance of an Assistant Secretary of Defense for Operational Testing, an associated Defense Test Agency, and separate and explicit funding for the purpose.[21] Such a step, along with the panel's larger recommended scheme of Defense Department management, would separate a portion of the testing activity from the charter of the existing Directorate for Research, Development, Testing and Evaluation, which is dominated by development interests.

The lack of operational testing (or field experimentation) is central to our critique of the present weapon-system acquisition process. However, we also tried to show that a testing process is one aspect of an overall management information system, and that operational testing will be afflicted and hence degraded by the larger budgetary incentives impacting on the military bureaus. It might be suggested that these problems can be avoided through a Defense Department Test Agency doing the testing. However, the task would be so large that either a very big agency (and new bureaucracy) would be required; or a manageable test program would be inadequately small. It is our strong view that most testing should be done by the military departments themselves, with only monitorship by the Office of the Secretary of Defense (and a Defense Test Agency not reporting through Research-and-Development channels) with the Defense Test Agency concentrating its positive test activity on those tests that have a high joint-service content. The services must have a positive incentive to do rigorous testing themselves, and this incentive can be created only through the budget. The Blue Ribbon Defense Panel, unfortunately, was silent on these aspects of the subject.

3. *Employ a "Fly Before You Buy" Weapons Acquisition Philosophy.*

This recommendation has both information and incentive content. It could be one version of the next recommendation—"Cease Concurrency of Weapons Develoment and Procurement"—insofar as its implementation would necessitate testing of a prototype or several competing prototypes before major procurement begins. In this sense, "Fly Before You Buy" becomes a way of getting additional knowledge about the "performance" of a system. But in its slogan form, the recommendation is silent about the nature of the testing program itself. If it means that one or a few development prototypes engage in a "flyoff," or a "contest," to determine which system is "best," a question remains regarding the criteria the test measures. On the one hand, the test may measure only physical-performance characteristics—that is, which system can fly the fastest, shoot the most accurately, and so on. Hence, these kinds of tests would measure the degree to which previously specified performance characteristics are met or exceeded. But the specifications may be off the mark in terms of providing a weapon with much combat utility.

On the other hand, it might be urged that the prototype, or several competing ones, be subject to operational tests. As a general rule, this may not be a bad idea. In fact, situations can be imagined when through prior operational testing it is possible to determine that a particular set of design features, permitted by a technical change, can provide a substantial gain in combat utility. In such cases, incorporating those changes in a new model of an existing system may be the rational thing to do. On occasion, operational testing might even suggest that an entirely new weapon concept is the best way to go, even if its cost of development and production are unknown by a factor of two or three. In such a case, we see no intrinsic objection to a concurrent development-and-procurement program; and having several "different" prototype programs could entail redundant effort and expense. However, to the extent that there might be an element of confusion on this point, a distinction should be made between operational testing (or field experimentation) that is undertaken before the performance specifications of a future system are established, and "operational acceptability" testing of prototype systems. The latter kinds of testing, which could have a strong operational flavor, would implement the "Fly Before You Buy" procurement policy.

Most students who advocate the "Fly Before You Buy" acquisition philosophy are also critical of concurrent development and procurement. Behind the advocacy of this position is the idea that it would permit creating more economic competition between weapons suppliers, and even a sharper division of labor between weapons developers on one hand and manufacturers on the other. By "economic competition" we mean competition in such matters as price and performance, as contrasted with proposal writing and promises. The overall force of these and related recommendations is to try to find ways to transform the private-sector weapons industry into something that more closely behaves like a free-enterprise activity, as contrasted with an "arsenal system."

4. *Cease Concurrency of Weapon Development and Procurement; Contractually Separate Development From Production.* These are actually two separate proposals, although the proposal that development be separated from procurement would imply elimination of concurrency. Much of the rationale for the "Fly Before You Buy" philosophy derives from this line of advocacy.

The argument for the elimination of concurrency is based upon a rejection of the idea of attempting to conceptualize a weapon system, consisting of a number of key subsystems some or all of which are as yet undeveloped, and proceeding to force the state of the art in one or more of specialized technical fields in order to get the major system at some specific future date. The effort to force the state-of-the-technical art as well as to get the various untried subsystems to mesh well in the larger-system context is very costly. For example, the Army's Main Battle Tank program illustrated the latter kind of problem: any one (or even several) of the design objectives might have been relatively easy to achieve. But mating a large number of them—e.g., the automatic loader, the caseless ammunition, and the missile; to say nothing of the vehicle, engine, and suspension system—proved to be formidable and costly. Because this development strategy gobbles up a large amount of resources, there are fewer resources to undertake exploratory research and development on a variety of technical approaches to find out which ones are, in fact, the best. Exploring a variety of technical approaches, to include physical experimentation, is a way of acquiring better information on technical feasibility. The major problem in technical development is coping with uncertainty. The "weapon-system" approach, it is argued, precludes exploring diverse technical solutions, because it is decided to follow the leads that seem most feasible and attractive at an inappropriately early time.[22]

The recommended development strategy that follows from this line of criticism is that a weapon system should not be conceived unless it is composed of subsystems that themselves are thoroughly developed and tested, each of which is hopefully, an item selected as a result of having pursued multiple technical approaches to the subsystem developments. By virtue of having selected the best subsystem, the pressure to try to force the state of technical art (say, like improved chemical milling to achieve a desired weight reduction) is eliminated. Problems can still arise in "mating" the diverse subsystems. These latter problems are a matter of the art of design and often are formidable in their own right. But they should not be compounded many times with each of many subsytems.

The contractual separation of development and production derives support from two complementary points. First, it would eliminate the present incentive for a firm to "buy into" a development program in the expectation that the production phase of the program (including spare-parts sales during the system's operating life) permits recouping any loss on the devlopment. Needless to say, this incentive contributes to optimistic cost estimating. A second rationale for the contractual separation is based on the belief that the "non-weapon system" strategy will save resources (on the development phase) so as to provide the means to support a large number of independent and smaller development-and-design teams, which makes the objective of pursuing multitechnical approaches operational.

This set of interrelated recommendations focuses on technical development and coping with the uncertainties of attaining technical feasibility of enhanced physical performance. It is silent on the question of whether the particular performance specifications that describe a system are the best ones to provide operational effectiveness. As has been stated previously in this book, even if technical developments proceeded without the cost overruns and were even achievable at lower cost, which the nonconcurrency strategy might very well permit, there still might not be very useful weapons in the abscence of testing that relates technical performance to effectiveness criteria.

It should be emphasized, however, that there is no conflict between adopting the nonconcurrent technical-development strategy, on one hand, and conducting increased operational testing, on the other. Indeed, they are complementary strategies. One deals with technical uncertainty; the other, with tactical, or operational uncertainty. Operational testing provides guidance to military users and technologists regarding which enhanced performance may provide the best tactical payoff. Thorough technical development of major subsystems provides items that, by improvisation, could be tested in an operational context—for example, a new airborne radar can be rigged to an existing aircraft and tested in an operational context; or an antitank missile could be tested before an entire vehicle is designed around it.[23]

5. *Nationalize Weapons Development and Manufacturing Firms.* This proposal has been advanced by Professor John Kenneth Galbraith.[24] The reasons for his advocacy of this position are not those that a socialist would advance; rather, they derive cogency from the behavior of defense firms. Large defense firms are so intertwined with the Defense Department bureaucracy that they are indistinguishable from government arsenals. Moreover, many defense firms employ large amounts of government-owned plant and equipment, from which private stockholders derive profits and a leverage on their equity capital. Hence, a question can be raised as to just what is the role of the profit (and loss) incentive in this business. This point is underscored by the effort of the government to succor firms from loss, as illustrated by the case of Lockheed obtaining a specially legislated loan. There is little competition, and the profit motive is mainly harnessed to clever proposal writing and lobbying with administrative and political decision makers. So if they are arsenals already, why should they not be owned outright by the government?

Some might agree with Galbraith's line of reasoning, given the way the existing weapon-system acquisition process has operated. Further, a case can be made that this system has not turned in a spectacular performance by way of providing useful weapons: the performance, as was the case with bygone arsenals, is, at best, very mixed. For these reasons, in the absence of more fundamental changes in the system, nationalizing defense firms will not change anything in terms of contributing to the country's national security. Some might argue that profits that private firms presently earn would be saved. However, it is our bet that the newly created arsenals would absorb that amount, if not more, and transform them into civil-servant and government-employee payrolls. Such a large number of employees might even increase the pressure that lobbying exerts on the decision-making process. For these reasons, the recommendation that defense firms be nationalized does not cope with real problems and it evades the task of trying to find ways to institute real competition in the defense sector.

6. *Decentralize Defense Department Management.* The concepts of centralized and decentralized management are ambiguous, although decentralized management is often treated as a "good thing." Unless one is fairly precise about what one means by "decentralized management," more of it can lead to mischief. In some circles, it can mean that the Office of the Secretary of Defense merely lets go of its power, or is reduced in power, to permit the military services (and even subcomponents of each service) to deal directly with Congress, or the congressional committees in particular. This was the pre-World War II U.S. model. However, it did not work well. It would work less well today given the increased complexity of defense management. Moreover, such a system would still be "centrally managed" to the extent that congressional committees (a rather high authority) try to make fine-grained decisions through budgets. That the overall program would lack coherence and consistency, as between its many components, masks the point.

In such a case, the system is simply not managed at all because of a failure to work out a clear division of labor between the many parties which, in fact, must participate in the management of large, complex organizations.

7. *Employ Better Contracting Arrangements, a "Should Cost" Approach to Development and Acquisition, and Tighter (Including Standardized) Cost-Accounting and Auditing Techniques.* These proposals are advanced as techniques that would assist in reducing cost overruns.[25] Specification of development-and-procurement contracts, particularly prices, is difficult, given the idiosyncratic nature of each program. No contracting technique employed thus far is devoid of potential to create problems. Hence, a "cost-plus-fixed-fee" form has been most frequently used in development programs (a substantial departure from this approach was the C-5A program).[26] Problems center around setting the appropriate fee, and clear identification of costs. On the fee, for example, a high ratio of sales to a firm's investment (the latter of which can be small because of government progress payments taking care of much working-capital requirements,

and the use of government plant and equipment) can permit extremely high or "excessive" profits. But profits can be partially masked, or absorbed by "expenses"; hence costing standards are necessary to control this behavior (a point discovered early in the effort to regulate public utilities and railroads). Yet there are no standard cost-accounting techniques to which defense firms must adhere. For these reasons, information forthcoming from defense firms has a peculiar quality: it provides limited insight on how the system operates; it does not permit careful monitorship of the resource-using activity; it facilitates obfuscation.

The idea of "should costing" is that of eschewing historical cost experience as a basis for government evaluation of industry cost estimates (and proposals), to rely instead upon production-engineering expertise (using techniques like time and motion studies) employed by government experts. In this fashion, it is hoped that standards for production efficiency could be established, and with this sort of tool it could be attempted to inspect (and police?) the activity of firms.

Most proposals along these lines came from "disinterested outsiders," such as scholars, and an occasional "insider" such as Admiral Rickover). This approach has also been strongly advocated by Senator Proxmire, as a result of his subcommittee hearings on procurement with its speical emphasis on the C-5A program.

Recommendatons of this type are unsatisfying because they are incomplete. Apart from the facts that doing these things is technically and in some respects inherently difficult if not impossible to carry out, the principal reason is that the military services—which are the "operators" in this business in that they actually negotiate and write the contracts, monitor the plant, audit the books, and so on—have no strong incentive to do so. The perverse incentives, created and sustained by the civilian masters (including those in Congress who play the pork-barrel game), will afflict attaining the objectives of improving development and manufacturing efficiency just as it inhibits raising and addressing the hard questions about weapon-system effectiveness. Moreover, a case can be made that advocacy of "Should Costing" and "Improved Cost Accounting and Auditing Techniques" evades addressing the main problems insofar as they are merely devices that seek to make an unsound acquisition strategy workable. Making the industry more competitive is an alternative strategy. There is much opportunity to employ *fixed price* contracts, where the possibility of bankruptcy (and an equal possibility of "excessive" profits for the really efficient producer) evoke healthy incentives. Of course, this approach requires that high officials have the crassness and courage to permit an occasional firm to go bankrupt. (It should be recognized, incidentally, that bankruptcy does not necessarily mean a loss of jobs, skills, or other resources; it merely means that stockholders might be wiped out, and a change in management).

In the years since the Defense Department has operated under a changed administration that confronted the management problems prevalent during the previous twenty-five years, some changes have been announced and promulgated. In the weapon-acquisition area, the ideas of the "Fly Before You Buy" and prototype testing philosophy have been voiced,[27] and there has been a stated intention to place more emphasis upon operational testing and evaluation,[28] a guarded endorsement of decentralized management (which has been termed "participatory management"),[29] and the adoption of a "fiscal guidance" approach as a tool for involving the military services in the budgetary dialogue.[30]

The "fiscal guidance" concept offers the greatest potential for fundamental reform insofar as it resembles our proposal that the military services be given more aggressive budgetary freedom and stronger incentives to economize. However, these guidelines thus far have been unclear as to just how much freedom the military services have to make tradeoffs within the major force-structure categories. At the same time, they had zero impact on specific weapons choices. Although the services are invited to make recommendations involving changes in the force structure, they are subject to OSD approval. The fiscal guidelines are built up from a rather fine-grained set of assumptions, with some variations in these assumptions, regarding the overall force structure. They also postulate a set of estimates for research and development. Finally, a large amount of the program budget falls in the category of "general support," and this is allocated as between the force-structure elements by means of crude estimating techniques.

There are mixed interpretations in the military services of what these guidelines really mean. In some quarters they are viewed to be a set of detailed force-structure guidelines; in others, fiscal guidelines. Since the guidance is silent on the point, there are no clear signals that a service can retain any "savings" that would result from its action. For these reasons the services approach the subject gingerly, since it will be reasoned that higher authority might accept the cost-saving elements of a proposed tradeoff but not go along with the other half of the trade that would entail an expenditure increase. Also, there is the possibility that the services will economize on support functions and training in ways that could degrade capability and ability to conduct sustained operations. (There has been a noticeable reduction in Air Force and Navy flying hours since 1970.) Hence, the readiness problem and the means of auditing it must be addressed before the fullest potential that the fiscal guideline approach can afford improved capability.

Although the fiscal-guidelines concept could change things in a major way, the incentive problem still remains. (However, cuts in defense spending, and especially major reduction in the real resources available for development and procurement owing to increased manpower costs and the incidence of inflation, might operate to give the military services some blunt incentives to economize.) Nor is the incentive increased to improve the information system and to do operational testing. Further, the precise direction that the hoped-for increased stated emphasis on operational testing will take is still to be worked out, and is thus unclear. There is the question of the role of the staff section in the Office of the Secretary of Defense in this activity. Will it seek actively to do most of the testing, or will it prod the services to do the lion's share? In the latter case, stronger service-testing commands will have to be established, which will necessarily upset and diminish the present power status of materiel and systems commands. For this reason, the change will be resisted for some time unless there is either strong prodding from higher authority or strong positive incentives impacting on service chiefs and their immediate colleagues to do more operational testing.

The precise meaning of "participatory management" as a way of achieving a more decentralized management was unclear, which is perhaps why it has not produced any noticeable changes. The once highly active Systems Analysis Staff has been somewhat muzzled, which has provided a more hospitable setting in which to receive the recommendations of the Service Chiefs. It also appears that the senior military have more opportunity to make their views known to Congress than they did during the McNamara period (nor has there been any noticeable reduction in the legislative liaison activity of the military services). Although Congress, including the important military committees, have become more skeptical of Pentagon offerings, much fine-grained decision-making impacting on resource allocation is still done by the highest authorities. There are some signs that its skepticism is moving Congress to make some of the detailed decisions itself, through the crude mechanisms of authorizing legislation and appropriations. Some of these initial decisions were, no doubt, called for. However, if the practice increases and becomes extensive, it would be highly unfortunate.

Only if the military services are placed under broad enough budgetary constraints to give them an incentive to achieve efficiency can defense management be improved in a substantial way. To make this change, however, careful attention must be given to the old-standing relationships between the executive and congressional branches of the government. To move in the direction of "decentralization" in the relationship between the Office of the Secretary of Defense and the military services, by way of granting more responsibility to the military, will not provide much progress if Congress is not also willing to give up some of its age-old prerogatives by way of dispensing favors that flow from the fisc. Like the Office of the Secretary of Defense and the President, it, too, should focus on the big issues, and forego attempting to play the old games that have long characterized congressional-bureaucrat arrangements. Congress, too, should content itself with dealing in major force-structure categories, the funding those categories require, and the associated military issues that have a high-level foreign-policy content. If Congress could make what surely would be a difficult transition from its more than one-hundred-year habit of dealing with detailed line-item budgets, the initial steps taken in the Defense Department in recent years could well turn out to be momentous. Should the executive branch merely permit the military services to deal unilaterally (in the older, informal ways) with Congress, and if Congress responds in the old way, the country's military capability will suffer. If anything, the near future promises to be a critical period of transition.

How much could be saved if military managers could have maximum incentive to economize? If there is waste in the form of overly sophisticated weapons of dubious combat utility, and owing to poor management practices motivated by the existing advocacy processes, then the country obviously could have as much fighting capability as it now has if that waste were eliminated. However, we may need a substantial increase in real combat effective units owing to the currently unrecognized low level of capability associated with weapons that do not work. In posing the question this way, no savings are due to lower levels of major force elements, say, like battalions or air wings committed to NATO. Whether some of the savings might be "plowed back" into providing additional but lower-cost and equally effective combat units, however, is a matter that should be addressed to the context of broader defense and foreign-policy deliberations. Our answer to the question is between $13 to $23 billion a year, relative to present defense budget of about $80 billion.[31]

The breakdown of this estimate of annual savings in billions is as follows:

Procurement	$10
Overhaul and spares	2.5–10
Military personnel	1.3–2.5
Total	$12.8–$22.5

The key to this estimate is procurement, because weapons and equipment are "levers" or multipliers that drive the other major cost elements of modern military forces. Procurement savings would be of two major kinds. First, new technical improvements would be tested and evaluated in a critical way, and much of the costly sophistication would be dispensed with. There would be less concurrency in development and procurement, and technical improvements that provide additional combat utility could be attained at less cost. More austere weapons, in some instances, at anywhere from a third to a fifth as costly as current ones (and more effective as well), would begin to appear in important functional areas as a result of a different, overall development-and-procurement strategy.

A second important source of procurement saving can come from more efficient use of equipment and design of the force structure. This kind of saving is especially relevant to land forces, although it should have some applicability to the Navy and Air Force. Presently, U.S. battalions are loaded down with vehicles and assorted specialized equipment. Much of this can be thinned out by "pooling" resources at higher echelons and specialized organizations, to be allocated to line organizations on an "as needed" basis.[32] In addition, tracked vehicles are often used for functions where less costly trucks can serve; trucks built to military specifications could be partially replaced by less costly commercial-type trucks. And with the right budgetary incentives, the Army's newly rich aviation community might substitute some less expensive, small fixed-wing aircraft to do some of the things presently done by expensive helicopters. For these reasons, it is our estimate that the present $20 billion level of procurement could be cut by half for a saving of $10 billion.[33]

It is characteristic of high-cost equipment to be more costly to maintain. This point seems to be acknowledged by military managers, and reflected by planning-cost factors (which are used for making budgetary estimates) for such items as major depot maintenance and overhaul, spare parts, and fuel. These factors for most systems run between 5 to 10 per cent per year of the acquisition cost, with a preponderance toward 10 per cent. If we assume that equipment has an average life of 10 years, procurement running at $20 billion a year meant a total asset inventory of $200 billion. If it settled down to $100 billion, the total inventory reduction would be $100 billion. Some of the inventory assets, however, are munitions stocks. The ten-year assumed weighted average life may be on the high side. Hence we postulate an inventory reduction of between $50 to $100 billion. Application of the 5 and 10 per cent factors to these amounts provides the $2.5 to $10 billion estimated saving on major overhaul and spares.

Maintenance is also done in operating military units and on shipboard by military personnel. These military personnel require other military personnel to support them—cooks, drivers, doctors, dentists, who, in turn, require still more drivers, cooks, and so on. This is why, in the U.S. Army during World War II, only about three out of ten men were fighters, and the chance is good the ratio is lower today. Presently, military pay costs run about $25 billion a year (total personnel-related costs are considerably higher). To this amount we again applied a saving factor ranging from 5 to 10 per cent (which may well underestimate actual field maintenance savings), to derive an annual cost-saving estimate of between $1.3 and $5 billion. This last estimate is conservative, especially if the military services had the incentive to economize over the full spectrum of manpower utilization: headquarters staffs could shrink drastically (especially if the need for politico-budgetary advocacy fell to zero), some cooks, drivers, and clerks might be converted to riflemen, and more attention might be given to ease of maintenance in ship and aircraft design.

As with pregnancy, it may be that in government activity there really is no such thing as a "little bit" of inefficiency. When it is fueled by perverse incentives driving specialists who produce the information, carry out the administrative actions, and thereby control the countless details of many complex specialties, the results impact upon all resource using activities of the organization. The mass of detail permits obfuscation; the obfuscation prevents critical review and control. Indeed, attempted detailed control increases the incentive to prevent outside review. Hence $13 to $23 billion of waste, in the form of procurement and support costs for weapons and force elements of dubious combat value, out of a total defense budget of $80 billion may not be difficult to understand.

A possible saving of $13 to $23 billion, however, poses a sober thought. To achieve savings of that magnitude presents awkward consequences for many interested parties, even if all the savings were to be plowed back into the military forces. Payrolls and land values in many parts of the country would be adversely affected. (Some military installations might be shut down.) The favors distributed to constitutents by the military who cater to Congress would be less. Both Congressmen on key military committees and high-level civilian officials in the executive branch would have to give up some of the "feeling of power" derived from making or approving the many fine-grained decisions. There are many vested interests in continuing the present style of peacetime military management. It is, indeed, a Military-Congressional-Scientific-Worker-Local Land Owner-Industrial Complex. The chance of changing it is not great unless the principals have some serious talks with themselves, and each other. It is hoped they will be serious, and soon, since it is a question of national security.

NOTES

CHAPTER 1

1. For a summary of the literature see Reinhard Bendix, "Bureaucracy," *International Encyclopedia of the Social Sciences* (New York: Free Press, Vol. 2, 1968), pp. 206–219.
2. See Joseph Kraft, "J. Edgar Hoover—The Compleat Bureaucrat," *Commentary*, Vol. 39 (February 1965), pp. 59–62; and Tom Wicker, "What Have They Done Since They Shot Dillinger?" *The New York Times Magazine*, (December 26, 1969), pp. 4 ff.
3. See Max Weber, "Bureaucracy," translated from *Wirtschaft and Gesellschaft*, by H. H. Gerth and C. Wright Mills, in *From Max Weber: Essays in Sociology*, (New York: Oxford Univ. Press, 1946; first published in 1922), pp. 196–98.
4. *Ibid.*, pp. 198–99, 203.
5. *Ibid.*, p. 203.
6. See Samuel P. Huntington, *The Soldier and the State* (Cambridge: Harvard Univ. Press, 1959), pp. 8–10.
7. *Ibid.*, p. 9.
8. C. Northcote Parkinson, *Parkinson's Law and Other Studies in Administration* (Boston: Houghton Mifflin, 1957), pp. 2–14.
9. See Gordon Tullock, *The Politics of Bureaucracy*, (Washington, D. C.: Public Affairs Press, 1965). However, Parkinson also has useful offerings on this phase of the subject, See *op. cit.*, Ch. 8, pp. 78–89.
10. See Anthony Jay, *Management and Machiavelli*, (New York: Bantam Books, 1967).
11. Tullock, *op. cit.*, pp. 42–43.
12. Dean Acheson, *Present at the Creation: My Years in the State Department* (New York: W. W. Norton, 1969), p. 15.
13. See Jay, *op. cit.*, pp. 36–44.
14. Weber, "Bureaucracy," *op. cit.*, pp. 232–33.
15. See William A. Niskanen, Jr., *Bureaucracy and Representative Government* (Chicago: Aldine-Atherton, 1971), for a rigorous demonstration and extension of this view; and upon which this discussion is based.
16. For an account, see Arthur Smithies, *The Budgetary Process in the United Sates* (New York: McGraw-Hill, 1955), pp. 49–100.
17. Aaron B. Wildavsky, *Politics of the Budgeting Process* (Boston: Little, Brown, 1964).
18. Aaron B. Wildavsky, "Budgeting as a Political Process," *International Encyclopedia of the Social Sciences* (1968), Vol. 2, p. 192.
19. Quoted in Richard E. Neustadt, "Politicians and Bureaucrats," *The Congress and America's Future*, ed. by David B. Truman (Englewood Cliffs, N. J.: Prentice-Hall, 1965), p. 109.
20. For an account of the interest these programs hold for Congress, see Robert Haveman and Paula Stephan, "The Domestic Program Congress Won't Cut," *The Reporter* (February 22, 1968), pp. 36–37.

21. See the editorial, "Preserve the Shuttle," *American Aviation,* February 3, 1969, which simultaneously expresses dismay over DOT's support of rail transit between Washington and New York and notes the "very interesting" fact that the first DOT secretary recently became a railroad president.
22. Neustadt, *op. cit.,* pp. 103–05.
23. See Lester W. Milbrath, *The Washington Lobbyists* (Chicago: Rand McNally, 1963), pp. 179–89, 207–56.
24. Irving Brinton Holley, Jr., *United States Army in World War II, Special Studies, Buying Aircraft: Materiel Procurement for the Army Air Forces,* (Washington, D. C.: Department of the Army, 1964), p. 570.
25. Neustadt, *op. cit.,* p. 114.
26. Wildavsky, "Budgeting as a Political Process," *op. cit.,* p. 195.
27. See Richard F. Fenno, "The House Appropriations Committee as a Political System: The Problem of Integration," *American Political Science Review,* Vol. 56, 1962, pp. 310–24.
28. See Otto A. Davis, M. A. H. Dempster, and Aaron Wildavsky, "A Theory of the Budgetary Process," *The American Political Science Review,* Vol. 60 (September 1966), pp. 529–47, which presents empirical support of this assertion.
29. For a more rigorous and technical treatment of the phenomenon, see Joan Robinson, "Rising Supply Price," reprinted in George J. Stigler and Kenneth Boulding, eds., *Readings in Price Theory* (Chicago: Richard Irwin, 1952), pp. 231–41.
30. See Anthony Downs, *An Economic Theory of Democracy* (New York: Harper and Row, 1957), for the pioneering work on this approach. A further important effort is James M. Buchanan and Gordon Tullock, *The Calculus of Consent: Logical Foundations of Constitutional Democracy* (Ann Arbor: Univ. of Michigan Press, 1962).

CHAPTER 2

1. See, e.g., Carl J. Friedrich, *Man and His Government: An Empirical Theory of Politics* (New York: McGraw-Hill, 1963), p. 322.
2. For an excellent treatment of this subject, which focuses particularly on the American setting, see Huntington, *The Soldier and the State, op. cit.,* pp. 80–97, 143–62, which emphasizes the tensions created by the gap between the value system characteristic of a democratic, egalitarian society and the values necessary to sustain a military organization. See, also, Morris Janowitz, *The Professional Soldier* (Glencoe, Ill.: Free Press, 1960), esp. pp. 79–174 for empirical findings regarding the military selection and promotion process.
3. For an interesting development and extension of such an hypotheses, see Vincent Davis, *The Admiral's Lobby* (Chapel Hill: Univ. of North Carolina Press, 1967). Davis contends that the Navy's officer corps had a twofold problem: as sailors in a predominantly land-oriented society and as military men. Army officers, on the other hand, partly owing to assignments and association with state national guards, have more opportunity to encounter civilians in many walks of life and parts of the country. Similarly, the airplane had commercial applications, and no small amount of romantic appeal to civilians; hence, military airmen were able to establish rapport with "other" elements of American society. According to Davis, naval

officers were thus badly "outgunned" on the domestic political front; and therefore found it necessary purposefully to develop the apparatus which is the title of his book.

With no intention to denigrate the quality of Davis' endeavor, it must be noted that all Army officers might not share his view. In his diary, General Stillwell remarks about the Navy's apparent favored position *vis-à-vis* President Roosevelt with a pungency only exceeded by that which he inflects upon Chiang Kai-shek. see Theodore H. White, ed., *The Stillwell Papers* (New York: Macfadden, 1962), p. 25.

4. See Huntington, *op. cit.,* pp. 464–66.
5. See Richard J. Willey "Taking the Post Office Out of Politics," *The Public Interest* (Spring 1969), 57–71; and Meg Greenfield, "What's the Matter With the Mails?" *The Reporter* (February 11, 1965), 21–25.
6. See Joseph A. Pechman, *Federal Tax Policy* (Washington, D.C.: Brookings, 1966), esp. pp. 50–75, 283–85, with regard to ambivalence. On one hand, the federal income tax caters to populist, egalitarian sentiments by virtue of its steeply progressive statutory tax rates. On the other hand, the operative system—owing to its complex of exemptions, deductions, and income exclusions—is considerably less progressive.
7. See Chester I. Barnard, *The Functions of the Executive* (Cambridge: Harvard Univ. Press, 1942), pp. 217–27 for a discussion of the formal and informal organizations and their respective communications systems.
8. See, e.g., James T. Bonner, "The Distribution of Benefits from Cotton Price Supports," in Chase (ed.), *Problems in Public Expenditure Analysis, op. cit.,* pp. 223–48.
9. Charles L. Schultze, *The Politics and Economics of Public Spending* (Washington, D.C.: The Brookings Institution, 1968), p. 51.
10. See, for example James Q. Wilson, "Corruption Is Not Always Scandalous," *New York Times Magazine,* April 28, 1968, which puts the subject in such a perspective.

CHAPTER 3

1. See George H. Stein, *The Waffen SS: Hitler's Elite Guard at War, 1939–1945* (Ithaca, New York: Cornell Univ. Press, 1966), pp. 60–92, and esp. 197–211.
2. See John W. Wheeler-Bennett, *The Nemesis of Power: The German Army in Politics 1918—1945* (New York: Viking Press, 1964), pp. 333–82, for a detailed account of how Hitler outmaneuvered the army during the period that his power position was vulnerable.
3. For an account of the change see William A. Niskanen, "The Defense Resource Allocation Process," in *Defense Management,* Stephen Enke, ed. (Englewood Cliffs, N. J.: Prentice Hall, 1967), esp. pp. 7–15; and Charles J. Hitch, *Decision-Making for Defense* (Berkeley: Univ. of Calif. Press, 1965), pp. 30–39.
4. Walter Millis, *Arms and Men: A Study in American Military History,* (New York: G. P. Putnam's Sons, 1956), pp. 60–64, for a summary of Jefferson's implementation of his philosophy.
5. Russell F. Weigley, *History of the United States Army* (New York: Macmillan Co., 1967), p. 122.
6. *Ibid.,* pp. 131–32.

7. The Admiral's motivation was suggested by Wellington. See Elizabeth Longford, *Wellington: The Years of the Sword* (New York: Harper & Row, Publishers, 1969), p. 282n.
8. Huntington, *The Soldier and The State, op. cit.*, p. 195.
9. *Ibid.*, pp. 198–99.
10. Lynn Montross, *War Through The Ages*, 3rd ed., (New York: Harper & Brothers, 1960), pp. 337–40.
11. *Ibid.*, p. 355.
12. *Ibid.*, p. 356.
13. For an account of the École's founding, its illustrious faculty, and, especially, its subsequent impact on the intellectual world by way of creating both logical positivism and what came to be termed "social engineering" (by engineers and physical scientists, of course), see F. A. Hayek, *The Counter-Revolution of Science: Studies on the Abuse of Reason* (Glencoe, Illinois: Free Press, 1952), pp. 105–88.
14. Quoted in Huntington, *op. cit.*, p. 197.
15. J. P. T. Bury, ed., *The New Cambridge Modern History, X, The Zenith of European Power: 1830–70*, (Cambridge: University Press, 1967), p. 294.
16. *Ibid.*, p. 287.
17. Quoted in *Ibid.*, p. 282.
18. See Huntington, *op. cit.*, pp. 230 ff. for a more extensive treatment of the development, and upon which this discussion is based.
19. For the most comprehensive source on the background of the Navy's system, see Julius Augustus Furer, *Administration of the Navy Department in World War II* (Washington, D.C.: Department of the Navy, 1959), pp. 1–32 plus chapters dealing with each of the Navy's wartime bureaus; see also Albion and Connery, *Forrestal and the Navy, op. cit.*, pp. 38–58, for a somewhat more critical view of the Navy's system.

   The Army's Technical Service system is treated throughout Weigley, *History of the United States Army, op. cit.* For a general view, with emphasis upon field logistics and wartime supply, see James A. Huston, *The Sinews of War: Army Logistics 1775–1953*, Army Historical Series (Washington, D.C.: Office of the Chief of Military History, United States Army, 1966). For more specific information of the Army's system, with reference to pre-World War II equipment development, see Constance McLaughlin Green, Harry C. Thomson, and Peter C. Roots, *United States Army in World War II, The Technical Services; The Ordnance Department: Planning Munitions for War* (Washington, D.C.: Office of the Chief of Military History, Department of the Army, 1955), pp. 199–200; Dulany Terrett, *United States Army in World War II, The Technical Services: The Signal Corps: The Emergency*, to December 1941 (Washington, D.C.: Office of the Chief of Military History, Department of the Army, 1956).
20. A. Goodwin, ed., *Cambridge Modern History, VIII, The American and French Revolutions* (Cambridge: Univ. Press, 1965), pp. 192–93.
21. Frank E. Comparato, *Age of Great Guns* (Harrisburg: Stackpole Co., 1965), pp. 36–42.
22. See Robert V. Bruce, *Lincoln and the Tools of War* (Indianapolis: Bobbs-Merrill Co., 1956), esp. pp. 99–117, for an account of Lincoln's involvement with rifles. Lincoln personally played a role in many other weapon acquisitions, generally over the objection of the Ordnance Department. This book provides a good account of this little-known facet of Lincoln's

capacity and ability. For example, the country's first aircraft carrier, in the form of balloons launched from a vessel on the Potomac, may be credited to him insofar as he pushed the idea through the bureaucracy (see *Ibid.*, pp. 85–88).

23. For an account of the development, see Sidney B. Brinckerhoff and Pierce Chamberlin, "The Army's Search for a Repeating Rifle: 1873–1903," *Military Affairs* 32 (Spring 1968), pp. 20–30.

24. Comparato, *Age of Great Guns, op. cit,* p. 183.

25. *Ibid.,* p. 196.

26. *Ibid.,* p. 194.

27. *Ibid.,* pp. 194–95.

28. *Ibid.,* pp. 195–202.

29. Green, Thomson, and Roots, *op. cit.*

30. See *The War Reports of Marshall, Arnold, and King* (Philadelphia: J. B. Lippincott, 1947), p. 261.

31. Robert Greenhalgh Albion and Robert Howe Connery, *Forrestal and the Navy* (New York: Columbia Univ. Press, 1962), p. 53.

32. Quoted in *Ibid.,* p. 52.

33. Harold and Margaret Sprout, *The Rise of American Naval Power, 1776–1918,* (Princeton: Princeton Univ. Press, 1939), pp. 166–67. It was observed by Mr. Dooley "that the first qualification of a Secretary of the Navy was that he should never have seen salt water outside of a pork barrel" (*Ibid.,* p. 181n.).

34. See Louis Smith, *American Democracy and Military Power: A Study of Civil Control of Military Power in the United States* (Chicago: Univ. of Chicago Press, 1951), pp. 121–22. See, also, Sprout, *op. cit.* pp. 190–98, 270–72, 278–80.

35. Elting E. Morrison, *Admiral Sims and the Modern American Navy* (Boston: Houghton Mifflin Co., 1942), pp. 84–88.

36. An important exception was made in 1908, after a bitter struggle which led to the protest resignation of the chief of the Bureau of Navigation, with hospital ships. President Theodore Roosevelt apparently had to make the final decision backing the Navy surgeon general's position that medical officers should command hospital ships. See Furer, *op. cit.,* pp. 497–98.

37. Quoted in Albion and Connery, *op. cit.,* p. 46.

38. *Ibid.*

39. Furer, *op. cit.,* p. 341.

40. *Ibid.,* pp. 343–44.

41. The Bofors system had been designed by Krupp, who had also acquired during the 1920's about a third ownership interest in the Swedish firm through stock purchases. The endeavor was part of the process by which Germany kept its hand in weapons development during the period the Treaty of Versailles was in effect.

42. Furer, *op. cit.,* p. 338.

43. *Ibid.*

44. Quoted in *Ibid.,* p. 339.

45. Quoted in *Ibid.*

46. For a recent and balanced treatment of the subject, see Merton J. Peck and Frederic M. Scherer, *The Weapons Acquisition Process: An Economic Analysis* Graduate School of Business Administration, (Cambridge: Harvard U. 1962), pp. 68–97, 582–83.

47. See Weigley, *op. cit.,* pp. 286–87, for a fuller account.

48. *Ibid.*, p. 287.

49. Furer, *op. cit.*, pp. 29–30.

50. For an account of the planning and procurement difficulties associated with the war with Spain, see Huston, *op. cit.*, pp. 273–91.

51. Forrest C. Pogue, *George C. Marshall: Ordeal and Hope: 1939–1942* (New York: Viking Press, 1965), p. 293.

52. For the story, see Mark Skinner Watson, *United States Army in World War II, The War Department, Chief of Staff: Prewar Plans and Preparations* (Washington, D.C.: Historical Division, Department of the Army, 1950).

53. For a detailed description of the organizational changes, see Otto L. Nelson, Jr., *National Security and the General Staff* (Washington, D.C., Infantry Journal Press, 1946), pp. 347–96.

54. See Pogue, *op. cit.*, pp. 289–301, for an account of how Marshall handled the campaign. A very important force that figured in this reorganization was the status of the Army Air Corps, and Marshall's relationship with Gen. H. H. Arnold. The reorganization also created the quasi-independent Army Air Force. For a good account of this aspect of the subject, see John D. Millett, *United States Army in World War II, The Army Service Forces, The Organization and Role of the Army Service Forces* (Washington, D.C.: Office, Chief of Military History, Department of the Army, 1954), pp. 25–26.

55. See Elias Huzar, *The Purse and the Sword: Control of the Army by Congress through Military Appropriations, 1933–1950* (Ithaca: Cornell Univ. Press, 1950), pp. 23–25.

56. See William W. Pierson, Jr., "The Committee on the Conduct of the Civil War," *The American Historical Review*, 22 April 1918, reprinted in Gordon B. Turner, ed., *A History of Military Affairs in Western Society Since the Eighteenth Century* (New York: Harcourt, Brace and Company, 1952), pp. 179–86.

57. See Huzar, *op. cit.*, Table III, p. 141, for evidence to support this point.

58. *Ibid.*, pp. 223–34.

59. *Ibid.*, pp. 300–03.

60. The link between the Army and agricultural interests had a firm precedence in Central Europe, and was reinforced by the Germans (and later the French) overcompensating landowners for damage inflicted on crops during maneuvers.

61. For a more detailed account of the confusion, ambiguity, and frustration that befell both military planners and congressmen during the 1920's and 1930's in their joint planning and programming effort related to air matters, see Irving Brinton Holly, Jr., *Buying Aircraft: Materiel Procurement for the Army Air Forces, op. cit.*, pp. 43–79.

CHAPTER 4

1. Karl von Clausewitz, *On War*, trans. Matthijs Jolles (New York: Modern Library, 1943), pp. 237–44.

2. *Ibid.*, p. 238.

3. *Ibid.*, p. 239.

4. *Ibid.*, pp. 240–41.

5. *Ibid.*, p. 242.

6. *Ibid.*, p. 243.

7. *Ibid.*, p. 244.

8. *Ibid.*

9. *Ibid.*, p. 139.
10. *Ibid.*, pp. 386–404.
11. *Ibid.*, p. 179.
12. *Ibid.*
13. *Ibid.*, p. 16.
14. *Ibid.*, p. 15.
15. Naval warfare, in the modern sense of concept, is a relatively recent development, which got underway around Elizabethan times. Specifically, it involved "deep-water" ships, relying exclusively upon sail for propulsion instead of combinations of sail and oars, and upon cannon for primary armament. Prior to this period, war at sea was essentially infantry warfare, and soldiers usually commanded the operation and determined the tactics. For an account of the galley warfare of the pre-Elizabethan period, see E. B. Potter and Chester W. Nimitz, eds., *Sea Power: A Naval History* (Englewood Cliffs, N.J.: Prentice-Hall, 1960), pp. 1–20.
16. There was, however, a major difference of view between the "formalist" and "melee" tactical schools of thought, which focused on the precise nature of the doctrine that governed the final engagement. For an account, see Potter and Nimitz, *op. cit.*, pp. 36–41, 48–51.
17. For a more extensive discussion of the technology of wooden ship construction, see Robert Albion, *Forests and Sea Power: The Timber Problem of the Royal Navy, 1652–1862* (Hamden, Conn.: Archon Books, 1965), esp. pp. 3–38. This book also treats the entire range of politics and military-procurement problems of the period's "timber-military complex."
18. Ships with less than fifty guns came to be frigates (or cruisers in the modern sense) and tended to standardize on thirty-six and forty-four guns. Frigates were employed for scouting and commerce raiding.
19. Quoted in Philip Guedalla, *Wellington* (New York: Harper and Brothers, 1931), pp. 169–70. Sir John also referred to it as "littoral warfare."
20. Potter and Nimitz, *op. cit.*, pp. 55–59.
21. Alfred Thayer Mahan, *The Influence of Sea Power Upon History, 1660–1783*, (New York: Hill and Wang, 1957), p. 1.

    The emphasis upon colonial and imperial power, which underlies part of Mahan's thinking, has a striking similarity to, and affinity with, Marxian theory, which has not gone unnoticed. See Vincent Davis, *The Admirals' Lobby, op. cit.*, pp. 106–09.
22. J. P. T. Bury, *The New Cambridge Modern History*, vol. 10, *The Zenith of European Power, op. cit.*, pp. 276–77.
23. For a good account of the period, with emphasis on the technological turbulence and how experimental evidence from assorted nineteenth-century naval actions was interpreted, see *Ibid.*, pp. 228–42.
24. Quoted in Correlli Barnett, *The Swordbearers: Supreme Command in the First World War* (New York: William Morrow, 1964), p. 100.
25. For some good studies of the subject, see I. B. Holley, Jr., *Ideas and Weapons: Exploitation of the Aerial Weapon By the United States During World War I* (New Haven: Yale University Press, 1953); Vincent Davis, *The Politics of Innovation: Patterns in Navy Cases* (Denver: Monograph Series in World Affairs, University of Denver Social Science Foundation, 1966–67); and Clark G. Reynolds, *The Fast Carriers: The Forging of an Air Navy* (New York: McGraw-Hill, 1968), esp. pp. 1–112, 380–401.
26. For an elaboration of the innovative process and the development of a

theoretical model that tries to explain the essential qualities of capitalistic economic system as a mechanism that facilitates the innovative process in economic relationships, see J. A. Schumpeter, *The Theory of Economic Development* (Cambridge: Harvard Univ. Press, 1934); for a testing of his model by reference to statistical and historical evidence, see also Schumpeter's *Business Cycles*, 2 vols. (New York: McGraw-Hill, 1939).

27. A. Goodwin, ed., *The New Cambridge Modern History, VII: The American and French Revolutions, 1763–93, op. cit.*, p. 196.
28. Frank E. Comparato, *Age of Great Guns* (Harrisburg: Stackpole Co., 1965), pp. 13–14.
29. *Ibid.*, pp. 13–15.
30. Reynolds, *The Fast Carriers, op. cit.*, pp. 65–78, 88–96, 161–69.
31. *Ibid.*, pp. 53–59.
32. *Ibid.*, pp. 128–29.
33. *Ibid.*, pp. 99–108, 169–204.
34. Even a thoughtful writer whose work is sympathetic to the Navy (Vincent Davis, *The Admirals' Lobby, op. cit.*, p. 136) feels that "the most grievous failure of naval officers during the pre-1941 decade in terms of appreciating the significance of technological change was their neglect of aviation developments."

    This statement is unlike ones that employ the usual examples of horse cavalry retention, or the machinegun densities on the eve of World War I. The record indicates (1) the U.S. Navy pioneered naval carrier tactics and techniques; (2) it possessed seven modern carriers when World War II started, a force that compared favorably with Japan's; and (3) most important, the carrier forces achieved the strategically important victory of the Coral Sea and the decisive one of Midway by mid-1942.

    The force of Davis' observation may be that the country would have been better served if it had had fewer battleships and more carriers when the war broke out. But this smacks too much of hindsight.
35. See Sir Llewellyn Woodward, *Great Britain and the War of 1914–1918* (London: Methuen, 1967), pp. 139–42.
36. For a detailed account of the German World War I innovation in infantry tactics, see *Historical Trends Related to Weapons Lethality: Basic Historical Studies, Annex I* (Washington: Historical Evaluation and Research Organization, 1964), pp. 77–82; for the best account of the German World War II organization and doctrine, see F. O. Miksche, *Attack: A Study of Blitzkrieg Tactics* (New York: Random House, 1942).

CHAPTER 5

1. Another phenomenon associated with military application of the airplane is the enormous literature it has generated. Advocates and critics concerned with the airplane appear to have been the most compulsive writers in military affairs. It is also true that World War II was probably one of the best-treated wars, at least from the American vantage point, in terms of historical writing whereby qualified historians were accommodated by the military services. There is the postwar *Strategic Bombing Survey*, of which there was both a British and American version. *The United States Strategic Bombing Survey* (Washington, D.C.: Government Printing Office, 1945–47),

consists of 316 volumes. Finally, most writings on particular World War II campaigns, phases of the war effort, or critical battles, have something to offer on the role of air.

Intertwined with the role of the airplane in World War II is the part that technologists, and intellectuals generally, played in military decision making; and there is an abundant and growing literature on this phase of the subject. This role will be treated at greater length in the next two and subsequent chapters.

The focus in this chapter is primarily on the management, organizational, and doctrinal, impact of the airplane. Principal literature sources employed were W. F. Craven and J. L. Cate, eds., *The Army Air Forces in World War II, vol. 1, Plans and Early Operations* (Chicago: Univ. of Chicago Press, 1948), esp. pp. 3–150; U.S. Army Air Defense School, *Air Defense: An Historical Analysis, vols. 1 and 2* (Fort Bliss, Texas: June 1965); and Harry Howe Ransom, "The Politics of Air Power—a Comparative Analysis," *Public Policy*, edited by Carl J. Friedrich and Seymour E. Harris (Cambridge: A Yearbook of the Graduate School of Public Administration, Harvard University, 1958), pp. 87–119.

For further insight about the political process in Britain during World War I that impacted upon the decisions that led to the establishment of the RAF and its focus on strategic bombing, see Andrew Boyle, *Trenchard* (London: Collins, 1962), pp. 191–316; for a somewhat "pro-Navy" view of the prewar American political setting, see Vincent Davis, *The Admirals' Lobby, op. cit.*, pp. 48–100. For an excellent account of how the U.S. Navy came into the air age, see Archibald D. Turnbull and Clifford L. Lord, *History of United States Naval Aviation* (New Haven: Yale Univ. Press, 1949). The full emergence of Navy air doctrine did not occur until mid-1944. Its development is excellently treated in Reynolds *The Fast Carriers, op. cit.*

2. F. W. Lanchester, *Aircraft in Warfare: The Dawn of the Fourth Air Arm* (London: Constable and Company, 1916).

3. *Ibid.*, pp. 187–89.

4. *Ibid.*, pp. viii–ix.

5. *Air Defense: An Historical Analysis, op. cit.*, vol. 1, pp. 8, 28.

6. *Ibid.*, p. 30.

7. Eugene M. Emme, ed., *The Impact of Air Power* (Princeton, N.J.: D. Van Nostrand, 1959), pp. 6–7. See Doyle, *Trenchard, op. cit.*, pp. 296–312, for an account of the operation.

8. Doyle, *Trenchard*, pp. 307, 311.

9. See Bernard Brodie, "Strategy," *The International Encyclopedia of the Social Sciences, vol. 15* (New York: Free Press, 1968), pp. 281–88.

10. Giulio Douhet, *The Command of The Air*, trans. Dino Ferrari, (New York: Coward-McCann, 1942).

11. R. B. Wiernam, ed., *The Cambridge Modern History, III: The Counter-Reformation and the Price Revolution, 1559–1610 (Cambridge: Univ. Press, 1968), pp. 347–52.*

12. See Ransom, *op. cit.*, pp. 89–98, for a brief but good summary of the British development.

Masked in the British policy deliberations was an increasing dissatisfaction on the part of some high civilian policy makers toward Sir Douglas Haig. However, no one individual or faction seemed able or willing to bite the bullet and fire Haig. It is also noteworthy that Lord Trenchard, senior British airman, first commander of the RAF, and subsequently regarded as the British personification and father of strategic bombing, retained a steadfast loyalty to Haig during the war, and adhered (despite blandishments from civilian politicians) to the notion that his primary mission was to support the ground forces. See *Trenchard, op. cit.,* pp. 191–239, for an account of this gamy phase of civil-military relations, which involved Jan Christian Smuts, Lord Curzon, Lloyd George, and the Admiralty, which was seeking to get a larger piece of the action. In effect, civilian "statesmen" were operating to induce one military officer to reduce the support he was providing another officer.

13. See P. H. Colomb, (vice admiral) *Naval Warfare: Its Ruling Principles and Practice Historically Treated,* 2nd ed. (London: W. H. Allen, 1895), pp. 3–6, for the coining of the term, a discussion of the practice, and the forces that led to its dimunition by the late sixteenth century.

14. For an account of the evolution of British World War II bombing policy and strategy, see F. M. Sallagar, *The Road to Total War: Escalation in World War II,* 4-465-PR (Santa Monica, Calif: The RAND Corporation, April 1969), pp. 95–191.

15. Craven and Cate, *op. cit.,* p. 6.

16. *Ibid.,* p. 10.

17. *Ibid.,* p. 7.

18. *Ibid.,* p. 10.

19. *Ibid.,* p. 9.

20. See Wavel, *Generals and Generalship, op. cit.,* p. 30.

21. See Craven and Cate, *op. cit.,* pp. 50–51, for a brief summary of the ambiguity that prevailed in the late 1930s.

22. *Air Defense: An Historical Analysis,* vol. 2, *op. cit.,* pp. 133–38.

23. See Burton H. Klein, *Germany's Economic Preparations for War* (Cambridge, Mass.: Harvard Univ. Press, 1959), pp. 232–33.

24. See, especially, William Mitchell, *Winged Defense: The Development and Possibilities of Modern Air Power—Economic and Military* (New York: G. P. Putnam's Sons, 1925), pp. 16–17.

25. Craven and Cate, *op. cit.,* p. 39.

26. *Ibid.,* p. 46.

27. *Ibid.,* pp. 58–59.

28. *Ibid.,* pp. 40–41. And it was in this form that Mitchell cast his campaign by 1925. See his Winged Defense, *op. cit., passim.*

29. In his *Winged Defense,* pp. 111–12, Mitchell did point out that traditional coast artillery was redundant, and suggested that the funds that could be saved should be reallocated both to field artillery and aircraft.

30. Craven and Cate, *op. cit.,* p. 598.

31. An interesting recent treatment of the decision-making process bearing upon the World War II use of airpower is contained in Harold L. Wilensky, *Organizational Intelligence: Knowledge and Policy in Government and Industry* (New York: Basic Books, 1967), pp. 24–34. Wilensky, drawing upon the *Strategic Bombing Survey,* views the decision-making bearing upon World War II strategic bombing and use of the airplane as a manifestation of institutional pathology, and an "intelligence failure" similar to the deci-

sion to produce the Edsel, and the complex of information failures that produced Pearl Harbor.

Wilensky's treatment of the British-American air offensive is an extension of the work of other scholars who have appraised the operation. For example, Burton Klein, in a more charitable tone, concludes that "The mistake of Sir Arthur Harris and his followers is simply that they anticipated history in imputing to their blockbusters the destructive power of atomic bombs." *Germany's Economic Preparations for War, op. cit.,* p. 235.

As part of the same stream of critical literature is C. P. Snow's account of the conflicting "scientific advice." offered to Winston Churchill regarding the effectiveness of strategic bombing, and the implication that Churchill was a "captive" of his scientific adviser, F. A. Lindemann, who advocated the RAF Bomber Command's strategy. See, C. P. Snow, *Science and Government* (New York: New American Library, 1962), esp. pp. 104–15.

These scholarly appraisals of the decision-making process suffer from a failure not to pursue the subject after it is demonstrated that the strategic air offensive against Germany did not win the war. But if the worth of the intellectual exercise is to probe the decision-making process, it seems the scholars are obligated to go the full route. It is appropriate to ask what was the ultimate cause of Germany's defeat? The answer can be found in Germany's military manpower losses, which by September of 1944 stood at 3.875 million, out of a total of 13 million that had been mobilized. By May 31, 1944, prior to the Normandy invasion, Germany had experienced losses of 3.285 million.

Had the U.S. and British decision makers possessed foresight equivalent to the scholar's hindsight, and had they allocated more resources to land forces and less to air forces, a major invasion could have been launched perhaps a full year or more earlier. One consequence of this alternative scenario is that the Russians would have experienced fewer casualties. This is not to suggest that Churchill explicitly reasoned along these lines. However, it is not unreasonable to assume that Churchill was knowledgeable enough about war to recognize that it could very well be a straightforward killing and associated exchange process, with its main incidence on men in the age groups that provide the best infantry. And, if the air offensive did not work, there were ample Russians to chew up German manpower. So perhaps the British-American air offensive was not such a bad allocation of resources after all.

32. One such case arose in the Pacific with the covering of the Leyte landing and the well-publicized failure of Admiral Halsey to guard the San Bernardino Strait when he was lured to chase a force of empty Japanese carriers. The incident had its roots in the fact that the Navy did not want to entrust their fast carrier force to the control of General MacArthur, who, the Navy felt, might expend them to support his ground operation; and clearly, MacArthur was not about to place command of the Philippines operations under a Navy admiral. Fortunately, the Japanese admiral who announced his arrival in the landing area by the splash of 18.1-inch shells got cold feet, and disaster was avoided. For an account of the affair, including a well documented exposition of the Navy's position on central management of its carrier forces, see Reynolds, *The Fast Carriers, op. cit.,* pp. 255–85.

CHAPTER 6

1. There are numerous sources that recount the story of radar, its associated spawning of operational research, and the subsequent growth of operational research. Many of these sources are biographical or autobiographical, and as such are often flawed but enriched by manifestations of strong egos or character evaluations. A relatively recent addition to the literature, and detached in tone, at least, is the official history treating the RAF. See Air Ministry, *The Origins and Development of Operational Research in the Royal Air Force* (London: Her Majesty's Stationery Office, 1963). The best biography or autobiography, in our view, is Sir Robert Watson-Watt, *The Pulse of Radar* (New York: Dial Press, 1959). Sir Robert is credited by all parties (including himself) as having been the inventor of radar. He also claims to be the inventor of operational analysis, and not without some justification. The lack of modesty in his autobiography, however, appears justified both by the absence of attempts to denigrate the endeavors of scientific peers or colleagues, and a revealed sensitivity to nontechnical considerations.

   For a good discussion of higher-level policy making (and politics) bearing upon the air-defense problem in pre-war Britain, see Frederick, the Earl of Birkenhead, *The Professor and the Prime Minister* (Boston: Houghton Mifflin Co., 1962), esp. pp. 117–219, a sympathetic biography of one of the most controversial figures involved in the British war effort—F. A. Lindemann (later Lord Cherwell)—who was Churchill's scientific adviser. With particular reference to the air-defense problem, see also Ronald W. Clark, *Tizard* (Cambridge, Mass.: M.I.T. Press, 1965), esp. pp. 105–63.

   Although the British deserve credit for the "invention" of radar as an operational system, discovery of its narrower technical underpinnings were not exclusively British. For a good account of other developments, see Dulany Terrett, *United States Army in World War II: The Technical Services, The Signal Corps: The Emergency (to December 1941)* (Washington, D.C.: Office of the Chief of Military History, Department of the Army, 1956), pp. 35–48. See also, Peck and Scherer, *The Weapons Acquisition Process, op. cit.,* pp. 31–37.

2. *Operational Research in the RAF, op. cit.,* p. 2.
3. *Ibid.*
4. Quoted in *Ibid.,* p. 3.
5. For an account of the higher-level political travail that led to the formation of the parliamentary subcommittee, see *The Professor and the Prime Minister,* pp. 177–219.
6. *Ibid.,* p. 3.
7. See, especially, C. P. Snow, *Science and Government: The Godkin Lectures at Harvard Univ., 1960* (New York: New American Library, 1962). As an antidote to Snow's appraisal of Lindemann, the serious student should also read Birkenhead's *The Professor and the Prime Minister, op. cit.*
8. Denis Richards, *Royal Air Force 1939–1945, vol. 1, The Fight at Odds* (London: Her Majesty's Stationery Office, 1953), p. 25.
9. Quoted in *The Pulse of Radar, op. cit.,* p. 278.
10. *Ibid.* pp. 278–79.
11. For the account of the expansion in the RAF, see *Operational Research in the RAF, op. cit.,* pp. 43–91.
12. *Ibid.,* pp. 40–41.

13. *Ibid.*, p. 41. For a highly readable account of the application of operational-research techniques to the submarine and shipping phases of the war, intertwined with his views on the methodology of operational research and insights about some of the higher-level bureaucratic issues related to the British strategic bombing effort, see P.M.S. Blackett, *Studies of War: Nuclear and Conventional* (New York: Hill and Wang, 1962), pp. 169–234.

14. Florence N. Trefethen, "A History of Operations Research," in Joseph McCloskey and Florence Trefethen, eds., *Operations Research for Management* (Baltimore: Johns Hopkins Press, 1954), p. 13.

15. *Ibid.*

16. W. F. Craven and J. L. Cate, eds., *The Army Air Forces in World War II, vol. 6, Men and Planes* (Chicago: Univ. of Chicago Press, 1955), p. 42.

17. *Operational Research in the Royal Air Force, op. cit.*, p. 42.

18. Irvin Stewart, *Organizing Scientific Research for War: The Administrative History of the Office of Scientific Research and Development* (Boston: Little, Brown, 1948), pp. 7–9.

19. *Ibid.*, pp. 10–11.

20. *Ibid.*, pp. 35–37.

21. *Ibid.*, p. 38.

22. *Ibid.*, p. 129.

23. For a brief summary of the office's activity, see *Ibid.*, pp. 128–50. For a more detailed account, see, Lincoln R. Thiesmeyer and John E. Burchard, *Combat Scientists: Science in World War II* (Boston: Little, Brown, 1947)

24. *Ibid.*, pp. 9–11.

25. *Ibid.*, p. 12.

26. *The Pulse of Radar, op. cit.*, pp. 324–325.

27. Russell L. Ackoff, "Operations Research," in *International Encyclopedia of the Social Sciences* (New York: Free Press, 1968), pp. 290–94.

28. Walter Goerlitz, *History of the German General Staff: 1657–1945*, trans. Brian Battershaw (New York: Praeger, 1963), p. 179.

29. For a fuller account of the story, see *Ibid.*, pp. 179–203. See also, Correlli Barnett, *The Swordbearers, op. cit.*, pp. 269–369, for a more vivid account, including a fascinating description of how Ludendorff underwent a loss of nerve when the offensive's failure became apparent. Equally fascinating and more significant for the future of Germany is the manner by which the German army bureaucracy was able to survive intact a domestic revolution in November 1918, the resignation of the Kaiser, and the transition to the republic. See John W. Wheeler-Bennett, *The Nemesis of Power: The German Army in Politics 1918-1945* (New York: Viking Press, 1964), pp. 3–45.

30. For a good account of the operation, see Potter and Nimitz, *Sea Power, op. cit.*, pp. 412–31.

31. Rear Adm. Sir Murray Sueter, *The Evolution of the Tank* (London: Hutchinson, 1937).

32. This and the following section draws upon R. F. Harrod, *The Prof* (London: Macmillan, 1959); and also G. D. A. Macdougal, "The Prime Minister's Statistical Section," in D. N. Chester, ed., *Lessons of the British War Economy* (Cambridge: Univ. Press, 1951), pp. 58–68. Both Harrod and Macdougal were members of the section.

33. Macdougal, *op. cit.*, p. 60.

34. *Ibid.*, p. 59.

35. Harrod, *op. cit.*, p. 186.

294   PLOWSHARES INTO SWORDS

36. *Ibid.*, pp. 186–187.
37. *Ibid.*, pp. 3–5.
38. *Ibid.*, p. 206.
39. Winston S. Churchill, *Their Finest Hour: The Second World War* (Boston: Houghton Mifflin Co., 1949), pp. 695–97. This particular memorandum may not have been a creation of the staff, since Churchill himself was highly knowledgeable about military affairs. It is likely, however, that he laid out the general idea, and that the staff developed the quantitative estimates.
40. Harrod, *op. cit.*, pp. 198–99.
41. Churchill, *op. cit.*, p. 168.

CHAPTER 7

1. Bruce L. R. Smith, *The RAND Corporation: Case Study of a Nonprofit Advisory Corporation* (Cambridge: Harvard Univ. Press, 1966), pp. 30–91.
2. Directive of the Secretary of Defense, December 11, 1948.
3. For what might now be considered a classic study, which also has the merit of being in the open literature, see A. J. Wohlstetter, F. S. Hoffman, R. J. Lutz, and H. S. Rowen, *Selection and Use of Strategic Air Bases*, R-266 (Santa Monica: RAND Corporation, April 1954); for an account of how the substantive findings of this study were disseminated, taken, and acted upon by the Air Force, see Smith, *op. cit.*, pp. 195–240.
4. For an account, from the viewpoint of an economist, see Stephen Enke, "Using Costs to Select Weapons," *American Economic Review* 55, (May 1965), 416–26, esp. 416–20. For the RAND "manifesto" on military cost-effectiveness analysis, see Charles J. Hitch and Roland McKean, *The Economics of Defense in the Nuclear Age* (Cambridge: Harvard Univ. Press, 1960).
5. Hitch and McKean, *The Economics of Defense in the Nuclear Age*, is the standard and pioneering work. It still verges on being the "last word" on the subject. Subsequent offerings have merely added refinements that cannot be very profitably exploited, given the complex of bureaucratic and political problems that bedevil any attempt to make government operations more efficient.
6. See *Ibid.*, pp. 159–81 for an extended discussion of the problems.
7. Ray S. Cline, *The War Department Washington Command Post: The Operations Division* (Washington, D.C.: Office of the Chief of Military History, Department of the Army, 1951), pp. 50–106. In the same reorganization, by placing the Technical Services under the Services of Supply (which later came to be called the Army Service Forces), under the command of General Somervell, the chiefs of the Technical Services were removed from the headquarters. The third major component of the Army, which was responsible for training and the "user" side of the Army's land forces, was the Ground Forces, under the command of General McNair. It is significant, after the war's end, that the Army returned to its prewar organization. Various reasons may be offered for reverting to the old organization. The best one is that the Technical Services, and their ways of doing business, were deep rooted in the Army. The in-fighting could be more profitably carried out in the headquarters.
8. John Miller, Jr., *United States Army in World War II, Guadalcanal: The First*

Offensive (Washington, D.C.: Historical Division, Department of the Army, 1949), pp. 8–16.

9. Charles F. Romanus and Riley Sunderland, *Stilwell's Command Problems: China-Burma-India Theatre* (Washington, D.C.: Office of the Chief of Military History, Department of the Army, 1956), pp. 314–28.

10. For an account of how these problems nagged Navy planners and thinkers even during the final phases of the war in the Pacific, after the Japanese fleet was rendered incapable of operating, see Reynolds, *The Fast Carriers, op. cit.* pp. 321–50.

11. See Robert Debs Heinl, Jr., *Soldiers of the Sea: The United States Marine Corps, 1775–1962* (Annapolis: U.S. Naval Institute, 1962), pp. 514–23, for an account of this post-World War II fight, which also involved President Truman.

12. Charles J. Hitch, *Decision-Making For Defense* (Berkeley: Univ. of Calif. Press, 1965), p. 15.

Hitch, *Ibid.*, pp. 3–18, provides a succinct discussion of the pre-1961 era of defense management. There is, however, an extensive literature on the subject. See, for example, Warner R. Schilling, Paul Y. Hammond, and Glenn H. Snyder, *Strategy, Politics, and Defense Budgets* (New York: Columbia Univ. Press, 1962); Paul Y. Hammond, *Organizing for Defense,* (Princeton: Princeton Univ. Press, 1961); and Samuel P. Huntington, *The Common Defense* (New York: Columbia Univ. Press, 1961); and Demetrios Caraley, *The Politics of Military Unification: A Study in Conflict and the Policy Process* (New York: Columbia Univ. Press, 1966). As emphasized above, the Navy's position was critical relative to reorganization proposals, it reacted strongly, and the significance of the events cannot be fully appreciated unless the Navy's role is understood. For a sympathetic focus on the Navy's political strategy, see Vincent Davis, *Postwar Defense Policy and the U.S. Navy, 1943–46* (Chapel Hill: Univ. of North Carolina Press, 1962).

13. For an account of how the Navy overcame the Air Force's monopoly, by a combination of technical developments and political adroitness, see Vincent Davis, *The Politics of Innovation, op. cit.,* pp. 7–22.

14. See James Gavin, *War and Peace in the Space Age* (New York: Harper & Brothers, 1958), p. 155.

15. See Maxwell Taylor, *The Uncertain Trumpet* (New York: Harper, 1959), p. 92.

16. *Ibid.,* pp. 82–83.

17. The best account of the purely organizational changes is in Hammond, *Organizing for Defense, op. cit.,* pp. 227–66, 288–320. This book also contains an excellent treatment of the organizational evolution of the old War and Navy departments, and relates that background to the postwar Defense Department developments.

18. *Ibid.,* pp. 315–19.

19. *Ibid.,* p. 318.

20. *Ibid.,* p. 316.

21. *Ibid.,* p. 311.

22. Quoted in *Ibid.*

23. *Ibid.,* pp. 319–20.

24. See *Department of Defense, Five Year Defense Program,* extract of the Department of Defense Program Structure Handbook, 7045.7-H, (Washington,

D.C.: Comptrollers Office of the Secretary of Defense, n.d.), pp. 44–86, for a listing of the individual program elements. Detailed definitions of the elements is obtainable from the component users of the element codes—e.g., Air Force, Defense Communications Agency, and so forth.

25. The combination of a program accounting (and costing) system, which tries to relate inputs to outputs, and cost-effectiveness (or cost-benefit) analysis, is loosely referred to as the Planning, Programming, and Budgeting System (PPBS). However, cost-effectiveness analysis can be applied without a program accounting system, and vice versa. Most students and critics of the subject nevertheless associate the two concepts. The heated criticism is directed toward the analysis and, more specifically, the decision makers who use the analysis and the staffs who serve those decision makers.

Criticism and defense of PPBS produced rich, and occasionally, pungent literature. For starters on recent offerings, see "Planning-Programing-Budgeting," *Hearings before the Subcommittee on National Security and International Operations of the Committee on Government Operations*, 90th Congress, First Session, Part 1, Aug. 23, 1967; Part 2, Sept. 27 and Oct. 18, 1967, (Washington D.C.: U.S. Government Printing Office, 1967). Part 1 contains statement and testimony by former Budget Director Charles L. Shultze; Part 2, of Alain C. Enthoven, former Assistant Secretary of Defense (Systems Analysis); also see, *Hearings on Military Posture and an Act (S-3253)*, Committee on the Armed Services, House of Representatives, 90th Congress, Second Session, Hearings before the full Committee, 3 April–27 May, 1968, pp. 8853–920, for an interchange between Dr. Enthoven and committee members and which provides insight on certain congressional sentiments regarding executive-branch use of systems analysis.

For a recent defense of the system, and an informative account of both the style of Systems Analysis Office and many of the issues it addressed in the Defense Department during the Kennedy-Johnson administration, see Alain C. Enthoven and Wayne K. Smith, *How Much is Enough? Shaping the Defense Program, 1961–1969* (New York: Harper & Row, 1971).

26. For an account of this and related procedural aspects of the decision-making cycle, see William Niskanen "The Defense Resource Allocation Process," in *Defense Management*, Stephen Enke, ed. (Englewood Cliffs, N.J.: Prentice-Hall, 1967), pp. 11–15.

27. William W. Kaufmann, *The McNamara Strategy* (New York: Harper & Row, 1964), pp. 217–30. See, also, Enthoven and Smith, *op. cit.*, for an account of the decision and the analysis of the issue, pp. 251–62.

28. See Hitch, *op. cit.*, pp. 54–55.

29. Kaufmann, *op. cit.*, p. 247.

30. See "Memorandum for the Secretary of the Army," April 19, 1962, and "Memorandum for Mr. Stahr," April 19, 1962, presented in Enthoven and Smith, *op. cit.*, pp. 101–04.

31. "The Army's Rifle Procurement and Distribution Program," Committee on Armed Services, U.S. Senate, May 31, 1967, p. 3. See also "Report of the Special Subcommittee on the M-16 Rifle Program," Committee on Armed Services, House of Representatives, October 19, 1967, pp. 5326–27.

32. See, for example, Samuel A. Tucker, ed., *A Modern Design For Defense Deci-*

sion: A McNamara-Hitch-Enthoven Anthology (Washington, D.C.: Industrial College of the Armed Forces, 1966.)

33. See "Planning-Programing-Budgeting," Part 2, *op. cit.*, pp. 86–89. The program, in terms of numbers of aircraft to be procurred, however, was the object of an interchange between the Air Force and the Systems Analysis Office. See Enthoven and Smith, *op. cit.*, pp. 262–66.

CHAPTER 8

1. The principal critic of the process, and founder of an ongoing RAND study effort focusing on development and procurement, was Burton H. Klein. For a nonacademic exposition of his criticism of the approach, see "A Radical Proposal for R. and D.," *Fortune* (May 1958), 112 ff. For a more technical exposition see Burton H. Klein, "The Decision Making Problem in Development" in Richard R. Nelson, ed., *The Rate and Direction of Inventive Activity: Economic and Social Factors (Princeton: Princeton Univ. Press, 1962), pp. 477–97.* See also A. W. Marshall and W. H. Meckling, "Predictability of Costs, Time, and Success of Development," *Ibid.*, pp. 461–75.

   A more recent product of the RAND effort is Thomas Marschak, Thomas K. Glennon, Jr., and Robert Summers, *Strategy for R&D: Studies in the Microeconomics of Development,* (New York: Springer-Verlag, 1967). This volume also contains an interesting number of case studies, but which are confined mainly to air weapons *(Ibid.)*, pp. 49–139).

   For a balanced presentation on the pros and cons of alternative weapons development and procurement strategies, see Peck and Scherer, *The Weapons Acquisition Processes; An Economic Analysis, op. cit.*, esp. pp. 17–54, 425–507.

2. Marshall and Meckling, *op.cit.*, p. 467.
3. *Ibid.*, p. 473.
4. *Ibid.*, p. 474.
5. *Generals and Generalship* (New York: Penguin Books, 1941), p. 16.
6. A variety of terms is in fact used. The British employ "Operational Requirements." The U.S. Navy's concept is "Scientific Operational Requirements." For the Army, the concept is called a "Qualitative Materiel Requirement." Each of these terms is misleading, since it refers to combinations of physical and physical-performance attributes that are expressed in engineering performance or physical terms. The frequent use of the word "operational" could imply utility or combat effectiveness. The implication is clearly unwarranted.
7. The attempt to reorient the NATO defense posture was perhaps the major U.S. foreign policy endeavor of the early 1960's, and for which Secretary McNamara took on the role of attempting to find the military means. For an account, see Kaufman, *The McNamara Strategy, op. cit.*, pp. 47–135, esp. pp. 102–34. See, also, Alain C. Enthoven, and K. Wayne Smith, "What Forces For NATO? And From Whom?", *Foreign Affairs* (October 1969), 80–96.
8. See E. C. Cornford, "Technology and the Battlefield," *Adelphi Papers*, no. 46 (London: Institute for Strategic Studies, March 1968), pp. 47–59, esp. pp. 48–52, for a succinct treatment of the technical and some operational aspects of the tank/antitank problem.
9. For an excellent treatment of armored vehicles—including tactics, organi-

zation, and the mechanics of design—see Richard M. Ogorkiewicz, *Armor: A History of Mechanized Forces* (New York: Praeger, 1960), esp. pp. 115–38, 282–365. For a succinct coverage of the U.S. Army, including data on existing, standard vehicles, see U.S. Army Armor School, *History and Role of Armor* (Fort Knox, Kentucky, February 1966). The term "tank" may generically describe any armored, track-laying combat vehicle. The family could therefore include self-propelled artillery, personnel carriers, scout vehicles, and others. More specifically, however, the term has come to refer to a general-purpose fighting vehicle, mounting a high-velocity gun in a turret with a 360-degree traverse, plus machine guns or smaller-caliber automatic weapons. Vehicles with a high velocity or similarly powerful weapon, but without the turret, are normally considered "tank destroyers."

10. Alan Clark, *Barbarossa: The Russian German Conflict, 1941–45* (New York: William Morrow, 1965), p. 54.

11. The tank-destroyer concept was controversial with its inception during the phase of hammering out the force structure on the eve of and during World War II. Tankers advocated employing tanks for the job, which also reflected the view that a larger portion of the army's force structure be allocated to armored divisions. However, General Leslie McNair, head of the Army Ground Forces, was a strong advocator of more specialized capabilities, to be organized in nondivisional units and allocated on an "as needed" basis. Specialized tank-destroyer battalions, and a school at Fort Knox, was the result of McNair's influence. For an account of this phase of the story, see Kent Roberts Greenfield, Robert R. Palmer, and Bell I. Wiley, *United States Army in World War II, The Army Ground Forces, The Organization of Ground Combat Troops* (Washington, D.C.: Historical Division, Department of the Army, 1947), pp. 72–84, 423–30.

In the North African campaign the tank destroyers "fell apart" and did poorly. It should also be pointed out that in the first American encounters with the Afrika Corps, few American concepts or organizations, including its armored division organization, stood up very well. Nor was our tactical air sparkling, as illustrated by the point that the medium-bombardment groups first deployed to North Africa had to be taken off operational status to retrain. It was simply a problem of green troops and commanders going against professionals. However, lessons were learned. In the Ardennes campaign, the tank destroyers, particularly those with self-propelled guns, when accompanied by infantry did very well, and the record was documented by careful operational analysis conducted by British teams. See, also, Hugh M. Cole, *United States Army in World War II, European Theater of Operations, The Ardennes: Battle of the Bulge* (Washington, D.C.: Historical Division, Department of the Army, 1965), *passim.*

12. Cornford, "Technology and the Battlefield," *op. cit.*, pp. 50–51.

13. *Ibid.*, p. 51.

14. See Department of the Army Field Manual, FM-17-36, *Divisional Armored and Air Cavalry Units* (Washington, D.C., Headquarters, Department of the Army, October 1965), esp. pp. 10–87 for a treatment of the organization, equipment, and missions of the armored cavalry troop and platoon.

15. See *History and Role of Armor, op. cit.*, p. 27.

16. For an indication of this concern, see Gavin, *op. cit.*, pp. 49–50, 64–65.

17. It would not be effective against sophisticated armored forces.
18. This section draws upon Committee on Armed Services, House of Representatives, *Report of the Armed Services Investigating Subcommittee, Review of Army Tank Program* (Washington: Government Printing Office, July 9, 1969); and *Review of Army Tank Program, Hearings of the Armed Services Investigating Subcommittee (March and April 1969)*.
19. *Review of Army Tank Program: Report, op. cit.*, pp. 1–2.
20. See Department of the Army Field Manual, FM 17–12, *Tank Gunnery* (Washington, D.C., Headquarters, Department of the Army, 1964), pp. 8–29.
21. *The Army Tank Program: Report, op. cit.*, p. 2.
22. See, Hearings Before a Subcommittee of the Committee on Appropriations, House of Representatives, 90th Congress, *Department of Defense Appropriations For 1969, Part 2, Research, Development, Test and Evaluation* (Washington: Government Printing Office, 1968), pp. 30–31, 494–95, for a summary of these characteristics.
23. For an account of the suspension system, the engine program, and the joint development project, see Edwin H. Burba (Maj. Gen., U.S.A.) "MBT–70: The New U.S./F.R.G. Main Battle Tank" *Ordnance*, (March–April 1968), pp. 475–79.
24. *Review of the Army Tank Program, op. cit.*, p. 6.
25. *Ibid.*, p. 37.
26. *Ibid.*, pp. 4–5.
27. *Ibid.*, p. 5.
28. *Ibid.*
29. *Ibid.*, p. 6.
30. *Ibid.*, p. 27.
31. *Ibid.*, p. 26.
32. *Ibid.* p. 27.
33. *Ibid.*, p. 21.
34. *Hearings, op. cit.*, p. 417.
35. See Department of the Army Field Manual, FM 17–12, *Tank Gunnery, op. cit.*, pp. 97–102.
36. *Review of Army Tank Program: Hearings, op. cit.*, p. 78.
37. *Report, op. cit.*, p. 27.
38. FM 17–12, *Tank Gunnery, op. cit.*, pp. 57–58.
39. *Review of Army Tank Program: Report, op. cit.*, p. 25.
40. *Ibid.*, p. 7.
41. *Ibid.*, p. 18.
42. *Ibid.*, p. 17.
43. *Ibid.*, p. 32.
44. *Ibid.*, p. 32. The congressional report notes that the driver of one Sheridan in Vietnam lost his life from the fire that resulted when ammunition "ignited almost instantaneously" with a rupture of the vehicle's hull near the stowage due to a mine explosion.
45. *Ibid.*, "A total of 41 misfires were recorded."
46. *Ibid.*, p. 27.
47. See, for example, *Hearings, op. cit.*, pp. 338–52, which contains large segments of "blanked-out" testimony in the exchange between committee members and the Army project manager regarding the MBT-70 program.

48. *Ibid.*, p. 349.
49. *Ibid.*, pp. 345 ff.

CHAPTER 9

1. See Hearings before a subcommittee of the Committee on Appropriations, House of Representatives, 91st Congress, *Department of Defense Appropriations for 1970, Part 5, Research, Development, Test and Evaluation* (Washington: Government Printing Office, 1969), pp. 621–22.
2. For an account, see Committee on Armed Services, House of Representatives, "Report of the Special Subcommittee on the M-16 Rifle Program" (Washington, D.C.: Government Printing Office, October 19, 1967).
3. Specifically, it was to employ a flechette projectile, which is fin-stabilized, as contrasted with a spin-stabilized bullet. The flechette concept began to attract attention during the middle 1950's. For a discussion of the SPIW and other advanced small arms concepts, see Col. John S. Wood, Jr., "Future Infantry Small Arms," *Ordnance* (July–August 1969), 75–77.
4. The flechette principle underlying the SPIW concept posed numerous technical uncertainties. It was also an unknown in terms of its tactical worth insofar as some preliminary studies indicated that an M16 (formerly the AR-15) with modifications could be more effective at certain ranges than the SPIW. For the latter finding, see Ballistic Research Laboratories "An Effectiveness Evaluation of the AR-15 Rifle with a Muzzle Attachment and Comparison With Other Rifle Concepts (U)," BRL Memo Report No. 1512, (Aberdeen, Maryland, October 1963). This and similar studies were based on technical-engineering data, and was theoretical in nature. As such, they should not preclude an exploratory development designed to provide hardware that can be tested. But the absence of any physical testing did not deter commitment to a full-scale weapon-system development program, and it is this practice toward which the criticism in the text is directed.
5. Jerome B. Wiesner and Herbert F. York, "National Security and the Nuclear-Test Ban," *Scientific American* (October 1964), p. 33.
6. Senate Hearings before the Committee on Appropriations, 91st Congress, First Session, *Department of Defense Appropriations, Fiscal Year 1970*, Part 3 (Washington, D.C.: Government Printing Office, 1969), pp. 56–7.
7. See *Ibid.*, pp. 1047–48.
8. See the *Washington Post* article, "Air Force Electronic Gadgets Assailed," June 28, 1969, pp. A1, A4.
9. See Marschak, Glennon, and Summers, *Strategies for R&D, op. cit.*, p. 128, for a summary of the problems afflicting "operational" aircraft.
10. Hearings before the Committee on Armed Services, United States House of Representatives, 91st Congress, First Session, *Hearings on Military Posture*, Fiscal Year 1970, Part 1 of 2 Parts (Washington: Government Printing Office, 1969), p. 2399. For a journalistic account of the North Dakota happenings, see Richard Pollak, "Missileland," *Harper's Magazine* (October 1969), 82–91.
11. Hearings before the Committee on Armed Services, United States House of Representatives, 91st Congress, First Session, *Hearings on Military Posture, Fiscal Year 1970, Part 2* (Washington: Government Printing Office, 1970), pp. 3266–69.

12. See Senate Hearings before the Committee on A-propriations, 91st Congress, First Session, *Department of Defense Appropriations, Fiscal Year 1970, Part 3* Washington, D.C.: Government Printing Office, 1969), pp. 182, 232.
13. *Ibid.*, pp. 207, 247.
14. *Ibid.*, p. 207.
15. *Ibid.*, p. 237.
16. *Ibid.*, p. 251.
17. See *The Army Tank Program: Hearings, op. cit.*, p. 345.
18. *Army Green Book*, 1967, *op. cit.*, p. 162.
19. See Harould D. Langham, *Historical Summary, United States Army Combat Developments Command Experimentation Center, 1 November 1956–30 June 1964* (Ford Ord, California, n.d.), p. 117.

CHAPTER 10

1. See Air Ministry, *The Origins and Development of Operational Research in the Royal Air Force, op. cit.*, p. xx, for the suggestion of this point.
2. For an account of the development, see Sidney F. Giffin, *The Crises Game* (New York: Doubleday, 1965), pp. 13–40.
3. The Blue/Red dichotomy in simulations is that the player's side is blue; the opponent's red. The convention has nothing to do with the East-West conflict of the past twenty-five or so years. The Germans, whose development of war gaming provides part of the intellectual foundation for present practice, instituted the color code. The Germans adopted blue for their side.
4. R. B. Braithwaite, *Scientific Explanation* (New York: Harper and Brothers, 1953), p. 90.
5. A. S. C. Ehrenberg, "Models of Fact: Examples from Marketing," *Management Science* (March 1970), p. 435.

CHAPTER 11

1. See Herbert A. Simon, "Causation," *International Encyclopedia of the Social Sciences*, vol. 2, (New York: Macmillan-Free Press, 1968), pp. 352–53.
2. Theodore Mommsen, *The History of Rome*, abridged by C. Bryans and F. J. R. Henry (New York: Philosophical Library, 1959), p. 258.
3. See Greenfield, *et al.*, *The Army Ground Forces, op. cit.*, p. 271.
4. *Ibid.*, pp. 108–10.
5. Archibald D. Turnbull and Clifford L. Lord, *History of United States Naval Aviation* (New Haven: Yale Univ. Press, 1949), pp. 270–83.
6. Recounted in Edward L. Katzenbach, Jr., "Twentieth Century Horse Cavalry," in *Public Policy*, Carl J. Friedrich and Seymour E. Harris, eds., (Cambridge: Harvard Univ. Press, 1958), p. 136.

CHAPTER 12

1. The Air Force prior to late 1957 had its Proving Ground Command, which was founded in 1941, and located at Eglin Field. Its head reported to the chief of the air staff. It no doubt developed a tradition and capability for operational testing. In 1957, the decision was made to put it under the Air

Force Research and Development Command, and its resources were combined with the Air Force Armament Center, also located at Eglin. Hence its resources and efforts became oriented toward the development phase of the procurement cycle.

2. Department of the Navy, Office, Chief of Naval Operations, *OPNAV Instruction 3960.1D* (Washington, D.C., 4 December 1967), Enclosure (1), p. 2.
3. *Ibid.*, p. 3.

CHAPTER 13

1. Langham, *Historical Summary*, op. cit., p. 3. For a further account of *Project Vista*, see Gavin, *War and Peace in the Space Age, op. cit.*, pp. 129–35.
2. See testimony of Major General George Brown in Hearings before a Subcommittee of the Committee on Appropriations, House of Representatives, 89th Congress, *Department of Defense Appropriations, for 1967, Part 5, Research, Development, Test, and Evaluation* (Washington, D.C.: Government Printing Office, 1966), p. 543.
3. *Ibid.*
4. *Ibid.*
5. *Ibid.*
6. *Ibid.*, p. 551.
7. *Ibid.*, p. 550.
8. *Ibid.*, p. 544. Around this period, Sandia's main business of testing atomic weapons was at its lowest level.
9. *Ibid.*, pp. 548–49.
10. *Ibid.*, p. 547.
11. Hearings before the Subcommittee of the Committee on Appropriations, House of Representatives, 90th Congress, *Department of Defense Appropriations for 1968, Part 3, Research, Development, Test, and Evaluation* (Washington, D.C.: Government Printing Office, 1967), p. 592.
12. Quoted from *1966 Hearings For FY 1967, op. cit.*, pp. 544–55. For the reference in the 1967 statement of the JTF–2 deputy commander, Rear Admiral Eugene Fairfax, see *Hearings for the FY 1968 Budget, op. cit.*, p. 595.
13. Hearings for FY 1967, *op. cit.*, p. 541.
14. See, *Report of the Special Subcommittee on the M–16 Rifle Program*, of the Committee on Armed Services, House of Representatives, 90th Congress, First Session, October 19, 1967 (Washington, D.C.: Government Printing Office, 1967).
15. The original propellant, designated "IMR 4475" was supplanted by the ball propellant designated "WC 846." The latter propellant produced a higher port pressure, which caused the weapon to cycle more rapidly than its design configuration. It also produced more visible fouling.
16. This was a propellant designated "IMR 8208M," which produced port pressures greater than the original "IMR 4475," and hence behaved similar to the offending ball propellant. For a further discussion see the letter of W. F. Jackson, Director, Research and Development Division, E. I. Dupont (dated April 11, 1968) to Representative Ichord, Committee on Armed Services, House of Representatives, 90th Congress, in *Hearings on Military Posture* (Washington, D.C.: Government Printing Office, 1968), pp. 8780–82.

17. See Jackson letter to Representative Ichord, *op. cit.*, p. 8781, which states, "It is abundantly clear that such a malfunction situation did not exist with the unmodified M16 rifle from the fact that Colt had, by preference, used ammunition loaded with IMR 4475 to make factory acceptance tests of rifles." This statement is slightly misleading and no doubt purposefully worded so as to avoid offending the Army. Acceptance tests are made by the manufacturer, but for the customer; and are monitored by government representatives. The ammunition/propellant choice for acceptability testing could not have occurred without the Army's knowledge.

18. See Hearings Before a Subcommittee of the Committee on Appropriations, House of Representatives, 90th Congress, *Department of Defense Appropriations for 1969, Part 2, Research, Development, Test and Evaluation* (Washington, D.C.: Government Printing Office, 1968), pp. 542–43.

CHAPTER 14

1. Statement and testimony by Pierre Sprey, Hearings Before the Committee on Armed Services, United States Senate held in December 1971, *Weapon Systems Acquisition Process* (Washington, D.C.: Government Printing Office, 1972), pp. 240, 262. Sprey compiles data indicating that the Army's proposed new Main Battle Tank (which was was recently terminated by congressional committee action) would have cost 35 times more than World War II tanks; an air-to-air firing attempt will be two thousand times more costly with present-day missiles than it was with the 6.50-caliber machineguns in World War II fighter aircraft; and that aircraft like the F-14 and F-15 currently under development, if they cost only $10 million each, will be one hundred times more costly than World War II fighters of the P-51 vintage. (All these comparisons are in *real terms*—i.e., adjusted for the effects of inflation.)

2. We emphasize that this is the peacetime role. In a major war, like World War I, and especially World War II, the military services both were constrained in terms of aggregate resources and had strong incentives to economize on their use. As illustrated by the Army during World War II, there was an incentive to deploy divisions overseas quickly. The constraints, successively, were primary raw materials, such as steel, shipping space, and, toward the end of the war, infantry replacements. Many difficult decisions were made within the Army, and in a hard-nosed way. It should also be pointed out that these decisions were made primarily by the "user" side of the Army, with the Technical Services playing a subordinate (and proper) role. For an account of the experience illustrating these points, see Kent Roberts Greenfield, Robert R. Palmer, and Bell I. Wiley, *The Organization of Ground Combat Troops: The United States Army in World War II, op. cit.*

3. There was an understanding between the comptroller, whose office contained until 1965 the Systems Analysis Directorate, and the director for research and development, to keep out of each other's territory.

4. At the time of the Agadir crisis of 1911, General Joffre was asked by his prime minister whether France had a 70 per cent chance of victory should a war occur. Joffre's reply was negative, whereupon the immediate decision of the civilian superior was to negotiate. See Alfred Vagts, *A History*

of Militarism: Civilian and Military, revised edition (New York: Free Press, 1959), p. 335.

5. However, a number of case studies have been compiled that underscore the relationship and provide insights. See Harold L. Wilensky, *Organizational Intelligence, op.cit.*

6. For a hint of this point, see "5000 Extra Tanks Found," *Washington Post*, October 30, 1970, p. A-1. The tanks in question, of which about twelve hundred were American M-60's were those kept in a reserve, prepositioned status in Europe. Although they were not actually "lost," the press account asserts that their existence was not known to "top-level Pentagon officials." In 1967, the Senate Armed Services Committee tracked how the Army's statements of rifle assets and requirements behaved in a strange way during the period of the Vietnam buildup, when the size of Army was increasing while the requirements for rifles was decreasing. During this period the Army might have been seeking to minimize its purchase of M-16's while it was trying to develop, on a crash basis, a new system (the SPIW) of its own conception. See U.S. Senate, Committee on Armed Services, *The Army's Rifle Procurement and Distribution Program*, (Washington, D.C.: Government Printing Office, May 1967).

7. For a study of both the production (supply) and the demand side of government statistics, especially with regard to the civilian side of government, see The President's Commission on Federal Statistics, *Federal Statistics*, 2 vols., (Washington, D.C.: Government Printing Office, 1971).

8. See, for example, Enthoven and Smith, *How Much is Enough?*, *op. cit.* pp. 313–20, which lists data deficiencies on both the cost and effectiveness side. The force of their recommendations on what to do about the problem appears to be expanded effort at the Office of the Secretary of Defense level.

9. For a critique of the emphasis on such systems, see Leon G. Hunt, "Management Information Systems," in *Federal Statistics*, vol. 2, *op.cit.*, pp. 437–54.

10. Numerous examples of threat exaggeration by military organizations can be listed over different periods and countries. Notable in recent U.S. experience was the "missile gap" that may have figured in the outcome of the 1960 Presidential election. Through the 1950's and early 1960's it was held that the Soviets had over 175 full-strength, highly trained divisions (plus more that could be fleshed out by mobilization) that "threatened" to overrun Western Europe. This belief importantly contributed to the development and deployment of tactical nuclear weapons, to be integrated with our "conventional" air and land forces. For an account of how questions were raised about this estimate and how it came to be deflated, see Enthoven and Smith, *How Much Is Enough?*, *op. cit.*, pp. 132–42. In "fairness" to the military, however, it should be noted that other bureaucracies trot out their "threats" to buttress the case for existing and proposed programs (and hence, budgets). The "energy crisis" is currently coming into vogue, perhaps because it happily serves the needs of a number of diverse federal bureaucracies.

11. One of the perennial difficulties in military management is determination of the appropriate "allowances" authorized for such units as battalions, air wings, and so on, with regard to supporting such equipment as trucks,

tools, and specialized maintenance personnel. There is a tendency for tables of organization and equipment of combat units to become "overloaded" with "impedimentia" (as the Romans termed it) and the people necessary to care for it. These resources also become the "requirements" that the taxpayers are ultimately asked to finance. To base readiness criteria on percentages of authorized allowances actually has nothing to do with measuring readiness, since it implicitly assumes that the official specifications are the "correct" mix of the diverse inputs. One of the worthwhile by-products of a readiness-evaluation program based on performance activities is that it can provide insight on how units might be best designed. For example, if unit "A" is consistently able to perform its mission with less than its authorized complement of mechanics (or cooks, or jeeps), the design of that type of unit could be modified in ways gratifying for both the taxpayer and the military service.

12. A similar recommendation has been made by the President's Commission on Federal Statistics for other federal programs. See *Federal Statistics*, vol. 1, *op.cit.*, letter of transmittal of Chairman W. Allen Wallis to President Nixon, and pp. 158–69.

13. For a suggestion on how the Army might restructure its operational testing organization, see J. A. Stockfisch, "Operational Testing," *Military Review* (May 1971), pp. 68–82.

14. See Blue Ribbon Defense Panel, *Report to the President and the Secretary of Defense on the Department of Defense* (Washington, D.C.: Government Printing Office, July 1970), esp. pp. 62–110. It should be pointed out that the panel treated the entire spectrum of Defense Department management, and did not focus exclusively on weapons acquisition. Separate appendixes dealing with range of subjects have been published. Those most pertinent to weapons acquisition are *Appendix F: Staff Report on Operational Test and Evaluation* and *Appendix E: Staff Report on Major Weapon Systems Acquisition Process.*

15. They were on *Economy in Government Procurement and Property Management*, (Washington, D.C.: Government Printing Office, 1968); and *The Economics of Military Procurement* (Washington, D.C.: Government Printing Office, 1970). An extension of this stream of inquiry by the Joint Economic Committee, which addressed some broader policy issues as well as procurement practices, is *The Military Budget and National Priorities* (Washington, D.C.: Government Printing Office, 1969).

16. See *Weapon Systems Acquisition Process, op.cit.*

17. See, for example, Enthoven and Smith, *How Much is Enough?, op.cit.*, esp. pp. 309–37; Richard F. Kaufman, *The War Profiteers* (Indianapolis: Bobbs-Merrill Company, 1970); Murray L. Weidenbaum *The Modern Public Sector: New Ways of Doing the Government's Business* (New York: Basic Books, 1969); Adam Yarmolinsky, *The Military Establishment: Its Impacts on American Society* (New York: Harper & Row, 1971), pp. 411–20.

18. See Kaufman, *op. cit.*, esp. pp. 232–37; and Joint Economic Committee, *The Economics of Military Procurement: Report of the Subcommittee in Government*, (Washington, D.C.: Government Printing Office, 1969), pp. 29–31.

19. *Ibid.* pp. 30–31.

20. Enthoven and Smith, *op.cit.*

21. *Report to the President and the Secretary of Defense on the Department of Defense*, op.cit. pp. 88–91. See also the statement and testimony of Gilbert W.

Fitzhugh to the Senate Armed Services Committee *Hearings, op.cit.,* pp. 3–53. (Fitzhugh was Chairman of the Blue Ribbon Panel.)

22. This was the force of the criticism of Air Force Research and Development strategy as it had evolved by the late 1950's, and which became a theme in The RAND Corporation weapon-acquisition studies. See Burton H. Klein, "A Radical Proposal for R and D," *Fortune,* (May 1958), 112 ff.

23. As we noted in the text, "Fly Before You Buy" and "ceasation of concurrency in development and procurement" are related and complementary ideas, and are viewed as ways to inject more vigorous and effective competition into the industrial side of the "military-industrial complex." Some students strongly recommend a further step to achieve this end is to permit firms other than the developer to compete for the procurement contract, or even to encourage certain firms to specialize in design and development. Such an approach appears to exist in the aircraft sector of the Soviet Union. (It is somewhat ironic if the Soviet Union's weapons industry behaves more like an old-fashioned private-enterprise one than does that of the United States.)

24. See, for example, John Kenneth Galbraith, "The Big Defense Firms Are Really Public Firms and Should Be Nationalized," *New York Times Magazine* (November 16, 1969), 50 ff.

25. For a brief advocacy of these and related recommendations, see U.S. Congress, Joint Economic Committee, *Report on Economy in Government Procurement and Property Management* (Washington,D.C.: Government Printing Office, 1968), esp. pp. 8–10.

26. In procurement contracts, since the late 1950's, increasing reliance was placed on incentive fees, whereby a firm could enjoy a higher fee as a function of "cost performance." This approach, as contrasted with cost plus fixed fee, gives contractors an incentive to overestimate costs. The incentive to achieve real efficiency is unknown. For discussion of these practices, see Irving N. Fisher, *Cost Incentives and Contract Outcomes: An Empirical Analysis,* Memorandum RM-5120-PR (Santa Monica, Calif.: RAND Corporation, September 1966).

27. See Secretary of Defense Melvin R. Laird's *Annual Defense Department Report, FY 1973: National Security Strategy of Realistic Deterrence,* statement before the Senate Armed Services Committee, February 15, 1972 (Washington, D.C.: Government Printing Office, 1972), p. 143.

28. *Ibid.,* p. 139.

29. *Ibid.,* p. 131. See also Secretary Laird's Statement, *Fiscal Year 1971 Defense Program and Budget,* before a joint session of the Senate Armed Services and Appropriations Committees, February 20, 1970 (Washington, D.C.: Government Printing Office, 1970), pp. 76–77.

30. See Secretary Laird's FY 1971 Statement, *Ibid.,* p. 78.

31. The FY 1972 (Total Obligation Authority) is around $78 billion; the FY 1973 Department of Defense proposed budget is $83 billion.

32. The tendency for lower-level organizations to acquire equipment and specialized personnel skills is endemic, and a version of one of Parkinson's laws. Hence, it is necessary, occasionally, to purge such organizations. In the military, this requires taking a hard look at unit Tables of Organization and Equipment and the overall force structure itself, revising both, and maintaining continued vigilance over the "requirements" formulation

process. For a case study of how this is done, see Kent Roberts Greenfield, Robert R. Palmer, and Bell I. Wiley, *The Organization of Ground Combat Troops: The United States Army In World War II (op.cit.)*, esp. 290–373. It should be pointed out that this World War II drive to attain efficiency was carried out within the Army, implemented by a subordinate agency clearly charged with the responsibility, under the command of Lt. Gen. Lesley McNair. The main motivation was to maximize combat forces to be deployed overseas, when the constraints were critical materials and shipping space.

33. Recall that in our first chapter the idea that a maximizing bureaucrat, behaving like a discriminating monopolist in the private sector, could at a limit extract an amount from the "consumer" sufficient to permit an activity up to twice the appropriate size. This presumption was applied only to the procurement side of military budgeting insofar as it is the most "political."

BIBLIOGRAPHY

BOOKS AND MONOGRAPHS

Acheson, Dean, *Present at the Creation: My Years in the State Department.* New York: W. W. Norton, 1969.

Ackoff, Russell L. "Operations Research," in David L. Sills, ed., *International Encyclopedia of the Social Sciences,* vol. 11, pp. 290–94. New York: Macmillan-Free Press, 1968.

Air Defense: An Historical Analysis, vols. 1 and 2. Fort Bliss, Texas: United States Army Air Defense School, 1965.

Air Ministry. *The Origins and Development of Operational Research in the Royal Air Force.* London: Her Majesty's Stationery Office, 1963.

Albion, Robert. *Forests and Sea Power: The Timber Problem of the Royal Navy, 1652–1862.* Hamden, Connecticut: Archon Books, 1965.

Albion, Robert Greenhalgh and Connery, Robert Howe. *Forrestal and the Navy.* New York: Columbia University Press, 1962.

Balchin, Nigel. *The Small Back Room.* Boston: Houghton Mifflin, 1945.

Barnett, Correlli. *The Swordbearers: Supreme Command in the First World War.* New York: William Morrow & Co., 1964.

Barnard, Chester I. *The Functions of the Executive.* Cambridge: Harvard University Press, 1942.

Bendix, Reinhard. "Bureaucracy," in David L. Sills, ed., *International Encyclopedia of the Social Sciences,* vol. 2, pp. 206–17. New York: Macmillan-Free Press, 1968.

Birkenhead, Frederick (Earl of). *The Professor and the Prime Minister.* Boston: Houghton Mifflin, 1962.

Blackett, P. M. S. *Studies of War: Nuclear and Conventional.* New York: Hill and Wang, 1962.

Bonner, James T. "The Distribution of Benefits from Cotton Price Supports," in Samuel B. Chase, Jr., *Problems in Public Expenditure Analysis,* pp. 223–48. Washington, D.C.: The Brookings Institution, 1968.

Boyle, Andrew. *Trenchard.* London: Collins, 1962.

Braithwaite, R. B. *Scientific Explanation.* New York: Harper, 1953.

Brodie, Bernard. "Strategy," in David L. Sills, ed., *International Encyclopedia of the Social Sciences,* vol. 15, pp. 281–88. New York: Macmillan-Free Press, 1968.

Bruce, Robert V. *Lincoln and the Tools of War.* Indianapolis: Bobbs-Merrill, 1956.

Buchanan, James M. and Tullock, Gordon. *The Calculus of Consent: Logical Foundations of Constitutional Democracy.* Ann Arbor: University of Michigan Press, 1962.

Caraley, Demetrios. *The Politics of Military Unification: A Study in Conflict and the Policy Process.* New York: Columbia University Press, 1966.

Churchill, Winston S. *Their Finest Hour: The Second World War.* Boston: Houghton Mifflin, 1949.

Clark, Alan. *Barbarossa: The Russian German Conflict, 1941–45.* New York: William Morrow & Co., 1965.

Clark, Ronald W. *Tizard.* Cambridge, Mass.: The M.I.T. Press, 1965.

Clausewitz, Karl von. *On War,* tr., Matthijis Jolles. New York: Modern Library, 1943.

Cline, Ray S. *United States Army in World War II: The War Department Washington Command Post: The Operations Division.* Washington, D.C.: Office of the Chief of Military History, Department of the Army, 1951.

Cole, Hugh M. *United States Army in World War II: The European Theater of Operations: The Ardennes: Battle of the Bulge.* Washington, D.C.: Office of the Chief of Military History, Department of the Army, 1965.

Colomb, P. H. *Naval Warfare: Its Ruling Principles and Practice Historically Treated,* 2nd ed. London: W. H. Allen, 1895.

Comparato, Frank E. *The Age of Great Guns.* Harrisburg: Stackpole, 1965.

Cornford, E. C. "Technology and the Battlefield," *Adelphi Papers,* No. 46. London: The Institute for Strategic Studies, March 1968.

Craven, W. F. and Cate, J. L. *The Army Air Forces in World War II,* 6 vols. Chicago: The University of Chicago Press, 1948–55.

Davis, Vincent. *The Admirals' Lobby.* Chapel Hill: The University of North Carolina Press, 1967.

———. *The Politics of Innovation: Patterns in Navy Cases.* Denver: Monograph Series in World Affairs, University of Denver Social Science Foundation, 1966–67.

———. *Postwar Defense Policy and the U.S. Navy, 1943–46.* Chapel Hill: The University of North Carolina Press, 1962.

Douhet, Giulio. *The Command of the Air,* tr. by Dino Ferrari. New York: Coward-McCann, 1942.

Downs, Anthony. *An Economic Theory of Democracy.* New York: Harper & Row, 1957.

Emme, Eugene M., ed. *The Impact of Air Power.* Princeton, N.J.: D. Van Nostrand, 1959.

Enthoven, Alain C. and Smith, Wayne K. *How Much Is Enough? Shaping the Defense Program, 1961–1969.* New York: Harper & Row, 1971.

Fisher, Irving N. *Cost Incentives and Contract Outcomes: An Empirical Analysis,* Memorandum RM-5120-PR. Santa Monica, Calif.: The RAND Corporation, Sept. 1966.

Friedrich, Carl J. *Man and His Government: An Empirical Theory of Politics.* New York: McGraw-Hill, 1963.

Furer, Julius Augustus. *Administration of the Navy Department in World War II.* Washington, D.C.: Department of the Navy, 1959.

Gavin, James. *War and Peace in the Space Age.* New York: Harper & Row, 1958.

Gibbon, Edward. *The Decline and Fall of the Roman Empire, 180 A.D.-395 A.D.,* vol. 1. New York: The Modern Library, n.d.

Giffon, Sidney F. *The Crises Game.* New York: Doubleday, 1965.

Goerlitz, Walter. *History of the German General Staff: 1657–1945,* tr. Brian Battershaw. New York: Praeger, 1963.

Green, Constance McLaughlin, Thomson, Harry C., and Roots, Peter C. *United States Army in World War II: The Technical Services The Ordnance Department: Planning Munitions for War.* Washington, D.C.: Office of the Chief of Military History, Department of the Army, 1955.

Greenfield, Kent Roberts, Palmer, Robert R., and Wiley, Bell I. *United States Army in World War II: The Army Ground Forces: The Organization of Ground Combat Troops.* Washington, D.C.: Historical Division, Department of the Army, 1947.

Guedalla, Philip. *Wellington.* New York: Harper and Brothers, 1931.

Hale, J. R. "Armies, Navies and the Art of War,: in R. B. Wiernam, ed., *The New Cambridge Modern History, Vol. 3: The Counter-Reformation and the Price Revolution, 1559–1610,* pp. 171–208. Cambridge: Cambridge University Press, 1968.

Hammond, Paul Y. *Organizing for Defense.* Princeton: Princeton University Press, 1961.

Harrod, R. F. *The Prof.* London: Macmillan, 1959.

Hayek, F. A. *The Counter-Revolution of Science: Studies on the Abuse of Reason.* Glencoe, Illinois: The Free Press, 1952.

Heinl, Robert Debs, Jr. *Soldiers of the Sea: The United States Marine Corps, 1775–1962.* Annapolis: U.S. Naval Institute, 1962.

Hitch, Charles J. *Decision-Making for Defense.* Berkeley: University of California Press, 1965.

——— and McKean, Roland. *The Economics of Defense in the Nuclear Age.* Cambridge, Mass.: Harvard University Press, 1960.

Historical Trends Related to Weapons Lethality: Basic Historical Studies, Annex I. Washington: Historical Evaluation and Research Organization, 1964.

History and Role of Armor. Fort Knox, Kentucky: U.S. Army Armor School, February 1966.

Holley, I. B., Jr. *Ideas and Weapons: Exploitation of the Aerial Weapon by the United States During World War I.* New Haven: Yale University Press, 1953.

Holley, Irving Brinton, Jr. *United States Army in World War II Special Studies: Buying Aircraft: Materiel Procurement for the Army Air Forces.* Washington, D.C.: Office of the Chief of Military History, Department of the Army, 1964.

Huntington, Samuel P. *The Common Defense.* New York: Columbia University Press, 1961.

———. *The Soldier and the State: The Theory and Politics of Civil-Military Relations.* Cambridge, Mass.: The Belknap Press of the Harvard University Press, 1959.

Huston, James A. *The Sinews of War: Army Logistics 1775–1953:* Army Historical Series. Washington, D.C.: Office of the Chief of Military History, United States Army, 1966.

Huzar, Elias. *The Purse and the Sword: Control of the Army by Congress Through Military Appropriations, 1933–1950.* Ithaca: Cornell University Press, 1950.

Kaufman, Richard F. *The War Profiteers.* Indianapolis: Bobbs-Merrill, 1970.

Kaufmann, William W. *The McNamara Strategy.* New York: Harper & Row, 1964.

Janowitz, Morris. *The Professional Soldier.* Glencoe, Ill.: The Free Press, 1960.

Jay, Antony. *Management and Machiavelli.* New York: Bantam Books, 1967.

Katzenbach, Edward L., Jr., "Twentieth-Century Horse Cavalry," in Carl J. Friedrich and Seymour E. Harris, eds., *Public Policy,* Cambridge, Mass.: Harvard University Press, 1958.

Klein, Burton H. *Germany's Economic Preparations for War.* Cambridge, Mass.: Harvard University Press, 1959.

———. "The Decision-Making Problem in Development" in Richard R. Nelson, ed., *The Rate and Direction of Inventive Activity: Economic and Social Factors*. Princeton: Princeton University Press, 1962.

Lanchester, F. W. *Aircraft in Warfare: The Dawn of the Fourth Air Arm*. London: Constable and Company, 1916.

Langham, Harould D. Historical Summary, United States Army *Combat Development Command Experimentation Center, 1 November 1956–30 June 1964*. Fort Ord, Calif.: n.d.

Lewis, Michael. "Armed Forces and the Art of War: Navies," in J. T. B. Bury, ed., *The New Cambridge Modern History: The Zenith of European Power: 1830–70*, vol. 10, pp 274–301, Cambridge: Cambridge University Press, 1967.

Longford, Elizabeth. *Wellington: The Years of the Sword*. New York: Harper & Row, 1969.

Macdougal, G. D. A. "The Prime Minister's Statistical Section," in D. N. Chester, ed., *Lessons of the British War Economy*. Cambridge: Cambridge University Press, 1951, pp. 58–68.

Marshack, Thomas, Glennon, Thomas K., Jr., and Summers, Robert. *Strategy for R&D: Studies in the Microeconomics of Development*. New York: Springer-Verlag, 1967.

Marshall, George C., Arnold, H. H., and King, E. J. *The War Reports of Marshall, Arnold, and King*. Philadelphia: J. B. Lippincott, 1947.

Miksche, F. O. *Attack: A Study of Blitzkrieg Tactics*. New York: Random House, 1942.

Miller, John, Jr. *The United States Army in World War II: The War in the Pacific: Guadalcanal: The First Offensive*. Washington, D.C.: Historical Division, Department of the Army, 1949.

Millett, John D. *United States Army in World War II: The Army Service Forces: The Organization and Role of The Army Service Forces*. Washington, D.C.: Office of the Chief of Military History, Department of the Army, 1954.

Millis, Walter. *Arms and Men: A Study in American Military History*. New York: G. P. Putnam's Sons, 1956.

Mitchell, William. *Winged Defense: The Development and Possibilities of Modern Air Power-Economic and Military*. New York: G. P. Putnam's and Sons, 1925.

Mommsen, Theodore. *The History of Rome*, Abridged by C. Bryams and F. J. R. Henry. New York: Philosophical Library, 1959.

Morrison, Elting E. *Admiral Sims and the Modern American Navy*. Boston: Houghton Mifflin, 1942.

Montross, Lynn. *War Through The Ages*, 3rd ed. New York: Harper & Row, 1960.

Nelson, Otto L., Jr. *National Security and the General Staff*. Washington, D.C.: Infantry Journal Press, 1946.

Niskanen, William A., Jr. *Bureaucracy and Representative Government*. Chicago: Aldine-Atherton, 1971.

———. "The Defense Resource Allocation Process," in Stephen Enke, ed., *Defense Management*. Englewood Cliffs, N.J.: Prentice-Hall, 1967.

Ogorkiewicz, Richard M. *Armor: A History of Mechanized Forces*. New York: Praeger, 1960.

Parkinson, C. Northcote. *Parkinson's Law and Other Studies in Administration*. Boston: Houghton Mifflin, 1957.

Parry, V. J. "The Ottoman Empire: 1566–1617," in R. B. Wierman, ed., *The New Cambridge History; Vol. 3.: The Counter-Reformation and the Price Revolution, 1559–1610*. pp. 347–76. Cambridge: Cambridge University Press, 1968.

Pechman, Joseph A. *Federal Tax Policy*. Washington, D.C.: The Brookings Institution, 1966.

Peck, Merton J. and Scherer, Frederic M. *The Weapons Acquisition Process: An Economic Analysis*. Boston: Harvard University, Graduate School of Business Administration, 1962.

Pierson, William W., Jr. "The Committee on the Conduct of the Civil War," The American Historical Review, vol. XXII (April 1918), reprinted in Gordon B. Turner, ed., *A History of Military Affairs in Western Society Since the Eighteenth Century*, pp. 179–86. New York: Harcourt, Brace and Company, 1952.

Pogue, Forrest C. *George C. Marshall: Ordeal and Hope: 1939–1942*. New York: The Viking Press, 1965.

Potter, E. B. and Nimitz, Chester W., eds. *Sea Power*, Englewood Cliffs, N.J.: Prentice-Hall, Inc., 1960.

Ransom, Harry Howe. "The Politics of Air Power—A Comparative Analysis," *Public Policy*, ed. by Carl J. Friedrich and Seymour E. Harris. Cambridge, Mass.: A Yearbook of the Graduate School of Public Administration, Harvard University, 1958.

Reynolds, Clark G. *The Fast Carriers: The Forging of an Air Navy*. New York: McGraw-Hill, 1968.

Reich, Charles A. *The Greening of America*. New York: Random House, 1971.

Richards, Denis. *Royal Air Force 1939–1945, Vol. 1, The Fight at Odds*. London: Her Majesty's Stationery Office, 1953.

Robinson, Joan. "Rising Supply Price," in George J. Stigler and Kenneth Boulding, eds., *Readings in Price Theory*, pp. 231–241. Chicago: Richard Irwin, 1952.

Romanus, Charles F. and Sunderland, Riley. *The United States Army in World War II: The China-Burma-India Theater: Stillwell's Command Problems*. Washington, D.C.: Office of the Chief of Military History, Department of the Army, 1956.

Sallagar, F.M. *The Road to Total War: Escalation in World War II*. R-465-PR. Santa Monica, Calif: The RAND Corporation, April, 1969.

Schilling, Warner R., Hammond, Paul Y., and Snyder, Glenn H. *Strategy, Politics and Defense Budgets*. New York: Columbia University Press, 1962.

Schumpeter, Joseph A. *Business Cycles: A Theoretical, Historical, and Statistical Analysis of the Capitalistic Process*, 2 vols. New York: McGraw-Hill, 1939.

———. *The Theory of Economic Development: An Inquiry into Profits Capital, Credit, Interest, and the Business Cycle*, tr. from the German by Redviers Opie. Cambridge, Mass.: Harvard University Press, 1934.

Schultze, Charles L. *The Politics and Economics of Public Spending*. Washington: The Brookings Institution, 1968.

Simon, Herbert A. "Causation," in David L. Sills, ed., *International Encyclopedia of Social Sciences*, vol. 2, pp. 350–6. New York: Macmillan-Free Press, 1968.

Smith, Bruce L. R. *The RAND Corporation: Case Study of a Non-profit Advisory Corporation*. Cambridge: Harvard University Press, 1966.

Smith, Louis. *American Democracy and Military Power: A Study of Civil Control of Military Power in the United States*. Chicago: University of Chicago Press, 1951.

Smithies, Arthur. *The Budgetary Process in the United States*. New York: McGraw-Hill, 1955.

Snow, C. P. *Science and Government: The Godkin Lectures at Harvard University, 1960*. New York: New American Library, 1962.

Sprout, Harold and Margaret. *The Rise of American Naval Power, 1776–1918*. Princeton: Princeton University Press, 1939.

Stein, George H. *The Waffen SS: Hitler's Elite Guard at War, 1939–1945*. Ithaca: Cornell University Press, 1966.

Stewart, Irvin. *Organizing Scientific Research for War: The Administrative History of the Office of Scientific Research and Development*. Boston: Little, Brown and Co., 1948.

Sueter, Murray. *The Evolution of the Tank*. London: Hutchinson & Co., 1937.

Taylor, Maxwell. *The Uncertain Trumpet*. New York: Harpers, 1959.

Terrett, Dulany. *United States Army in World War II: The Technical Services The Signal Corps: The Emergency (to December 1941)*. Washington, D.C.: Office of the Chief of Military History, Department of the Army, 1956.

Thiesmeyer, Lincoln R. and Burchard, John E. *Combat Scientists: Science in World War II*. Boston: Little, Brown and Co., 1947.

Trefethen, Florence N. "A History of Operations Research," in Joseph McCloskey and Florence Trefethen, eds. *Operations Research for Management*. Baltimore: The Johns Hopkins Press, 1954.

Tucker, Samuel A., ed., *A Modern Design for Defense Decision: A McNamara-Hitch-Enthoven Anthology*. Washington, D.C.: Industrial College of the Armed Forces, 1966.

Tullock, Gordon. *The Politics of Bureaucracy*. Washington, D.C.: Public Affairs, 1965.

Turnbull, Archibald D. and Lord, Clifford L. *History of United States Naval Aviation*. New Haven: Yale University Press, 1949.

Vagts, Alfred. *A History of Militarism: Civilian and Military*, rev. ed. New York: The Free Press, 1959.

Watson, Mark Skinner. *United States Army in World War II: The War Department Chief of Staff: Prewar Plans and Preparations*. Washington, D. C.: Historical Division, Department of the Army, 1950.

Watson-Watt, Robert. *The Pulse of Radar*. New York: Dial Press, 1959.

Wavell, Archibald. *Generals and Generalship*. New York: Penguin Books, 1941.

Weber, Max. "Bureaucracy," translated from *Wirtschaft and Gesellschaft* by H. H. Gerth and C. Wright Mills, in *From Max Weber: Essays in Sociology*. New York: Oxford University Press, 1946; first published in 1922.

Weidenbaum, Murray L. *The Modern Public Sector: New Ways of Doing the Government's Business*. New York: Basic Books, 1969.

Weigley, Russell F. *History of the United States Army*. New York: The Macmillan Co., 1967.

Western, J. R. "Armed Forced and the Art of War, 2: Armies," in A. Goodwin, ed., *The New Cambridge Modern History, Vol. 8, The American and French Revolutions, 1763–93*. Cambridge: University Press, 1965.

Wheeler-Bennett, John W. *The Nemesis of Power: The German Army in Politics 1918–1945*. New York: The Viking Press, 1964.

White, Theodore H., ed. *The Stillwell Papers*. New York: Macfadden, 1962.

Wildavsky, Aaron B. "Budgeting As a Political Process," in David L. Sills, ed., *International Encyclopedia of the Social Sciences*, vol. 2, pp. 192–198. New York: Macmillan-Free Press, 1968.

———. *Politics of the Budgeting Process*. Boston: Little, Brown and Co., 1964.

Wilensky, Harold L. *Organizational Intelligence: Knowledge and Policy in Government and Industry*. New York: Basic Books, 1967.

Wohlstetter, Hoffman, F. S., Lutz, R. J. and Rowen, H. S. *Selection and Use of Strategic Air Bases, R-266.* Santa Monica: The RAND Corporation, April 1954.

Woodward, Llewellyn. *Great Britain and the War of 1914–1918.* London: Methuen & Co., Ltd., 1967.

Yarmolinsky, Adam. *The Military Establishment: Its Impacts on American Society.* New York: Harper & Row, 1971.

PERIODICALS

Brinckerhoff, Sidney B. and Chamberlin, Pierce. "The Army's Search for a Repeating Rifle: 1873–1903," *Military Affairs,* Vol. XXXII, Spring 1968, pp. 20–30.

Burba, Edwin H. "MBT-70: The New U.S./F.R.G. Main Battle Tank," *Ordnance,* March-April 1968, pp. 475–479.

Davis, Otto A., Dempster, M.A.H., and Widavsky, Aaron. "A Theory of the Budgetary Process," *The American Political Science Review,* Vol. LX, September 1966, pp. 529–547.

Ehrenberg, A. S. C. "Models of Fact: Examples from Marketing," *Management Science,* Vol. 16, March 1970, pp. 435–45.

Enke, Stephen, "Using Costs to Select Weapons," *American Economic Review,* May 1965, pp. 416–26.

Emtjoven, Alain C. and Smith, K. Wayne. "What Forces For NATO? and From Whom?," *Foreign Affairs,* October 1969.

Fischer, John. "The Easy Chair," *Harper's,* April 1970, pp. 28ff.

Galbraith, John Kenneth. "The Big Defense Firms are Really Public Firms and Should Be Nationalized," *The New York Times Magazine,* November 16, 1969, pp. 50 ff.

Greenfield, Meg. "What's the Matter With the Mails?" *The Reporter,* February 11, 1965, pp. 21–25.

Haveman, Robert and Stephan, Paula. "The Domestic Programs Congress Won't Cut," *The Reporter,* February 22, 1968, pp. 36–7.

Klein, Burton H. "A Radical Proposal for R and D," *Fortune,* May 1958, pp. 112ff.

Kraft, Joseph. "J. Edgar Hoover-The Compleat Bureaucrat," *Commentary,* Vol. 39, February 1965, pp. 59–62.

Pollak, Richard. "Missileland," *Harper's,* October 1969, pp. 82–91.

Stockfisch, J. A. "Operational Testing," *Military Review,* May 1971, pp. 68–82.

Wiesner, Jerome B. and York, Herbert F. "National Security and the Nuclear-Test Ban," *Scientific American,* October 1964, pp. 27–35.

Wicker, Tom. "What Have They Done Since They Shot Dillinger?," *The New York Times Magazine,* December 26, 1969, pp. 4ff.

Willey, Richard J. "Taking the Post Office Out of Politics," *The Public Interest,* Spring 1969, pp. 57–71.

Wilson, James Q. "Corruption Is Not Always Scandalous," *The New York Times Magazine,* April 28, 1968, pp. 64 ff.

Wood, John S., Jr. "Future Infantry Small Arms," *Ordnance,* July-August 1969, pp. 75–77.

United States
Government Publications

Blue Ribbon Defense Panel. *Report to the President and the Secretary of Defense, 1 July 1970.* Washington, D.C.: Government Printing Office, 1970.

Fitzhugh, Gilbert W. "Blue Ribbon Panel Report," Statement to Committee on Armed Services, 92nd Congress, 1st Session, *Weapon Systems Acquisition Process.* Washington, D.C.: Government Printing Office, 1972.

Hunt, Leon. "Management Information Systems," in *Federal Statistics,* vol. 2, pp. 437–54. Washington, D.C.: Government Printing Office, 1971.

Laird, Melvin R., *Fiscal Year 1971, Defense Program and Budget.* Washington, D.C.: Government Printing Office, 1971.

————. *Annual Defense Department Report, Fiscal Year 1973: National Security Strategy of Realistic Deterrence.* Washington, D. C.: Government Printing Office, 1972.

The President's Commission on Federal Statistics, *Federal Statistics,* 2 vols. Washington, D.C.: Government Printing Office, 1971.

Sprey, Pierre M. "Expanding the Range of Choice in Weapons: Austere Alternatives," Statement to Committee on Armed Services, 92nd Congress, 1st Session, *Weapon Systems Acquisition Process.* Washington, D.C.: government Printing Office, 1972.

Department of the Army Field Manual, FM 17-36, Divisional Armored and Air Cavalry Units. Washington, D.C.: Headquarters, Department of the Army, October 1965.

Department of the Army Field Manual, FM 17-12, Tank Gunnery. Washington, D.C.: Headquarters, Department of the Army, 1964.

Department of Defense, Five-Year Defense Program (Extract of the Department of Defense Program Structure Handbook, 7045.7-H). Washington, D.C.: Comptroller's Office, Office of the Secretary of Defense, n.d.

Department of the Navy, Office, Chief of Naval Operations, OPNAV Instruction 3960.ID. Washington, D.C.: 4 December 1967.

United States Congress

Subcommittee on Economy in Government of the Joint Economic Committee, 90th Congress, 1st Session, *Report on Economy in Government Procurement and Property Management.* Washington, D.C.: Government Printing Office, 1968.

Subcommittee on Economy in Government of the Joint Economic Committee, 91st Congress, 1st and 2nd Sessions, 92nd Congress, 1st Session, *The Acquisition of Weapons Systems.* Hearings, 4 parts. Washington, D.C.: Government Printing Office, 1970–1971.

Subcommittee on Economy in Government of the Joint Economic Committee, 91st Congress, 1st and 2nd Sessions, 92nd Congress, 1st Session,

The Military Budget and National Economic Priorities. Hearings, 2 parts. Washington, D.C.: Government Printing Office, 1969.

United States Senate

Committee on Armed Services, 90th Congress, 2nd Session, *Hearings on Military Posture and an Act (S-3253).* Washington, D.C.: Government Printing Office, 1968.
Committee on Armed Services, 91st Congress, 1st Session, *Hearings on Military Posture, Fiscal Year 1970, Parts 1 and 2.* Washington, D.C.: Government Printing Office, 1970.
Committee on Armed Services, 92nd Congress, 1st Session, *Weapon Systems Acquisition Process.* Washington, D.C.: Government Printing Office, 1972. *Department of Defense Appropriations, Fiscal Year 1970, Part 3.* Washington, D.C.: Government Printing Office, 1969.
Subcommittee on National Security and International Operations of the Committee on Government Operations, 90th Congress, 1st Session, *Planning-Programming-Budgeting. Parts 1 and 2.* Washington, D.C.: Government Printing Office, 1968.
Preparedness Investigating Subcommittee of the Committee on Armed Services, 90th Congress, 1st Session, *Army Rifle Procurement and Distribution Program.* Washington, D.C.: Government Printing Office, 1967.

United States House of Representatives

Armed Services Investigation Subcommittee of the Committee on Armed Services, 91st Congress, 1st Session, *Review of the Army Tank Program: Hearings.* Washington, D.C.: Government Printing Office, 1969.
Armed Services Investigation Subcommittee of the Committee on Armed Services, 91st Congress, 1st Session, *Review of the Army Tank Program: Report.* Washington, D.C.: Government Printing Office, 1969.
Committee on Armed Services, 90th Congress, 1st Session, *Hearings before the Special Subcommittee on the M-16 Rifle Program.* Washington, D.C.: Government Printing Office, 1967.
Committee on Armed Services, 90th Congress, 1st Session, *Report of the Special Subcommittee on the M-16 Rifle Program.* Washington, D.C.: Government Printing Office, 1967.
Subcommittee of the Committee on Appropriations, 89th Congress, 2nd Session, *Department of Defense Appropriations for Fiscal Year 1967, Part 5, Research, Development, Test, and Evaluation.* Washington, D.C.: Government Printing Office, 1966.
Subcommittee of the Committee on Appropriations, 90th Congress, 1st Session, *Department of Defense Appropriations for Fiscal Year 1968, Part 3, Research, Development, Test, and Evaluation.* Washington, D.C.: Government Printing Office, 1967.
Subcommittee of the Committee on Appropriations, 90th Congress, 2nd Session, *Department of Defense Appropriations for Fiscal Year 1969, Part 2, Research, Development, Test, and Evaluation.* Washington, D.C.: Government Printing Office, 1969.
Subcommittee of the Committee on Appropriations, 91st Congress, 1st Session, *Department of Defense Appropriations for Fiscal Year 1970, Part 5, Research, Development, Test, and Evaluation.* Washington, D.C.: Government Printing Office, 1970.

INDEX

Browning automatic rifle, 53
Browning, John, 53
Budget-maximization
  and military threat assessment, 252
  techniques to achieve, 10–13
Budget, Bureau of the, 14
  See also "Management and Budget, office of"
Budgetary process
  advocacy in, 42
  bureaucrat as actor, 13
  characteristics of, 19
  within Congress, 19, 30
  military
    aggregative, 261–265
    and Bureau Chiefs, 251
    civilian role, 137, 256–257
    and professionalism, 85
    in World War II, 62
  as scenario, 21
  and specification of objectives, 14
Budgets
  struggle over, 29
  military and role of Congress, 62–64
  and politics, 14
Bureau head
  as budget maximizer, 9–10
  as follower, 27
  as leader, 13
  outward-directed political behavior of, 31
  and suppression of internal controversy, 13
  role of subordinates toward, 34
  views toward cabinet officer, 18
Bureaucracy
  as Byzantine court, 2
  conservatism of, 81
  contrasted with feudalism, 4
  definition of, 1–2
  ideal image of, 2–4
  officer corps as military, 2
  public as contrasted with business, 7–8
  and professionalism, 3
  tactics within, 6
  relationship to democracy, 4
  role of knowledge in, 241–242
  result of U.S. Civil Service reforms, 8
  effect of growth on Congress' behavior, 17
  as "feudal system," 6
  financial support of, 7
  Foreign Service as, 5–6
  growth since 1930s, 14
  varied views on, 2–8, 23–24
  Max Weber on, 2–4
  and written documents, 26

Bureaucratic behavior
  and dual communication systems, 33–35
  and individual behavior, 6
  obfuscation and propaganda, 12
  special relevance to national security, 36–37
Bureaucrats
  as "actors," 2, 13
  as advocates, 29
  attitude toward President, 18
  as dedicated public officials, 24
  expertise of, 24–27
  as instruments, 21, 35
  as maladroit, 24
  motives of, 30–33, 35
  as mutually suspicious, 6
  sensitivity to constituents of powerful Congressmen, 17–18
  as "victim" of budgetary scenario, 22
Bureaus
  Cabinate officers as spokesmen for, 15–16
  and constituency interactions, 16
  and interaction with Congress and executive branch, *Figure,* 15
  as providers of instrumental services, 16
  mature vs. immature, 28–30
  and relation to Congress, 250
  subgroups within, 13
"Bureau system," military, 45, 50–59
  See also "Arsenal system," "Technical Services"
Bush, Vannevar, 112–113, 125

Cabinet, President's, 15–16
Caesar, Julius, 38
Cameron, Donald, 59
"Cannon Kings," 53, 54
Capital-intensive projects, 11
Capital ship
  as aircraft carrier, 73
  as 74-gun ship, 70
C-130, 145
C-5A, 144, 250, 272, 273
Carnot, Lazare, 47
Cate, James, 86
Cavalry
  criticism of during Civil War, 39–40
  role of, 68
  armored, 160–161
"Centralized management," 247
  as military doctrine, 100–105
Centurion tank (British), 206
Chaparrel missile, 233
Chennault, Gen. Claire L., 81, 132
Cheyenne helicopter, 158

Chief of Naval Operations, Office of, 60, 65
Chippawa, Battle of, 46
Christie, Walter, 54
Churchill, Winston S., 106, 108, 117
  and F. A. Lindemann, 119–120
  use of analysis staff, 120–123
  and World War I policy role, 119
Citizens, 21
Clausewitz, Gen. Karl von, 67–69, 102
Close air support
  reliability of, 105
  quality of, 234
Civilian control of military
  ambigious meaning of, 245–246
  aspects of, 38–39
  pre-World War II, 58–60, 64–65
  and weapons procurement, 245
Civil-military relations
  Jeffersonian image of, 46–48
  and naval forces, 48–49
Civil Service reforms, 8
Civil War, 50
  criticism of cavalry, 39–40
  as seedbed of professional officer corps, 49–50
"Cold War," 252
Cologne, bombing of, 92
Combat Arms (Army)
  Chiefs of, 60
  intedependence between, 67
  vs. Technical Services, 41
Combat Developments Command, 229–230
  Combat Service Support Group of, 230
  Combined Arms Group of, 230
  disdain for testing, 231–233
  establishment of, 219–220
Combat Development Experimentation Center, 229, 238
"Combat Scientists," 114–115
Combustible ammunition, 164, 168–169
Committee on the Conduct of [Civil] War, 61
Competition, 7
Compton, Karl T., 114, 117
Computer simulations, 128
Conant, James, 112
Concurrency, 150–152
  recommendations to cease, 269–271
  Main Battle Tank as example, 269
Congress, U. S.
  aviation appropriation in World War I, 92
  and Army budgets, 62–63
  budget constraint on Fleet exercises, 64

and committee system, 17
and constituents, 16–17
on the "defensive" since 1930s, 17
House appropriations subcommittees, 19
interaction with bureaus and executive branch, Figure, 15
and Navy budgets, 63–64
willingness to enter imperial age, 63–64
Congressional Military Committee, 65
Conservatism
  justification for, 40
  toward weapons, 247
Constitutents, 15–16
Constitution, U. S., 60–61
Consumers' Surplus, 9
Contintenal Army Command, 229, 230
Cornwallis, Gen. Charles, 71
Corporateness
  qualities of, 3
Corps of Engineers, 16
Cost controls, proposals for, 272–274
Cost-effectiveness analysis, 108
  origins of in Britain, 122–123
  under McNamara, 144–145
  and user outlook, 250
Cost overruns, 151–152
  and contracting techniques, 272–273
Cost underestimation, 10–12
Council of National Defense, 112
Craven, Wesley, and James Cate, quoted, 86
Cromwell, Oliver, 38
"Cross-ravaging," 91

Dahlgren, Adm. John, 53
Daniels, Josephus, 59, 65
Dawes, Charles G., 16
"Daylight Precision Bombing," 98
"Decentralized management," 272
"Defense intellectuals," 106
Decision-making process, 42–43
Defense Department
  service views on, 132–134
  Reorganization Act of 1958, 138–139, 142
  impact on weapons development, 152
Development Concept Paper, 147–148
Development of Weapons (pre-World War II)
  French arsenals and artilley, 51–52
  French naval, 71–72
  quality of U.S., 54
Discriminating Monopolist
  bureaucrat as, 8–10
  in private sector, 8–9
Distribution, 20–21

Money creation, 14
Moore, Gen. Sir John, 71
Mortars, infantry
as artillery, 68
"Mossbacks," 40

"N-square law" of combat, 87
Napoleon, 48, 76, 78, 80
Napoleon, Louis III, 53
National Academy of Sciences, 112
National Defense Research Committee, 112–113, 125
National security
and bureaucratic behavior, 36–37
National Science Foundation, 125
NATO, 135, 136
and armored forces, 157–158
National Security Act of 1947, 134
National Security Council, 134, 135
Nationalization of weapons firms, 271–272
Naval aviation, 97–98
Naval forces
and civil-military relations, 48–49
19th Century technical transformation of, 69–70
Naval Institute, 50
Naval Power
as employed by England, 70–72
Naval tactical doctrine and "capital ship," 71
Naval War College, 50
Naval operations
in period of wood-and-sail ships 49
and ship design, 70
Navy Systems Command, 217
Navy, U. S.
budgets and ship construction, 63
condition of during post-Civil War period, 55
dichotomy between "line" and "staff" officers, 56
"shore establishment" vs. "Fleet," 54–55
transition to steam, 55–56
Nelson, Horatio, Adm. Viscount, 49
Neville, Gen. Robert, 83
New Deal, 14, 29
New Orleans, Battle of, 46
Nixon, Richard M., 265
Norden, C. L., 98
Nuclear weapons, 124, 125
and rise of analysis, 130–131
See also "Strategic war"

Obfuscation, 279
opportunity for, 36–37
techniques of, 12
Oerlikon 20 mm. antiaircraft gun, 57, 80
Office of Field Service (of OSRD), 114–115
OSRD (Office of Scientific Research and Development), 113–114, 125, 139
Officer corps
bifurcation of, 36, 40–41
as innovators, 81
insulation from politics, 36–37
introversive quality of, 25
as "military bureaucracy," 2
origins of in U.S., 48
Office of Naval Research, 125
155 mm. howitzer, 54
155 mm. self-propelled howitzer, 146
105 mm. gun-howitzer, 54
ONTOS anti-tank weapon, 161
Operational effectiveness, 155
measurement of, 187–188
Operational research, 107
contrasted with cost-effectiveness analysis, 128–131
contribution to World War II, 189
expansion of during World War II, 109–111
of land warfare, 110–111
and technical research, 112–115
"invention" of, 108–109
in U.S. military during World War II, 111–115
in World War II as compared with present, 116–117
See also "Cost-effectiveness analysis," "Operational testing," "Models."
Operations Evolution Group, 125
OPTEVFOR (U.S. Navy), 222–224
Operations Research Group, 125
Operations Research Office, 126, 131, 186
Oral briefings, 33–35
Ordnance, Bureau of (Navy), 56–57
Ostfriesland (German), 209
Ottoman Turks, 89–90, 95

Packenham, Gen. Sir Edward, 46
Paixhains, Henri Joseph, 71
Panama tests
of Sheridan/Shillelagh, 167
of M16 rifle, 243
Panther tank (German), 159
Panzerfaust, infantry anti-tank weapon, 158
Parkinson, C. Northcote, 4, 9, 29
Parkinson's "laws," 5
Parliament (British)

and bureaucratic motive to avoid exposure, 13
and bureaucratic budgetary motive, 12
and expertise, 10
and operational research, 117
Secretary of Defense, Office of
legislative changes affecting, 138–139
Self-serving behavior, 10–11
Senate Armed Services Committee, 265
Service "Centers" (Army), 217
Seven Years' War, 77
and English naval operations, 71
75 mm. gun (French), 51–52
Shadow costs, 11
Sheridan/Shillelagh
engineering difficulties of, 166–170
military characteristics of, *Table* 8.1, 163
See also "Shillelagh missile"
Sherman, Gen. William T.,
disgust with War Secretary, 58
as force for professionalism, 50
as Grant's pupil, 49
Shillelagh missile, 162, 183, 190, 250
adapted to M60 tank, 165
"Ship-of-the-line," 70
and advent of steam, 71–72
SS (Shutzstaffel), 38–39
Sidewinder missile, 145, 233
Sims, Adm. William S., 56
Simulations of combat, 191–193
See also "Models"
Single-round hit probability, 180–181,
185
Skybolt missile, 144
Social cost of capital, 11
Spaatz, Gen. Carl, 111
Spanish-American War, 59
SPIW (Special Purpose Infantry Weapon),
173–174
Specialization
and central management, 102
within military services, 41
Spencer rifles, 52
Springfield Arsenal, 52–53
Springfield rifle, 1903 model, 52–53
Sputnik, 139
Stennis, John, 265
"Sticky bomb," 122
Stillwell, Gen. Joseph, 132
Stoner rifle, 209
Strasbourg (France), arsenal in, 51
Strategic Air Command, 25, 217, 220, 235
Strategic war
analysis of, 127–128
concepts of, 89–90
models of, 203–204
and terrorizing civilians, 89–90

Stuka dive bomber (German), 175
Subculture, military, 39–40
"Suboptimizing," 130
Swinton, Lord, 108–109
"Systems analysis," 127
See also "Cost-effectiveness analysis"
and "Operational research"
Systems Analysis Directorate, 138, 139,
190
activities of, 144–145
and "bean counting," 254–255
method of operating, 146
and research and development, 147–
148
and user outlook, 249

Tactical Air Command, 217, 220
Tactics
bureaucratic, 6
18th century infantry, 76–78
machine gun, 207
Talos missile, 135
T-34 tank (Soviet), 159
Tank
design evolution of, 158–159
origin of, 119
gunnery, 163–164
tactics, 183–187
Tank-destroyer
concept, 159–160
in World War II, 185–186
Tartar missile, 233, 237
Taxation, 14
in-kind, 4
public aversion to, 17
as source of financial support of
bureaucracy, 7
Tax policy, 31
Technical change
British Admiralty's response to French,
72
and innovation, 78–81
and stimulation of bureaucratic rivalry,
40–41
"Technical Service Problem," 59
"Technicism," 157
Technical services, 41
conservatism of, 156–157
Army's disestablishment of, 229
and relation to Congress, 250
restoration of power in Army after
World War II, 60
skills in programming, 139–140
Technical tradeoffs, 155–156
Technologists
accomplishments during World War II,
151

SOE ✓
UA
17
U5
S6 —

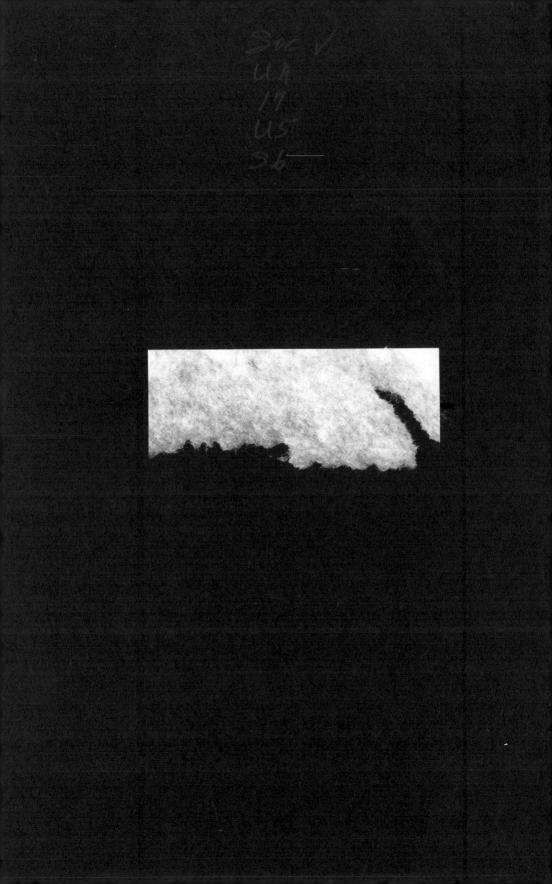